Women and the Politics of Education
in Third Republic France

Women and the Politics of Education in Third Republic France

LINDA L. CLARK

OXFORD
UNIVERSITY PRESS

OXFORD
UNIVERSITY PRESS

Oxford University Press is a department of the University of Oxford. It furthers the University's objective of excellence in research, scholarship, and education by publishing worldwide. Oxford is a registered trade mark of Oxford University Press in the UK and certain other countries.

Published in the United States of America by Oxford University Press 198 Madison Avenue, New York, NY 10016, United States of America.

© Oxford University Press 2023

All rights reserved. No part of this publication may be reproduced, stored in a retrieval system, or transmitted, in any form or by any means, without the prior permission in writing of Oxford University Press, or as expressly permitted by law, by license, or under terms agreed with the appropriate reproduction rights organization. Inquiries concerning reproduction outside the scope of the above should be sent to the Rights Department, Oxford University Press, at the address above.

You must not circulate this work in any other form and you must impose this same condition on any acquirer.

Library of Congress Cataloging-in-Publication Data
Names: Clark, Linda L., 1942– author.
Title: Women and the politics of education in Third Republic France / Linda L. Clark.
Description: New York, NY : Oxford University Press, [2023] |
Includes bibliographical references and index.
Identifiers: LCCN 2022058347 (print) | LCCN 2022058348 (ebook) |
ISBN 9780197632864 (hardback) | ISBN 9780197632888 (epub)
Subjects: LCSH: Women teachers—Training of—France—History—19th century. |
Women teachers—Training of—France—History—20th century. |
Teachers colleges—France—History—19th century. | Teachers colleges—
France—History—20th century. | Women in education—France—
History—19th century. | Women in education—France—History—20th century. |
Church and education—France—History. | Secularization—France—History. |
France—History—Third Republic, 1870–1940.
Classification: LCC LB1725.F8 C53 2023 (print) | LCC LB1725.F8 (ebook) |
DDC 371.100820944—dc23/eng/20230118
LC record available at https://lccn.loc.gov/2022058347
LC ebook record available at https://lccn.loc.gov/2022058348

DOI: 10.1093/oso/9780197632864.001.0001

Printed by Integrated Books International, United States of America

Contents

Acknowledgments	vii
Introduction: Women, Normal Schools, and the Politics of the Third Republic	1
1. Directrices and Their Mission in Republican Normal Schools	8
2. Training Future Teachers: Knowledge, Values, Conduct	43
3. Representing Republican Education: Directrices, Official Observers, and the Public	82
4. Directing Normal Schools in *Petites Patries*: Brittany and the Vendée, Algeria	118
5. Approaches to Feminism	152
6. Old Issues, New Challenges: From World War I to World War II	183
Epilogue: Beyond the Third Republic	218
Notes	237
Selected Bibliography	283
Index	301

Acknowledgments

The assistance and advice provided by archivists and librarians in France and by colleagues on both sides of the Atlantic have helped me enormously in the process of doing the research for this book and writing it. When I decided to look into the professional careers and experiences of an important but previously unstudied group of women, the directrices of normal schools whose role was central to the implementation of the Third Republic's education policies launched when Jules Ferry became minister of public instruction in 1879, the first steps were to identify these women in *annuaires* and then to find their personnel files at the Archives Nationales in Paris. The help of archivists was crucial because when I began the Archives Nationales did not have the current data base for personnel files for the education ministry (series F17). As the number of individuals I was pursuing multiplied, M. Paul Bureau kindly gave me access to the boxes of index cards with file numbers kept in his office. Mme Armelle Le Goff and Mme Édith Pirio also provided valuable assistance, including facilitating access to files requiring special authorization because of the younger age of some later directrices.

Noting in the publications of Jacques Ozouf and Mona Ozouf that the pre-1914 teachers surveyed by them in the early 1960s sometimes referred to experiences as normal school students or to normal school personnel who taught them, I went to the research facility of the Musée National de l'Éducation in Rouen to sample the files of women teachers in the Enquête Ozouf. The staff members there were always helpful and more recently have provided electronic access to files, with the proviso that the respondents remain anonymous.

I also extend my sincere thanks to librarians at the Bibliothèque Diderot of the Université de Lyon 3, where the collections on the history of education, formerly at the Institut Pédagogique National in Paris, are now housed. Similarly, I am indebted to librarians at the Bibliothèque of the Université d'Angers, Belle-Beille, the site of the holdings of the Centre des Archives du Féminisme. I thank Christine Bard for putting me in touch with France Chabot at the library. Finally, I owe thanks to numerous staff members at

viii ACKNOWLEDGMENTS

the Bibliothèque Nationale in Paris and to Carol Armbruster, formerly at the Library of Congress.

While this book was a work in progress, the suggestions of colleagues were often invaluable. I owe a major debt to Rebecca Rogers for keeping me up to date on recent French publications on the history of education and for asking probing questions and providing criticism. At several meetings of the Society for French Historical Studies, I benefited from the comments of Barry Bergen, Sarah Curtis, Karen Offen, and Jean Pedersen. I also thank Jean Pedersen for sharing research materials with me and offering advice. Marie-Paule Ha taught me a great deal about the situation of women teachers in colonial Indochina. Another big thank you goes to Stéphanie Dauphin of the Université d'Arras for inviting me to participate in a conference devoted to "les enseignantes" (women educators) in 2018 and for editing my contribution to a forthcoming collection of essays. The conferences in Arras in 2018 and 2019 brought renewed contact with Marlaine Cacouault and her work on women secondary school professors in the twentieth century.

For assistance with my search for illustrations or obtaining permission to use previously published images, I want to thank Claude Poitrenaud, Alexis Ballart, Joëlle Rochas, Alvin Pfenninger, Anne-Claude Guérin, and Jean-Marc Rousseau, Jérome Chevruel of the Archives départmentales de la Mayenne, and the photographic service of the Musée National de l'Éducation (MUNAE).

In the preparation of the manuscript for publication by the Oxford University Press, I benefited greatly from the advice and encouragement of senior editor Nancy Toff and also from the help provided by Zara Cannon-Mohammed.

Last and not least, my big personal debt is to my husband William Weber, who sometimes took time off from his own research on the history of music to help me with taking notes or pictures when time was limited during trips to France for research.

Women's normal schools were in cities with departmental prefectures, with the exceptions of Aix-en-Provence (Bouches-du-Rhône), Douai (Nord), Coutances (Manche), Rumilly (Haute-Savoie), and Miliana (Alger). The departments of the Moselle-and Bas-Rhin, and most of the Haut-Rhin were annexed by Germany 1871–1918.

Map based on Eugen Weber, *Peasants into Frenchmen: The Modernization of Rural France, 1871–1914* (Stanford: Stanford University Press, 1976).

Introduction

Women, Normal Schools, and the Politics of the Third Republic

In October 1880 Jules Ferry, France's premier and minister of public instruction, responded to a letter from the bishop of Châlons-sur-Marne, who had asked whether Ferry realized that the *directrice* (directress) of the new *école normale* (normal school) in the Marne department was a Protestant. Her religion, the bishop claimed, made her unsuitable for a post in a largely Catholic department. The woman in question, Mme Hélène Granet, was an experienced *institutrice* (woman teacher) from Nîmes, where she had trained at the *cours normal* for Protestant women. Ferry replied that the *directrice*'s religion should not cause concern because her duty was to respect the "liberté de conscience" (freedom of belief) of all students. Furthermore, he added, her respect for all faiths would set an excellent example for future women teachers trained at the normal school.[1]

For historians of French education during the Third Republic, this interchange exemplifies aspects of the well-known controversy between the new republican government and the Catholic church over changes in public education. For historians of French women, the interchange highlights the important role that republican leaders assigned to women employed in public education during a crucial period of reform. The work of normal school *directrices* was central to the republican project.

The political background to the educational reforms associated with Jules Ferry is well known. In early 1879 a republican majority assumed leadership of both legislative houses of the Third Republic (1870–1940), the regime established after the defeat of the Second Empire of Napoleon III (1852–70) in the Franco-Prussian War of 1870–71. Emboldened by recent electoral victories over monarchist and Bonapartist opponents, republicans embraced policies intended to enhance the new democratic government's chances for longevity, an obvious concern in a country that, since the Revolution of 1789–99, had experienced two Bonapartist regimes, two monarchies, the

---

Women and the Politics of Education in Third Republic France. Linda L. Clark, Oxford University Press.
© Oxford University Press 2023. DOI: 10.1093/oso/9780197632864.003.0001

2 WOMEN AND THE POLITICS OF EDUCATION IN FRANCE

short-lived Second Republic of 1848–52, and the upheaval of the Paris commune of 1871. The content of the education of the next generations of voters was thus a pressing issue. Republicans like Ferry believed that moral and civic instruction and history lessons in schools would play an essential role in winning support for the new government, which embraced the motto of *liberté, égalité, fraternité*, first coined in 1790.

Women could not participate in the universal suffrage that men enjoyed, but the Third Republic, like previous regimes, recognized the important influence exercised by women within family circles as wives and mothers, and so gave new attention to girls' education. Whereas the great majority of boys attending public schools were taught by laymen well before the Third Republic, a majority of girls until the late 1870s had women teachers belonging to Catholic religious orders. Because of the Catholic Church's support for monarchy in the old alliance of "throne and altar" perpetuated in reaction to the Revolution of 1789, republican leaders planned to end the Catholic presence in public schooling. The Ferry laws of June 16, 1881 and March 28, 1882 made primary education compulsory and, in public schools, free and secular (*laïque*). It was the requirement of *laïcité* that laid the basis for the raging arguments that continued for decades.[2] Public education was obviously not the only major issue in the protracted controversies between Catholics and anticlerical republicans, but it occupied a central place in the war of words, and sometimes deeds, that historian Gordon Wright termed France's "last religious war."[3] Hostile Catholics would long label the republican school "une école sans Dieu" (a school without God).[4]

Teachers loyal to the Republic were essential for the effective implementation of the new education laws. Accordingly, in 1879 the legislature had undertaken reforms in the training of lay teachers. The law of August 9, 1879, dubbed the Paul Bert law after its sponsor, required each department to maintain a normal school (*école normale*) for training women teachers (*institutrices*) as well as one for training men (*instituteurs*). French usage of the term *école normale* to designate a model pedagogical institution that provided "norms" for teaching practices dated from the Revolution and the short-lived creation of an *école normale* in Paris in 1795. The first normal school in a department was one for men in Strasbourg (Bas-Rhin), created in 1810 and modeled on teacher training provided in German "seminars." During the July Monarchy (1830–48) the Guizot law of 1833 spurred the creation of more men's normal schools, previously limited in number, and by 1879 most departments already maintained a men's normal school.[5] For women teachers, however, training had often occurred in *cours normaux*

INTRODUCTION 3

(normal courses) in private schools, many of them run by religious orders. The Bert law aimed to create a new cadre of lay women teachers, trained by other lay women rather than by nuns. Thus from 1879 to 1890, sixty-nine new normal schools for women were opened, but only seven more were needed for men.[6] The new women's normal schools at the departmental level necessitated, in turn, the preparation of women to administer them and provide instruction, and for that purpose a higher normal school, the *école normale supérieure de l'enseignement primaire*, was opened in late 1880 in Fontenay-aux-Roses, just south of Paris. Fontenay-aux-Roses and departmental normal schools offered women teachers a more advanced level of professional preparation than many public or private institutions provided previously.

Certainly women's schools of various types existed before 1879 and played an essential role in educating several generations of teachers, as historians Françoise Mayeur, Anne Quartararo, and Rebecca Rogers have demonstrated, but with the Third Republic came a new standardization of training and curricula and also a distinct improvement in teachers' professional status.[7] The expansion of primary schooling in France was well under way before the 1870s and was often, historians generally agree, a response by public authorities to demands from families and employers aware of the economic value of education. In the case of girls and young women, the availability of more schooling because of new legislation also spurred social trends that would influence women's ambitions.[8]

The *directrices* of the Third Republic's normal schools for women, assigned an important role in educating the next generations of girls and young women, have not previously been studied in detail.[9] Whereas women who headed boarding schools and the first women secondary school professors have attracted historians,[10] studies of women in French primary education have largely focused on teachers and not on the women who trained them.[11] Anne Quartararo's study of nineteenth-century women's normal schools, before and after 1870, highlights the experiences of their students.[12] The normal school directrices were a relatively well-paid group of professional women at a time when women in France and elsewhere in the Western world were also demanding access to employment in other professional domains, notably medicine and the law, previously restricted to men and long deemed appropriate only for men.[13]

Normal school directrices were, first and foremost, educators, but in the context of the 1880s and beyond, they were also central to educational politics both at the local and the national level. Within a department the

4 WOMEN AND THE POLITICS OF EDUCATION IN FRANCE

directrice was typically the most prominent woman representing public education and, as such, was watched carefully and judged by friends and foes of the Republic.

Not surprisingly, women who headed the new public secondary schools for girls, created by the Camille Sée law of December 21, 1880, also faced public scrutiny and Catholic hostility, but their schools served a different, and much smaller, social clientele and had a mission that was not professional training but rather providing to future middle-class wives and mothers a more advanced education than that offered by the primary schools for pupils aged six to thirteen.[14] In the parlance of the day, the primary schools (*écoles primaires*), for which normal schools trained teachers, served the "children of the people" (*enfants du peuple*). During the Third Republic the difference between primary and secondary schools was as much one of social class as of age, for secondary schools were long not free and many offered fee-paying elementary classes.

Who were the women called upon to provide the role models for the next generations of republican women teachers? How did they fulfill their responsibilities, and how did their experiences at work influence their thinking about a variety of topics, including the role of women in French society? The social and educational backgrounds of 193 women who headed normal schools between 1879 and World War I indicate why Félix Pécaut, director of studies at Fontenay-aux-Roses, characterized many of them as "filles sorties du peuple" (daughters of the people) who would train other "filles du peuple" to educate "les enfants du peuple."[15] Yet the directrices' career trajectories, detailed in their personnel files, testify to a degree of ambition unusual for contemporary women, and their profession made upward social mobility possible for those from humble origins. Their personnel files, a major documentary basis for this study, often contain correspondence which permits their voices to be heard.

In women's normal schools, directrices were not only leaders but also the teachers of courses in pedagogy, psychology, and moral education (*instruction morale*). Colleagues with the rank of professors or *maîtresses* taught French grammar and literature, history, geography, mathematics and sciences, art, music, foreign language, and *travail manuel* (manual work), which for young women meant sewing. Many lessons necessarily covered the Republic's expectations for teachers and, more specifically, for women teachers. Official documents and training at Fontenay-aux-Roses spelled out such expectations, which included the essential point that woman's most important duty was that of wife and mother. Thus directrices, like colleagues teaching other subjects, often commented on gender roles in their presentations inside and outside the classroom, and sometimes they published their views in pedagogical journals. The *institutrice* (woman teacher) trained at a departmental normal school should, ideally, become a role model for girls and women in the local community where she worked. At the same time, she should heed expectations for appropriate womanly conduct and attitudes. Yet because women teaching in normal schools, as well as the teachers they trained, had careers exemplifying an alternative to domesticity, it is unsurprising that a number would eventually push against the boundaries of prevailing gender norms, especially if they had experiences with unfairness related to gender.

Beyond the normal school, directrices necessarily had dealings with a variety of male officials and other individuals. Although the women's normal schools were often described as "lay convents" (*couvents laïques*) shut off from a larger society, many outsiders paid attention to their activities and readily voiced opinions about them. The directrice interacted with her school's local surveillance committee, the chief departmental education inspector (*inspecteur d'académie*), the rector (*recteur d'académie*) responsible for the regional educational administration, local officials and notables, and, of course, the parents of students. If subjected to criticism, a directrice had to learn to defend herself, even as she also sought support from administrative superiors, some of whom might be severe critics. French public education was, and remains, highly centralized, but local attitudes and situations could affect the experiences of a normal school's staff and students, especially in areas known for local particularities, such as the Breton departments and the Vendée in western France or the three departments of colonial Algeria.

By 1914 the women's normal schools of the Third Republic and their directrices were well established. At the opening ceremony in November 1913 for the new facilities for the Seine-et-Oise department's normal school, relocated from Versailles to Saint-Germain-en-Laye, directrice Juliette Mayaud celebrated the triumph of normal schools over their opponents. Under "assaults . . . since their origin" by enemies eager for their failure, women's normal schools were now "thriving more than ever," she affirmed. Premier Louis Barthou, present for the occasion, proceeded to laud the accomplishments of the Republic's teachers.[16]

Some directrices and their colleagues, like other women teachers, were also drawn before 1914 to the expanding French feminist movements, particularly as the issues of equal pay, married women's legal status, and women's suffrage attracted more attention and brought into focus the question of women's relationship to the Third Republic. Indicative of how, over time, directrices developed concerns that extended beyond normal school walls, their interest in reforms to benefit all women would continue.

During World War I, which disrupted the functioning of many normal schools, women educators at all levels demonstrated their loyalty to the Republic, often taking on extra responsibilities or replacing male colleagues called to military service. In the ensuing interwar decades normal school directrices continued to engage with republicanism and challenges to it, remaining defenders of *laïcité*. They also participated in debates about the need for new pedagogical methods (*éducation nouvelle*) and for restructuring public education to create an *école unique*. In addition, many addressed matters of professional status, feminism, pacifism, and other public issues. Between October 1914 and 1940, 120 new directrices were appointed as older directrices retired or, in some cases, assumed different duties.

Then came a professional as well as national crisis under the collaborationist Vichy Regime (1940–44), established after the defeat of France by Nazi Germany. Many directrices experienced major disruptions in careers as the new government closed normal schools and replaced them with "institutes of professional formation." For some directrices, World War II became an occasion for resistance, passive or, in certain cases, more active. The postwar provisional government and the ensuing Fourth Republic (1946–58) revived normal schools but with important alterations, and the Fifth Republic made still more changes before eventually replacing them with "university institutes" for training teachers.

A notable expansion of post-primary education after 1945, in response to public demand, and the significant restructuring of public schooling after 1958 understandably brought into question not only the continuing need for the old normal schools focused only on primary education but also the rationale for separate men's and women's schools. As women's position in the workplace and the larger society evolved, *mixité* (coeducation) became the norm at various levels of schooling during the 1960s and 1970s.[17] Yet even as normal schools were reconfigured more than once before their closure after 1989, they continued to exhibit the legacy of the Third Republic.[18]

The normal school directrices had learned since 1879 to exercise authority and to become strong advocates for their institutions and the teachers they trained. In the process of defending the Third Republic, directrices had to understand its workings, and with an understanding of what a democracy

INTRODUCTION 7

purported to be, many became aware of, and often uncomfortable with, the limitations that laws and customs placed upon women, even as educational opportunities for women were expanded. Several generations of directrices thus endeavored to teach their students to reconcile women's traditional place in the family with professional duties and also to understand the importance of the social and political dimensions of their role as educators.

1
Directrices and Their Mission
in Republican Normal Schools

"The woman must belong to science or she belongs to the Church."[1] This much quoted statement from a speech by republican deputy Jules Ferry in Paris in April 1870, less than six months before the collapse of Napoleon III's Second Empire, well capsulizes Ferry's approach to policies for the education of girls and young women when he became minister of public instruction in 1879 and, later, premier.[2] Like many other republicans of the 1870s and subsequent decades, Ferry framed the central contemporary political struggle as one between the vestiges of the Old Regime (*ancien régime*) and the legacy of the French Revolution of 1789, which had abolished legally defined social classes and issued the Declaration of the Rights of Man and the Citizen. This political conflict pitted supporters of monarchy or Bonapartism against republican supporters of a new government based on universal manhood suffrage.

The conflict between republicans and the Catholic church was rooted in the religious policies of the French Revolution and the post-revolutionary alliance of "throne and altar." Catholic bishops recognized, Ferry stated, that holding women's loyalties was the key to influencing her children. If women were to become mothers who encouraged the next generations of children to be loyal to a democracy, they must, anticlerical republicans argued, be lured away from priestly influences. For men alienated by the alliance of monarchy and church and far more likely than women to shun religious observances during the nineteenth century, Ferry and republicans also held out the prospect that improvements in women's education could lead to more harmonious households in which there was a "mariage des âmes" (marriage of minds) because wives and husbands would share similar beliefs.[3]

The major educational reforms launched after republicans finally gained control of both legislative houses in early 1879 featured plans for curricular changes and improvements in teaching in public schools, especially girls' schools. The law of August 9, 1879, sponsored by deputy Paul Bert, was

Women and the Politics of Education in Third Republic France. Linda L. Clark, Oxford University Press.
© Oxford University Press 2023. DOI: 10.1093/oso/9780197632864.003.0002

the first major step toward altering the composition of the teaching staff in girls' public schools. It required departments to maintain normal schools for women as well as for men, and its supporters expected it to have greater impact on girls' education than on that of boys because of the gender differences recorded in statistics on schooling.

Although nearly as many girls as boys attended school in 1878, 83 percent of boys in public primary schools were taught by laymen (1,889,000 of 2,287,000), whereas only 51 percent of girls in public schools were taught by laywomen (876,000 of 1,706,000). In private schools run by religious orders, girls (501,000) were four times more numerous than boys (122,000). Adding pupils in nonreligious private schools brought the number of schoolboys to 2,489,000, 4 percent more than the 2,390,000 schoolgirls; and girls were somewhat more numerous among the 620,000 children not attending schools. In all types of schools, religious teachers instructed 57 percent of girls, but only 20 percent of boys, and they often lacked a teaching certificate (*brevet*), officially required for lay teachers in public schools since 1819 but not for the religious for whom a letter of obedience sufficed until 1880, when it was the only qualification held by 16,000 women.[4] The education statistics of the 1870s reflected the feminization of religious practice and religious orders in post-Revolutionary France.[5]

Ferry was not the first education minister eager to see more girls instructed by lay teachers, but his efforts proved more far-reaching. Religious influence in public schools had increased in the aftermath of the Revolution of 1848 and the short-lived Second Republic (1848–52) when legislators unnerved by continuing social unrest blamed it partly on lay male teachers, trained in the normal schools promoted by minister François Guizot during the July Monarchy (1830–48). The Falloux law of 1850 permitted a significant increase in religious teaching orders' presence in public schools. Before 1850, 13 percent of boys and 45 percent of girls in public schools had religious teachers; by 1866, 19 percent and 53 percent, respectively. As families increasingly sought more schooling for children, Victor Duruy, Napoleon III's liberal education minister (1863–69), promoted the creation of more public schools but could do little to reverse staffing trends. His introduction of public secondary courses for girls in 1867 also provoked sharp attacks from Catholic authorities.[6] The "Syllabus of Errors" issued by Pope Pius IX in 1864 had explicitly condemned the idea that public schools should be "freed from all ecclesiastical authority . . . and should be fully subject to the civil and political power."[7]

The Third Republic's first education minister, Jules Simon, hoped to make primary schooling compulsory and free in public schools, but he and Adolphe Thiers, the provisional president, were ousted in 1873 by the "Moral Order," the royalist and Catholic majority in the governing constitutional assembly. This action was among the central episodes in the conflict between monarchists and republicans that dominated the 1870s and provided the immediate backdrop for subsequent republican policies in education and other areas. The constitutional assembly elected in 1871 after France's loss of the Franco-Prussian War had a substantial monarchist majority, but because of protracted rivalry between supporters of the Bourbon and Orleanist claimants to a restored monarchy, the assembly instead passed the constitutional laws of the Third Republic in 1875. After the next elections gave republicans control of the Chamber of Deputies, the lower legislative house, another political crisis occurred when the monarchist president Marshal Patrice de MacMahon, Thiers's successor, dismissed the government on May 16, 1877, and called for a new election. Contrary to monarchist hopes, this election returned another republican majority in October 1877.

The era of full republican control of the government began once republicans gained a majority of the indirectly elected Senate and MacMahon resigned in January 1879. Ferry received the education post in premier William Waddington's cabinet and quickly appointed directors of primary and secondary education who would play a major role in implementing reforms. Ferdinand Buisson, director of primary education and a liberal Protestant, oversaw the implementation of policies for primary schools and the normal schools whose graduates would staff them. The landmark Ferry laws of 1881–82 made primary schooling compulsory for children aged six to thirteen and made public primary schools free and secular. Serving in twenty-five cabinets between 1879 and 1896, Buisson provided substantial administrative continuity as coalition ministries changed frequently.[8]

In August 1879, when the Bert law was passed, women's normal schools functioned in only eighteen of the eighty-nine departments of France and Algeria. Women in religious orders directed seven of them and laywomen the other eleven. Nine of the lay schools were recent creations, opened between 1872 and 1876 in departments where local republicans persuaded *conseils généraux* (general councils) to invest more in girls' education, in advance of any new national assistance.[9] In departments lacking a women's normal school there was typically a *cours normal*, an extended pedagogical course offered in a private institution, run either by laywomen or the religious, and for which some students received departmental scholarships (*bourses*). Between 1879 and 1890, sixty-nine new normal schools for women were opened, but only seven more were needed for men.[10]

Ferry's decree of July 13, 1880, addressed the need to train women directors and professors for departmental normal schools by creating a higher normal school, the *école normale primaire supérieure de l'enseignement primaire*, soon opened in Fontenay-aux-Roses. The prestigious *École normale supérieure* for men in Paris, short-lived in 1794–95, had been reestablished by Napoleon I and was a training ground for men seeking careers in secondary education. Men staffing departmental normal schools for teachers were to receive separate training because of the structural separation of primary and secondary schooling, dating from 1808 and persisting throughout the Third Republic. Thus a three-month course for men was started in 1881, and in December 1882 an *école normale supérieure de l'enseignement primaire* opened in Saint-Cloud. Training for women professors for the new girls' secondary schools created by the Sée law of 1880 was provided in a third new *école normale supérieure*, opened in Sèvres in December 1881. New professional credentials for departmental normal school personnel, awarded after written and oral examinations, accompanied the more rigorous training for them: a certificate of aptitude for professors, and another certificate for direction, which also qualified men—and eventually women—to inspect primary schools.

The First Republican Directrices: Identities and Problems during Years of Transition

By the time that Fontenay-aux-Roses welcomed its first students in late 1880, Ferry and Buisson already had appointed directrices for thirteen normal schools created since August 1879 and also made decisions to retain or dismiss the directrices of older schools. The educational preparation of previous directrices and the first new appointees in 1879 and 1880 would not match that of future graduates of Fontenay-aux-Roses, but Ferry and Buisson wanted to create momentum for normal school reform rather than wait longer. Although the Bert law specified a four-year timetable for opening new normal schools, officials in Paris frequently encountered delays because of political resistance in some departments to funding new facilities and problems with the actual construction. Typically the normal school was in the same town as the department's prefecture, the administrative center.[11]

12 WOMEN AND THE POLITICS OF EDUCATION IN FRANCE

Who were the veteran directrices in place before 1879, who were the first new appointees, and how did they adjust to the republican educational project? Of the eleven laywomen heading normal schools before 1879, all but one continued under the new administration, some for longer terms than others. Appointed between 1872 and 1878, before the creation of new credentials soon required for normal school assignments, the veteran directrices held the same *brevets* as primary schoolteachers. Five had taught in public schools, four in private schools, and one in both. Born between 1815 and 1847, they had an average age of nearly forty-eight in 1879. Seven were single, two widowed, and only one was married.

The paths of the veteran directrices to previous appointments often told a story of useful familial and political connections. When the *conseil général* of the Saône-et-Loire department decided to replace a religious *cours normal* (pedagogical course) with a normal school in Mâcon in 1872, one of the department's primary school inspectors pushed successfully for the appointment of his sister, Césarine Baudry, age forty-five, a teacher in a Breton department, the Côtes-du-Nord, for twenty-five years.[12] To open the Seine department's normal school in Paris in 1873, minister Simon turned to Joséphine de Friedberg, a forty-nine-year-old widow and head of a girls' *école primaire supérieure* (higher primary school) in Paris since 1867. The connections of her father, a retired army officer, with the Seine prefect, Baron Georges Haussmann, had facilitated her first appointment during the Second Empire to inspect *salles d'asile* (nursery schools) in 1860.[13]

After Paul Bert and other republicans on the Yonne department's *conseil général* voted in 1872 to replace a congregational *cours normal* with a normal school in Auxerre, the directrice selected was Léonie Ferrand, age thirty-five, a successful public schoolteacher for thirteen years. Her ability to cope with clerical hostility and her careful role during the *seize mai* political crisis of 1877 garnered praise from republicans.[14] Similarly, Marie Porte, a teacher in a rural area and then a normal school *maîtresse* in the Isère department before becoming the directrice of the new normal school in Amiens (Somme) in 1876, was later commended for her perseverance when conservatives cut off funding for the school in May 1877. Senator René Goblet, the mayor of Amiens and a republican deputy, helped her find the resources to keep the school open until the academic term ended.[15]

The only lay directrice not retained in 1879 was Victorine Lanaud, head of the Jura department's normal school in Lons-le-Saunier since 1858. Founded in 1842 and run by laywomen, the Jura school, like other older normal schools, had strong religious traditions and instructors who were unmarried. It was the degree of religiosity, not religious practice per se, that separated Lanaud from other lay directrices. Before the Ferry law of March 28, 1882, the curriculum of primary schools included religion, and normal schools also engaged a Catholic chaplain (*aumônier*) and, in some cases, a Protestant pastor. The education commission of the Jura *conseil général* and the chief departmental inspector (*inspecteur d'académie*) questioned Lanaud extensively in August 1879, and the rector of the academy of Besançon soon informed Ferry that he, the prefect, and a majority of the *conseil général* recommended her dismissal. The teachers she had trained, wrote rector Jules Lissajous, formed "a sort of occult congregation imbued with a Jesuitical attitude," rather than "l'esprit laïque" desired by republicans. Lanaud had discouraged students from marrying and upon their graduation asked them to promise that as teachers they would follow their parish priest's advice.[16]

The personnel files of the ten experienced directrices who were retained identify at least seven as practicing Catholics, an identity often cited positively by previous inspectors and rectors.[17] Thus in 1873 Baudry's "fervent Catholicism" was judged a fine example for students. Friedberg, a Catholic, had affirmed the importance of religious instruction for students of all faiths in late 1873 when the Catholic press alleged that normal schools were hostile to religion. Porte's piety was termed "solid." To laicize the existing normal schools in Rumilly (Haute-Savoie) and Besançon (Doubs) in 1880 and Ajaccio (Corsica) in 1882, the education administration tapped the Catholic directrices Baudry, Véronique Bonnet, and Suzanne Lemercier, respectively.

Other veteran directrices were reassigned to open new republican normal schools. Porte was sent from Amiens to Lyon in 1879, Émilie Bonbled from Montpellier to Melun (Seine-et-Marne) in 1880, and Amélie Garcin from Moulins (Allier) to Épinal (Vosges) in 1881. Still later, Amélie Sage, formerly in Miliana (Alger) and Saint-Étienne (Loire), opened the school in Saint-Brieuc in the Côtes-du-Nord, one of the Breton departments highly resistant to republican education. Friedberg, well regarded in Paris, was elevated to the role of directrice of the new *école normale supérieure* in Fontenay-aux-Roses, where she shared authority with its *directeur d'études* (director of studies), Félix Pécaut, a liberal Protestant with pastoral training. In departmental normal schools the directrices themselves supervised studies, but administrative superiors regularly evaluated their work. Friedberg's reassignment put Ferrand in charge of the Seine normal school.

14   WOMEN AND THE POLITICS OF EDUCATION IN FRANCE

The ten veteran directrices were clearly valuable to the republican administration as educational reforms began in 1879, but only three (Porte, Ferrand, Sage) remained after 1890. Six had retired or died, and one was dismissed. Several had faced administrative criticism for retaining religious practices or symbols that the new government did not want inside secular normal schools. Although normal school personnel and students were free to continue religious worship outside the school, the injection of religion into the school itself conflicted with the republican commitment to religious neutrality. Thus Garcin was faulted in 1881 for placing religious decorations in the Moulins school and in 1886, in Épinal, for giving too much attention to religion when she presented the new program of secular moral instruction. She "no longer represents the desired type of normal school directrices," inspector general Pierre Leyssenne judged in 1881. When criticism of Lemercier as too clerical mounted in Aix-en-Provence in 1882, Buisson summoned her to Paris for a conference. Accusations of clericalism plus faulty financial management led to the transfer of Sage, a teacher in a private school until 1878, from Miliana in Algeria to Saint-Étienne in 1884.[18] Porte, the youngest "veteran," had the longest career as a directrice, working until 1907. Credited in 1880 with reducing the hostility in Lyon to the new normal school which rivaled a religious order's longstanding preparation of teachers, she made her students aware of the struggles faced as normal schools were founded during the "heroic era of the école laïque."[19]

To staff additional normal schools, Ferry, advised by Buisson, also appointed eighteen new directrices in 1879 and 1880, selecting experienced teachers after assessments of their commitment to republican goals. New instructors were hired as well, most of them still designated as *maîtresses* because the title of normal school *professeur* did not exist until new certification was created in June 1880.[20] Eleven of the beginning directrices launched new normal schools, six replaced directrices reassigned to open new schools, and one replaced Lanaud in the Jura. Although they ranged in age from 27 to 60, an average age of 37 made them a decade younger than the ten veterans. Eleven were single when appointed, 5 were married, and 2 widowed.

Because directrices had to reside in their normal schools, some officials initially questioned married women's suitability for the post and also the appropriateness of husbands or sons living in close proximity to young women students.[21] The rejoinder to such concerns was the insistence that a republican wife and mother provided a better role model for future teachers than celibate nuns. Pécaut would write in the *Annuaire de l'enseignement primaire* in 1892 that directrices were "secular women (*séculières*) who prepare [students] for secular life, which is why nothing is more natural than to see mothers of families in charge" of normal schools. Indeed, he added, "domestic life" would enhance directrices' experience and make them better able to draw on "the hidden resources of feminine nature, and exercise their supervision more maternally."[22] Republican France, unlike many other countries, did not bar married women from teaching or other employment in the public sector.[23] In normal schools the need to accommodate not only the directrice but possibly also family members necessitated enlarging her living space when existing facilities were remodeled or new schools constructed. After 1900, as noted below, the incidence of married directrices increased.

Only 6 of the 18 new directrices in 1879 and 1880 had taught previously in an older normal school, 2 of them for just a year. The others had experience in public or private schools, and five also had worked for individual families. Before the considerable expansion of teaching opportunities for laywomen in public education, credentialed lay teachers often turned, of necessity, to private schools, some of which offered instruction that was the equivalent of secondary education, as Rebecca Rogers demonstrated. Yet until the Sée law of 1880, no public school for girls used the "secondary" designation of *collège* or *lycée* because since 1853 all girls' schools were officially classified as "primary."[24] The expansion of public schooling after 1879 substantially diminished the clientele for nonreligious private institutions, and many of their teachers sought work in public schools, which offered job security and a pension.

How well individual women made the transition from fee-paying private institutions to public normal schools varied, but of the five new directrices of 1879–80 whose appointments ended within five years, four had spent most of their careers in private schools. In Rouen, Léontine Rey ran an important boarding school (*pensionnat*) for nearly twenty years, and for six years the Seine-Inférieure department subsidized a *cours normal* in her school. Because local officials strongly supported her, Ferry chose her in 1879 to inaugurate the normal school based initially in her facility and rented by the department. One optimistic inspector general expected that Rey, with her fine character traits, would effect change in young Norman women who seemed "dull-witted and apathetic" (*lourdes et apathiques*). By 1881, however, Louis Liard, the new rector of the academy of Caen, judged that she did not understand how the role of a normal school differed from that of a boarding school, and Buisson complained that she was among the former boarding school

16 WOMEN AND THE POLITICS OF EDUCATION IN FRANCE

women "peu disciplinables." Some local republicans and the journal *Le petit rouennais* also branded her a partisan of "clericalism," citing the placement of a crucifix in her office and in each classroom. In late 1883 a disappointed Rey, then age fifty, resigned and planned to open a private course.[25]

Similar issues ended Anna Cougoul's direction of the normal school that she opened in 1880 in Carcassonne (Aude) in southern France. An *instituteur*'s daughter from the Puy-de-Dôme department, she had run a private school in Clermont-Ferrand for six years and then given private lessons before becoming a normal school *maîtresse* in Montpellier in 1878. The Montpellier experience evidently did not prepare her to guide subordinates, one of whom denounced her for clericalism and provoked some students to do the same. After the rector of the academy of Montpellier, Gustave Chancel, condemned her harsh and capricious treatment of her staff and insisted upon her termination, she returned to private school teaching in 1882.[26]

Unlike Rey and Cougoul, Eugénie Hippeau faced attacks from Catholics and monarchists after she opened the normal school in Perpignan (Pyrénées-Orientales) in 1880. They complained that she did not require students to go to confession. Her republican loyalties notwithstanding, she was dismissed after only a year because of professional incompetence, her appointment at the age of sixty, with no experience in public education, having been a favor to her husband, a retired professor.[27]

With the exception of Cougoul, the first new directrices with prior normal school experience worked until retirement or death. Berthe Tailleur, a *maîtresse* at the Mâcon normal school since 1872, opened the Clermont-Ferrand school in 1879, returning a year later to Mâcon, where she remained for twenty-five years. Marie-Thérèse Georgin, daughter of the director of the men's normal school in the Isère, was a *maîtresse* since 1872 at the women's normal school outside Grenoble and became its directrice in 1880 when Bonnet left to laicize Besançon. She would direct two other schools before becoming an inspectress of *écoles maternelles* (nursery schools) in 1887 in the Seine department, where her father was a primary school inspector. Anna Bergin, a *maîtresse* since 1873 at the normal schools in Moulins and Chartres, opened the school in Versailles (Seine-et-Oise) in 1879 and directed four others before her death. In Amiens the reassignment of Clémence Moret, Porte's successor in 1879, to open the normal school in Dijon enabled Pélagie Doisnel, a *maîtresse* for one year, to become the school's third directrice in 1880. She remained until retirement in 1907. Marie Lusier, an experienced teacher trained by nuns at the old religious normal school in Orléans, became a *maîtresse* at the Mâcon school in 1879 and soon received orders to open the first two women's normal schools in the academy of Poitiers: Tours (Indre-et-Loire) in 1880 and Niort (Deux-Sèvres) in 1882.[28]

Nine former public school teachers became directrices in 1879 and 1880 without having held a normal school post, seven of them assigned immediately to launch new normal schools, and Moret doing so as a second assignment. The ninth teacher replaced Lanaud. The schoolteachers and normal school *maîtresses* appointed in 1880 all secured certification as normal school directrices, as did former teacher Louise Chasteau, named in December 1879 to open the school in Troyes in the Aube department after she impressed Paul Bert during the oral part of the certifying examination.[29] Joséphine Karquel, a teacher in the Meurthe-et-Moselle department since 1854, had headed a big girls' school in Nancy with three hundred students; her record prompted the local parliamentary deputation and the mayor of Nancy to push for her appointment in 1879 to open the normal school in Maxéville, just outside Nancy. Although the republican press sometimes attacked her for clerical leanings, administrators and political supporters affirmed her loyalty to public education, and her tenure lasted until she retired in 1889 at age fifty-seven.[30]

Unlike most directrices, former teacher Hélène Granet was a Protestant, an identity sometimes controversial, as indicated in the "Introduction." Her parents were public school teachers in Nîmes (Gard), as were three uncles, and her husband was a secondary school professor. She had begun teaching in 1867 in Nîmes and eventually directed a large Protestant public school, previously headed by her mother, which enrolled 140 girls. Many public schools still had religious designations before the Ferry law of 1882. Credentialed to direct normal schools in July 1880, Granet was the first of the graduates of the Protestant *cours normal* in Nîmes to lead a normal school.[31]

Yet before Buisson advised Ferry to choose Granet to open the normal school in Châlons-sur-Marne, he had explored sending her to launch other schools and met resistance because of her religion. The prefect of the Côte-d'Or acknowledged her "superior talents" but strongly opposed naming a Protestant to Dijon, where replacing a Catholic *cours normal* was already controversial. The *conseil général* of the Pyrénées-Orientales did not want her in Perpignan, where the directice selected subsequently would face Catholic ire. In the Marne department the prefect posed no objections, despite the grumblings of some members of the new normal school's oversight committee. The bishop protested, as did the archbishop of Reims, but Ferry firmly backed Granet. By April 1881 inspector general Pierre Brouard could report that her "tact" and "intelligence" had enabled her to win much support and largely dispel concerns about her Protestant identity. Success in Châlons led to her selection in 1883 to start the normal school in Douai in the populous Nord department, where she died in 1884 at the age of thirty-eight, soon after childbirth.[32]

The opening in late 1880 of the *école normale supérieure* for preparing women for departmental normal school posts soon permitted selecting directrices and professors from among the first women to profit from its offerings, women likely to have more understanding of republican educational goals than predecessors. The first students were welcomed in mid-November 1880 at the Seine department's normal school in Paris but relocated in early December to the permanent facilities in a refurbished chateau in Fontenay-aux-Roses south of Paris.

Both contemporary accounts and later treatments of the Fontenay school emphasize the centrality of Félix Pécaut's role as the director of studies until 1896.[33] He was, stated former student Sophie Lauriol, "the venerated guide . . . who made the school so dear to us" and remained "the light of our conscience."[34] Although Fontenay also had two directrices at the outset—Chasteau, with the title of *directrice* of studies, and Friedberg—Pécaut was the dominant figure, setting its tone for years to come. He recommended

École normale supérieure, Fontenay-aux-Roses. *Postcard, Author's collection*

the hiring of professors, chosen from the ranks of men teaching in Parisian secondary schools or at the Sorbonne, and he briefly addressed students at the start of each school day with an informal talk (*causerie*). Those talks covered many topics, some of which appear in his posthumous *Quinze ans d'éducation* (1902), and the nature of republican moral instruction (*morale laïque*) loomed large.[35] Directrices would later start their departmental normal school's instructional day with similar conversations.

At Fontenay directrice Friedberg's role was one of overseeing students' well-being, providing counsel, and attending to aspects of daily operations. Pécaut would praise her as a "valiant directrice" and "true woman" (*vraie femme*) with considerable "savoir-faire," stating also that he valued her intelligent collaboration. She exercised her authority "with ease and dignity, without going beyond her role or her sex."[36] Former students also felt comfortable appealing to Friedberg for support, as when normal school directrice Aurélie Lacroix asked her to help another classmate, now married and pregnant, with an impending reassignment, Lacroix writing that in this case "a woman can truly defend another woman."[37] Chasteau, the other directrice, unmentioned in many commentaries on Fontenay, resigned in May 1881 to avoid revocation for reasons Buisson and Pécaut left unexplained in her dossier.[38]

Under Pécaut's leadership Fontenay-aux-Roses was sometimes characterized as a "Port Royal laïque," a reference to the Cistercian nuns' abbey where Jansenism, with its emphasis on stern morality, struck roots in the seventeenth century, much to the displeasure of Jesuits and more than one pope. Because Jansenists, so named after theologian Cornelius Jansen, had often been regarded as Calvinistic Catholics, the characterization was also a reminder of Pécaut's Protestant religious origins and training. Aware of the Port Royal comparison, Pécaut himself spoke of the special "esprit" of Fontenay, insisting that it meant the opposite of a dogmatic approach to learning and denying that Fontenay was like a "cloister."[39] The ideal was rather to develop the ability to think for oneself and in the process to understand oneself. Although likened to Protestantism for its emphasis on the individual, the Fontenay "esprit" could also be compared to what Catholic students of Kantian philosophy absorbed in secondary schools. Indeed, the first professor offering lessons in moral instruction at Fontenay was Henri Marion, a Catholic sharing the new ideals for *laïcité* and toleration in public education. The "esprit" of Fontenay was also akin to the "esprit" of Saint-Cloud, the higher normal school that prepared directors and professors for

20   WOMEN AND THE POLITICS OF EDUCATION IN FRANCE

the men's departmental normal schools and was headed from 1882 to 1899 by Édouard Jacoulet, like Friedberg a practicing Catholic.[40]

Director Buisson at the ministry of public instruction and Pécaut at Fontenay were certainly among the prominent leaders of public education with Protestant backgrounds during the period of reforms initiated by Ferry, himself married to a Protestant. Adversaries fixated on the idea that republican education represented a "Protestant peril"[41] also found other targets: Pauline Kergomard, the most prominent of the four inspectresses general of *écoles maternelles*; Julie Velten Favre, widow of politician Jules Favre and the first directrice of the higher normal school in Sèvres training women for secondary school posts; Élie Rabier, the ministry's director of secondary education by 1889; and inspector general Jules Steeg, a former pastor and deputy who succeeded Pécaut at Fontenay in 1896. On the local level, Protestants assigned to normal schools could be subject to Catholic hostility, as in the case of directrice Granet. Yet not all Protestants, a minority of 2 percent of the French population, held identical views on *laïcité* and on educational issues.[42]

The policies for secularizing public education would not have been enacted without the votes of many liberal and often anticlerical republicans from Catholic backgrounds. What advocates of republican education shared, regardless of religious origins, was the belief that public schools could make an essential contribution to the formation of a society composed of essentially rational individuals who had a sense of responsibility to others that the official curriculum and schoolbooks would term "devoirs envers les autres."

The duties presented in republican schooling for most women were traditional.[43] Through education they would become better informed wives and mothers. Although the women educators who trained future teachers in normal schools represented, as professional women, an alternative to tradition, they too were instructed to present the destiny of most women as domestic. Fontenay students heard a message of "equality in difference," meaning that men and women were "equal" as human beings but destined to different roles in life. Professor Marion, who inaugurated the Fontenay courses in psychology and moral instruction, told students that although men and women were equal morally, the "profound difference" between them meant that a husband's greater authority in marriage was natural, and he warned that a wife who wanted to free herself was forgetting "her own nature" and "true destiny."[44] His message was consistent with French law, dating from Napoleon I, that dictated wifely "obedience" to husbands until 1938. Pécaut routinely counseled Fontenaysiennes that their role required reserved behavior and "modesty." Although their work might draw on "certain qualities of force and reason wrongly seen as exclusively virile," they should "remain women" (*rester femmes*). To reconcile a normal school directrice's task with women's traditional domestic duty, he likened her nurturing of students to the role of a mother and compared her counseling of professors to that of an older sister.[45]

Such statements were obviously consistent with longstanding beliefs that women, single or married, had maternal qualities that made them the natural teachers of children. Indeed, by the late nineteenth century, advocates for expanding women's opportunities in public life in France and elsewhere were also contending that women's nurturing qualities would be valuable outside the home in other endeavors and occupations. These arguments for transforming "motherhood from women's primary *private* responsibility into *public* policy" are now often termed "maternalism" by historians.[46] Long popular with many feminists, maternalist arguments were compatible with notions of "equality in difference."

During its first two years Fontenay-aux-Roses welcomed two categories of students. A competitive entry examination (*concours*), first administered in October 1880, was open to young women at least twenty years old who held the advanced *brevet* for teaching, formerly termed the *brevet complet* but soon retitled the *brevet supérieur*. Those successful would follow a full program of study, eventually set at two years for preparation of professors but initially shorter because of the urgent need to staff new normal schools. That need also led to admitting a second category of students for a short three-month course, intended for experienced teachers or women already working as normal school *maîtresses*. New *concours* were held twice in 1881 and twice in 1882, after which one annual *concours*, offered for specialization in either *lettres* or sciences, was deemed sufficient; the short course was discontinued after the spring of 1882.[47]

Apart from pedagogical instruction, Fontenay provided students with more grounding in traditional academic subjects—literature and composition, history and geography, mathematics and sciences—than previous normal school professors had received. Fontenay professors also were expected to make students think about how they might eventually teach those subjects to sixteen-to-eighteen-year-old students in departmental normal schools. What professors covered in lectures was reinforced by *répétitrices*, Fontenay alumnae employed to help students review the content of lectures and prepare for the examination certifying professors. *Répétitrices* themselves often used the extra time at Fontenay to prepare for their own certification as directrices.[48]

Recognition of the problematic attitudes or deficiencies in the work of some of the directrices appointed since 1879 also prompted the decision in 1882 to offer a special third year for their training, an opportunity open to Fontenay graduates and other women already certified as normal school professors. The extra year focused on pedagogy and administrative matters, and those attending made presentations on topics they would later teach, presentations critiqued by fellow students and professors and providing models for how they might critique their own students' practice teaching in the primary school (*école annexe*) attached to a normal school.[49] Directrices also needed to make judgments about whether normal school professors under their supervision taught a specific subject in a way that students could understand.

When they assumed posts in departmental normal schools, the directrices and professors encouraged at Fontenay to think for themselves would need to consider what degree of independence in thought and deed was compatible with their gender and professional duty. Typically they left Fontenay with pride in the training received and confidence in their abilities that proved to be valuable psychological armor.

The adjustments made at Fontenay during its first two years were necessary in a period of transition for educational policy. Changes in women educators' training were also mirrored in the backgrounds of the next thirty-six normal school directrices, appointed from 1881 to 1883. Although they again differed considerably in age, ranging from 25 to 58, they were a younger group than predecessors, with an average age of 33, because for the first time women trained at Fontenay-aux-Roses—24 of the 36—became directrices. Many of the Fontenaysiennes had experienced only a few months there, however. With a few exceptions, these new directrices were expected to hold the *certificat d'aptitude à la direction des écoles normales*, either when first assigned or to have an initial status of *déléguée* changed to directrice. Only three appointees in 1882 lacked it, and as of 1883 a woman "delegated" without it could not remain a directrice. Although nine of sixteen directrices named in 1883 began as *déléguées*, all but one were credentialed by 1887.

Several directrices named in the still transitional years between 1881 and 1883 would have important and highly visible careers, but others—particularly those lacking Fontenay training—had difficulty adapting to new expectations for reasons like those for which previous directrices had been faulted. Of the seven appointed in 1881, three were ousted before 1890, two of them because of complaints that they injected religiosity into their schools. In 1881 Marthe Expilly, then age twenty-eight and with a ten-year background in private school teaching in Marseille, quickly came into conflict with the chief departmental inspector in the Drôme because she wanted a bishop to bless the new normal school in Valence, located in a rented facility formerly housing a boarding school for Protestant boys. Alice Logé-Hervé's retention of Catholic devotional practices in the La Rochelle normal school, which she opened in 1883 as her second assignment, prompted protests from parents of Protestant students and her demotion to professorial rank in 1887.[50]

Two older directrices with private school backgrounds also served only briefly. In Saint-Étienne, Caroline Stromeyer Boissiere, a fifty-six-year-old widow appointed in 1882, served for less than eighteen months because, judged the rector of Lyon, she treated the normal school like her own private school. Since 1851 she had taught in or headed private institutions in Alsace, including a Protestant *cours normal* in Strasbourg, but eventually left after the German annexation. Eugénie Calloch, age fifty-eight and also with a private school background before her appointment to Le Mans in 1883, had to leave in 1886 because, Buisson explained, she had the habits of a "maîtresse de pension" (boarding school headmistress) who treated professors like "sous-maîtresses" (underlings), rather than as collaborators, and students as "enfants" (children), rather than as future teachers, and so caused disharmony in the school. She was appointed, he added, when not enough qualified directrices were available to fill all normal school slots, a judgment not unique to her case. Because of familial and political connections, Boissière and Calloch received alternate assignments as departmental inspectesses of *écoles maternelles*, Boissière in Toulouse and Calloch in Quimper.[51]

Unlike the former private school headmistresses whose stints as directrices were cut short, Emma Mathieu coped better, her time at Fontenay in 1880–81 facilitating her adjustment. For a woman then age forty-seven, the adjustment was sometimes problematic, but at the four normal schools she headed before retiring in 1897, inspectors and rectors supported her, albeit not always enthusiastically.[52]

All but four of the directrices appointed from 1881 to 1883 held or later acquired certification for directing normal schools, but Zoé Bourguet, who did not, could still have, like Marie Porte in Lyon, a prestigious career. Her selection at the age of thirty-eight for the first of several leadership roles was due to a combination of meritorious previous work and valuable

24   WOMEN AND THE POLITICS OF EDUCATION IN FRANCE

social skills. Although departmental normal schools were expected to train modest teachers able to relate well to children of *le peuple* and their parents, directrices selected for especially prominent posts had to be able to interact effectively with multiple urban constituencies. Bourguet, like Friedberg, to whom she was sometimes compared, was considered a "femme d'élite" (elite woman) whose experience in education and wielding authority compensated for a lack of formal credentials other than teaching *brevets*. Her mother, Marthe Muret, was the first directrice of the Protestant *cours normal* in Nîmes, opened in 1841 with support from both the Gard department—where Protestants comprised a third of the population—and the Protestant consistory. Succeeding her mother in 1868, Bourguet headed an institution with seventy-five students in 1882, including some from the neighboring Lozère and Hérault.[53]

Supporters in the Gard wanted Bourguet to direct the department's new normal school, citing in her favor the success of several *cours normal* graduates at Fontenay, but Pécaut judged that appointment too risky. Comparing the division between Catholics and Protestants in the Gard to a "volcano," he warned Buisson to consider "appearances" and avoid making the new normal school seem like a continuation of the Protestant *cours*.[54] Instead, Bourguet, the wife of a business agent, was delegated in April 1882 to open the normal school in Périgueux (Dordogne) in the southwest, and a few months later she received a more prestigious appointment, direction of the École Pape-Carpantier.

The École Pape-Carpantier dated from 1848 when the short-lived Second Republic chose Marie Pape-Carpantier (1815–78) to head the new *école normale maternelle* in Paris for training teachers for *écoles maternelles*, the nursery schools originally called *salles d'asile* (literally, rooms of asylum). The Second Empire soon renamed it a *cours pratique* for teachers in *salles d'asile* but retained Pape-Carpantier, who directed it until the monarchist Moral Order dislodged her in 1874. The name École Pape-Carpantier was adopted in December 1878, as the national political climate changed, and in 1881 the *salles d'asile* were retitled *écoles maternelles*, a change indicating that these schools for children aged two to six were indeed schools rather than charitable refuges for children of the poor. Ferry reorganized the school and transferred it to suburban Sceaux in 1882 as part of a plan to create a *cours normal des écoles maternelles* in each of the seventeen administrative academies for education, instructors for these *cours* to be trained at the École Pape-Carpantier. For several years it functioned as a kind of annex of Fontenay, with oversight by Pécaut, but in 1886 the plan for *cours normaux*

DIRECTRICES AND THEIR MISSION IN SCHOOLS   25

was discarded in favor of training *école maternelle* teachers in normal schools.[55] Bourguet then became the second directrice of the normal school in Versailles, and after Ferrand's death in 1894 she headed the normal school in Paris, regarded as the "premiere" departmental normal school.[56]

Like Bourguet, Lucie Saffroy, a young directrice named in 1881, eventually achieved special prominence. Born in 1855 in Auxerre, she was one of six children of a baker (*boulanger*) and was an orphan when she began teaching in the Yonne department where deputy Bert wielded great influence. She was, in fact, one of five public school directrices from the Yonne, who became normal school directrices between 1879 and 1883. In Joigny, Saffroy had boosted enrollment at the girls' primary school, laicized in 1878, from 22 to nearly 200, an accomplishment cited by the rector of Dijon when he recommended her admission to a Fontenay short course in March 1881. Having obtained the new certification for normal school professors in 1880, she qualified after Fontenay for the directrices' credential. In October 1881 she opened the normal school in Aurillac (Cantal), which replaced a religious *cours normal*, and then six weeks later succeeded Ferrand in the Yonne's well-established school in Auxerre. Two more directing assignments followed in 1883, the number of her postings not unusual for effective directrices during the formative decade for normal schools. After inaugurating the normal school in Bourges (Cher), another site of clerical opposition to replacing a religious preparatory course, she was reassigned a few months later to replace Rey in Rouen.[57]

Friedberg's death in 1890 created the opening that brought Saffroy back to Fontenay-aux-Roses as its second directrice. Having watched Saffroy's career progress, Friedberg persuaded Pécaut that she had the necessary experience and maturity that younger Fontenay graduates lacked. Saffroy, proud of her rural origins, proved to be less socially adept than Friedberg, a "femme du monde." Her assertiveness irritated Pécaut and his successor, Jules Steeg, who called her challenges to his authority intolerable and insisted that the ministry remove her in 1897. Finishing her career in Paris as an *inspectrice primaire* (primary school inspectress), a much prized post, Saffroy in 1903 was among the first republican women educators decorated by the Legion of Honor, recognition previously accorded to Friedberg and Kergomard.[58]

Directrice Jeanne Lacoste also would have a distinguished career, culminating at Fontenay. Yet among the sixteen directrices appointed in 1883, she was one of only four without Fontenay training. From a distinctly working-class background, she was born in 1858 in the Paris suburb of

26 WOMEN AND THE POLITICS OF EDUCATION IN FRANCE

Ivry, the daughter of a stationer's employee and a maid, and she became a milliner's apprentice after completing primary school. Through independent study and courses offered by the Society for Elementary Instruction (Société pour l'Instruction Élémentaire), she obtained *brevets* and in October 1879 began teaching in a primary school in Saint-Denis. Two months later she qualified as a normal school *maîtresse* and was assigned to the new school in Tours. Certified as a professor in 1882, the ambitious Lacoste in 1883 obtained certificates for normal school direction and secondary school teaching. She then became the second directrice of the recently opened normal school in Agen (Lot-et-Garonne) and in 1885 moved to the year-old school in Toulouse. She also added another secondary school title to her impressive resumé, that of *agrégée des lettres*, obtained in 1884 through a new examination separate from the prestigious *agrégation* for men.[59]

Lacoste was praised in Agen by inspector general Pierre Bertrand, who found her judgment surprisingly mature for a young person, but she fared less well in Toulouse with inspector general Leyssenne, who thought that she had received too much praise too soon. He judged her lacking in modesty and prudence, qualities that she should exhibit to students destined for teaching careers. Yet the essential point is that criticism did not destroy Lacoste's self-confidence or career prospects. During the 1890s, after marriage to lycée professor Émile Dejean de la Bâtie, she became the Republic's first *inspectrice primaire*, assigned to Versailles in 1891 and later to Paris, by then the mother of three sons. Regarded by Steeg as a "very distinguished woman," she succeeded Saffroy at Fontenay and after Steeg's death in 1898 no longer had to share authority with a *directeur*.[60] Dejean de la Bâtie's career, continuing until retirement in 1917, was testimony, like that of Saffroy, to the new opportunities that the Third Republic offered to determined women from humble origins.

Collective Profiles of 193 Directrices, 1879–1914

The individual stories so far recounted were part of the experiences of the large group of 124 directrices of the 1880s, for whom collective profiles will indicate more about aspects of their personal and professional identities, to be compared as well with those of another 69 directrices appointed between 1890 and 1914. By 1890, a decade after passage of the Bert law, each department had a normal school for women or, in several cases, shared a school with a neighboring department.[61] The number of directrices named between August 1879 and 1890, obviously exceeding the number of departments (eighty-nine), points to noticeable turnover in staffing during the first decade of the republican normal school. Some women failed to do the work satisfactorily. Directrices who succeeded in one post, particularly if they opened a normal school replacing a Catholic training course, might be sent to open another. A directrice's difficulties in a locality also led to reassignments or removals, and some changes simply reflected personal preferences, such as being closer to family members or wanting a different climate. During the 1880s, eighty-five of the directrices headed at least two normal schools.

Most normal schools were in small provincial towns, which women from large urban areas might dislike, but women from similar places were familiar with their social dynamics. The 124 directrices of 1879–89 were born in fifty-three different departments, including those in Alsace-Lorraine annexed by Germany in 1871, and three foreign countries.[62] More directrices came from northern and eastern France than from other regions, a representation correlating with the long history of greater availability of schooling for both boys and girls in these areas. Historians, like nineteenth-century statisticians, have emphasized that literacy rates for men and women were noticeably higher in departments north of a line running from Geneva, Switzerland, to Saint-Malo in the northwest than they were below it.[63] There was also a correlation between traditions of high literacy and areas with significant concentrations of Protestants, who valued education for both sexes as essential for Bible reading and whose presence since the Reformation often spurred Catholics in the same areas to open competing schools.

Fourteen directrices of the 1880s came from the three eastern departments in the administrative academy of Nancy, as compared to only 5 from the Breton academy of Rennes, which had seven departments, or 4 from the south central academy of Clermont-Ferrand with six departments. Eleven directrices were from the Seine department, 10 of them Parisians. The 9 directrices of the 1880s from the Gard, the largest number from a southern department and second only to the Seine, included at least 6 trained at the Protestant *cours normal*, where a tenth named in 1894 also studied. The 69 directrices appointed after 1889 added to the geographical diversity in backgrounds, with birthplaces in sixteen departments unrepresented previously, including the department of Alger, the home of 2. The later directrices raise the Seine totals to 14, the Gard to 13, and the academy of Nancy to 18. The big academy of Paris, comprised of the Seine and eight other

28 WOMEN AND THE POLITICS OF EDUCATION IN FRANCE

departments, provided the largest contingent: 25 of 193 directrices named before 1914.

When Pécaut characterized the social origins of normal school directrices in 1892, he described them as "filles du peuple" (daughters of the people) who prepare other "filles du peuple" to educate "les enfants (children) du peuple."[64] Expected to train primary schoolteachers for children from humble or poor families, perhaps similar to their own, these "daughters of the people" were not to be educators of bourgeois children in secondary schools. Normal school directrices typically came from relatively modest middle-class families or from working-class families with aspirations to higher status. Their backgrounds thus more closely resembled those tabulated by Jacques Ozouf and Mona Ozouf for nearly 2,100 men and women primary schoolteachers, whose careers began before 1914, than those of the young women who were admitted during the 1880s to the *école normale supérieure* in Sèvres to prepare for secondary school careers.[65] Families with limited means were more likely to assume that daughters might need to work than were prosperous middle-class families, and teaching, the first profession widely available to women, was eminently respectable.

Perhaps not surprisingly, public education was the single most common employer for directrices' fathers, engaging 23 percent (43) of the 189 whose work has been identified, a figure slightly higher than the Ozoufs' tabulation of fathers in education (19 percent for *instituteurs*, 20 percent for *institutrices*) or Jean-Noël Luc and Alain Barbé's identification of 21 percent of the fathers of 688 male students at Saint-Cloud before 1914.[66] Most of the directrices' fathers in education were *instituteurs*, but five rose to the rank of primary school inspector, either before the daughter was born or later, and another directed a men's normal school. Two fathers had secondary school or university careers, and five were in private education. For mothers, public records identify nearly a third (62) with occupations, before or after marriage, 17 of them working as teachers in public or private schools, including the mothers of directrices Granet and Bourguet. Although teachers earned small salaries, especially before the Third Republic, their modest education provided them with a modicum of "cultural capital," a facility with language and familiarity with aspects of knowledge and culture that might promote chances of upward social mobility.[67]

Other occupational backgrounds for directrices' fathers included work in local government offices or the police for 23 and the military for another 6. Employment in public service, the background of 38 percent of fathers when educators are included, made families well aware of its advantages for daughters needing to work—notably job security and pensions. Commerce and trade engaged twenty-seven fathers, and seven were employees. Fifty were artisans or workers, the artisans typically better off economically than other manual laborers. The employed mothers included 25 workers or servants and 2 midwives. Three of those workers were among the five unmarried mothers. Only eighteen families (9 percent) made a living from agriculture, at a time when it was still the largest sector of the French economy. Although many directrices' families lived in small rural communes, directrices were noticeably less likely to come from modest agricultural backgrounds than were pre-1914 male students at Saint-Cloud (23 percent) or the male teachers in the Ozoufs' survey (19 percent), but only slightly less likely than that survey's women teachers (11 percent).[68] The extra education needed to become a teacher, let alone a normal school professor or directrice, was harder for rural daughters to acquire than for town dwellers.

To support a daughter's ambition for more education, families often made financial sacrifices. The Third Republic's compulsory schooling extended only to the age of thirteen, although children passing the certificate of primary studies might leave sooner, and many children had no choice but to begin working once schooling ended. Success on a competitive examination (*concours*) for normal school entry at the age of sixteen required additional study at a public *cours complémentaire* (complementary course) or *école primaire supérieure* (higher primary school), or at a private school. Because post-primary schooling did not exist in many small towns, some young women sought additional instruction from a local teacher, who often encouraged their ambitions. Normal schools were free after 1879, but a student and her father had to pledge that she would teach for at least ten years. She also needed the required clothing and linens, a *trousseau* sometimes subsidized by departmental authorities.

Extra schooling thus placed a burden on families with limited income, as some directrices' personnel files indicate. Aglaë Bancilhon, born in 1861 and educated at the Protestant *cours normal* in Nîmes, was one of seven children of a blacksmith. Adèle Tourret from Nîmes was the daughter of a railroad employee and a seamstress. Émilie Desportes from Angers was the oldest of six children of a clerk who later became a teacher. The advantage of being a teacher's child was evident in the case of Cornélie Bertrand, born in 1852 and the oldest of seven children; she reported in 1886, as the directrice in

30 WOMEN AND THE POLITICS OF EDUCATION IN FRANCE

Digne (Basses-Alpes), that four of her siblings were teachers in the Bouches-du-Rhône department. Directrice Marie Marsy and a younger sister who became a normal school professor were two of the ten children of an *instituteur* in the Nord department.[69]

Unfortunately, the information in directrices' personnel files about their earliest education is often incomplete. Their teaching *brevets* were recorded, but frequently without mention of prior study. When early schooling was cited for directrices of the 1880s, it was often in private institutions. Sometimes parents or other relatives were their first teachers, three directrices reporting that their mothers ran private schools. To pass the examination for a primary school teaching credential, at least nineteen women had prepared at a *cours normal*, usually run by a Catholic order but sometimes by laywomen. In the Aude department Joséphine Conte, born in 1863 in a small rural commune, enrolled in the congregational *cours normal* in Carcassonne and completed studies at the republican normal school replacing it in 1881. Mathilde Guny, a teacher's daughter born in 1864, experienced a similar transition in 1882 in Laon in the Aisne.[70] Of the 10 women trained before 1879 at one of the older normal schools, 4 were taught by nuns (3 in Orléans, one in Besançon), and another 2 attended the Lons-le-Saunier school directed by the pious Victorine Lanaud. For many directrices named during the 1880s, Fontenay-aux-Roses provided their first encounter with detailed information about what the Third Republic's normal schools should be and what was expected of their new women leaders.

Predictably the directrices appointed after 1889 had more exposure to republican education at a younger age. By 1886 a *brevet élémentaire* was required to enter a normal school, where students then prepared for a *brevet supérieur*. Of the 23 directrices named during the 1890s, at least 10 attended a normal school, and 3 others obtained *brevets* after study at one of the new public secondary schools for girls. Directrices designated between 1901 and 1914 were even more likely to have attended a departmental normal school—at least 29 of 46 (63 percent); another 12 received *brevets* after secondary school education, and one after a higher primary school.

Just as directrices' educational preparation evolved during the 1880s after the opening of new normal schools and Fontenay-aux-Roses, so too did their profiles of prior teaching experience. The ten pre-1879 directrices had all taught in public or private schools, but only Porte was also a normal school *maîtresse*. Of the 114 directrices appointed between 1879 and 1889, nearly half (56) had taught in a public school (42 before 1879, 14 during the Ferry era), and nearly half (56) had private school teaching or tutoring experience.

Eleven were also normal school *maîtresses* before 1879, and 38 more held that title during the next few years, most of them soon obtaining the new certification for professors, on their way to advancing to the rank of directrice. The directrices named during the 1890s had comparable teaching backgrounds, 12 having taught in public schools and 6 in private ones before obtaining normal school posts. Primary school teaching experience was more unusual, however, for appointees after 1900; only 17 of 46 had been *institutrices*. Entering Fontenay-aux-Roses immediately after study at a departmental normal school put women on a fast track for career advancement, enabling them to go directly to professorial posts in normal schools or higher primary schools.

Fontenay-aux-Roses prepared two-thirds of the directrices of the 1880s for the requisite certification for normal schools. While Lucie Saffroy and Emma Mathieu were among the women clearly profiting from a Fontenay short course between 1880 and 1882, younger Fontenaysiennes who became directrices went through the two-year training for professors and then acquired directing certification through either independent study or Fontenay's special year for preparing directrices. Fifty-two directrices of the 1880s benefited from the extra year, 16 of them having no previous Fontenay training. All but 3 of the 23 appointees of the 1890s were Fontenaysiennes, and 12 of them attended the extra year, discontinued after 1895 because qualified directrices were no longer in short supply. Fontenay alumnae were also nearly three-fourths (34) of the 46 directrices designated between 1901 and the outbreak of war in 1914, but 12 others followed an alternate professional route.

The non-Fontenaysiennes were, for the most part, normal school graduates who became teachers and then found a way to study for and pass the certifying tests for normal school professors and directrices. That alternative route remained because after the creation of Fontenay-aux-Roses and Saint-Cloud, some primary schoolteachers, especially men, argued successfully that it was unfair to deny individuals who did not attend these new higher normal schools the chance to advance to posts in school inspection or normal schools.[71]

Most of the 124 directrices of the 1880s (88 percent) were unmarried when first appointed. Whereas the pre-1879 directrices and those without Fontenay training included 9 married women and 6 widows, only one of 81 directrices from Fontenay was married when initially assigned, and she was an older woman admitted to the special preparatory year for directrices. Eventually 34 more directrices of the 1880s did marry, including 28 Fontenaysiennes, but

32   WOMEN AND THE POLITICS OF EDUCATION IN FRANCE

three-fifths of the 1880s cohort remained single. The first Fontenay-trained directrices were also a noticeably younger group. Although they ranged in age from 23 to 47 when first appointed, their average age was 28, as compared to age 40 for the others. The minimum age for directrices was set at twenty-five in 1880 and raised to thirty in 1887, but the pressing need for directrices led to the selection of twenty-six below the required age during the 1880s.

Because of the large number of directrices named before 1890, only 23 new directrices were assigned during the next decade, most of them (19) initially single but another 5 later marrying. Typically several years older than the first directrices from Fontenay, they ranged in age from 26 to 43, with an average age of nearly 32, and eight were under 30, the required age. The 46 directrices named after 1900 were still older as a group, with an average age of 35, and as an older group were more often married when first designated (12 married, one widow). Later marriages for another eight made them the cohort with the highest marriage rate (46 percent) and also representative of the increasing social acceptance of marriage for professional women.[72]

The openings for new directrices after 1889 occurred because of the retirements, deaths, dismissals, resignations, or reassignments of directrices of the 1880s, fifty-eight of whom no longer served by 1900. In only four cases was marriage a factor in departures, three women resigning to accommodate a husband's career and a fourth returning to professorial status. In social history, marriage is often a key to upward social mobility for women, but for many directrices whose careers already had led to higher social status, marriage simply maintained that status. The most typical employment of the husbands of 79 married or widowed directrices was in public education, which engaged 48 of them. Thirteen others were in public service or the military. Many of the husbands also experienced social promotion through careers in education. One was an inspector general, 5 were *inspecteurs d'académie*, 3 held posts in universities and 15 in secondary education, 5 were primary school inspectors, one directed a normal school, and 13 were professors in normal or higher primary schools. Only one was an *instituteur*, and 4 were chief clerks in the office of the *inspecteur d'académie*. Occasionally rectors or inspectors judged a directrice to be superior, intellectually or professionally, to her husband.[73]

At least 70 percent (55) of the married directrices were mothers, and 19 had three or more children. Only one directrice had to return reluctantly to professorial status because of difficulty combining child-rearing with a directrice's duties.[74] Sadly, three directrices died soon after childbirth.[75]

DIRECTRICES AND THEIR MISSION IN SCHOOLS   33

Whether single or married, most directrices (139) headed more than one normal school. Typically they directed two or three, but 53 led four or more. Although many working-class women and men in search of jobs were also on the move from rural areas to larger towns and cities during the later nineteenth century,[76] the geographical mobility experienced by normal school directrices and professors, as well as by secondary school counterparts, was unusual for women, including women educators. Most primary schoolteachers remained rooted in the departments where they were born or educated. Especially during the 1880s, when many new normal schools opened, experienced and competent directrices received several assignments. Camille Layet directed the schools in Perpignan and Tours before opening new ones in Beauvais in 1884 and Avignon in 1886 and then, after marriage, obtaining a transfer in 1892 to Melun, closer to Paris, her birthplace. Ernestine Béridot from Nîmes, assigned to direct the school in Montpellier in 1882, next opened schools in Oran in 1883, Toulouse in 1884, and Mont-de-Marsan in 1886. Partly because of her husband's work as a civil servant, she held three more posts before retiring in 1915 from the school in Draguignan (Var).[77] Eight other directrices also launched two normal schools during the 1880s.

Frequently directrices requested transfers to be closer to families or to escape from isolated locations, such as Mende in the Lozère department, or politically difficult situations, such as the Vendée or Morbihan departments, each with 8 directrices before 1914. The schools having the largest number of changes in leadership were Perpignan with 15 directrices, Saint-Etienne with 13, Gap with 12, Lons-le-Saunier and Moulins with 11, and Grenoble, Mende, and Oran with 10. The appointments of Marguerite Paringaux between 1882 and 1913 provided a veritable tour de France: Grenoble, Melun, Évreux, Rodez, Chambéry, Cahors, and finally Foix, where she was born in 1854. Marguerite Ginier, a Parisian, directed five normal schools— Perpignan, Bourges, Troyes, Agen, Besançon—before returning to Paris as a primary school inspectress in 1904 and soon becoming active in the Fontenay-aux-Roses alumnae association.[78]

Unsurprisingly, directrices asked to leave schools in cities or towns they found agreeable far less often. Lyon, Orléans, Chartres, Angers, Poitiers, and Limoges had only two directrices before 1914; and Bordeaux, Pau, La Rochelle, Niort, Rennes, Rouen, Évreux, Nancy, and Nevers, three. The normal school in Angoulême (Charente) was the only one to have a single directrice. Emma Frugier launched it in 1884, her second posting, and

34 WOMEN AND THE POLITICS OF EDUCATION IN FRANCE

remained until retirement in 1920, the rector in 1908 describing the school as her "petite république."[79] For some married women whose husbands were also in education, it was convenient to remain in the same place because of the difficulty of obtaining two posts in the same city. Alix Rambault, mother of five, spent thirty years directing the normal school in Limoges where her husband was a teacher (*maître*) in the men's normal school. Adèle Dollé and her husband, a higher primary school professor, remained in Pau for more than thirty years after they married in 1892. Rouen proved an agreeable location for Alcidie Menat, the directrice from 1890 to 1925, and her husband, a normal school professor.[80]

Clearly the vast majority of the 193 directrices named before August 1914 were committed to their work: nearly all pursued careers that lasted until retirement or death. The exceptions were 16 who left, voluntarily or involuntarily, 15 of them during the 1880s.[81] A large majority (137) retired or died as normal school directrices. Of the others, 20 retired or died as directrices or professors in higher primary or secondary schools, 4 as normal school professors, and 16 as *inspectrices*, more often of *écoles maternelles* than primary schools.[82] Careers typically lasted until the interwar years for younger directrices appointed after 1890. Whether or not they received training at Fontenay-aux-Roses, normal school directrices had become *fonctionnaires* (civil servants) loyal to the Third Republic and contributed thereby to the creation of a new image of what women could accomplish in an educational post carrying significant responsibility. Like women heading the new girls' secondary schools, they needed administrative ability as well as talent for teaching.

Celebrating and Debating Women's Role in Public Education

The Third Republic placed its educational accomplishments on display in 1889 when it celebrated the centennial of the French Revolution of 1789, to which it traced its roots and political values. During the year France hosted an international exposition and a number of special congresses, including an international congress on primary education that was an occasion for showcasing the democratic Republic's recent provision of more educational opportunities, including opportunities for women educators.

By 1889 the goal of secularizing public schools, central to the foundational Bert and Ferry laws, had been furthered by the Goblet law of October 30, 1886, which required that lay teachers replace members of religious orders still teaching in public schools. The law set a five-year timetable for replacing men, but women religious teachers would be replaced only when they retired or withdrew from public schools. That gender difference stemmed from recognition of important practical and political realities: girls in public schools were nearly four times more likely than boys to have teachers from religious orders; the number of lay *institutrices* was still limited, and nine departments lacked normal schools; and resistance to laicizing girls' schools in some locales dictated political caution. The Goblet law also reorganized the departmental council (*conseil départemental*) of primary education whose functions, under the leadership of the prefect and the chief departmental inspector (*inspecteur d'académie*), included reviewing recommendations for promoting or disciplining teachers and opening new schools.

The restructured departmental education council no longer included religious leaders but retained political representation with four members from a department's *conseil général*, chosen by their colleagues. Educators were better represented than previously, when only the *inspecteur d'académie* and one primary inspector had membership, for the Goblet law added the directors of the men's and women's normal schools, a second primary inspector, and two men and two women teachers elected by colleagues. Private education (*enseignement libre*) would have delegates present at meetings only when the conduct of one of its teachers was under discussion. The Goblet law underscored the Republic's goals of religious neutrality in public schools and an enhanced status for teachers. Unsurprisingly, some of the women trained at Fontenay hailed the changes in the council, including the addition of women for the first time, as an example of the Republic's commitment to "liberal" and "laic" values, and they saw a welcome correction to the 1850 Falloux law, which had made teachers subordinate to the clergy. The election of teachers' representatives, with a voice in disciplinary issues, was indicative of belief in democratic self-government, opined Angélina Petit in 1887.[83]

Women's inclusion on departmental education councils had not come without controversy. During debate in the Chamber of Deputies and before the final legislative proposal specified the election of two women teachers, bishop Charles-Émile Freppel of Angers, a monarchist deputy, had argued against including the normal school directrice, calling it inappropriate for

36   WOMEN AND THE POLITICS OF EDUCATION IN FRANCE

her to be the only woman on the council and suggesting instead that she communicate with the council by sending written statements. Republicans then countered that placing women teachers on the council would give the directrice female colleagues, and by the time both legislative houses approved the law, an earlier proposal to have teachers elected by men and women colleagues had been revised to specify that male teachers would select two colleagues, as would women teachers.[84]

The year of the Goblet law also marked another milestone for women educators with the election in December 1886 of Pauline Kergomard, an *inspectrice générale* of *écoles maternelles*, to the Conseil Supérieur de l'Instruction Publique (Higher Council of Public Instruction). Although there was no requirement to include a woman on this influential advisory body, reorganized in 1880 and dominated by men from secondary schools and universities, Kergomard became the first woman to win one of the six seats reserved for representatives of primary education. In campaigning she presented her candidacy as that of "the mother and the woman," a careful use of traditional terminology to make the untraditional argument that women educators deserved a special advocate on the council.[85]

The international congress on primary education in August 1889 provided a public occasion for highlighting women's place in the politics of republican education, and Kergomard, normal school directrices, and other women educators contributed to the discussion of women's roles. To document recent progress, inspectors compiled reports on the history of primary schools, nursery schools (*écoles maternelles*), normal schools, and the *écoles normales supérieures* for primary education. The congress's formal agenda featured three major topics: vocational education, the *écoles annexes* attached to normal schools, and roles appropriate for women educators. Aspects of the latter topic proved by far the most controversial. Well before the congress, teachers and normal school personnel submitted position papers (*mémoires*) to Octave Gréard, vice-rector of the academy of Paris, and in the quasi-official *Revue pédagogique* Kergomard published a much discussed article on women educators' roles and advocated their appointment as primary school inspectresses.[86]

There was widespread agreement in the pre-congress *mémoires* and at the congress about women's special abilities as teachers of very young children and girls but substantial disagreement about two questions.[87] Should women be the preferred teachers for one-room coeducational schools (*écoles mixtes*) in communes whose populations of fewer than five hundred did not warrant the maintenance of separate schools for boys and girls? And should women inspect primary schools, as Kergomard strongly advocated? The Goblet law, article 6, specified that *écoles mixtes* should have women teachers, but in 1889 male teachers were still a majority in such schools, and many people believed that men could better handle the older boys they enrolled.[88] Because localities often preferred a male teacher who could also serve as secretary to the mayor, a public function presumed to be unsuitable for women, the law authorized departments to grant temporary exemptions to communes requesting a man for an *école mixte*. Legislators in 1889 were debating the admission of women to the corps of 450 primary school inspectors, and the law of July 19, 1889, passed shortly before the congress, permitted their appointment but did not mandate it.

Men and women who commented on women educators' roles in 1889 routinely cited assumptions about women's personalities and intellect to bolster their views, in the process sometimes revealing variations in contemporary attitudes concerning gender. There was much agreement about differences between men's and women's personalities but disagreement about how such differences might affect women's ability to fill certain positions. In the Aude department the personnel from the men's and women's normal schools in Carcassonne met together, with the *inspecteur d'académie* presiding, and professor Marie Szumlanska drew up the *mémoire* on their deliberations. Women's "natural aptitudes and tastes" made them educators "par excellence," she wrote, adding that their opportunities in education should be enlarged as much as possible because teaching was "the only liberal career" women could easily enter. The directrice, Marguerite Jalambic, also opined at the meeting that women as educators were often superior to men. On the question of women becoming primary school inspectors, the Aude's *inspecteur d'académie* expressed full support, but some male professors objected that *inspectrices* would make judgments on the basis of first impressions and lack impartiality—to which women colleagues replied that because of an *inspectrice*'s prior experience as a teacher or professor, there should be no fear that feminine "*nervosité*" (nervousness) would prevent her from making fair judgments.[89] In Mende (Lozère) normal school personnel also endorsed the appointment of *inspectrices*, adding that directrices might play a role in inspection as well.[90]

Unlike women at the normal schools in the Aude and Lozère, Pauline Gaudefroy, directrice of the normal school in Tulle (Corrèze), expressed reservations about women school inspectors, even as she championed

38   WOMEN AND THE POLITICS OF EDUCATION IN FRANCE

women teachers for *écoles mixtes*. She called the post of inspector the educational role "the least compatible" with women's duties as wives and mothers because it posed complications which women educators typically did not face, such as the need to travel. Positions requiring women's travel were more to the taste of Americans than to the French, she wrote. Although Gaudefroy did not reject the woman inspector "in principle," she doubted that many *inspectrices* were needed, and she suggested that normal school directrices could play a useful supporting role in school inspection. If directrices were sometimes allowed to be absent from normal schools to visit girls' primary schools, they could thereby advise women teachers, not all of whom were normal school graduates.[91] Similarly, women at the normal school in Perpignan, directed by Adrienne Guinier, envisioned a role for directrices in inspection but saw it as simply rendering assistance to an inspector because they believed that a woman's qualities and deficiencies did not suit her for an inspector's work.[92]

In a detailed *mémoire* submitted in late May, Marie Simboiselle, the recently appointed directrice of the normal school in the Hautes-Alpes, responded to Kergomard's article in the *Revue pédagogique* on women educators' accomplishments and added her own observations about recent changes in society and attitudes. Because women now had access to various careers closed to them twenty years earlier and demonstrated their ability to succeed in new professional roles, Simboiselle thought that most people no longer questioned woman's "intellectual value" or "intrinsic value." Although she believed that women were more dominated by "sentiment" and men by "reason," she argued that the equilibrium between the two sexes made the transformation of existing social norms possible. Thus if a woman became an *inspectrice* or a directrice, she would remain, above all, an *institutrice* "by nature" with her own children and the children of others. Simboiselle, then age thirty-one and not yet married, also believed that especially intelligent women could surpass the "limits assigned by nature."[93]

At the international primary education congress, attended by more than 1,500 people from August 12 to 16, 1889, the advocacy for primary school inspectresses and women in charge of *écoles mixtes*, led by Kergomard, provoked more controversy among French delegates than any other issue. Although some countries, such as Germany, offered examples of men as the heads of girls' schools, French delegates, male and female, were firmly committed to the tradition of assigning only women to head *écoles maternelles*, girls' schools, or women's normal schools. Kergomard, as an *inspectrice générale* of *écoles maternelles*, occupied a post that the French state had been assigning to women since 1837. Yet many male inspectors and other educators objected vehemently to allowing women to be primary school inspectors, and women themselves were divided, as the pre-congress *mémoires* indicated.[94]

Opponents at the congress again marshaled arguments about women's supposed psychological deficiencies for inspection posts and contended that the travel required was too rigorous for a woman and unsuitable for a woman traveling alone. These arguments prevailed with a majority of the largely male and mostly French delegates to the congress's "second section," which deliberated on women educators' roles. They approved a resolution stating that men should continue to be the only inspectors of girls' primary schools because the job was "incompatible with woman's nature and her role in the family" and because a woman could not always have "the necessary authority to intervene effectively with local administrations." Yet the section did not apply the same critiques to inspectresses for *écoles maternelles*, resolving instead to support their continuation, even though they too had to travel and exercise authority. As with its resolution favoring men, not women, for *écoles mixtes*, the second section was voicing displeasure with what French law made possible.[95] Pronouncing women unfit for certain posts was also, of course, an effort to preserve men's dominance in those posts.

National politics were injected into the congress's debates by primary inspector Charles Delapierre from Paris, who insisted that the Republic would be endangered if women became inspectors for all girls' primary schools. He foresaw "republican instruction, patriotic and neutral from the standpoint of religious dogma in boys' schools, and probably a different instruction in girls' schools" where the "patriotic idea" would be weakened.[96] His warning showed little confidence in the effectiveness of either the laic policies adopted for girls' public schools or the teaching of republican civics lessons to girls.

Although Delapierre did not explicitly mention women's normal schools, he evidently doubted that some teachers they trained were sufficiently loyal to the Republic. Certainly many parents encouraged daughters who were normal school students to attend church services, and the generations of women teachers trained before 1914 were more religiously observant and less likely to be freethinkers than men teachers.[97] Delapierre's perspective was not uncommon, but by the late 1880s when rectors and inspectors had occasion to comment on the religious practice of normal school directrices and professors, they typically deflected public complaints about such practice

40 WOMEN AND THE POLITICS OF EDUCATION IN FRANCE

by defending educators' right to religious liberty, so long as they did not proselytize inside the normal school.[98] In other words, educational officials recognized that one could be a Catholic and support the Republic.

Kergomard responded at the congress in 1889 to those who doubted women's republican loyalties. During the congress's debate on assigning women teachers to one-room *écoles mixtes*, opponents of the policy like Delapierre expressed fear that "republican influence" in coeducational schools would be lost without a male teacher. In reply, Kergomard conceded that not all women had accepted the Republic, but she then insisted that a "republican woman teacher in each village and hamlet" would provide the best way to ensure that women and their children shared republican ideals.[99]

The woman at the congress who was most outspoken in opposition to women as primary school inspectors was an older normal school directrice from Tarbes in the Hautes-Pyrénées, Léontine Heurtefeu, then age fifty, a year younger than Kergomard. Heurtefeu prefaced her remarks to the full congress by stating that she spoke with regret because she did not believe it suitable for women to speak in public. Evidently she did not think that the students and professors she routinely addressed inside the normal school constituted a public, even though political and educational leaders often emphasized that the normal school prepared young women for a "public function."[100] Like male opponents of inspectresses, she cited presumed psychological differences between men and women: men were directed by reason and could wield authority; women, directed by "the heart" and "sensibility," could not. Heurtefeu also dismissed the arguments that male inspectors sometimes abused their authority and acted inappropriately with women and that women teachers would feel more comfortable confiding in a woman inspector. She doubted that the alleged abuses occurred and contended that an honorable woman (*honnête femme*) could confide in an honorable man and knew how to protect herself.[101]

All normal school directrices were invited to attend the congress as official delegates, and at least ten were delegates to the second section deliberating on women's roles, but of the ten only Gaudefroy submitted a *mémoire*, and only Heurtefeu's views appeared in the published summary of debates.[102] Three other women educators did speak up in favor of inspectresses: Augustine Lebrun, a normal school professor from Versailles; and Blanche Scordia and Marie Rauber, both teachers in Paris.[103]

Under the leadership of vice-rector Gréard, who presided over the final discussions, the full congress modified some of the second section's resolutions, notably by recommending that primary school inspection posts be assigned to women "on a trial basis." The resolution was a compromise, reached after the congress rejected endorsing women's access to inspection posts on the same basis as men. In his summation of the deliberations concerning inspectresses, Gréard remarked pointedly that the congress, dominated by French delegates, had proved to be "less liberal" than French law. Surprised also that more women did not object to being denied access to inspection posts, Gréard stated that he had more confidence than some women themselves in women's "sharp judgment and reason."[104]

The minister of public instruction, Armand Faillières, delivered remarks to conclude the congress and remind attendees of the educational accomplishments of the Third Republic. He thanked foreign as well as French participants but focused on French matters, calling the recent law of July 19, 1889, a fitting celebration of the centennial of the Revolution because it stipulated that the state would take charge of paying teachers' salaries, thus making primary education truly an "enseignement d'État." He did not mention, however, that the new law continued the tradition of paying women educators, whether in primary schools or normal schools, less than male colleagues. The Republic relied on teachers to demonstrate that it offered a society "of peace as well as emancipation," Faillières stated, and women teachers' contribution was as vital as that of male teachers. *Institutrices*, through their work in girls' schools, would provide French democracy with women who were "educated, strong, virtuous."[105]

Clearly Faillières and numerous republican officials valued the work that women teachers, trained in normal schools, would do to educate new generations of republican wives and mothers. Yet that very emphasis on the centrality of women's domestic role also provided arguments against extending women's public roles, as the proceedings of the 1889 congress indicated. The benefits offered to women by Paul Bert, Jules Ferry, and other leaders of the first republican educational reforms were only a "relative emancipation of the mother-citizen (*mère-citoyenne*)."[106]

It fell to the normal schools, and particularly to their directrices, to take the lead in creating a model for the new woman teacher loyal to the Third Republic and its policies. By 1889 the misunderstandings about the nature of republican educational policies, and particularly *laïcité*, exhibited by some of the veteran directrices and first appointees after 1879, were far more rare, notably because women trained at Fontenay-aux-Roses had entered the ranks of normal school personnel, comprising three-fourths (64) of the

42 WOMEN AND THE POLITICS OF EDUCATION IN FRANCE

86 directrices in October 1889. Despite doubts still expressed by various male officials and colleagues or the general public about women's ability to wield authority, or wield it fairly should they become *inspectrices primaires*, directrices' success in leading normal schools was a challenge to the disparagement of women's abilities. The directrices provided valuable instruction and helpful advice as they trained future teachers and tried to give them confidence in their abilities.

2

Training Future Teachers

Knowledge, Values, Conduct

The normal school directrice wielded considerable authority within her school. Her duties were administrative, pedagogical, and moral. She monitored the teaching effectiveness of professors and instructors, the academic efforts and behavior of students, and the work of the *économe* who organized the provision of meals, cleaning of facilities, and purchasing of supplies. In addition, she regularly submitted reports on the school's functioning to administrative superiors. All students also encountered the directrice in the classroom where she gave lessons in *morale* (moral instruction), psychology, and pedagogy. Certainly all normal school instructors were expected to be appropriate role models for future teachers as they endeavored to make them more knowledgeable, but the directrice had special responsibility for helping students understand what would be expected of them in their future classrooms and in the communities where they taught. As the directrice provided guidance, how would she balance the task of helping young women become confident in their intellectual abilities with the obligation to remind them of traditional expectations for feminine conduct?

In some localities the directrices and professors saw part of their mission, especially with first-year students, as one of "civilizing." Schools, transportation networks, and the army would all play a role in further integrating rural areas into the nation and turning "peasants into Frenchmen."[1] For three years normal school students ages sixteen to eighteen resided in an *internat*, a boarding facility where they could acquire habits and values that some families might not have provided. Thus if some students arrived lacking proper table manners, they would acquire them in the normal school dining room. They also learned about practices for personal hygiene, even if facilities were limited in some schools.

Contemporaries frequently likened the organization of women's normal schools to that of Catholic convents, terming them *couvents laïques*. Lengthy

Women and the Politics of Education in Third Republic France. Linda L. Clark, Oxford University Press.
© Oxford University Press 2023. DOI: 10.1093/oso/9780197632864.003.0003

École normale d'institutrices de Limoges. *Postcard, Author's collection*

periods of silence were imposed, and during an academic term students could leave the normal school only at designated times, either in groups escorted by school personnel or individually with family members or other people approved by parents. Students wore long black dresses with high necklines and kept hair pinned up in a chignon, away from their faces. The daily schedule, set by the directrice in consultation with professors and subject to administrative approval, typically extended from about 5–5:30 a.m. to 9–9:30 p.m. and on days with classes could include up to six hours for instruction, plus recreation after lunch and in the late afternoon, and several hours for study.[2] Although male normal school students also experienced a regimented existence and wore a professional "uniform" when outside the school, they enjoyed more freedom of movement. Republican leaders wanted the conduct of normal school students to be above reproach, and a sheltered existence for women students in a carefully monitored facility served that objective.

Directrices often commented on the *internat*'s moralizing effect, made possible, they believed, because it removed students from confining or undesirable home environments. That conviction reflected the views of Félix Pècaut, who considered the *internat* essential for providing normal school students with a "complete education" for life and not just knowledge about subjects they would teach.[3] The Marne department's first directrice, Hélène Granet,

École normale d'institutrices de Limoges, dormitory, c. 1900. © *Réseau Canope – Le Musée National de l'Éducation, Rouen, 1979.17801*

reported in 1881 that some students from urban centers arrived with habits and attitudes that are "not ours," but she expected that in their new surroundings these problems could be corrected.[4] Céline Mazier, who opened the normal school in Blois (Loir-et-Cher) in 1880, judged the *internat* valuable for creating an esprit de corps among new republican teachers, adding that it met French societal expectations for giving young women more protection than seemed customary in the contemporary United States or England.[5] These directrices' comments well illustrate how women students would experience social values and corporate identity in nineteenth-century French normal schools.[6] While providing young women with academic training, the school's personnel also endeavored to teach them how to live.

Another directrice's discussion of the normal school's "civilizing" objectives reached a broader audience than the unpublished comments cited above, for it was published in the quasi-official *Revue pédagogique* in 1886. Sponsored by the ministry of public instruction, this review was circulated to a large national readership representing various ranks in primary education. The unnamed author of the "Notes d'une directrice d'école normale" was

46 WOMEN AND THE POLITICS OF EDUCATION IN FRANCE

actually Louise Martin-Schaefer, a Parisian who had trained at Fontenay-aux-Roses during its first two years and was in her second directing post, the Meuse department's normal school in Bar-le-Duc, which she opened in 1885. Marriage in 1884 to the chief departmental inspector (*inspecteur d'académie*) for the Aube, her previous posting, likely added to her familiarity with administrative expectations for directrices. Discussing the goal of improving behavior, Martin noted that teaching first-year students new habits of order and cleanliness was more difficult than one might expect. For example, maintaining silence in study rooms could be problematic because young women liked to talk. She also perceived that for many students the normal school offered a more physically comfortable setting and better food than their homes had provided, But, she quickly added, such amenities did not alter the goal of training teachers who were "fortes et simples" (strong and modest) and definitely not "déclassées" uprooted from any social moorings.[7]

The routine and discipline for Martin's students included assembling on Saturday evenings to hear her present evaluations ("notes") for each student in each subject. Her regular meetings with instructors (*le conseil des professeurs*) provided the detailed information on students' progress. After concluding the Saturday session with a general summary and sometimes singling out students whose course work was poor, she left the room so that each student could reflect on the individual and collective evaluations. The next morning students were asked to share their reflections.[8] Directrices hoped that such sessions would motivate students to try harder in the future. No doubt the public ranking of students discouraged some, even as it promoted competition among others.

As the directrice imposed discipline on students' academic work and behavior, she was also expected to maintain an atmosphere that was familial. She was, in effect, like a "mère de famille" (mother) to her charges, just as her male counterpart was likened to a "père de famille" (father). With younger instructors, she should try to give advice as an older sister might. Repeatedly the inspectors and rectors who evaluated directrices praised them for displaying "maternal" concern and faulted them for deficiencies in this regard. Thus inspector general Félix Cadet characterized Mme Martin as gentle, gracious, and maternal. Alix Rambault, directrice of the Limoges normal school which she opened in 1883, was praised for making it like a "true family" but was also told more than once that her maternal good nature should not become too indulgent. Other directrices, such as Gabrielle Athané, received similar cautions. Residing in the directrice's apartment in the normal school, Rambault and her husband, an instructor at the men's normal school, provided a model republican household with a family eventually including five children.[9]

Administrators' emphasis on the value of directrices' maternal qualities well exemplifies the numerous late nineteenth-century "maternalist" discourses deployed in Western nations by advocates of enlarging women's public and professional roles.[10] Although a majority of directrices remained unmarried, they were about as likely to be characterized as maternal as were married colleagues. Thus in 1890 rector Émile Charles commended directrice Marie Porte in Lyon for being a "mère de famille" for both students and professors. Rector Gaston Bizos praised directrice Herminie Bousquet in Montpellier in 1898 as a "good mother" who prepared teachers to be "good housekeepers" (*ménagères*). Berthe Tailleur, a directrice since 1879, remained an excellent "maternal teacher," inspector general Guillaume Jost reported in 1896.[11] Such descriptions of single women were consistent with longstanding beliefs that women were inherently maternal in nature, their qualities of sweetness, gentleness, and self-abnegation making them the ideal teachers of young children. Women educators themselves typically shared such notions, as *mémoires* written for the 1889 education congress indicated, and they conveyed them in behavioral advice offered to students. When male officials judged a directrice lacking in "maternal sentiment," they might also call her "more feared than loved."[12]

Credited with providing a welcoming and familial atmosphere in normal schools, directrices were also severely criticized if they failed to maintain appropriate discipline, detect misdeeds on the part of students or instructors, or prevent or stem major conflicts among instructors. The typical annual review by an inspector or rector termed the students in many normal schools "docile"—a word used repeatedly—and hardworking, but there were exceptions. In 1885 students in Vannes (Morbihan) circulated letters with songs deemed unsuitable. Their directrice, Élise Legros, who had opened the Breton school in 1884, eventually found and seized the offending material but nonetheless received an official reprimand (*blâme*) for not discovering it sooner. Eugénie Jacquemin, age twenty-seven when she assumed her first directing post in 1887 in Blois (Loir-et-Cher), encountered a hostile instructor determined to incite students against her, and she also identified students who circulated notes mocking various staff members. Although she, like Legros, eventually found the unacceptable material and reported it, she was moved to another school in 1889.[13]

48 WOMEN AND THE POLITICS OF EDUCATION IN FRANCE

Normal school students were allowed to receive letters only from their parents and others approved by parents, and the envelopes of incoming correspondence were checked to verify that they came from approved parties before they were handed to students. Some students managed, however, to have other students bring in letters or to obtain them surreptitiously while outside the school if a professor escorting them on walks was not watchful. Directrice Léonie Pieyre was transferred from Aix-en-Provence in 1890 after she failed to report promptly on an exchange of letters between a student and an unapproved male correspondent and also because she did not stop inappropriate contact between a woman instructor and a professor at the men's normal school. Nathalie Bourgoise, the interim directrice in La Roche-sur-Yon (Vendée) in March 1887, was officially reprimanded for negligence because she had not detected the pregnancy of the normal school's cook, who gave birth on the premises. In Aurillac (Cantal) in 1903 directrice Célina Sabatier and the director of the men's normal school were both faulted because their students secretly exchanged letters and seven of Sabatier's students went into town without wearing the prescribed hat.[14]

Not only students' unacceptable correspondence but also possession of unapproved books figured in a later incident in the Moulins (Allier) normal school in 1906. Directrice Caroline Hoël ordered the premises searched after a professor saw a student reading Rousseau's *Confessions*, and she found more offending material, including novels by such popular authors as Gustave Flaubert, Paul Bourget, Alphonse Daudet, and Émile Zola. There were also letters revealing that some students conversed with students from the men's normal school and the lycée. Hoël's report on her findings prompted the chief departmental inspector to investigate further, and he and the rector faulted her for not discovering the novels sooner. Complicating administrators' decisions about punishing the dozen students involved in misconduct was the fact that parents' connivance was detected in a majority of cases and that some parents worked in public education. Rector Alfred Coville reported to the director of primary education in Paris that these students came from a region where morality was "très faible" (very weak) and that Hoël's lack of vigilance had allowed three months to pass before the problematical novels were found. The normal school should be a place of "haute culture morale" (high moral culture), not a reflection of local failings, he wrote. At the end of the academic year Hoël, then nearly fifty, was transferred to the normal school in the Haute-Savoie.[15]

The most severe punishment of a directrice was meted out to Henriette Loiret, a widow removed from her post in Troyes (Aube) and excluded from future employment in public education in 1889 because of complaints that she allowed students to be too affectionate with each other and was too affectionate with some of them herself. In the evidently rare cases when a directrice or professor learned of students making gestures deemed inappropriate toward other students or actually sharing a bed, the students were typically dismissed from the school, unless administrators accepted explanations that their contact had been innocent. Surveillance of students day and night was intended to prevent such occurrences. In Loiret's case, the attendant publicity complicated the usual administrative tendency to treat incidents with sexual overtones discreetly and in veiled language.[16]

Linked to the familial model favored for normal schools was the assumption that cooperation could outweigh conflicts among its members. Ideally, in the *internat* students should learn more about getting along with others and develop greater self-control, interpersonal skills that would enhance their ability to function successfully later in communities where they taught. The directrice, professors, instructors, and *économe* were expected to provide models of collegiality as they worked for the success of the institution.[17]

Unsurprisingly, senior administrators deplored cases of serious conflict. In Valence in 1895 not only professors but also students were divided into two camps, and the rector placed the blame on Sophie Veyron-Lacroix, a fifty-five-year-old directrice (with no Fontenay training) whose favoritism toward some individuals antagonized others.[18] Disputes between a directrice and the *économe* in charge of housekeeping were frequent, as in Tarbes in 1888, Clermont-Ferrand in 1889, and Draguignan in 1894, and explain why aspiring directrices might face a question on their certifying examination about the respective duties of the directrice and the *économe*.[19] Bitter clashes between a directrice and professors resentful of her authority or feeling abused by that authority were also not unusual, and the clashes not hidden from public view could fuel local gossip. They were also the basis for fictional plots. Louise-Marie Compain's *L'Un vers l'autre* (1903), later serialized in the *Revue de l'enseignement primaire*, recounted the heroine's disillusionment with the life of a normal school professor; and Élise Albert and C. Arnaud's novel *Normaliennes* (1914), first serialized in *L'École émancipée*, depicted rivalries among students as well as professors.[20] Depending upon the severity of real-life conflicts, one or more of the women involved might be reprimanded and/or transferred.[21]

Teaching and Monitoring the Curriculum

The reforms introduced by the Ferry law of March 28, 1882, enriched the curriculum of public primary schools and required that a secular "moral and civic" instruction replace "moral and religious" instruction. As a new subject, *la morale laïque* had to be explained to current and future teachers. In primary schools teachers could use new textbooks for moral instruction, replete with lists of behavioral do's and don't's, which told young pupils about their duties to family, friends, community, and the nation. Textbooks for reading had stories about good and bad behavior that reinforced moral lessons. In the normal schools the directors and directrices prepared their students to teach *morale*. They explained why the Third Republic had adopted a *morale laïque*, clearly aiming to influence their students' thinking. When young women first came to the normal school, wrote Mme Martin, they were accustomed to religious practices but, presumably, had done little or no personal reflection about the reasons for adhering to rules of conduct. At the morning meeting with students to open an instructional day, Martin, like Pécaut at Fontenay, used conversations and literary or philosophical texts to prod them to think about such topics as the nature of goodness (*bonté*) and sincerity and to examine their own consciences. The goal was to promote independent thinking and replace blind acceptance of authority.[22]

Training at Fontenay-aux-Roses, from the outset, exposed all students to courses in psychology, moral instruction, the history of educational thought, and pedagogy. Henri Marion, a lycée professor of philosophy who inaugurated the psychology course, presented it as a basis for approaching the teaching of *morale*. Understanding human psychological as well as physical development would provide insight into how children learned to make choices between good and bad conduct and ideas. Although Marion soon ceased to teach at Fontenay when he assumed a new chair at the Sorbonne in the "science of education" in 1883, his *Leçons de psychologie appliquée à l'éducation* (1882) and *Leçons de morale* (1882), both based on lecture notes taken by Fontenay students, became important texts for instruction in departmental normal schools. An eighteenth edition of the psychology text appeared in 1926 and a twentieth edition of *Leçons de morale* in 1927.[23]

Fontenay and then Saint-Cloud, as *écoles normales supérieures*, paved the way for making the study of pedagogy more important and bringing it into institutions of higher education. The universities of Bordeaux, Lyon, and Montpellier created chairs in the "science of education" in 1884, to be followed by others.[24] Gabriel Compayré, formerly a professor of philosophy at the University of Toulouse, introduced Fontenay's course on pedagogy and the history of educational thought in 1880–81, before his election to the Chamber of Deputies; his *Histoire de la pédagogie* (1884) and *Cours de pédagogie théorique et pratique* (1886) also became staples for departmental normal schools.

Women attending Fontenay's special third-year preparatory course for directrices, started in 1882, gained experience in making presentations on subjects in the normal school curriculum. Emma Frugier, assigned in 1882–83 to discuss lessons on *morale* for normal school students, emphasized that because of its importance not only a directrice but also other professors should incorporate it in lessons. As future teachers learned how to present moral duties (*devoirs*) in primary schools, they should also develop their own strong sense of duty for which they would make sacrifices. Moral instruction in normal schools should be separated from all religious dogma, Frugier continued, but still recognize "religious sentiment" and find "in a single name, God," the ideal of perfection. To inspire this sentiment in students, professors themselves needed "a profound conviction." After Frugier spoke, director Pécaut provided a critique of her comments on "religious sentiment." He insisted that *la morale laïque* had a rational basis and thus was grounded in more than a belief in God. Although there were textbooks available for moral instruction, he advised that directrices could best influence students by combining the exposition of moral topics with a skillful posing of questions.[25]

Frugier's presentation at Fontenay reflected a close reading of the recently issued instructions for the primary school curriculum, framed by the Conseil Supérieur de l'Instruction Publique (CSIP) to comply with the law of March 28, 1882. Although the law did not mandate teaching "devoirs envers Dieu" (duties to God)—a disappointment to Jules Simon and many senators—the CSIP, under the influence of philosophy professor Paul Janet, incorporated "devoirs envers Dieu" in the program for *morale* in the *cours moyen* for children aged nine to eleven. Official instructions issued in July 1882 told teachers not to expound at length on the nature of God but to make two basic and essentially deistic points. They should associate "the name of God with the idea of the first Cause and perfect Being (*Être parfait*)," without any linkage to a specific religion; and they should help students understand the duty of "obedience to the laws of God" as revealed by "conscience and reason."[26]

52 WOMEN AND THE POLITICS OF EDUCATION IN FRANCE

The concern with striking a proper balance between references to a divinity and purely secular messages about values and conduct would long preoccupy republican educators, such as the eleven normal school directors and directrices who contributed to a discussion in the *Correspondance générale de l'instruction primaire* in 1894–95.[27] For many schoolteachers, Jules Ferry provided the most understandable interpretation of republican expectations for moral instruction, stating in his circular of November 17, 1883, that it was essentially the "old code of conduct . . . of our fathers." Although Catholic critics branded the public school an "école sans Dieu" (school without God), its curriculum included "duties to God," even if, in practice, attention to the topic varied greatly—according to the preferences of teachers, inspectors, and local communities—and was further ignored after the separation of church and state in 1905. There were thus "contradictions" in the *laïcité* of Ferry.[28]

The linkage of psychology to moral instruction in normal school teaching was addressed by future directrice Adèle Tourret at Fontenay in 1887. Assigned to explain how a directrice should introduce psychology to students, she first noted that many arrived with limited experiences. From milieus where many people were poorly educated and lacked large vocabularies, students often came unprepared for an intelligent exchange of views. To assume the responsibility of educating children, they needed to understand people, and to understand others they should first understand themselves. Directrices could begin by asking students to recall how they had experienced suffering, worries, and joys—an approach that would accustom them to looking inside themselves. Then they would be ready to understand the development of a child's personality as a progression from physical activity and sensation to the development of intelligence, moral sensibility, and will power. Finally, students would reach an understanding of the "duality" in human nature, marked by lifelong individual struggles against one's "inferior nature" so that reason would control one's life and choices.[29]

Such exercises at Fontenay prepared women to respond successfully to pedagogical questions on examinations for certifying directrices. When Aglaë Bancilhon, Tourret's classmate and like her a Protestant from the Gard, had to write in 1887 about how teachers could further the development of a "moral personality," she stressed that to influence pupils, they must first learn to direct themselves. The normal school, through its curriculum and discipline, would help future teachers acquire that essential self-control and intellectual independence. In a century when "all beliefs" were subject to critical analysis, it was crucial, she wrote, that young women develop the ability to think for themselves. Faulting Rousseau's pedagogical treatise *Émile* for treating the girl Sophie like an "agreeable toy" for the male, she complained that many people who considered themselves "liberals" still feared that a woman's intellectual development would cause her to lose "charm." A woman, like a man, deserved her own life and was "not made simply to please." Bancilhon clearly equated a woman's full moral development with more independence and intellectual growth than was traditional, but like many colleagues also felt the need to say that such development did not harm essential feminine traits.[30]

Directrices' obligation to present *la morale laïque* clearly and persuasively also accounts for the pedagogical question on the 1891 examination for their certification: what should primary schools and normal schools convey about "l'esprit laïque"? The essays of two of the future directrices drew pointed contrasts between laic and ecclesiastical mind-sets. Isabelle Ruet, age forty-two and a normal school professor who had taught previously in a boarding school, equated "l'esprit laïque" with confidence in "human nature" and "human reason." Whereas Ruet had profited from Fontenay's third-year program, Louise Sahuc, a graduate of the normal school in Miliana (Algeria) in 1886, prepared for the examination by teaching for a year at a normal school in southern France.[31]

Sahuc knew that enemies of republican education often misrepresented "l'esprit laïque," and she recognized that a directrice might have to explain it to worried parents. The laic mind-set is "liberal," she wrote, and can prepare students to exercise their will and reason freely, the opposite of passive obedience. It was thus essential for educating the future citizens of a "free country" (*pays libre*). Countering attacks on the republican school as "sans Dieu," she insisted that teachers could create respect for the "magnificent work of the Creator" without "the formulas of a [religious] credo." *Laïcité* was the opposite of "cet esprit ascétique qui mutile l'oeuvre de Dieu" (this ascetic spirit which mutilates the work of God). It enabled a teacher to promote "the development of reason and judgment" and teach a child "that he is not only the brother of those who share his religion, but of all men, whatever their religious convictions." The republican school should thus teach not only love of France but of all humanity.[32]

As Sahuc's essay indicated, the normal school curriculum also linked the goal of promoting independent thinking and individual responsibility to lessons in "civic duties." Citizens in a nation with universal suffrage were

54   WOMEN AND THE POLITICS OF EDUCATION IN FRANCE

expected to be patriotic, obey laws, pay taxes, respect compulsory schooling requirements, perform military service, and exercise their right to vote. Women were excluded from voting and the military, but as mothers and teachers they needed to be able to explain civic duties and the workings of the republican government to girls as well as boys. Because of the current debate on votes for women in England, Compayré had warned against such advocacy in his manual for civic instruction in normal schools. Men and women were equal as "moral persons," he wrote, but a wife's subordination to a husband was "normal" in marriage and because of "the special functions that nature imposes on mothers, it would be difficult and dangerous to bring the weaker sex into the agitations inseparable from political life," especially because this might introduce "division and trouble" in a household. In France, he added, women did not seem inclined to ask for political rights, an opinion understandable in the mid-1880s although it ignored the current advocacy of Hubertine Auclert and a limited number of other Frenchwomen.[33]

The curriculum for civic instruction in women's normal schools was reduced to "essential notions" in 1889, and it excluded keeping records for the local mayor's office (*mairie*), an extra role restricted by custom to male teachers. Women's normal schools were to emphasize the "particular duties of the mother of a family, the housekeeper and the woman teacher,"[34] topics for which educators might still use the late seventeenth-century texts written for upper-class girls by the abbé Fénelon and Mme de Maintenon.[35]

In addition to teaching *morale* and psychology, directrices gave lessons on the history, theory, and practice of pedagogy, particularly emphasizing pedagogical practice during the third year. They introduced students to works by leading educators and offered advice on how to organize a class and impose discipline. Normal school students could apply pedagogical lessons in the *école annexe*, a primary school where they observed one or more *institutrices* and eventually taught some classes. Most women's normal schools had an *école maternelle annexe* as well. For lessons, directrices could draw on Compayré's popular *Histoire de la pédagogie*, which surveyed educational thought from the ancient world to the present and briefly treated the significant expansion of women's education during the 1880s. Yet, as in his manual for civic instruction, Compayré favored preserving certain differences between the education of men and women. Discussing the ill-fated Marquis de Condorcet, an advocate of "equality of education" for men and women during the French Revolution, he praised him for disputing the longstanding denigration of women's mentality but pronounced, "He is evidently in error when he dreams of the perfect identity of instruction for the two sexes, when he forgets the particular destiny of women and the special character of their education."[36]

The directrice, as the authority on pedagogy, also checked on the classes of professors and instructors to ensure that they followed the national curriculum for a subject—French, history and geography, natural and physical sciences, mathematics, foreign language, art, music, *travail manuel*—and presented it at a level appropriate for normal school students preparing to teach in primary schools. Thus future directrices training at Fontenay gave presentations on subjects other than the basic pedagogy and *morale* that they were to encourage professors to incorporate in lessons. Indeed, the third year of the science curriculum complemented the emphasis on duties specific to women in *morale* lessons by including "domestic economy," which covered housekeeping, laundry and ironing, meal preparation, and keeping accounts. History professors, who covered ancient history through the Third Republic, could use third-year lessons on the Revolution of 1789 or the constitution of 1875 to reinforce the directrice's teaching on civic duties and democratic values. At Fontenay future directrice Philippine Semmartin, who laicized the normal school in Orléans in 1887, spoke about teaching children to respect the "legitimacy" of republican institutions; and Léonie Pieyre discussed how studying history contributed to intellectual and moral development, including an appreciation of liberty. In 1889, civics lessons were moved to the history curriculum.[37]

Living and learning in the normal school did not turn students into "déclassées," scornful of their humble origins, directrice Martin had confidently asserted in 1886. Yet students certainly acquired more formal knowledge of literature, history, and science than that possessed by many parents of the children of "le peuple" whom they would teach. Such learning did not make *normaliennes* particularly unusual in urban settings, but in a small town or rural village their level of culture might well stand out. The same was true for their greater facility with the French language, which occupied more classroom time in normal schools than any other subject. Directrice Mazier in Blois had observed in 1880 that students from the countryside often arrived speaking poorly accented French but would likely improve through contact with their instructors and students from urban areas.[38]

For decades to come, normal schools, especially in some regions far from Paris, wrestled with the difficulties of improving language skills. Adrienne Guinier, the fourth directrice of the laicized school in Ajaccio in Corsica,

56 WOMEN AND THE POLITICS OF EDUCATION IN FRANCE

observed in 1887 that French was by far the most difficult subject for her students because many on the once Italian island came with a poor command of French, despite success on entry examinations. Their language and manners improved at the normal school, she reported, but she bemoaned the enduring "prejudices" that neutralized efforts to "civilize" Corsica, acquired by France in 1768 yet seemingly "French only in name." More than two decades later, directrice Hélène Odoul in the mountainous southern department of Lozère indicated that students still arrived at the school in Mende with a problematic accent but, after three years, left with that accent nearly gone. Language issues remained more difficult for normal schools in Brittany, for as inspector general Pierre Pécaut (son of Félix Pécaut) reported in 1913 after evaluating the school in the Côtes-du-Nord, French was not the "native language" of many students.[39]

To supplement the formal instruction in French grammar, composition, and literature given by professors, directrices often added activities to encourage reading and provide cultural enrichment. For example, after supper Louise Martin might ask a student to read aloud while others did sewing for themselves or the poor. The reading on these occasions was not from textbooks but rather from books that were "easy and amusing," such as Hector Malot's *Sans famille* or translations of Charles Dickens's *Christmas Carol* or Harriet Beecher Stowe's antislavery classic, *Uncle Tom's Cabin*.[40] Recreational reading was intended to encourage teachers to continue to read and learn after leaving the normal school so that they would become more knowledgeable in the classroom. Reading might also, some commentators believed, provide solace to those who felt isolated in small towns and villages, especially if they faced hostility to the public school.[41]

Martin's discussion of recreational reading appeared soon after five other directrices had responded to director Buisson's request in the *Revue pédagogique* in 1885 for information on reading practices in normal schools. Whereas the names of the men who replied were published, the directrices were identified only by their normal school or initials, and Martin's article was signed as "Z." Identifying a school of course allowed anyone who checked the *Annuaire de l'instruction publique* or *Annuaire de l'enseignement primaire* to find their names. Directrice Mazier in Blois reported introducing oral readings on Thursday and Sunday afternoons while students did sewing, the *travail manuel* required in women's normal schools. From Limoges Rambault wrote that she did the oral readings herself and often chose poetry or drama, explaining that because classical theatre was new to many students they did not liken this exposure to an extra lesson. Heurtefeu in Valence sent a list of novels in the school library and reported that she allowed students to read one or two per week on their own. She distributed the books herself, however, in order to discover individual preferences. The comments from "L. S." were noticeably different because of her reservations about group reading practices. Not all students could grasp the meaning of a text quickly, and interruptions for explanations might make the activity seem like another class. Furthermore, she opined, many novels could overexcite a group of young women, even if they were fine for individual reading, and parents also might object that reading novels wasted time.[42]

Unlike the cautious L. S., Jeanne Lacoste in Toulouse admitted that her selections for recreational reading might seem bold because she often chose articles from journals like the *Revue des deux mondes* or even newspapers like *Le Temps*. If she judged that an entire article was unsuitable, she did the reading herself to omit problematic passages. She defended her choices by asking, "why should our girls not be introduced to this fine literary movement, this intellectual life we are so happy to experience?" To provoke discussion of good and bad taste in dress, she obtained the *Journal des modes*, using one article to mock the "absurde frange" (ridiculous bangs) that hid the part of a woman's face "where intelligence and thought were so well reflected."[43] Her letter, like those from other directrices, illustrated how one might exercise judgment about acceptable literary content for students, while also heeding official expectations. Buisson, by publishing much of Lacoste's letter, seemingly indicated approval of her choices, but some months later inspector general Leyssenne faulted her for turning a lesson on Fénelon's treatise on girls' education into an imprudent "glorification of woman" unsuited to the modest needs of young women from the countryside destined to return there.[44]

Leyssenne's critique exemplified a tension built into the republican effort to train more knowledgeable teachers, male and female. More knowledge, academic and practical, might well inspire some teachers to aim for more than a primary school post that was generally respected but not especially well remunerated. Some officials also sought to limit women teachers' aspirations by reminding normal school directrices that they should not be creating overly "learned women" (*femmes savantes*). Indeed, Aurélie Lacroix, trained at Fontenay, included that caution in her response in 1885 to the question on the directrices' certifying examination about how to advise normal school professors obliged to cover an ambitious and detailed curriculum. Normal

58 WOMEN AND THE POLITICS OF EDUCATION IN FRANCE

school graduates, she wrote, should be intelligent women but not "bas bleus" (bluestockings), and professors should recognize that good teaching required making wise choices about what parts of a subject deserved more or less emphasis. Inspector general Jean Clerc praised directrice Hoël in 1891 for training good teachers with a modest bearing, not *savantes*, at the normal school in Vannes, and the rector of Montpellier bestowed similar praise on Herminie Bousquet in 1898.[45]

Nonetheless, the goal of better educating *le peuple* also inspired educators to advocate bringing more learned culture to the children of humble families. Directrice Marthe Magnier addressed this in remarks in January 1886, on the occasion of education minister René Goblet's visit to the recently opened normal school in the Bordeaux suburb of Caudéran. Previously, she stated, the "enfants du peuple" were denied a true "culture d'esprit" (culture of the mind) as well as liberty, but now the Republic's normal school provided them with teachers whose knowledge and moral convictions assured the future of French democracy. Two decades later directrice Eugénie Jacquemin in the Drôme would defend the public school's mission in a report to the congress of the Ligue contre la Misère (League against Poverty), a philanthropy that dispensed aid and studied the causes of poverty. Countering critics who blamed schools for promoting an exodus from poor rural areas, she cited economic reasons for the trend and defended efforts to bring "modern enlightenment" (*lumière moderne*) to the countryside. Certainly the teaching of science was useful for agriculture, but instruction should be more than technical or practical, she argued, because a democracy should not unfairly deprive rural students of poetry and music.[46]

Lessons in literature, singing, and drawing at the normal school prepared future teachers to cover that part of the curriculum. Some normal schools also offered the option of piano lessons, usually for a fee, but directrice Bourgoise's effort to add violin lessons in Quimper in 1900 was rejected by the chief departmental inspector, who feared that they might give teachers affectations that the Breton population would find odd. Subsequently transferred to Périgueux, she encountered different objections in 1903 from rector Bizos and inspector general Émilien Cazes, who ordered a halt to violin lessons because they thought that violin playing required ungraceful movements unsuitable for young women—that objection long hindering women violinists' efforts to gain recognition. In Évreux (Eure), the departmental inspector called directrice Marie Larivière's discussions of the art and monuments viewed during her travels inappropriate for preparing teachers for posts in modest milieus, but the rector of Caen countered that such diversions from everyday life did no harm.[47] Larivière was not the only directrice to add such personal observations to enrich lessons, thereby acquainting students with aspects of the *culture générale* prized by social elites and defying critics who wanted to limit the intellectual horizons of primary school personnel.

Advising Teachers on Professional Conduct

Directrices and professors, instructed at Fontenay-aux-Roses about the importance of preparing women teachers who well represented republican education, would, in turn, arm students in departmental normal schools with considerable advice about how to conduct themselves as teachers. Speaking to Fontenay classmates in 1882–83, future directrice Marie Peltier considered how a teacher should interact with pupils' families, stressing the need to enlist parents to second the school's efforts because they shaped so much of a child's character. Cooperation could consolidate the authority of both parents and teachers, and parents might acquire new habits of order and cleanliness. Yet the teacher must also exercise considerable tact to avoid offending parents. Particularly in rural areas she should remain modest and not affect an air of superiority that could distance parents from the school. Peltier further recommended sending parents reports about their children's progress, inviting them to the school on a Sunday to discuss their child, lending books to pupils, and teaching courses for adults. Teachers' visits to students' homes should be rare, however, because poor families might feel embarrassed about their modest abode and visits could appear to favor some families over others.[48]

Above all, Peltier stated, the teacher should preserve her independence by keeping some distance from others, thereby not seeming to take sides on divisive local issues. Her reserved behavior would show concern for all children in a town and enhance support for the Republic's schools. After leaving Fontenay, Peltier opened the normal school in Alençon (Orne) and soon experienced the difficulties of maintaining the recommended neutrality in a department where a long-established and popular religious school was replaced.[49]

A special aspect of advising teachers about public behavior was part of the administrative question posed in 1887 to candidates for certification as directrices. They were asked to detail how the Goblet law of 1886 had changed the departmental council (*conseil départemental*) for primary education and to indicate what advice they would give to women teachers elected to the council. The law, as noted previously, added the directors of the men's and women's normal schools and two men and two women teachers to the council, initially restricting the teachers eligible to serve to those heading a primary school with at least three classes or an *école annexe*, or to retired teachers. Several future directrices highlighted the precedent-setting inclusion of women, Adèle Tourret terming it a "bold and liberal" measure, an honor for women as well as a new responsibility. Marguerite Sicre thought it affirmed "the equality of man and woman . . . in aptitudes and knowledge." Nathalie Bourgoise even related it to women's legal status, stating that although the civil code did not recognize the "equality" of men and women, education laws were in advance of other laws.[50] Yet such bold statements were tempered by cautions indicative of how assumptions about women's "equality in difference" led to awareness of certain limits.

The behavioral advice that aspiring directrices proposed to offer women teachers on the departmental council mirrored current societal values and emphases at Fontenay-aux-Roses, where fourteen of the fifteen successful candidates had studied for one or more years, ten of them already having experience as temporary directrices (*déléguées*). Aglaë Bancilhon recognized that women's participation in a "public function" would be closely watched, and Clara Bonnel warned that the new honor also carried "peril." Thus respondents stated repeatedly than an *institutrice* should not forget that as a woman she was expected to conduct herself with modesty, simplicity, and prudence. Accordingly, some advised that certain questions, particularly political ones, were probably best left to more experienced and higher-ranking men with better judgment on such issues. Marie Dosser and Blanche Heigny even stated that a woman on the council should not speak until a man requested her opinion.[51]

Other aspiring directrices said, however, that women members should not hesitate to express opinions, especially in matters concerning young children and women teachers. Indeed, Angélina Petit stated that because critics of women's inclusion on the council had predicted their ineffectiveness because of excessive timidity, she would warn women to guard against being overly modest and not daring to voice an opinion contrary to that of their administrative superiors. Élise Legros advised combining independent thinking with caution when she concluded, "If for reasons of public interest . . . women teachers are obliged to leave the demi-obscurity where being a woman places them, they must on the departmental council guard against losing the reserve . . . that their sex imposes upon them." Dosser made the same point succinctly: "The woman must remain a woman even when she performs a man's role."[52] Presumably the future directrices realized that their advice for women teachers also applied to themselves. Their essays, combining behavioral limits with recognition of new steps toward equality, well illustrate the "relative emancipation" offered to women by republican reformers of the 1880s.[53]

The important question of how a woman teacher should fulfill her public duties while conducting herself in an appropriate feminine manner received extensive treatment in *L'Institutrice, Conseils pratiques*, published in 1895 by Louise Sagnier, an experienced directrice influenced by Pécaut. Born in Toulon in 1856, the daughter of an administrative agent of the navy, she had taught privately for five years before securing a normal school post in Aix in 1880 and then entering Fontenay-aux-Roses in 1881 to gain certification as a professor and as a directrice. Apart from a brief stint temporarily directing the normal school in Tours, she remained at Fontenay as a *répétitrice* until 1886, helping students review lessons and prepare for exams. By 1895 she had headed four normal schools, the last one in Grenoble, and wrestled herself with the issue of appropriate conduct. Two-thirds of Sagnier's 125 pages of "practical advice" concerned "private life," with chapters on hygiene, clothing, toilette, manners, and bearing. She also provided a list of photographs and etchings suitable for bringing art into the classroom. Her attention to many small details was warranted, wrote inspector general Steeg in a preface, because a woman teacher's conduct should provide a model for her community.[54]

Turning to the teacher in "public life," Sagnier stated pointedly that the duties of being "at the same time a woman and a *fonctionnaire*" might sometimes conflict. While her sex required reserved and modest behavior, her duties made others dependent upon her and placed her in a situation where everyone watched her acts and gestures, either because they were nosy, jealous, or hostile politically, or simply because they wanted assurance that their children were in good hands. Sagnier, like Peltier, counseled the teacher to keep a distance between herself and friendly parents because even if social isolation was difficult, her independent position could make her an agent of peace in a village. On her visiting cards, she should put Mlle or Mme before her family name and professional title, and not let her first name become public knowledge.[55]

Upon arrival in a new post, a teacher should first visit the mayor, with whom official dealings were likely. Then she should visit the local priest, as a matter of courtesy, but not visit again. Although a priest no longer had free access to a public school, Sagnier warned that he might try to lure a lonely teacher into sharing confidences in order to influence her. The *inspecteur primaire* (primary inspector) was her best adviser because, as the intermediary between teachers and the *inspecteur d'académie* (chief departmental inspector), he represented her interests. Yet the woman teacher should also not forget that her academic superiors were men, and that to gain and maintain their respect, she must preserve her dignity. Her school was always open to inspectors, but not her private lodging, whether inside or outside the school. To conquer their place definitively in contemporary society, women teachers must be seen as persons "bien élévées" (well-mannered).[56] Sagnier's advice book was successful enough to warrant a sixth edition by 1912.

Women teachers' sometimes difficult situation in rural towns and villages attracted much attention in the literary as well as pedagogical press in 1897 because of Léon Frapié's novel *L'Institutrice de province*, reviewed by Francisque Sarcey in *Les Annales politiques et littéraires*. Sarcey's synopsis of the miseries faced by Frapié's heroine provoked responses from men and women educators, to which he devoted another article. Their letters, he reported, were moving and revealing commentaries which also displayed common sense and good taste, but they were largely pessimistic. One woman's letter, which he excerpted extensively, detailed the unfair treatment imposed by the unsympathetic woman heading her school. Surprised also by revelations about some male teachers' hostility to women colleagues, Sarcey invited additional responses.[57] Ultimately nearly 60 women and men educators, including 34 *institutrices* and 20 *instituteurs*, sent letters, and many of the later ones were more positive than the first, as Sarcey reported in a third article.[58]

Three normal school directrices were among Sarcey's respondents, and their letters—not published—tried to convey optimistic perspectives without losing sight of problematic realities cited by teachers. Mme Rambault wrote that she was a village *institutrice* for nine years before becoming a normal school directrice, and in Limoges since 1883 she had trained about 150 teachers for the Haute-Vienne department, most of whom stayed in contact with her and shared confidences. Village life, she admitted, was often narrow and limited, marked by jealousies, frustrating when mothers complained that a teacher's standards of cleanliness were too high, and painful when competition between a congregational school and a public school closed some household doors to a teacher. She also recognized that conflicts between men and women teachers sometimes occurred. Yet many women teachers readily sent their daughters to the normal school, eager for them to become teachers as well. More than a hundred graduates had recently returned to the normal school to participate in starting an alumnae association (*association amicale*). To illustrate teachers' devotion to their work, she enclosed letters from nine recent graduates, some of them also expressing appreciation for her familial concern about their well-being. "We are," Rambault concluded, "une classe de femmes vaillantes."[59]

Lucienne March, the directrice in Nancy, also cited her correspondence with teachers to dispute Frapié's depiction of their great unhappiness. Informing Sarcey that she had read his first articles aloud at two meetings with teachers, she indicated that certain revelations shocked them, including reports that some desperate teachers considered suicide. It was unwise, she also complained, to discourage women who had to work from choosing a profession so well suited to their natural attributes and maternal instincts. Émilie Desportes, the directrice in Nevers since 1883, pointedly informed Sarcey that teachers in the rural Nièvre department were not "parisiennes déclassées" like Frapié's heroine and did not consider themselves to be above their humble situation. If education made them seem superior in their milieu, it also gave them the necessary moral authority to do their job effectively. Admittedly, many teachers faced rural isolation and material deprivation, and those in communes where a majority of children attended the *école congréganiste* were particularly unfortunate because the public school was seen as a lesser school, serving the poor and wards of public assistance. Yet Desportes, like March and Rambault, pronounced Frapié's depiction of a provincial teacher's life excessively bleak.[60]

Soon after discussion of Frapié's provocative novel began, the prestigious *Revue des deux mondes* published another negative portrayal of the Republic's women educators. Maurice Talmeyr's "Les Femmes qui enseignent" drew attention to the numbers of credentialed women teachers unable to find employment and presented unflattering pictures of the training provided by Fontenay-aux-Roses and the Seine department's normal school in Paris. Talmeyr termed the latter a "red convent," meaning politically leftist, and called its typical graduate "a revolutionary (*révolutionnaire*) with correct behavior." Buisson, professor of pedagogy at the Sorbonne since July 1896, promptly wrote a critical and sarcastic rebuttal for the widely read *Manuel général de l'instruction primaire*, soon reprinted in the *Revue pédagogique*; and former normal school directrice Sophie Lauriol echoed Buisson's defense of lay women educators and their training in the *Bulletin* of Fontenay's alumnae association."[61] In the newspaper *Le Radical*, inspector general Édouard Petit, active in the Ligue de l'Enseignement, termed Frapié's and Talmeyr's negative depictions of women educators part of a larger attack on republican education. He did not mention the Dreyfus Affair as part of the current context for that attack, which was also furthered by nationalist author Maurice Barrès's *Les Déracinés* (1897), a novel maligning republican secondary schools for giving young men unrealistic hopes of rising above their social origins and leaving them "uprooted."[62]

A decade later, directrice Albertine Eidenschenk's *Petits et grands secrets de bonheur* (1907), a book of advice for normal school students and women teachers, did not ignore the reasons for some women teachers' dissatisfaction, even as it displayed the stoicism and realism about their duties and situation evident earlier in Sagnier's book and directrices' letters to Sarcey. Presenting examples of her lessons in moral instruction at the normal schools in Oran (Algeria), Chambéry (Savoie), Saint-Brieuc (Côtes-du-Nord), and Douai (Nord), Eidenschenk cited Pécaut's inspiring message at Fontenay, where she had studied in 1884–86 and also worked, like Sagnier, as a *répétitrice*.[63]

Eidenschenk's practical advice included chapters on love and marriage, where she warned that men often played games with love. Advising the woman teacher to choose a husband who was her equal in education and status, she explained that marriage to a worker or peasant, many of whom were certainly honorable, would likely diminish a teacher's status in a village where, to retain respect, she should remain "a bit apart." A male teacher might well be an ideal mate who shared her aspirations, yet Eidenschenk also warned that some had bad habits and could be "egotistical" and "authoritarian." Marrying at too young an age was not advisable because the first years of teaching were usually the hardest. A new teacher should first pass the examination for a certificate of professional aptitude and further develop her own abilities, realizing that self-development would ultimately make her a better teacher and mother because by learning to live for oneself, one then learned to live for others. For women who did not marry, Eidenschenk counseled ignoring people who treated single women as lesser. Not all men or women wanted to marry, she added, and humanity gained from such "diversity."[64]

Eidenschenk herself, born in 1864, was the wife of a man fourteen years older who had been the chief departmental inspector in Oran where they met and married in 1894. Upon their return to France he accepted secondary school teaching posts so that she, after a five-year leave of absence and birth of two children, could again direct a normal school, without their functions being in conflict because an *inspecteur d'académie* was a directrice's immediate supervisor.[65]

As Eidenschenk's insistence on women teachers' need for personal growth suggests, she did not shy away from criticizing some of the traditional behavioral advice for women and, more broadly, the Republic's treatment of women. Commenting that republican men repeatedly pronounced that the purpose of women's education was to form good wives and mothers, not savantes, she complained that this emphasis kept women "enclosed"

Directrice Albertine Eidenschenk with family, École normale d'institutrices de Douai. *Courtesy of Archives de l'Université de Lille/Institut National Supérieur du Professorat et de l'Éducation (INSPE) Académie de Lille – Hauts de France, Fonds de l'École normale d'institutrices, and Alexis Ballart, archiviste*

66 WOMEN AND THE POLITICS OF EDUCATION IN FRANCE

in a "special role." Instead, she wanted education to be "boldly liberating" (*hardiment libératrice*) and to further a woman's development "for her own sake" and not simply to serve the needs of others. She cited old and enduring prejudices to explain why gains for women so far remained limited, despite the efforts of some progressive men. French women's legal status, especially if they were married, was thus still inferior to that of women in many other "civilized countries" because the Napoleonic code remained a "monument of injustice." Fortunately, she added, French customs were more advanced than the law, for women held a respected place in society and increasingly could work in professional capacities.[66] Elected to the Conseil Supérieur de l'Instruction Publique (CSIP) in 1904, Eidenschenk saw herself as a champion of women educators, and her critiques displayed familiarity with contemporary feminist advocacy.

Assessing Normal Schools after 1900

Normal school directrices, like other republican educators, were staunch defenders of public schools when critics launched attacks that seemed unfair, but in pedagogical journals and at congresses many also discussed deficiencies in their institutions and ways to improve them. Debates about whether the normal school curriculum packed in too much content dated from the 1880s and provoked interchanges about whether some topics had any value or utility for the social milieu in which normal school students would later teach. Questions were also raised about how well the sheltered existence in a normal school prepared future teachers, and particularly women teachers, to function in remote or hostile locales, like those faced by Frapié's fictional teacher or some of Sarcey's respondents. In 1900 Charles Bayet, Buisson's successor as director of primary instruction in the education ministry, created two commissions to study reform of the normal school curriculum. No woman served on the commission for sciences, and the only woman on that for "letters" was Mme Dejean de la Bâtie, the Fontenay directrice.[67]

Normal school directrices and professors took up the curricular discussion in the Fontenay alumnae *Bulletin* and followed it in the pedagogical press, sometimes making suggestions that annoyed defenders of giving teachers significant exposure to "general culture." The directrices of two important schools, Eugénie Kieffer in Douai (Nord) and Marguerite Ginier in Besançon

(Doubs), wanted to make foreign language optional, but Marie Garnier, directrice in Arras (Pas-de-Calais), disagreed, citing the superior linguistic skills, especially in English, of France's Dutch and German neighbors. Kieffer preferred more time for instruction in French, arguing that French was almost a foreign language in regions where a patois was still widely used. She also suggested eliminating ancient history and reducing the time allotted to literary history and sciences, thereby allowing more time for contemporary history and the "practical" subjects of pedagogy and "domestic economy."[68]

The biggest change in the revised normal school curriculum adopted in 1905 was the redesigned third year for men and women alike. Because of concerns that pedagogical training was neglected while third-year students focused on preparing for the *brevet supérieur* examination, the new program moved that testing hurdle to the end of the second year. The elimination of handwriting and less time for history and mathematics allowed more time in the third year for pedagogy and practice teaching. For both men and women there was greater emphasis on recent history, deemed essential for understanding "contemporary life," and a new requirement to incorporate local and regional history into the general history of France.[69]

Notable differences between the academic program for men and that for women continued. The number of hours allotted to mathematics for women was only half of that for men, and the difference was nearly as great for physical sciences. Like the previous program—which had included emphasis on women's duties as mothers, housewives, and teachers for courses in psychology, *morale*, and pedagogy and also offered "domestic economy"—the new program maintained gender specificity with references to "qualities that give a woman teacher authority" and the "particular destiny of woman" in her "domestic role and social role." Sewing remained in all years of the women's curriculum, and in the third year two hours of cooking were added, and *puériculture* (infant care) became part of hygiene lessons.[70]

The increased curricular attention to preparing women teachers to provide domestic instruction for the next generations of wives and mothers was a reflection of and response to current preoccupations in political circles and the general press. The widely used terms *solidarisme* and *dépopulation* denoted two of the major concerns. At a time when working-class activism was increasing, in the wake of legalization of labor unions (*syndicats*) in 1884, and socialists were attracting more followers, Radical republican leader Léon Bourgeois argued in articles and his book *Solidarité* (1896) that the preservation of "social peace" required a new level of cooperation between the middle

68 WOMEN AND THE POLITICS OF EDUCATION IN FRANCE

classes and the "popular" classes. A combination of legislating social reforms and promoting voluntary associations such as consumers' cooperatives and mutual aid societies was central to solidarism's agenda to promote cooperation and defuse social conflict. Teachers were urged to do their part through adult education courses or recreational programs for teenagers in need of activities because compulsory schooling ended at the age of thirteen.[71]

Solidarists wanted women teachers to help prepare future housewives to maintain clean and orderly households that would be a source of comfort to workers and potentially reduce their dissatisfaction. That theme was already explicit in educational literature for girls' schools in the 1880s but received more attention when the Ligue de l'Enseignement, a massive pressure group supportive of public education, made it a major focus at annual meetings and through the activities of its Comité des dames (women's committee), revived in 1900.[72] Directrice Jeanne Sourdillon of Tours well captured solidarist preoccupations in 1902 when she introduced her detailed article on *enseignement ménager* (housekeeping instruction), by stating its importance for the "moral and material uplifting of the popular classes" in a democracy.[73]

The heightened concern about *dépopulation* by the 1890s focused particularly on the noticeable difference between the size of the German and French populations and their respective birthrates, perceived as endangering France's future military preparedness. Pronatalists eager to boost the birthrate also promoted efforts to improve housekeeping and reduce infant mortality through attention to hygiene, hoping that well-kept homes would enhance family life and make couples eager to have more children. Although the effect of populationist propaganda on the birthrate was at best negligible, as various scholars have demonstrated, populationist discourse became increasingly pervasive, and the pedagogical press was only one place mirroring it.[74]

The addition of *puériculture* to the women's normal school curriculum meant not only formal lessons but also visits by third-year students to local child care facilities, public and private. Before such visits, students might practice with dolls, as directrice Adèle Dollé reported from Pau. Philippine Semmartin indicated that the proximity of the normal school in Orléans to the municipal crèche allowed students ample opportunities to learn how to care for babies, practice that would enable them as teachers to present such skills to the oldest primary school girls or school graduates who might come to special classes on Sundays. In Versailles directrice Julia Mayaud asked doctors to speak at the normal school and sent students to help at a local child care center. In some departments, however, such visits aroused objections to letting "pure young women" see naked infant boys. Directrices themselves also disagreed about the appropriateness of teaching *puériculture*. One directrice believed that it belonged only in courses for adults, but Albertine Eidenschenk gave Dr. Adolphe Pinard's textbook on *puériculture* to her young daughter, who applied its lessons to her dolls. While *normaliennes* practiced what Mayaud termed "improvised maternity," they evidently did not receive instruction about one topic in the hygiene program for men's normal schools: venereal diseases and dangers they posed "for the individual, his family, and society."[75]

Preoccupations with military preparedness and the birthrate also had an impact on discussions of public schools' role in promoting the physical fitness of soldiers and mothers. Physical education had been in the normal school program since the 1880s but for young women was often little more than walks and minimal exercises in restricted spaces or in the school courtyard. Dr. Philippe Tissié, head of the Girondin League for Physical Education, a private organization with a women's committee, found an ally in directrice Dollé in Pau, where he had settled. In 1903 they introduced a program of "rational gymnastics" based upon a model Tissié studied in Sweden when sent by the ministry of public instruction. After several years the normal school's doctor reported fewer common ailments, and inspector general Félix Martel, impressed by the results, asked Dollé to write a report, soon published in the *Annuaire de l'enseignement primaire*, complete with illustrations of exercises. Some teachers also reported that young pupils enjoyed the new exercises, but one indicated that in her village certain parents grumbled that little girls were being trained like soldiers. "Strong mothers make strong people" was Tissié's first sentence in a pamphlet republishing part of Dollé's report. Another directrice, Louise Murique, authored *Gymnastique des jeunes filles* (1906), intended for normal school students and presenting exercises to use with classes.[76]

Inspectors' reports on normal schools' compliance with the increased emphasis on domestic training after 1905 often cited delays in implementation. Some older directrices resisted change, and others questioned the appropriateness of more domestic instruction when so much else had to be taught. Calling directrices' interest in organizing *enseignement ménager* still too rare in 1908, inspector general Charles Coutant praised Léonie Viaud, directrice in Caen since 1896, for attention to housekeeping lessons even before 1905

École normale d'institutrices de Laval, c. 1900, Leçon de gymnastique. © *Réseau Canopé – Le Musée National de l'Éducation, Rouen, 1979.36669.22*

and for coping with her school's deficient facilities for them. In Bourges, inspector general Edmond Duplan commended a younger directrice, Nancy Perseil, for attaching as much importance to domestic education as to "intellectual culture," later adding when he evaluated her in Melun in 1911 that future teachers, sometimes scornful of humble tasks, needed the domestic emphasis to prepare to accept the realities of life. In normal schools with at least sixty students, a full-time *économe* was responsible for organizing, with the directrice's approval, students' participation in preparing meals and helping with cleaning. A science professor treated theoretical issues related to home economics. The new curricular attention to homemaking also prompted future directrice Marie Stolzenberg to suggest in an essay on her certifying examination in 1906 that adding a woman to a normal school's all-male supervisotry committeel would be beneficial.[77]

The deliberations on revising normal school curricula unfolded at the same time as multiple discussions, within and beyond educational circles, about making the institution less cloistered and more in touch with the larger society. Directrice Kieffer, in correspondence forwarded to primary education director Bayet, was among the severe critics of normal school life. A Parisian, born in 1858, she had taught in Athens in a boarding school and in Algeria in a public school before entering Fontenay in 1885 and becoming a directrice in 1887. She was in her third directing post in 1902 when she sought an appointment as an *inspectrice*, writing that life in an *internat* in the small city of Douai was "insupportable." Renewing the request in 1903, she admitted disliking the normal school's organization, curriculum, and "esprit." Appointments to inspect girls' primary schools in the Seine-et-Oise in 1905 and in Paris in 1912 better suited her. In the meantime, columnist Odette Laguerre, writing in the feminist journal *La Fronde*, advocated more interaction between normal schools and the larger society, drawing on letters from three current or future directrices. They partly confirmed but also modified her critiques, directrice Paringaux in Chambéry writing that some easing of discipline was already possible because current regulations were "very elastic."[78]

Similarly, directrice Dollé, in the *Manuel général de l'instruction primaire* in 1902, applauded recent tendencies to relax discipline in normal schools, contrasting the current "more liberal" discipline with that of the early 1880s when, as a young *maîtresse*, she had been faulted for being too lenient with students. Now she felt pleased that she had taken that earlier stand, her opinions drawing praise from normal school professors Suzanne Épinoux and R. Denoël, who also asked for more attention to "social education."[79] Inspector general René Leblanc in 1903 welcomed the easing of discipline under directrices Eidenschenk in Saint-Brieuc and Mayaud in Troyes.[80] As France faced a continuing shortage of teachers trained in normal schools, a shortage exacerbated by dismissals of teaching nuns and closure of some congregational schools, education minister Aristide Briand ordered another kind of easing of policy in 1906 when he announced that normal schools could admit qualified auditors, thereby rescinding an 1897 ban dictated partly by fears that students not residing in *internats* might be a corrupting influence.[81]

Pécaut's idea of the women's normal school, often perceived as a kind of "séminaire laïque," had become problematic, inspector general Duplan recognized in 1909, because it no longer suited married or younger personnel.[82] Other officials echoed that point, sometimes with regret. In a report on three younger professors' discontent with living conditions in Laval,

72 WOMEN AND THE POLITICS OF EDUCATION IN FRANCE

inspector general Georges Lamy did not fault directrice Peltier, stating instead that he wished that younger professors were less learned and had more simplicity so that they could cope with their destiny, presumably as older women had done. Similarly, rector Coville, evaluating directrice Camille Modrin in Guéret (Creuse) in 1910, characterized young professors as less devoted to aspects of their job outside the classroom because they wanted to pursue personal interests, including more study, and to enjoy more independence. Duplan actually expressed fear for the future of normal schools because of the difference between a dedicated directrice like Juliette Marie, trained by Pécaut, and newly credentialed professors who only wanted to teach and resented other tasks.[83]

Increasingly after 1900 a major source of tension between normal school directrices and professors was the monitoring of students, especially at night, a duty for which women received no extra compensation, unlike male normal school colleagues. The association of normal school professors, founded in 1902, often featured the issue in its *Bulletins*, highlighting differences between the men's and women's schools and also complaining that directrices who assigned surveillance duties were exempt from them. Residing in the normal school was required only for the director and *économe* of men's schools, but was prescribed for unmarried women professors as well as the directrice and *économe*. Married women professors living outside the normal school called surveillance an unfair burden on family life, professor Augustine Goué, mother of three young children, underscoring that point in the Fontenay-aux-Roses alumnae *Bulletin*. The single women who were authorized to live outside the school with parents or other family members made similar complaints, and those residing in the school argued that they, like students, needed sleep, especially as they grew older. By 1909, a third of all women normal school professors were married, as were 31 percent of directrices; in 1890, only 12 percent of professors had been married.[84]

Directrice Eidenschenk, as a member of the CSIP since 1904, addressed the issue of surveillance, presenting the minister of public instruction with a special report in late 1906, and the ministry eventually ordered a survey of the views of normal school personnel. In 1909 the CSIP, after a report by Eidenschenk, approved the text for a decree modifying policy. It provided compensation for nighttime surveillance, whether done by professors or qualified teachers from outside the school engaged as "auxiliaires." All women normal school personnel, including teachers in the *école annexe*, still had a role in daytime surveillance, now limited to five hours a week for those not residing in the school or ten hours for those who did.[85]

Commenting in *L'École nouvelle* on the significance of the new policy, primary inspector Albert Laugier, also a CSIP member, added a critique of Pécaut's legacy of "couvents laïques" and the "depressing atmosphere of the *internat*." Many women professors were understandably irritated by being required to live in close quarters with students, colleagues, and a sometimes authoritarian directrice, he wrote. Furthermore, younger professors were influenced by recent claims that individuals deserved a right "to live completely," that is, to enjoy a "personal life" as well as a professional life.[86] At a time when many French schoolteachers and their professional associations were posing demands for better treatment and higher pay, the airing of discontent on the part of normal school personnel was unsurprising.[87]

Students, Directrices, and the Normal School Experience

In light of the mounting critiques of women's normal schools as convent-like institutions failing to prepare students to understand social realities that they would encounter as teachers, evidence of students' perceptions of the normal school is instructive. Students' voices could occasionally be found in directrices' personnel files, either as letters to directrices or in inspectors' reports. Alumnae bulletins of departmental normal schools also published students' recollections, often as remembrances of deceased directrices or professors. In the Ozoufs' survey of pre-1914 teachers, conducted during the early 1960s, some respondents also commented on normal schools, particularly if they added pages to the printed questionnaire.[88]

Varied perspectives figure in the evidence for students' reactions to normal schools. Directrice Marie Lafforgue, retired in 1899 from her post in Miliana (Algeria), sent director Bayet a recent graduate's letter thanking her for her "maternal" concern and expressing appreciation of the school where she had developed self-awareness and learned to think. Mlle H. Couret thus confirmed that, in her case, the women's normal school had met the pedagogical objectives desired by republican officials. Similarly, Mlle Gazeau, a teacher who spoke on behalf of other graduates at a ceremony marking the first twenty years of the Angoulême normal school, stated in 1904 that they owed "all that is best in us, as women and as educators" to the school and

74   WOMEN AND THE POLITICS OF EDUCATION IN FRANCE

its dedicated directrice, Frugier. Her appreciation, like Couret's, was the antithesis of the mockery of a school's routine or of directrices and professors sometimes found in students' journals seized when a directrice or inspector conducted an investigation after detecting a problem. One such journal, belonging to a student from Paris, was found at the normal school in Le Mans (Sarthe) in 1883, its first year of operation, during a search prompted by the discovery of another student's secret correspondence with a young cleric. Directrice Jacquemin made a similar discovery in Blois, as noted above.[89]

When retired teachers later commented on pre-1914 normal schools and their directrices and professors, they often expressed gratitude. A woman who entered the normal school in Bourges (Cher) when it opened in 1883 called her three years there the happiest of her life. Saffroy, the first directrice, inspired students, and Mlle Magnier, the literature professor (and a future directrice), was their "idol" who opened their minds to the existence of a larger world. Another teacher also rated her years at the normal school in Arras (Pas-de-Calais) from 1899 to 1902 the happiest time of her life, a sentiment echoed by a teacher trained at the same time in Melun (Seine-et-Marne). After study in Digne (Basses-Alpes) from 1897 to 1900 another woman retained "excellent" memories of the devotion of the directrice (Cornélie Bertrand) and professors to their work and also of the comradeship among students. Albertine Eidenschenk was admired by students in Saint-Brieuc and then in Douai. Similarly, a teacher in the Haute-Sâone reported her "veneration" of directrice Marie Claude and Mlle Colson, a science professor, at the normal school in Vesoul just after 1900. Directrice Marie Thiébault in Dijon was praised for excellent leadership by a teacher who graduated in 1906, and directrice Perseil was remembered for exerting a happy influence in Bourges from 1905 to 1908.[90]

Magdeleine Bonnefon, the directrice in Chartres (Eure-et-Loir) for thirty-four years, trained teachers who were an "elite," one former student stated proudly, the school's graduates also including a niece who paid tribute to her aunt's influence on her.[91] A teacher in the Eure regarded directrice Larivière as her "mère spirituelle" (spiritual mother), and another confirmed that most classmates had excellent memories of her. Denise Billotey, the directrice in Paris as of 1902, also inspired much affection and respect.[92] At the normal school in the Corrèze a teacher who graduated in 1912 recalled encountering "superior people" (êtres supérieurs) who influenced her life. Although some teachers' fond recollections of normal schools did not cite the directrice or professors, in the case of a woman who experienced the school in Carcassonne (Aude) after 1912 as a "vie rêvée" (ideal life), it seems likely that at least one of them contributed to that memory.[93]

The critical and negative comments on normal schools sent to the Ozoufs include those from a teacher (later a normal school professor) who recalled the Clermont-Ferrand school (Puy-de-Dôme) in 1896–99 as a place with mediocre teaching, an aged directrice (Marie Ruault), and an "esprit" closed to the problems of life. A Bordeaux student in 1894–97 was equally unflattering about directrice Joséphine Gebelin, writing that she almost never smiled, seemed made of "stone," and was boring in the classroom. Jeanne Thomas, an experienced directrice, seemed "dry" (*sèche*) and "severe" to students in Le Mans in 1900. A graduate from Aix (Bouches-du-Rhône) after 1900 recalled a place with harsh discipline which conditioned students to limit their horizons and accept the humility of their situation. Discipline was equally strict in Châlons (Marne), another reported, and professors were indifferent toward students. Negatives also abounded in an account about the Bourges school in 1910–13: the building was cold and ugly, outside events did not penetrate it unless reported by students who had permission to leave on Sundays, and the directrice (Mme Lafourcade) seemed uninterested in students. A contrast to previously cited positive memories of Bourges, the account suggests how a change in directrices might affect students.[94]

Similarly, a teacher trained in La Rochelle (Charente-Inférieure) in 1906–09 regretted a lack of contact with the outside world and blamed the directrice (Constance Robert) for excessive caution in this regard. Another La Rochelle student was less critical, however. Admitting that Robert, known as a disciple of Pécaut, seemed too rigorous to many students, she nonetheless believed that Robert's high ideals made an impact on many of them, and her own memories of study there from 1911 to 1914 were happy. Another mixed assessment concerned the normal school in Besançon in the mid-1890s: it was closed like a "prison," but because directrice Ginier and the professors tried to make it agreeable for students, a teacher reported leaving with good memories.[95]

The difference that a change in leadership could make in students' experience in a normal school, particularly in regard to matters religious, was underscored by a teacher in the Saône-et-Loire. During her first year in Mâcon under directrice Tailleur, students felt pressured to attend mass. Then directrice Ruet, arriving in 1905, said that they were not in a "convent," made

76 WOMEN AND THE POLITICS OF EDUCATION IN FRANCE

it clear that church attendance was optional, encouraged independence, and urged them to be aware of and struggle against social injustice. Ruet's views were perhaps a half century ahead of her time, she wrote.[96] Directrices were obliged to remain neutral regarding students' religious views and practice, and they had to arrange for students wishing to attend church to be escorted, but in the wake of the controversy occasioned by the law separating church and state in December 1905, more directrices like Ruet evidently stressed that religious practice was an individual choice. Eidenschenk had already done this in Saint-Brieuc in 1903 and found that most parents favored letting their daughters decide for themselves about churchgoing. In Douai, after students spoke of being upset by the Catholic church's hostility to the separation law and the local priest's sermons attacking the normal school, she began explaining the politics of the controversy to students, reminding them that church attendance was their choice. "Most of us" stopped attending because of the calumnies, one graduate later wrote.[97]

Differences between the religious preferences of students and their parents also emerged, as directrice Sabatier reported from the south-central department of Cantal in 1907. Respecting the regulations of 1887, she had asked parents to indicate whether they wanted daughters to attend church, and in October 1906 parents of 36 of the 47 students favored it. Yet because students now had latitude to make this decision as well, by June 1907 only 8 to 12 went to services.[98] Indeed, professor Goué reported in July 1907 that several women's normal schools—not named—had permission to stop requiring a professor to take students to church services, presumably because parents did not request it or possibly had made other arrangements.[99]

After 1900, as previously, students' religious observances varied from department to department. In Bourges in the mid-1880s when the normal school was new, not going to confession was "mal vu" (badly regarded), and all but two students attended church, those two envied by some fellow students, a teacher recalled. Twenty-five years later nearly all students at the normal schools in Tarbes (Hautes-Pyrénées) and in Épinal (Vosges) continued to attend church, but by 1914 in urban Lyon only half of the students did so, and in La Rochelle and Grenoble, only a minority.[100] Already in 1903 professor Rachel Albert of La Rochelle had told La Fronde that most normal school directrices and professors were not practicing Catholics, suggesting that their example had an impact on students. She was reacting to feminist Odette Laguerre's claim that religiosity still prevailed in normal schools and among teachers they trained, and thereby impeded loyalty to the Republic and women's ability to think independently.[101]

A number of respondents in the Ozoufs' later survey indicated that they had ceased to be practicing Catholics while at the normal school or shortly thereafter, some explaining that they had learned to think independently but not citing any exertion of antireligious pressure by normal school personnel. Others mentioned the anticlerical influence of fathers or husbands or their own reactions to clerical attacks against the Republic.[102] In a journal begun in 1945 Thérèse Billard wrote that her loss of faith began at a higher primary school and continued at the normal school in Chambéry (Savoie) in 1906–09. She admired directrice Hortense Rostaing's teaching and conviction that through science and reason the world would steadily improve. When she later returned to Catholicism, she described a spiritual journey that drew on the idealism of Rostaing, her "chère directrice," even though she had reached different conclusions.[103]

In some locales peer pressure to attend church remained strong, as with the example of the Tarbes normal school. Thus teachers might later complain about the religious pressure still exerted by some normal school directrices after 1900. In the Deux-Sèvres a student in Niort from 1898 to 1901 revealed that her parents had told her to attend mass to avoid displeasing directrice Lusier, who reportedly had arranged the dismissal of a student who did not. When she tested the situation by refusing to go to confession, Lusier told her that she erred but did not order her to go. In Tours a student at the normal school from 1903 to 1906 recalled feeling harassed because her refusal to attend church greatly displeased directrice Sourdillon. Although group prayers were supposedly eliminated from normal schools, a student in Rennes in Brittany after 1902 reported that when prayers were said the only Protestant student remained seated, and she befriended her while many others kept their distance.[104]

The teaching of tolerance was prominent in other former students' recollections of their normal school's treatment of religion. As the French became bitterly divided during the Dreyfus Affair of the late 1890s, the education ministry ruled that it should not be discussed in classrooms. Yet an obvious antidote to the antisemitism heightened by the Affair was part of the examination for future directrices in 1898 when they were asked to discuss the importance of teaching future citizens about tolerance.[105] In La Roche-sur-Yon in the very Catholic Vendée department, a student at the time of the church-state separation in 1905 recalled that directrice Élise Labergère, a "disciple" of Pécaut, used great tact in her lessons on moral instruction for primary schools and cautioned them to avoid religious intolerance. At the normal school in Melun in 1909–12, directed by March and then Perseil, a student was quickly impressed by the range of ideas presented in classes and by the toleration regarding decisions to practice religion or to shun it. The contrast with the "meanness" (*mesquinerie*) of the nuns who first educated her led to a complete break with the ideas of her youth.[106]

The normal school experience, intended to enable students to think critically and independently, thus influenced individual decisions to reduce or abandon religious practice. Although 56 percent of retired women teachers in the Ozoufs' survey identified themselves as Catholic, while only 35 percent of men did so, many women qualified that identification by adding that they were nonpracticing or seldom religiously observant. Beyond the normal school, of course, members of the public, whether devout or anticlerical, long paid attention to the religious practice, or lack thereof, of students and normal school personnel. Some young teachers also encountered pressure to conform to religious norms in their communities.[107]

How much, in fact, did women's normal schools and their directrices change before 1914 in response to calls to make the schools more open to the larger society? In 1913 Marie Varlet, the directrice in Lyon, discussed their evolution in a report prepared for the education section of the International Congress of Women's Philanthropies and Institutions and Women's Rights. Her report was presented at the congress by inspectress general Kergomard. As the head of an urban school, Varlet did not view normal schools as excessively cloistered. She affirmed that they well prepared students for their lives as teachers but also saw weaknesses. The traditional *internat* retained a familial atmosphere and accustomed students to habits of order and cleanliness and the values of patriotism and "maternal feelings" for the less fortunate. Its communal life could thus promote the development of social virtues, but, she admitted, the sheltered and regulated life might leave some students "enclosed . . . in their personality" and give "small irritations" an exaggerated importance.[108]

Nonetheless, Varlet reported, current events now penetrated the Lyon school, through books and selected newspapers, and politics and major national events were often discussed. Students were also taken to public lectures, museums, and expositions. Each professor could be "a vehicle for new ideas," which students discussed. Perhaps "we even discuss too much,"

Varlet commented, but at least students knew that they had the right to be heard. Ideally, then, students left the normal school with a sense of their competence and their individual rights, but its "too intellectual" emphasis might not fully prepare them for "action" later in their communities. Normal school directrices and professors could best help students prepare for their future by displaying not only intellectual qualities but also "feminine qualities."[109]

In 1913, then, the combination of valuing "feminine qualities" and advocating more exposure for students to issues outside the normal school was not as controversial as it once had been. Marguerite Martin, the directrice in Nîmes, remarked in her report for the women's congress that woman's horizon had been much enlarged, new rights had been accorded to her, and soon "she will no longer be *l'éternelle mineure* (eternal minor)."[110] When an inspector general visited the normal school in Valence (Drôme) that same year and heard directrice Joséphine Desvignes use a lesson on women's duties in the family and in society to provoke discussion of pressing current problems, he judged the combination perfectly appropriate for third-year students.[111]

École normale d'institutrices de Lyon, 1909, Directrice Marie Varlet seated first row, third from right, with professors. © *Réseau Canopé – Le Musée National de l'Éducation, Rouen, 1986.01005.14*

80   WOMEN AND THE POLITICS OF EDUCATION IN FRANCE

The reports written for the 1913 women's congress by two students from Nîmes offered confirmation of the effectiveness attributed to normal schools by Varlet and their own directrice Martin. After three years of study and living at the normal school, the young Mlle Caldesaigue believed that she had acquired "initiative, [and] more energy in thought and action." Contact with other students had helped her "leave the restrained circle of my family and friends" and understand her duty to help others and her country. Mlle Mante was equally positive, stating that she had learned to better judge "the events of life" and to have patience with others, with whom she felt a "bond of solidarity."[112]

The normal school's contribution to the development of important personal and professional qualities, including a social conscience, did not eliminate criticisms of their cloistered nature, however. A student in Rumilly (Haute-Savoie) from 1911 to 1914 later compared the normal school to a "convent" and complained that newspapers were unavailable. Although Fontenay-aux-Roses, the higher normal school, had subscribed to the centrist *Le Temps* since 1880, newspapers were long excluded from departmental normal schools, to prevent the reading of those with strong political or antirepublican biases. The relaxation of rules that Varlet reported for the Lyon school in 1913 thus depended upon the discretion of a directrice and her immediate superiors. Several other teachers who attended normal schools after 1911 would recall that because of their schools' isolation from the outside world, the outbreak of war in August 1914 came as a complete surprise. Similarly, a teacher in the Oise also cited the lack of attention to recent history.[113]

As official reports by inspectors and rectors indicate, and as former students' comments confirm, the normal school directrice herself, aided by professors, typically set the tone for the school and often determined what graduates thought of their experience living and learning there. Certainly contrasting opinions abound in official reports and personal recollections, as two final examples well indicate. Teachers trained at the normal school in Épinal remembered Blanche Valin, the directrice as of 1912, as a stern and pious person inclined to mock students' rustic accents. "She did not like us, and we did not like her." On the other hand, a student at the Saint-Brieuc normal school from 1904 to 1907 called her first directrice, Mme Eidenschenk, "the greatest influence" on her life and long remembered Eidenschenk's morning talks as inspirational and "sublime."[114]

By 1914, professional experience and success in leading normal schools and teaching and advising students had given directrices like Eidenschenk a confidence in their abilities. That confidence emboldened them to contribute to debates not only on normal school issues but also on contemporary social issues, including the status of French women.

3

Representing Republican Education

Directrices, Official Observers, and the Public

"The directrices, let them not forget, are the object of a perpetual sur-veillance."[1] When Félix Pécaut made this assertion in the *Annuaire de l'enseignement primaire* in 1892, he called the students and professors with whom a normal school directrice lived and worked her most important au-dience, but he also cited various external observers. Throughout France a directrice was the most important woman representing public primary ed-ucation within a department. Only in the Seine department was the position of the directrice of the *école normale primaire supérieure* in Fontenay-aux-Roses, the counterpart of the *école normale supérieure* for women's secondary education in Sèvres, more prestigious.

The directrices of departmental normal schools necessarily interacted with a variety of male officials and, sometimes, a larger public. Although contemporaries often described women's normal schools as "lay convents," the directrices' exercise of authority had public dimensions, and many outsiders expressed opinions about directrices and their schools. The min-istry of public instruction required annual evaluations of normal school personnel by an inspector general, the rector of the regional administra-tive academy, and the chief departmental inspector (*inspecteur d'académie*). The directrice also had a public role as one of three women on the depart-mental council for primary education, and she reported regularly to the normal school's local surveillance committee. Because departments funded the school's physical facilities, the prefect and departmental general council (*conseil général*) necessarily received reports.

Moreover, Pécaut noted in 1892, the external observers of the directrices also included the press and other shapers of public opinion.[2] Local notables could provide a directrice and her school with valuable support, but they might also cause annoyance and distress or exacerbate difficulties. Thirteen years after the Bert law had mandated normal schools for women, Pécaut thus warned that the cause of secular education for women was "not yet

Women and the Politics of Education in Third Republic France. Linda L. Clark, Oxford University Press.
© Oxford University Press 2023. DOI: 10.1093/oso/9780197632864.003.0004

definitively won." Although enshrined in law and public institutions, it was still lagging in "moeurs" (customs).[3] Directrices thus remained alert to the need to defend their own schools and the goals of public education.

Directrices and Official Evaluators

In addition to the educational officials who evaluated the directrice's teaching and administration of a normal school, there was a local surveillance committee (*conseil d'administration*) that reviewed a school's financial accounts and ensured that facilities were safe and hygienic. Chaired by the *inspecteur d'académie*, the committee included four local notables chosen by the rector and two members of the departmental general council, selected by the political majority on the council. The committee met at least four times a year and members could enter the school to inspect its premises, but they could not judge teaching or other instructional matters. Detailing the committee's duties when she took the examination for certifying directrices, an experienced normal school professor wrote in 1906 that it could help a directrice understand a region's customs and prejudices and bring "an echo of normal life" to schools that were "perhaps still too closed (*fermées*)." Ideally, she added, members offered the benefits of worldly experience that a directrice lacked, but some might be indifferent or too meddlesome.[4]

Because the academic evaluators of normal school directrices and professors were men educated in secondary schools, universities, and often the prestigious and historic *École normale supérieure*, their reports sometimes mirrored a cultural bias with regard to both men and women working in the structurally separate world of primary education serving "children of the people." Pécaut, the dedicated champion of women's normal schools, called them institutions where women "from the popular classes . . . prepare other daughters of the people to teach the children of the people." Jacoulet at Saint-Cloud, like Pécaut at Fontenay, told students to remain modest.[5] In the dossiers of men and women normal school personnel, as well as in those of the nearly all-male primary school inspectorate, evaluators often made condescending remarks about the undistinguished manners or mentality of those they termed "les primaires."[6]

Comments about a directrice's appearance frequently figured in official evaluations of her teaching and leadership of the normal school. In the twenty-first century such comments would be deemed highly unprofessional,

84 WOMEN AND THE POLITICS OF EDUCATION IN FRANCE

but Pécaut provided insight into why many inspectors included them. The directrice's words were "without a doubt the great instrument for persuasion and reason," he wrote, but her facial features (*physionomie*), bearing, and dress could also affect her ability to exercise authority and inspire students.[7] Thus when the rector of Lyon, Émile Charles, evaluated Berthe Tailleur in Mâcon in 1879, he wrote that her main defect was "exterior: she is short, thin, not pretty, timid," and her "elocution is not very facile," but the rest is "excellent." Inspector Émile Anthoine judged Léonie Viaud, the directrice in Corsica in 1884, to be serious and a good professor, describing her as very tall, not feminine, and still with a bit of the appearance of a "campagnarde" (rustic woman)." Nine years later in Douai the chief departmental inspector praised her for restoring harmony and discipline in the normal school but also bemoaned her undistinguished appearance, as did rector Charles Bayet, who noted her lack of feminine qualities and said that she looked like a "cook." The inspector for the Loire thought that Léonie Pieyre was perhaps not the best educator for young women because she lacked natural distinction and had "allures vulgaires" (common features). Rating directrice Berthe Bourgoin, whose mother had taught in a village school in the Dordogne, the rector of Grenoble, Joseph Zeller, likened her appearance and manners in 1897 to those of "primaires," but found her suitable for the Privas normal school in the rugged Ardèche department. She also did not try to go beyond "her place" (*sphère*), he stated.[8]

As in Bourgoin's case, it was not unusual for evaluators to link comments about a directrice's appearance to a normal school's location. Thus inspector general Jost criticized Jeanne Pélissier in Ajaccio in 1892 for neglecting her appearance but added that in Corsica no one cared. Marie Porte, the directrice in Lyon since 1879, was faulted in 1896 by Compayré, the new rector, for lacking a sufficiently cultivated mentality and having manners that seemed vulgar in an important city. Noémie Robert, the temporary directrice in Gap in 1888, was described by inspector general Alexandre Vessiot as "a bit worldly" and thus out of place in a small Alpine town, and her successor Marie Simboiselle was also seen as too "mondaine" (worldly) by rector Jules Gérard. Later, however, inspector general Athanase Gilles praised Simboiselle, now Mme Peltier, for her ability to mingle in society in Laval (Mayenne). Similarly, her sister, directrice Jeanne Sourdillon, impressed inspector general Georges Lamy in 1907 as a "femme du monde" (woman of the world) whose image was perfectly appropriate for the city of Tours, where her husband was a secondary school professor and normal school students often came from a "remarkably refined milieu." The socially adept sisters had learned much from their father, head of a private school in Soissons (Aisne).[9]

Director Buisson at the education ministry provided one of the rare examples of criticizing a negative judgment about a directrice's appearance when he reviewed inspector general Leyssenne's comments on Marguerite Fontes, appointed to Grenoble after her training at Fontenay. Her "allures" and independent mind would never suit a woman who cared about her reputation, Leyssenne wrote in 1884. In a marginal note Buisson indicated his intention to tell Leyssenne that he found the review painful, more because of what it said about Leyssenne than about Fontes. Leyssenne's evaluation was unfair and lacked the "reserve" that a woman deserved, Buisson wrote.[10]

Nonetheless, comments about appearances and demeanor remained common in inspection reports for decades to come. Thus an inspector general in 1899 likened directrice Marie Laurain of Épinal to a "grande dame" of the eighteenth century, but without any charm or grace, and "lourde" (heavy) in body and mind. The rector of Rennes, Louis Gérard-Varet, thought that directrice Marie-Louise Buisson's problems with professors and students in Vannes in 1913 were compounded by a poor physical appearance, weak voice, and uncertain look. Describing Rachel Albert, the departmental inspector in Tarbes wrote in 1914 that because she was so short and thin, she did not have the appropriate appearance for a directrice. In the future such comments were likely moderated because educators of various ranks could request access to their personnel files at the ministry in Paris or their rector's offices. But in the late nineteenth and early twentieth centuries, unflattering verdicts about appearance or speech also figured in officials' reports about male normal school directors and primary school inspectors. The social divide between the secondary sector of public education and the primary sector, mirrored in evaluators' reports, remained throughout the Third Republic.[11]

More important, of course, than comments about physical appearance were evaluators' assessments of directrices' teaching and administrative abilities. Typically reports about teaching, whether for a directrice or professor, recorded the topic of a class, the quality of a presentation, and students' attentiveness and accuracy in responses. Directrices taught psychology, *morale*, and pedagogical theory and practice, and inspectors and rectors often concluded their reports with comments about how well such lessons inspired future teachers with a sense of their vocation and prepared them to serve pupils, communities, and the Republic. Judgments about whether a

86 WOMEN AND THE POLITICS OF EDUCATION IN FRANCE

directrice was better as a professor or administrator were also common. Thus inspector general Irénée Carré rated Louise Sagnier, directrice in Douai in 1889, as better in the classroom, a judgment similar to rector Jules Jarry's appraisal of Céline Mazier in Laval in 1890, and to departmental inspector Alphonse Darlu's verdict on Marguerite Jalambic in Carcassonne in 1898.[12] Whereas Sagnier returned to fulltime teaching in 1895, under circumstances discussed below, Jalambic had a long career as a directrice, capped by appointment in 1908 to a more prestigious post in Toulouse, from which she retired. Although seniority often figured in such moves, its significance was tempered by officials' assessments of whether a particular directrice merited a more important post and had the social skills to deal with a more varied public.[13]

In the case of Cornélie Bertrand, directrice in Digne (Basses-Alpes), administrative talents were rated higher than the pedagogical by inspector general Leblanc in 1897. Her accomplishments included opening the normal school in 1887 and later merging it with that of the Vaucluse department, which functioned for only six years before closure in 1892. Her "maternal" concern for students won departmental inspector Pierre Dauthuile's praise in 1896, but he also criticized her for trying to give them a "gilded life" (*existence dorée*), inappropriate for a poor department with a harsh climate and many isolated villages where teachers' lives were unlikely to be easy. The normal school was not a lycée, he wrote, thereby conveying that its students "from humble origins" (*naissance modeste*) should not develop middle-class expectations. Inspector Gabriel Roques, who spoke at her funeral in 1903, called his predecessor's fears "exaggerated" because she well knew the difficulties future teachers faced. She was, in fact, the oldest of seven children of a village schoolteacher. By 1903, she had trained at least half of the department's lay women teachers, for whom she remained, noted inspector general Martel, "intellectually and morally, the directrice." Roques's final tribute pronounced her "more than a directrice" because her service was "a veritable apostolate."[14]

Élise Legros, born in 1852, as was Bertrand, faced criticisms of both her teaching and leadership during twenty-three years as directrice of five normal schools. In 1890, when Buisson ordered her transfer from Le Mans (Sarthe), her third post, he complained to the minister that she was a mediocre directrice, first delegated in 1882 when there was a lack of more qualified directrices. A protégé of the veteran Yonne directrice Ferrand, Legros did spend a year at Fontenay in 1881–82 before being assigned to inaugurate normal schools in two departments hostile to republican projects: the Haute-Loire and Morbihan. Despite her obvious service to republican women's education, Buisson found her teaching inadequate and described her as jealous of her authority. She had refused several times to let an inspector general observe her teaching, explaining to inspector Carré in 1888 that his presence in her classroom would cause her to lose prestige with students. Inspector general Jost, who heard her teach in 1895 at the Vendée normal school, reported that she spoke before others with difficulty but had some real pedagogical aptitude. Her elocution was "difficult and embarrassed," the departmental inspector wrote in 1898, and her teaching of *morale* and pedagogy was merely "sufficient." At her last post in Quimper, rector Raymond Thamin found her timid and with no authority over subordinates other than through her personal example as an "excellent person." In 1905, at age fifty-three, she requested retirement.[15]

Criticisms in evaluations were certainly not unusual during many directrices' long careers, but some directrices nearly always received complimentary reviews. They include four who headed important normal schools in the Paris area, and a fifth in Montpellier, locations where hostility to women's normal schools was limited, as compared to some other areas. Alcidie Menat, the directrice in Rouen for thirty-five years, initially seemed "timid" but kind when inspector Leyssenne saw her in Chaumont, her first directing post, yet within a few years inspector general Jean Fraissinhes affirmed that she had the necessary qualities to lead an important school, and in 1896 Pécaut rated her one of the best directrices. She came to the role with certain advantages. Her father was a normal school director who had taught her about work and duty, she remarked, and for five years she taught in Rouen under directrice Saffroy, who recommended her for the Fontenay directing course. In 1890 when Saffroy became the directrice of Fontenay, Menat replaced her. Julia Mayaud, also a Fontenaysienne, advanced from her first post in Gap (Hautes-Alpes) in 1895 to an eventual fifth posting in 1906 in the Seine-et-Oise, where she remained for twenty-three years. She succeeded a "lamentable" directrice, departmental inspector Alfred Leune noted in 1910, and calmed divisions among the school's personnel.[16]

Two of the highly rated directrices were Protestants. Marcelline Cruvellier, from the Gard, held three directing posts, the last in Montpellier, where she stayed twenty years. Although she was often rated an "excellent" directrice, by 1917 an inspector general termed her simply a "good directrice old style." Nancy Perseil, a pastor's daughter, spent two years at Fontenay as a student and then served as a professor in Rouen for two years before returning to

88   WOMEN AND THE POLITICS OF EDUCATION IN FRANCE

Fontenay for another nine as a *répétitrice*. In 1902 she became the directrice in Rodez, where the departmental inspector remarked on her "natural distinction." His counterpart in Bourges, her next post, credited her with transforming the school's "esprit." She complained, however, before receiving the Bourges appointment in 1905, that she had been denied at least two other posts because of concern that her Protestant background—even though she was nonpracticing—might anger the local population. In 1910 she advanced to Melun (Seine-et-Marne), retiring there in 1931.[17]

Unlike the other four highly rated directrices, Denise Billotey, appointed to head the normal school in Paris in 1902, had not attended Fontenay or held a normal school post. The daughter of a painter of porcelain, she attended the Seine normal school from 1880 to 1883 and taught for nearly a decade in Paris girls' schools before obtaining the professorial certification that enabled her to advance to a higher primary school in Paris—the same certification as that required for normal schools. Billotey's familiarity with Paris schools, acquisition of the credential for directing, success as the interim directrice of the higher primary school in 1898–99, involvement with organizations promoting public schools, and her savoir-faire led to the appointment to succeed Zoé Bourguet at France's most prestigious departmental normal school, from which she retired in 1928.[18]

Because the professional relationship between a directrice and her immediate superior, the *inspecteur d'académie*, necessarily entailed regular contact, it is probably unsurprising that on five occasions before 1914 the relationship became a personal one leading to marriage, which then had professional consequences. The chief departmental inspector could not continue to evaluate his wife's work. The first of these marriages, that of Henriette Loiret-Griess in 1881, ended with the inspector's suicide in 1883. Whereas Louise Martin-Schaefer stopped working after 1888 because her husband remained an inspector, the husbands of Albertine Eidenschenk-Patin in 1897 and Adrienne Six-Polge in 1912 shifted to secondary school teaching, and the husband of Gabrielle Athané-Terrial, fourteen years her senior, retired just before they married. There was also one instance of an inspector general, Charles Petit-Dutaillis, marrying a directrice whom he had evaluated favorably while rector of Grenoble. After their marriage in 1917, Joséphine Petit-Dutaillis became an inspectress general of *écoles maternelles*.[19]

If a directrice married an inspector of primary schools, it was a union of colleagues of essentially equal status. Yet administrative superiors might try to avoid appointing the school inspector to the departmental council—so that he and his wife could not act as a bloc—and, similarly, to prevent their serving on the same departmental examination commission. In 1904, when a primary inspector married a professor who later became a directrice, inspector general Duplan opined that such marriages were inconvenient for both normal schools and school inspection because one of the two usually suffered, but he added that the administration would not want to forbid educators' marriage.[20]

Criticisms conveyed after official visits to a normal school by a directrice's immediate superiors, the chief departmental inspector and rector, might easily cause unhappiness, if not a loss of self-confidence. Beyond this obvious point of tension in professional relationships, there was also the potential for more serious conflict, as personnel files often reveal. Typically such conflicts involved the directrice and the inspector, with the rector often mediating or supporting one more than the other. Sometimes, however, clashes between a directrice and the rector occurred, and the ministry of public instruction might then order an inspector general to investigate. Such investigations also occurred if a rector decided that he could not resolve a conflict, or if complaints reaching Paris led the director of primary education or the minister himself to order an inquiry. The outcome would depend upon the issues, personalities, and localities involved, as was also the case when outsiders leveled charges against a directrice.

One example of how conflict between a directrice and a departmental inspector could also take on political dimensions occurred in Niort (Deux-Sèvres) in 1890 when Marie Lusier challenged Charles Causeret at a meeting of the departmental education council, criticizing his proposal to create an *école maternelle* in a location she thought unsuitable. The site, near a military base and a brothel, was rejected by the council. Subsequently the two argued about whether the directrice of the girls' lycée should serve on the examination commission for the *brevet supérieur* when a lycée student was a candidate, and the inspector alleged that Lusier was rude to him. Sent in 1882 to open the normal school in a western department "manifestly hostile," Lusier had enjoyed strong support from the rector of Poitiers, Édouard Chaignet, and at age forty-six felt secure in her position. In 1890, however, the rector was caught between Causeret, who wanted Lusier transferred, and Lusier, who, he admitted, lacked respect for Causeret. Because he respected both of them, Chaignet decided to defer to Buisson's judgment.[21]

As rumors about Lusier's situation circulated in Niort, the local notables on the normal school's oversight committee alerted republican deputy Antonin

Proust, who wrote to minister Léon Bourgeois on Lusier's behalf. When word of her likely transfer reached Niort, the committee protested to the ministry, as did Proust, and the editor of the *Mémorial des Deux-Sèvres*, Lusier's champion on previous occasions, also defended her. In the end, Lusier stayed in Niort, and Causeret moved to a more prestigious post in Poitiers. Evaluating Lusier and the normal school in 1893, inspector general Leyssenne reported that this "firm and clever" directrice had become a local "puissance" (power), with the result that departmental inspector Antoine Guillet hesitated to criticize her. The episode in 1890 revealed how an adept directrice could use the normal school's externally appointed supervisory committee to her advantage and also develop a political base that enabled her to outmaneuver supporters of her immediate superior, Causeret.[22]

A serious conflict in Le Puy (Haute-Loire) in 1892 between directrice Pauline Ebren and departmental inspector Étienne Carbasse included conduct by the inspector that would now be termed sexual harassment. When she arrived in 1887, Pauline Planchard found the inspector to be an ally in dealing with a city council hostile to secular public education, and he reviewed her work favorably. Problems arose after she married a professor at the men's normal school, and when one incident finally prompted her to write to the rector of Clermont-Ferrand, Léopold Micé, to request a new post, she cited a history of several "scenes" and the inspector's efforts to disparage her and undermine her authority with students and professors in the normal school. On March 27, she stated, Carbasse came to her office and made "propositions déshonnêtes" (disgraceful propositions), which she rejected. Micé immediately requested a deposition from both Ebrens. Already in December 1891 Henri Ebren had told an inspector general (unnamed) that Carbasse's wife was spreading slanderous rumors about his wife but that Mme Ebren did not want him to initiate legal action that would cause a local scandal. In 1892 Mme Ebren reported that Carbasse often came to the normal school for extended visits, without giving any prior notice, and that he spent time with one professor in particular. The rector's questioning of the school's *économe* and professors confirmed the Ebrens' allegations. Accordingly, he recommended moving the inspector, telling minister Bourgeois that he would report more about Carbasse orally.[23]

Rector Micé also wanted to move the Ebrens. He faulted Mme Ebren for tolerating Carbasse's unrestricted visits in the school, although he admitted that she had no prior notice of them. Ten days after her complaint reached Micé in April, the Ebrens were reassigned to the Jura; Carbasse was removed in May and soon retired.[24] In the twenty-first century rector Micé's criticism of Mme Ebren's failure to complain sooner seems unfair, because in normal circumstances a directrice was expected to conform to the chief departmental inspector's orders, and should she wish to lodge a complaint, she was required to send it to him for transmission to the rector. In instances when directrices decided to write directly to a rector, inspector general, or the director of primary education about a problem, they could, like Mme Ebren, be faulted for not respecting the norms of the administrative hierarchy.

As Lusier's situation in Niort indicated, directrices who became comfortable in a normal school and locality could unsettle male superiors if they seemed too independent. Emma Frugier, a Fontenaysienne assigned to open the Charente department's school in Angoulême in 1884, remained for thirty-six years. She was an *instituteur*'s daughter from the neighboring department of Charente-Inférieure. Early in her tenure and again in 1894 inspector general Leyssenne found her lacking in authority, but his colleague Jost disputed that verdict in1895, and another inspector general rated her one of the best directrices in 1900. With administrative approval, she added a fourth-year program in 1901 to prepare ambitious students for the Fontenay entry examination in "Lettres." Formal evaluations repeatedly noted her good relations with students and professors, although sometimes with a comment that her sense of discipline might be too "liberal." Then in 1907 departmental inspector Henri Rémond accused her of trying to free herself from the authority of her superiors, and rector Henri Cons added that her disdain for her "chefs" set a bad example for students. For some years, Cons remarked, Frugier seemed to consider herself the "independent sovereign in her small republic."[25]

Rémond's successor, Raymond Orth, complained that Frugier regularly urged students to claim their independence and rights but failed to instill respect for a legitimate hierarchy. It is possible that official concern about some primary schoolteachers' push for collective action lay behind that comment, but Frugier was never explicitly blamed for such organizing, engaged in by some normal school graduates such as Marie Mayoux. The criticisms of Frugier in 1907–08 came with no apparent thought of dislodging her, however, for the school functioned well, and she maintained ties with graduates through the association L'Amie de l'école that she helped found. Nonetheless, the criticisms may help explain some resistance to rewarding this "disciple of Pécaut" with the Legion of Honor, first proposed for her in 1912 but not

92 WOMEN AND THE POLITICS OF EDUCATION IN FRANCE

approved until her retirement in 1920, after an effort that included petitions signed by more than a hundred former students.[26]

For another experienced directrice, Adrienne Guinier, serious difficulties with a new departmental inspector, Denis Ginoux, occurred after nearly twenty years of leading the normal school in Draguignan (Var), which she had opened in 1889, her third post since training at Fontenay. Conflict with a student and her parents plus the intersection of that conflict with local educational politics compounded the situation. Marie-Louise Blanc, a first-year student, told her parents in July 1908 that the directrice's sister, professor Hortense Guinier, had scolded her inappropriately. The parents complained to Ginoux, who investigated and reported to rector Jules Payot that the Guinier sisters were "mauvaises" (bad) and wanted to be "absolute maîtresses" of the school. He added that the directrice was also disloyal to him. The student's father, employed by the administration of bridges and roads (*ponts et chaussées*), wrote directly to the rector as well. Soon after the next term began, directrice Guinier asked Payot to move Mlle Blanc to another normal school because she was insolent and creating a "scandal" in the school. By then Guinier also knew that in the town Blanc's father was making complaints that students learned about when they left on Sundays to be with families. The parents of some students did write to Payot in support of Guinier, but their letters would not be enough to counter the campaign by the Blancs, who claimed that the Guiniers treated their daughter like an outcast.[27]

A new political dimension was added in December 1908 when the prefect informed Payot that the Blancs had complained to premier Georges Clemenceau, who would request a report from minister Gaston Doumergue. Mme Blanc, an experienced teacher elected to the departmental education council, was an opponent of creating teachers' unions (*syndicats*), a position in line with Clemenceau's hostility to public employees' unions, which he expected local educational officials to combat.[28]

Rector Payot reported to Doumergue in January 1909, after visiting the normal school, that directrice Guinier had a "malevolent" nature and was, like her sister, a bad influence on the school. A retired professor wrote to primary education director Amédée Gasquet to attest to Guinier's professional and personal qualities, and Guinier herself submitted a long statement about the unfairness of the charges against her, adding that inspector Ginoux, since his arrival, had sought her ouster. He had used the Blancs' complaints for his own purposes, she alleged, and resorted to tricks that subordinates could

REPRESENTING REPUBLICAN EDUCATION   93

not counter, especially if they were women and trained to respect hierarchy and authority. When Ginoux was impolite to her in front of the school's professors, she could do nothing. As was often the case, the ministry in Paris waited until late in the school year to take decisive action. Guinier, learning that she would be reassigned to the Ardèche department, chose to retire, as did her sister. The circumstances leading to the unhappy ending of her thirty years of service to republican education had entailed not only conflict with a higher official but also clashing with a woman teacher who had local supporters and aligned herself with the national administration.[29]

Directrices and Public Controversies, Political and Personal

Because republican education, especially for young women, faced attacks from conservative politicians and the Catholic church for decades after 1879, officials like Pécaut warned directrices that they should not make "graves maladresses" (serious blunders) likely to compromise the reputation of public schools in provincial departments.[30] Public controversy was sometimes unavoidable, however, and occurred for various reasons, not all of which reflected missteps by a directrice. Some controversies were linked to the intertwining of politics and religion, others were tied to directrices' personal conduct, and sometimes political and personal issues overlapped. The directrices' superiors, the departmental inspector and rector, had to investigate complaints, while also recognizing their obligation to defend a subordinate unfairly attacked. If an accusation seemed baseless or petty, they might quickly drop it and simply counsel the directrice involved. If it was deemed very serious, the rector might ask the education ministry for help from an inspector general. In the end, as cases of conflict between a directrice and her immediate superior also indicate, the accused directrice might stay in her post with her reputation redeemed by administrative backing, or she might be moved to another post, sometimes at her own request.

The 1880s legislation secularizing the public school curriculum and teaching force unleashed the first conservative and Catholic attacks on the republican "school without God," often targeting women's normal schools and their directrices. In Lyon, France's second largest city, the new departmental normal school rivaled long established training by the Sisters of Saint-Joseph, and directrice Marie Porte had to overcome "prejudices."[31]

94 WOMEN AND THE POLITICS OF EDUCATION IN FRANCE

Of the nine departments in the academy of Paris, the Loiret was the last to fund a republican normal school, not doing so until 1887, because a normal school in Orléans run by a religious order had long functioned. There Philippine Semmartin, daughter of a retired lycée professor in Tarbes, faced a "difficult and delicate" laicization and won praise for her courageous and tactful handling of local circumstances. She led the school until her death in 1911. Élise Legros, sent to open the school in Le Puy in 1882, called the Haute-Loire a backward department with enemies poised to attack. In the Haute-Marne, continuing clerical hostility limited enrollment at the school in Chaumont, opened by Sophie Lauriol in 1883. In the Ardèche the work of Léonie Pieyre, the second directrice of the normal school, was appreciated by the rector of Grenoble, but because she was a Protestant he recommended in 1884 that if she left, a Catholic should replace her because of the "esprit" of the department.[32]

Resistance to republican schools in some of the seventeen administrative academies occurred in multiple departments. There was strong opposition in Brittany and the Vendée, where hostility to the Third Republic had roots in the Revolution of 1789, and many directrices sent to the seven departments in the academy of Rennes and to the Vendée department reported difficulties. Indeed, when education officials elsewhere characterized local problems, they found Brittany a useful basis for comparison. Although the rector of Caen, Edgar Zévort, often bemoaned the limitd spread of an "esprit laïque" in conservative Normandy, inspector general Adolphe Lénient judged in 1897 that "reactionary passions" in the region were not as "aggressive" as in Brittany. The Orne general council had resisted supporting the normal school in Alençon that replaced a popular religious school, and when Marie Peltier opened it in 1883, she encountered not only new students but also hostile students from the old school. The last normal school created in the academy of Caen was in Évreux (Eure), for which Buisson in 1888 selected Lauriol, who had already held two difficult posts since leaving Fontenay. By 1890, reported inspector general Jost, she was winning acceptance of the school in a "reactionary" department.[33]

There was also a noticeable lag in the south in the academy of Toulouse, where two of the eight departments, Aveyron and Tarn, lacked a normal school until 1889 and 1890, respectively, well beyond the target date of 1883 set in 1879. Clerical journals greeted directrice Marthe Janin with hostility when she arrived in Albi (Tarn) in 1890. Her successor, Augustine Languéry, soon bemoaned the "occult" influence exerted by the priest who was the confessor for many students and some professors, and she left after only a year. Léona Thomas, who opened the school in Rodez (Aveyron) in 1889, found a population that "by education and nature" was "defiant" of laic education and the "esprit libéral." For her work in a locale that was almost like an "enemy," she won Pécaut's praise. That experience probably gave her more endurance when she became the third directrice for Albi in 1893, for she remained until retiring in 1908.[34]

The first department where a new normal school closed was the Gers, also in the academy of Toulouse. From its start in 1886 in the town of Auch, it had the disadvantage of being in the fief of a leading Bonapartist politician, Paul de Cassagnac, whose newspaper *L'Autorité* used the slogan "For God, for France," a pointed attack on *laïcité*. Before the school in Auch opened, directrice Friedberg at Fontenay advised Buisson to pick a directrice who had "militant qualities" for a "poste de combat," and she recommended Marie Fontecave, a teacher's daughter who was "very firm" and understood the area's population because of her background in the Aude. She could oppose "violence with serenity, which is the true feminine force," and a quality that would enable her to dominate the situation. Fontecave remained until the school, with a small enrollment, closed in 1890, its students destined for the normal school in the Hautes-Pyrénées.[35]

Enemies of public education found new fuel for attacks in a situation at the normal school in Troyes in the Aube in 1889, the year when republicans celebrated the legacy of 1789 but also had to counter the political ambitions of General Georges Boulanger, popular with Bonapartists and many nationalists. Directrice Henriette Loiret, a widow, was at the center of a controversy generating the kind of bad publicity that republican leaders wanted to avoid. Two professors, Mlles Sandilhon and Bouley, went to Paris on March 9 to tell Buisson about affectionate relationships between students and between the directrice and some students. The allegations immediately triggered an investigation by the Dijon rector, Thomas Chappuis, and departmental inspector Régis Artaud. Chappuis's subsequent report highlighted revelations about the school's "moral situation" and also noted Loiret's clashes with some subordinates. The questioning of professors and students had confirmed reports of Loiret's "tendresses" (affections) and embraces, resisted by some *maîtresses* and students but accepted by others. Two students whose mothers were friends had slept in the same bed more than once. Eight students' depositions were also sent to Buisson. Loiret denied any impropriety, stating that she did not know

96   WOMEN AND THE POLITICS OF EDUCATION IN FRANCE

what Chappuis meant when he first accused her of "preferences" for some students.[36]

Rector Chappuis's verdict on Loiret's case was clear: he judged her "completely mad" and unworthy of another normal school post. The ministry quickly removed her on March 18 and sent directrice Clara Bonnel from Châlons as an interim replacement. Eleven third-year students, the most implicated in the scandal, were sent home temporarily, while Loiret prepared to leave, and when they returned with their fathers on March 30 to meet with inspector Artaud and Bonnel, those accused of misbehavior obeyed Artaud's instruction to ask forgiveness. The investigation had a last chapter in April when Bonnel searched students' desks and trunks and found incriminating letters written by Loiret and students. The evidence was "overwhelming," the rector reported. Loiret's revocation was a sad ending to the career of one of the first twenty-eight women to obtain a secondary baccalauréat before 1880 and also, briefly, a Fontenaysienne.[37]

Understandably, rumors about the normal school circulated in Troyes, and students talked to their parents. Local and national press coverage, largely in conservative papers, soon followed. The regional *Propagateur de la Champagne* reported on April 11 that the directrice's corrupting of the school was no surprise because it was an "école sans Dieu." Two days later it noted that most conservative papers in Paris were covering the "scandale laïque," including *L'Univers*, *La Croix*, *La Défense*, and *Le Moniteur universel*. Cassagnac's *L'Autorité* soon joined the condemnation, calling laicized girls' schools "écoles de démoralisation." A local Bonapartist paper, the *Libéral de l'Aube*, added salacious detail, stating that the directrice knew more about the poetry of the Greek Sappho than about the gospel and so turned the school's dormitory into a "petite Lesbos." In the meantime, the local republican paper *Le petit Troyen* tried to counter allegations about Loiret's career before she came to Troyes in 1885. The ultra-Catholic *L'Univers* published at least five articles on "Le Scandale de Troyes," and *La Croix*, at least nine articles. In all, clippings from or references to fifteen newspapers went into Loiret's personnel file.[38]

The Troyes normal school also figured in meetings of local and national representative bodies. In May, Count Armand, a member of the Aube general council, asked the prefect about the directrice's removal and was told simply that the ministry in Paris had made the decision. Conservative members of the general councils in two neighboring departments, the Yonne and Haute-Marne, also registered dismay about the Troyes school, and *Le*

Soleil then asked why the Aube council's republican majority did not express more concern. Loiret's critics also wondered why no legal action was taken against her. In fact, materials about the Troyes events were sent to the minister of justice, but no legal proceedings ensued, the judgment being that there was no assault on public morality. In the Chamber of Deputies on July 13, the royalist Alexandre Fairé used an opportunity to question minister Faillières and recounted a version of Loiret's personal and professional history. Denouncing public schools as "without God," Fairé asked why the government had entrusted her with important responsibilities. Loiret, while the directrice in Melun, was widowed when her husband, the *inspecteur d'académie,* killed himself in 1883; reassigned in 1884 to Bordeaux, she left after a year. Faillières responded briefly to the baiting questions, citing the administration's investigations and subsequent swift action. By July 1889 most republicans and their opponents were more concerned about the upcoming elections for the Chamber than about the months-long scandal.[39]

Conservative attacks on directrices and their normal schools for alleged misconduct were far more common than republican critics' attacks, but the latter were also disquieting for directrices. After early republican complaints about some older directrices who did not respect the new religious neutrality in public education during the 1880s, republican officials typically found less to question in this regard with the next cohort of directrices and usually supported them if they faced attacks. Shortly before 1900 and soon after, however, there were incidents where republicans criticized directrices for clericalism and lack of respect for *laïcité.* Although local circumstances varied, such critiques coincided with the pronounced splits in public opinion generated by the Dreyfus Affair as the French became increasingly divided between those who believed Captain Alfred Dreyfus, a Jew, innocent of treason, and those who did not. Whereas Dreyfusards argued that a democracy must guarantee fair treatment for every individual, anti-Dreyfusards contended that the overriding national interest precluded challenges to the verdict of an army court martial. Anti-Dreyfusards were frequently but not exclusively from the political and Catholic right, and many republicans long hesitated to take sides. Political divisions were later heightened by the July 1904 law banning members of religious orders from teaching in private schools and by the law separating church and state in December 1905. The left wing of republicanism, the Radicals and Radical Socialists, also felt increasing pressure from several socialist parties by the early twentieth century.

The resignation of directrice Marie Léonie Slawinska in Dijon in 1898 occurred after several years of administrative concern about her religious practices. Born in Nancy, the daughter of a tax official, she had held a teaching *brevet* since 1866 and taught privately before becoming a primary schoolteacher in Paris in 1880 and then obtaining credentials for both secondary and normal school teaching. In 1887 she placed first on the qualifying examination for normal school directrices but, because of her mother, opted for a professorship in Nancy until 1890 when she became the directrice in Chaumont. In Caen, her next post, departmental inspector Paul Dubuc reported that she attended mass daily, as she was free to do, even if that seemed excessive. Slawinska also had difficulty maintaining authority over personnel, and in Dijon her problems multiplied. Rector Bizos characterized her in 1897 as a "woman burning with a kind of mysticism" and lamented her conflicts with departmental inspector Pierre Deschamps. Quarrels among students and staff members prompted an investigation by Bizos and primary education director Bayet, Buisson's successor. Bayet's report to minister Alfred Rambaud faulted Slawinska for insubordination, lack of openness, and "Jesuitical allures." Although she was not formally dismissed, officials gladly accepted her resignation in January 1898, after which she taught in a Catholic school. No references to Catholic support for anti-Dreyfusards were in her personnel file, but recognition of the escalating conflict may have been implicit in concerns about her religiosity. Her resignation came just over a week after Clemenceau's newspaper *L'Aurore* published novelist Émile Zola's article "J'accuse," denouncing the army's handling of evidence and giving the Dreyfus Affair greater prominence.[40] Slawinska was not, in fact, an anti-Dreyfusard, as she later indicated.

By the time that Lieutenant Colonel Georges Picquart identified another army officer as the man guilty of the treason for which Dreyfus was unjustly convicted, the discussion of the Dreyfus Affair in public schools was forbidden. Pécaut, by leaving Fontenay-aux-Roses, could later speak publicly about Dreyfus, as his son Élie urged. Some educators who spoke out were placed on leave, including Paul Stapfer, dean of the faculty of letters at the University of Bordeaux, and Marie Baertschi, a professor at the normal school in Versailles.[41] Many educators and intellectuals would join the new Ligue des Droits de l'Homme (League of the Rights of Man), spearheaded by Senator Ludovic Trarieux. The army's imprisonment of Picquart in 1898 further outraged Dreyfusards, and late in the year *L'Aurore* and four other Paris newspapers asked readers to endorse protests on Picquart's behalf. Some 40,000 responses were received.[42]

Educators on the published lists of *protestataires* on Picquart's behalf sometimes included their professional identities, among them "L. March, directrice d'école normale Nancy," "Mlle C. Robert répétitrice Fontenay-aux-Roses" (a former directrice who returned to a normal school in 1900), and "Mme Perseil professeur d'école normale" (another Fontenay répétitrice and future directrice). There were also four professors at the men's normal school in Beauvais, at least two women normal school professors plus Baertschi, four women professors at the *école primaire supérieure* Edgar Quinet in Paris (including Sagnier), and some forty institutrices. Mlle Slawinska added her name, identifying herself as an "agrégée" of secondary education and former normal school directrice. Laurent Eidenschenk was among secondary school professors on the protest lists, but Mme Eidenschenk, on leave and waiting for another normal school post, was not.[43] A year later, however, she would ask pointedly in the Fontenay alumnae *Bulletin* whether public educators' obligation to maintain "neutrality" should always apply when students could hear crowds clamoring in the streets for the death of a group of citizens, a reference to cries of "down with the Jews" (*à bas les juifs*). Fontenay alumnae president Lauriol and directrices Paringaux and Lafforgue, present at Pécaut's funeral in August 1898, heard Buisson's eulogy—soon widely publicized—recognizing Pécaut's commitment to justice for all.[44]

Most normal school personnel evidently said nothing about the Dreyfus Affair to students, as the government dictated, but directrice Ebren in the Jura did not hide her Dreyfusard sympathies, according to a student in Lons-le-Saunier from 1895 to 1898, nor did a professor in Grenoble who discussed the Affair while on walks with students. Of the teachers who mentioned the Affair on questionnaires submitted to the Ozoufs during the early 1960s, most indicated that they learned about it from their families. A normal school student in Màcon from 1899 to 1902—after the presidential pardon for Dreyfus but before his exoneration in 1906—reported that a classmate's attempt to start a discussion of the Affair surprised other students. Even after 1905, according to a former student in Bourges, a popular professor regarded as advanced in her opinions refused students' requests to discuss the Affair, explaining that she was not allowed to do so. Yet if students heard their parents and neighbors debating the Affair and taking sides, they were likely to bring opinions back to the normal school, as a teacher in the Vendée

100 WOMEN AND THE POLITICS OF EDUCATION IN FRANCE

recalled in 1934, stating that the Affair "divided us into two clans" at the La Roche-sur-Yon school, but without the animosity then common.[45]

Against the backdrop of the Dreyfus Affair, *L'Aurore* featured allegations in December 1899 about "jesuitical" tendencies at the normal school in Versailles, directed by Louise Murique. Departmental inspector Pestelard then investigated and concluded that religious neutrality was scrupulously observed, reporting that the library held no religious books that might give offense and finding no reason to accuse Murique of clericalism. After *L'Aurore* published new allegations in January 1900, including complaints from teachers trained at the school, Pestelard spoke to fifteen teachers who had graduated within the last four years. Some were practicing Catholics, one was Protestant, and some held no belief. All reported good memories of the school and respect for personal convictions. Current students knew about *L'Aurore*'s attacks, and one third-year student talked to Murique on behalf of others because they wanted to protest against the allegations by writing to the inspector or having their parents write to the education ministry. Realizing that her role was to calm students and defuse a situation, Murique advised against letter-writing campaigns. Vice-rector Gréard defended her when he transmitted Pestelard's findings to minister Georges Leygues, stating that although her exercise of authority could be rigorous, she had an appropriate sense of her duties and "a love of young people." Then nearly fifty years old, Murique had headed three normal schools and written successful textbooks.[46]

Another republican press attack in 1900 targeted Jeanne Thomas, a directrice since 1884 and head of the normal school in Le Mans (Sarthe) since 1890. An article sarcastically titled "L'Enseignement dite 'laïque' " in *La Petite République* accused her of displaying "religious zeal" when she and a group of students went to a cemetery for the burial of a student's father but then left the procession to avoid participating in a civil burial. Only one professor stayed. The newspaper, tied to moderate socialist Alexandre Millerand, the minister of commerce, also complained that too many professors at women's normal schools attended mass with students, not explaining that students themselves could decide to attend church but, unlike male students, had to be accompanied by a professor. Education officials noted the critique but did no special investigation.[47]

In Grenoble directrice Honorine Jacquin faced a more difficult situation when some local republicans and socialists attacked her throughout one school year. An "open letter" in the *Tribune du sud-est* in August 1900 from some former students alleged that when the Republic was under attack—likely a reference to the Dreyfus Affair—she had tried to inspire despotism. One deputy then complained to the education ministry. Investigation by departmental inspector Raymond Rey and rector Auguste Boirac revealed the complexities in the local conflict. The relations between the directrice and certain personnel were bad, and many teachers were hostile to her husband, the chief clerk in Rey's office, with access to personnel records. Although Boirac and Rey calmed the situation, it erupted again when four Isère department deputies pressed for removing the Jacquins, as did a local socialist paper, *Le Droit du peuple*. On ministerial orders, inspector general Duplan investigated and in a report dismissed deputy Octave Chenavaz's allegation that Mme Jacquin was a religious fanatic. She was a nonpracticing Protestant, who asked students to start each day with a serious thought, not a pious one, a practice directrices learned from Pécaut at Fontenay.[48]

Duplan added, however, that Jacquin's concessions to Catholic students perpetuated practices problematical for a normal school. About eighty of the ninety students were taken to mass on Sunday and requested no meat on Fridays. During his visit on Saturday, March 29, many students asked to be taken to confession, and he opined that Jacquin, without offending beliefs, should have explained that it was better for them not to miss Saturday classes and that, with Easter vacation imminent, they would soon be with their families for religious observances. He also faulted her decision in 1898, just before the annual *brevet supérieur* exams, to allow third-year students to go to confession because she should have told them that believing that confession could affect test results was pure superstition. In a statement unlikely to be made publicly but revealing of some officials' attitudes toward the policy of religious "neutrality" at a contentious time, Duplan mused that if a normal school did not purge the religious beliefs that students brought with them, then professors, especially professors of literature and history, should ask themselves if they were partly responsible. He concluded that several normal school professors had conducted a "war" against Jacquin by denouncing her to the press and politicians. Neither she nor her husband had committed any "grave" mistakes, but he advised moving them and two professors to calm the situation. Although Duplan did not want relocation to seem like a victory for the Jacquins' adversaries, the couple saw her reassignment to Lons-le-Saunier as a disgrace they had to accept.[49] Similarly, Marie-Thérèse Allégret, unfairly accused of proselytizing for Protestantism in Bourg (Ain department) in 1895, had to accept reassignment to Nîmes.[50]

102   WOMEN AND THE POLITICS OF EDUCATION IN FRANCE

In the case of Émilie Desportes, directrice in Chaumont since 1898, it was her own religious practice that some officials found excessive. *La Petite République*, which had previously targeted Jeanne Thomas, reported in 1901 that before the *brevet supérieur* exams Desportes had allowed twelve of the sixteen third-year students to go to confession. Departmental inspector Alphonse Piétrement's investigation revealed that they had gone unaccompanied and also, on one Sunday, returned alone from mass while Desportes and her sister remained in church. She was known, he commented, to have little "esprit laïque." Transmitting the inspector's report to Paris, rector Charles Adam of Dijon added that Desportes was a "mediocre" directrice. Complaints about her religiosity resurfaced in 1904, and inspector general Leblanc learned that she often left the school to attend daily religious services. By then her antagonism toward the directrice of the local higher primary school had angered republicans on the city council and prompted the prefect to request her departure for the sake of normal school recruitment and the "esprit laïque" of the Haute-Marne's women teachers. Educational officials concurred, and Desportes retired in 1905.[51]

The heightened tensions between church and state also had an impact on directrice Nathalie Bourgoise in Bourges. Her acceptance of free Bibles from a Protestant evangelical society prompted professor Désirée Mus to ask departmental inspector Maurice Berteloot in March 1905 whether their use conflicted with the principle of "neutrality." Mus also questioned other practices by Bourgoise, such as the propriety of letting students wear masculine garb for theatrical productions. When inspector general Edmond Durand investigated, Bourgoise explained that she had obtained the Bibles for students because they were important as literature, comparable to Homer's *Iliad* and *Odyssey*. He then told her that in the present state of "religious evolution" the Bible was seen as an instrument of propaganda, and if this were not the case an organization might not have donated them. Accepting the Bibles indicated a lack of political savvy and might create problems for the administration, he warned. In the aftermath, Bourgoise was promoted but agreed to relocate to Chaumont, the post vacated by Desportes. Her adversary, Mme Mus, was warned that she must treat a directrice respectfully but could stay in Bourges where her husband taught at the men's normal school.[52]

As some of the political and religious controversies entangling directrices indicate, conflict with subordinates, students, supervisors, or other officials could draw public attention. Other well-publicized controversies centered on directrices' personal conduct and were seemingly independent of ideological conflict. Yet in departments where a normal school had a history of frequent turnovers in leadership, discussion of a directrice's conduct might well be linked to other local issues or rivalries, as was true for episodes in the careers of Louise Sagnier and Cécile Chaudron.

Sagnier faced an attack on her personal morality while heading the normal school in Grenoble, a difficult place for more than one directrice. Arriving in 1891 to assume her fourth directing post, she was its seventh directrice since 1879. In April 1895 Louis-Félix Lombard, a member of the Isère general council and former republican deputy, told the prefect about rumors concerning Sagnier and republican senator Mathias Saint-Romme. Departmental inspector Rey and rector Zeller investigated and reported to the ministry that ties between the families of Sagnier and Saint-Romme dated from friendships between their fathers and that their contacts were always in public and often in the company of other people, including Buisson's son Étienne. In provincial cities, Zeller added, even the most innocent and appropriate relations between men and women might arouse suspicions which malicious people and political factions could exploit to harm republican education. He admitted, however, that the directrice of Grenoble's higher primary school had contributed to the rumormongering. His conclusion that the incident showed why women educators should be reserved and prudent was precisely the advice that Sagnier herself gave to women teachers in her book published that same year. There was no doubt about her intelligence and aptitude for command, inspector general Duplan had reported, but he thought that the "narrow formalism of provincial life does not suit her." Sagnier finished her career as a professor at a higher primary school in Paris where her sister resided. Her successor in Grenoble, Jacquin, also faced travails, as noted above, and the school would have two more directrices by 1914, the last of whom, Anne-Marie Grauvogel, experienced political attacks from the Left.[53]

Cécile Tassin Chaudron, like Sagnier, encountered critics of her personal conduct in departments with high turnover for directrices. In 1899 she became the fifth directrice since 1883 for Mende in the Lozère (ten by 1914), and in Lons-le-Saunier in the Jura as of 1903 she was the tenth since 1879. Once again, issues religious and political were intertwined with personal attacks. Mende was an unpopular location geographically and culturally. A previous directrice, Marie Thiébault, called it a "desert" without intellectual resources and complained that even public schoolteachers and other *fonctionnaires* sent their daughters to religious schools. Élise Dalon,

École normale d'institutrices de Grenoble, 1892–93, Directrice Louise Sagnier, center, first row, with professors. *From Julien Clavel, Histoire de l'école normale d'institutrices de Grenoble (Grenoble: Allier, 1969), Collection des bibliothèques universitaires de Grenoble, BU Professorat Éducation. Courtesy of Joëlle Rochas, Conservatrice/Mission Coopération documentaire scientifique – BAPSO – Recherche, Université de Grenoble*

Chaudron's predecessor, was equally negative about the town's "esprit." When the unmarried Cécile Tassin, daughter of a print shop employee and a laundress in Versailles, arrived for her first directing post two years after completing Fontenay preparation for directrices, departmental inspector J. Dequaire identified her as "clearly laïque." Similarly, inspector general Charles Coutant soon praised her good influence on attitudes in a normal school that drew Catholics and Protestants from a region with "ardent" religious leaders. After she married Émile Chaudron, a professor of history at the collège in Mende in 1901, the journal *École laïque* reported approvingly that the couple had chosen to have only a civil marriage ceremony, and the Chaudrons feared that the unwanted publicity would provoke more intolerance. Subsequent problems with departmental inspector Guibaut in 1902 led Mme Chaudron to request a new post, calling Mende a "gossipy and clerical" mountainous village where she did wish to bring up her daughter.[54]

At Chaudron's next difficult post, Lons-le-Saunier, conflict inside the normal school attracted much public attention. Initially credited with restoring peace to a school divided into two factions under Jacquin, the previous directrice, Chaudron by 1905 faced complaints from some students and parents. Thus in 1906 departmental inspector Alfred Jeanperrin and rector Édouard Ardaillon investigated allegations that she made inappropriate comments in moral and hygiene lessons, the latter including *puériculture*, mandated since 1905. "Legends" about her audacity circulated in the department, inspector general Gilles later reported, but he found little truth behind them. Chaudron admitted to drawing from her own experience to talk to students about childbirth and also husbands' virtues and defects, and Ardaillon told her that some of her comments were ill-considered. He also scolded professors and students hostile to her, telling them to concentrate on their work.[55]

Contrary to Ardaillon's hope that difficulties were over when he sent a report to director Gasquet on March 19, the normal school turmoil and local gossip about it continued. A justice of the peace wrote to Ardaillon and the education minister to request a new investigation, citing a letter from his daughter and stating that he acted in the interest of "instruction laïque" because people in the town were now shouting questions at normal school students during their supervised walks. Other students also wrote to parents, perhaps prodded, as Ardaillon and Jeanperrin suspected, by professors hostile to Chaudron. The director of the *école annexe* at the men's normal school, M. Jeanjacquot, informed Ardaillon that he had intercepted and destroyed an anonymous letter destined for the *Jura socialiste* and probably written by a hostile professor. At the lycée some students boycotted Émile Chaudron's classes, and one mother of a normal school student threatened to keep her daughter at home if the directrice did not leave. An angry father forwarded a letter from his daughter, a third-year student, who stated that Mme Chaudron had discussed sexual relations, the pains of childbirth, houses of prostitution, "shameful maladies," and how a husband could know whether his wife was a virgin. She also called the directrice unpatriotic and intolerant of Catholicism. Indeed, she even complained that Chaudron said that the normal school should be "neutral" with regard to religion—which was, of course, what a directrice was supposed to convey.[56]

When director Gasquet summoned Chaudron to a meeting in Paris, the rector again defended her, asking that she not be treated harshly. Gasquet informed minister Aristide Briand that Chaudron acknowledged a basis for some allegations against her but also pointed out exaggerations. She had told students about suffering after the birth of her second child. In a lesson on colonization she stated that Europeans often brought not only civilized

106   WOMEN AND THE POLITICS OF EDUCATION IN FRANCE

advances but also vices, diseases, and alcoholism to indigenous populations. Like Ardaillon, Gasquet faulted her for using too many revealing examples from her own life and for warning students too explicitly about dangers women teachers might face. Some local problems, he concluded, might stem from her husband's dabbling in politics, adding that he was inferior to her in intellect and character.[57]

As news of Chaudron's audience in Paris circulated locally, other defenders of her competence wrote to Gasquet, including the directrice in Bar-le-Duc, Célina Géhin, formerly in Lons-le-Saunier from 1898 to 1901. Jeanjacquot wrote that after teaching in Lons for twenty-five years, he knew the tactics of enemies of the *école laïque*, whom he blamed for the attacks on both Chaudrons. Supportive letters from some students and parents also reached the ministry. Particularly important was the backing from the *amicale* (association) representing seven hundred Jura teachers. Its president, A. Vernier, a member of the departmental education council, called Chaudron a victim of maneuvers by hostile colleagues and other foes. In the context of 1906, enemies of public schools were angry about the ban on teaching by religious congregations and the separation of church and state.[58]

To restore calm in Lons-le-Saunier Gasquet recommended transferring Chaudron and several professors, but to show that she was not in disgrace, the ministry promoted her from fifth to fourth class in April, five days before reassigning her to the normal school in Troyes. Three professors were transferred or removed, two of whom also had defamed previous directrices. A grateful Chaudron, shaken by the ordeal, thanked Gasquet and later forwarded a letter signed in May 1906 by sixteen former students. They appreciated her "moral" and "maternal" advice, intended to protect future teachers, and credited her with helping to "liberate" their minds. On behalf of Jura teachers, Vernier thanked the ministry for dispensing justice for Chaudron.[59] What had begun inside the normal school as an attack on the directrice by hostile colleagues willing to draw students into their fight ended up assuming political and religious dimensions involving the larger community.

Activities and Contacts Outside the Normal School

Dedicated normal school directrices wanted contact with students to continue after they became teachers. They corresponded with them, sometimes visited their schools, and welcomed return visits to the normal school. By the 1890s education officials also urged directrices, as well as directors, to add structure to such contacts by encouraging the formation of *amicales des ancien(ne)s élèves* (alumni associations), which could meet at the normal school. Directrice Marie Crouzel, who founded the *amicale* in Coutances (Manche) in 1898, emphasized its benefits for both the normal school and teachers: professors could learn about students' experiences teaching "children of the people," and teachers could be reminded that *l'esprit laïque*, with its respect for reason and toleration, was the basis of French democratic institutions. In the Côtes-du-Nord directrice Marie Thiébault told her school's alumnae group that meetings could lessen teachers' feelings of isolation and provide a renewed sense of purpose if energies were flagging. Normal school personnel would also find out whether they had adequately prepared teachers for careers and life. By uniting, teachers would strengthen the "école laïque, school of progress, liberty, reason, fraternity." First published in the department's education bulletin, Thiébault's talk defining an *amicale*'s role in supporting public schools was reprinted in the *Revue pédagogique*.[60]

The first normal school *amicales* for women were founded in Paris in 1882, encouraged by directrices Friedberg and Ferrand, and in Rouen in 1887, spearheaded by Saffroy. Others started in Douai and Nancy by 1892. The creation of the Fontenay-aux-Roses association in 1894 inspired Legros to start one for the small Vendée school, which after ten years had prepared only eighty-five teachers. To overcome the initial objections of the departmental inspector, who worried that an alumnae group would further divide normal school graduates from other teachers, Legros opened it to all lay teachers. The bitter conflict generated by the Dreyfus Affair made associations of lay women teachers still more timely, and by 1899 at least sixteen existed, including the one in Thiébault's difficult Breton department. More than half of the women's normal schools had an *amicale* by 1914, although not all continued after directrices left or local interest declined. Frequently the directrice was an *amicale*'s president or honorary president. In at least one instance, however, conflict between a directrice and a teacher, the vice president, led the directrice, Eugénie Jacquemin, to step down as president, that conflict also contributing to her leaving the normal school in the Drôme in 1908.[61]

Many alumnae groups published bulletins to report on their annual or semiannual meetings, occasions for lectures and socializing. Pedagogical

108   WOMEN AND THE POLITICS OF EDUCATION IN FRANCE

topics and news about members and their families were also included. For members unable to attend meetings, perhaps because of the difficulty of travel from rural areas, the bulletins provided a link to the school. Directrice Rambault used the Limoges bulletin in 1905 to publish her critical reaction to Frapié's recent novel, *La Maternelle*, which recounted a teacher's miseries at a nursery school in a working class district of Paris. His characterization of *normaliennes* as pedantic *demoiselles* who looked down on the poor and were not true women or mothers drew her rejoinder that normal school students were the daughters of workers, small shopkeepers, and modest employees and thus clearly from "le peuple."[62] At the 1906 meeting of the big Rouen association, attended by 263 members, directrice Menat offered encouragement to those in the "many parts" of the department where people frightened by the word "laïque" still viewed women teachers with suspicion. The *école laïque*, she affirmed, taught children about the ideals of tolerance, love, truth, justice, *fraternité*, and social peace. In the Vendée bulletin in 1912 directrice Jeanne Palanque recounted a personal experience to try to help teachers unhappy in their current location. Before becoming a directrice, she had taught in Saint-Étienne, an industrial city where she learned to appreciate a working-class population which held under its "common appearance" an "inexhaustible reservoir of goodness." As feminist organizations became more active after 1900, some alumnae bulletins, such as those for the Seine and Seine-et-Marne, also provided information about feminist goals.[63]

In the *Bulletin* of the Fontenay-aux-Roses *amicale*, directrices and professors in normal schools and higher primary schools shared ideas about pedagogical, professional, and even social issues. Five directrices and two *inspectrices primaires*, formerly directrices, served as the *amicale*'s president before 1914 and used the *Bulletin* to report on meetings and invite comments. Marie Mahaut as president liked Thiébault's suggestion that the *Bulletin* discuss normal schools' role in community groups supportive of public schools, and she asked professor Émilie Flayol to report on examples of appropriate "social education." Flayol, a future directrice, did a survey and noted regretfully that many normal school colleagues remained sheltered and hesitated to act in groups, fearing that they would be talked about and seem diminished in feminine virtue in the court of public opinion.[64]

Some articles in the Fontenay *Bulletin* tackled topics more controversial than those typical in *amicales*' newsletters. For example, during the Dreyfus Affair, Eidenschenk, a member of the Fontenay *amicale*'s advisory council, drew on Pécaut's teachings to argue that there were limits to what

REPRESENTING REPUBLICAN EDUCATION   109

maintaining "neutrality" should mean in public education. He had said in 1886 that educators should not be neutral in debates pitting a republican regime of liberty against dictatorship. In teaching history, Eidenshenk stated, adherence to religious neutrality did not prevent professors from taking positions on topics like the role of religion in history. Old biases against Mohammed, Martin Luther, the Edict of Nantes, or the French Revolution should be discredited, as should support for the Catholic Inquisition or Napoleon. She also reported with dismay that lycée professors at a recent congress had refused to endorse a proposal to post the Declaration of Rights of 1789 in classrooms, claiming that it was not neutral. Such a stance allowed enemies of the Republic to use neutrality against it at a time when students truly needed to know about its values. Inspectress general Kergomard took a similar position in the feminist newspaper *La Fronde*.[65]

Directrices could reach a larger audience beyond the normal school by publishing textbooks and articles in pedagogical reviews. Predictably, their textbooks for primary schools usually offered fairly traditional lessons about appropriate feminine behavior and the importance of women's role in the home. Sagnier's reader for girls' schools, *La Fillette bien élévée* (1896), discussed personal hygiene, clothing, and correct behavior with parents, teachers, friends, and in the larger society—topics like those in her advice manual for teachers. At least 60,000 copies of her textbook were eventually published. Mayaud's *Politesse et bonne tenue* (1904) provided detailed behavioral advice for "enfants du peuple" in primary schools. Murique's *Maman et petite Jeanne*, first issued in 1891 and in a fourth edition by 1904, used a story to present younger girls with moral lessons on the family, school, and nation. Her *Économie domestique et hygiène* (1894), like other home economics textbooks, covered part of the girls' science curriculum and was in a seventh edition in 1911. Eidenschenk also assembled three volumes of readings for different levels in girls' primary schools, each volume published in multiple editions totaling more than 50,000 copies. Whereas her *Premières lectures des petites filles* (1911) were simple stories and fairy tales, *Les troisiémes lectures* (1913), comprised of excerpts from various authors, included examples of active women like Florence Nightingale.[66]

Changes in contemporary attitudes toward women and their roles were acknowledged explicitly in 1910 by primary inspector Alcide Lemoine and directrice Juliette Marie in their preface to *La jeune française*, a book of readings for older schoolgirls. They saw the "modern" woman's role in the family and society becoming larger and believed that the idea of woman as

110 WOMEN AND THE POLITICS OF EDUCATION IN FRANCE

man's "equal" was replacing the old view of her as an inferior to be treated as an "eternal minor." Yet they emphasized the primacy of women's domestic duties, termed as important as those of men. Knowing how to advise husbands, fathers, or brothers represented the highest form of women's "emancipation." Some selections indicated, however, that women often needed to work outside the home, and two featured a teacher and a hospital nurse.[67]

Professor Blanche Gauthier, promoted to directrice in 1914, would have an especially successful publishing history with a series of science textbooks, beginning in 1908–09 with two volumes of chemistry lessons (*Leçons de chimie*) for the first- and second-year courses in women's normal schools, and by 1923–24 in thirteenth editions. Her *Manuel de chimie* (1911) also covered homemaking (*enseignement ménager*) and was designed for higher primary schools and *cours complémentaires* (complementary courses) preparing students for the *brevet élémentaire* and normal school entry *concours*; by 1920 it was in a tenth edition. Her command of physics as well as chemistry, subjects once thought too difficult for women, was evident in several textbooks coauthored with higher primary school professor Léon Perseil, husband of Nancy Perseil, the directrice when she was a professor at the normal school in Bourges before becoming the directrice in Moulins. They published the two-volume *Leçons de physique* (1909–10) for women's normal and higher primary schools and a *Manuel de physique* (1912) for girls' higher primary schools; the *Leçons* were in an eighth edition in 1920, and the *Manuel* in a sixteenth in 1926. After curricular changes in 1920, they worked with a third author to make the physics *Leçons* suitable for both men's and women's normal schools.[68]

While less than a dozen directrices published books before 1914, at least forty contributed to national and regional pedagogical journals and alumnae bulletins, addressing curricular, professional, and social issues. Most attached their names to articles, but some continued to sign as "une directrice" well into the 1890s and even later. Their articles appeared in at least a dozen pedagogical reviews, including the *Manuel général de l'instruction primaire*, *Journal des instituteurs*, *Le Volume*, and *L'École nouvelle*, all read by many teachers. The circulation of the *Manuel général* once reached at least 60,000 and that of *Le Volume*, 40,000.[69] In *L'Instituteur*, *L'Union pédagogique*, and the *Correspondance générale de l'instruction primaire*, Léonie Heurtefeu published more than fifty articles, later available in a posthumous volume, *Pour nos institutrices, conseils pratiques* (1901), introduced by directrice

Dollé, who had known her since 1881.[70] Like Juliette Marie, some directrices also discussed changes in women's roles and after 1900 increasingly examined issues of inequality affecting women, as Eidenschenk did in her 1907 manual for teachers and many articles in *L'École nouvelle* and the *Manuel général*. Sagnier contributed to *Le Volume*.

As directrices wrote more often for professional journals and worked with their school's alumnae association, it is not surprising that some also began to speak on occasions outside the normal school, for they had acquired substantial experience talking to students and teachers. Although directrice Heurtefeu had opined at the education congress in 1889 that women should not speak in public, other colleagues became less hesitant when they perceived attitudes changing. In July 1897 Billotey, then a professor, began her address to students and parents at her higher primary school's annual prize ceremony by stating that it was "the first time that a professor at the *école* Edgar Quinet" had done this and the honor somewhat embarrassed her. She discussed the importance of education for French democracy and highlighted women educators' role, which was to make women aware of their

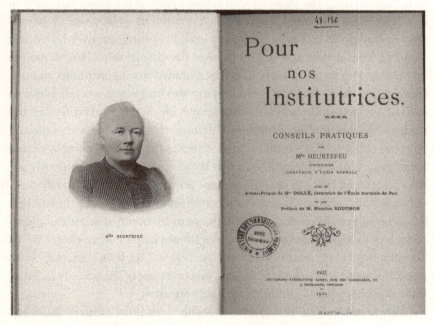

Directrice Léontine Heurtefeu, *Pour nos institutrices, Conseils pratiques* (Pau: Garet, 1901). *Courtesy of Bibliothèque Diderot, Université de Lyon 3*

112   WOMEN AND THE POLITICS OF EDUCATION IN FRANCE

duties. She also alluded to "the big feminist movement" struggling for "new rights." Excerpts from the talk appeared in the *Revue pédagogique*.[71]

Five years later, a woman speaking at a school's prize ceremony was still highly unusual. Directrice Frugier, invited to speak in a suburb of Angoulême in 1902, first thought of declining but then decided that if the mayor and town council had the courage to ask her, she should have the courage to speak. She would talk about "féminisme," she said, because the invitation itself was a feminist act. Recognizing that "féminisme" was often either mocked as absurd or viewed with alarm, she reassured her audience by presenting it as women's recognition of their self-worth and an inevitable result of more women needing to enter the workplace. Many women now managed to combine employment with domestic duties, she noted. In conclusion, she cited Jules Ferry's much quoted comments about republican education as the key to happy marriages because spouses could share beliefs and values. The precedent-setting nature of the talk, warmly applauded, was underscored by a local newspaper which published it, as did *La Fronde*.[72]

Pedagogical reviews also reported on educators' efforts to reach out to local populations, as urged by the Ligue de l'Enseignement and republican "solidarists." The quasi-official *Revue pédagogique* published parts of directrice Rose Lecomte's report on her creation of a *patronage* to benefit women workers in Le Puy in 1895. Sixty to eighty young women who worked in stores, households, or a factory came to the normal school's *école annexe* on Sunday afternoons for activities that included sewing, readings and discussion, practical advice on housekeeping and budgeting, remedial lessons in basic subjects, and musical entertainment. Normal school professors and students assisted, and a committee of "dames protectrices" provided modest financial support. For normal school students the sessions complemented their "professional education" in a way that Lecomte termed "less artificial" than practice teaching in the *école annexe*. Sometimes medical consultations were available, and sessions ended with refreshments. Lecomte hoped that the *patronage* might make a small difference in an "ocean of miseries," and an editor's note suggested that her example should inspire other efforts. What Lecomte began was continued by her successor, Charlotte Armanet, as an inspector noted approvingly.[73] Indeed, this extra use of the school's facilities and resources required administrative authorization.

Other examples of *patronages* or adult education courses launched by directrices before 1900 include Marguerite Ginier's Monday evening courses in Agen, Crouzel's Sunday gatherings for workers in Coutances, and the projects of Ebren in Lons-le-Saunier, Jacquin in Grenoble, Sabatier in Aurillac, Josephine Escande in Cahors, and Pieyre in Saint-Étienne. At the normal schools in Orléans and Blois, directrices and professors started correspondence courses to help girls in isolated rural areas prepare for the normal school entry *concours*.[74] On occasion, however, efforts at outreach drew criticism, as in 1900 when *L'Aurore* attacked directrice Céleste Léveillé's work on Red Cross fundraising because her name appeared on a committee list placed on a church door in Troyes. Rector Adam promptly assured the ministry that Léveillé was devoted to laic education, indicating also that Mme Loubet, wife of the president of the Republic, was the honorary president of the Red Cross organization in question. In provincial towns, he added, the wives of higher-ranking *fonctionnaires* joined such groups, and directrices' participation could draw teachers into this "patriotic" work.[75]

Beyond the local level, various organizations and national and international meetings attracted normal school personnel. The education ministry arranged congresses on primary education in conjunction with the international expositions of 1889 and 1900,[76] and the Ligue de l'Enseignement's annual meetings were also a draw, as were meetings of its local chapters, including the large Paris group. Paringaux and Billotey were among the directrices who made reports at Ligue meetings.[77] After 1900, the Ligue intensified efforts to encourage the formation of youth organizations for public school pupils, recognizing that there were already 2,350 Catholic *patronages* for boys and 1,800 for girls. Its *comité des dames* (women's committee) promoted such efforts for girls throughout France, while the group Coopération féminine, founded in 1901, focused on the Paris area.[78] The members of Coopération féminine, presided over by Ferry's widow, included Billotey, Fontenay directrice Dejean de la Bâtie, primary inspectresses Ginier and Kieffer, and some secondary school professors.[79] Normal school personnel and many teachers also joined a new society for the study of child psychology, founded in 1899 by Buisson, professor of the "science de l'éducation" at the Sorbonne after leaving the education ministry. Twenty-seven of the eighty-six directrices or their normal schools figured on the membership list in 1907.[80]

The Union pour la Vérité (Union for Truth), led by Paul Desjardins, a secondary school professor and lecturer at the women's higher normal school in Sèvres, also appealed to educators through publications discussing moral education, church-state relations, and social issues. With members of all religious persuasions who shared, according to Desjardins, the "spirit of

Fontenay" and Pécaut, the Union drew older directrices and normal school professors. Among the 229 women on a membership list of 779 in 1908 were 23 current or former directrices and 16 normal school professors, 16 higher primary school directrices and professors, plus 31 institutrices and 19 secondary school professors—a total of 105 educators, comprising 45 percent of women members. In the Union *Bulletin* in 1904 Eidenschenk published an expanded version of her reflections on public educators' obligation to remain "neutral" when attacked viciously by political adversaries.[81] The ecumenical nature of the Union meant that freethinkers were welcomed, but only two of the directrices who were members appeared on a list of more than 3,600 attending the International Free Thought Congress in Paris in 1905: Eidenschenk and Dollé, in the company of their husbands.[82]

With the goal of promoting contacts among educators from different nations, Buisson, elected a deputy from Paris in 1902, also spearheaded the creation of the Comité international des études pédagogiques in 1893, sharing the title of president with directrice Nathalie Bourgoise. The organization began after a group of French educators met with colleagues in Switzerland. Two of its five vice presidents were directrices Aurélie Lacroix of Foix and Jalambic of Carcassonne. Local chapters were formed, including one headed by Lacroix and another in the Ardennes led by Gabrielle Cligny, then at a higher primary school and later a normal school directrice. In the context of rising nationalism in conservative political quarters, an international trip provoked criticism of Bourgoise in September 1905. Seventy French teachers went to an exposition in Liège and then traveled to Frankfurt, attending a banquet hosted by German educational associations. There Bourgoise and a male colleague made remarks supportive of friendly Franco-German relations and expressed hope for an end to wars and an era of universal peace once national egotisms waned. The French ambassador to Germany, Georges Bihourd, promptly complained to premier Maurice Rouvier, registering dismay that pacifist views aired at recent meetings of teachers' *amicales* in France were echoed elsewhere. French teachers visiting a rival country should not offer opinions that made France look weak, he stated. Although Bihourd's letter went into Bourgoise's personnel file, no other negative consequences for her or the international group were indicated.[83]

The defense of basic professional interests understandably led a number of directrices into the Association des Inspecteurs primaires et Directeurs d'écoles normales (AIPDEN), founded in 1905 at a time when teachers' *amicales* were growing noticeably and becoming more vocal in the wake of the Associations law of 1901. Normal school professors had formed their own association in 1902. Directrices Eidenschenk and Billotey were elected to the first AIPDEN council of fifteen members, and Eidenschenk, now on the Conseil Supérieur de l'Instruction Publique, also became a vice president and thus one of five executive bureau officers.[84]

Normal schools faced an immediate danger in 1905 because Alfred Massé, the Radical republican deputy reporting for the Chamber's budget commission, recommended closing them and instead training teachers in secondary schools and new institutes tied to universities. Arguing that normal schools had inadequate academic offerings and enclosed future teachers in an "esprit primaire," he contended that contact with other students of similar age would broaden future teachers' outlook. Other commentators who faulted "l'esprit primaire" were anxious about the growth of syndicalist, socialist, and pacifist sympathies among teachers. To defend their institution and the teachers they trained, normal school directors and professors, including Eidenschenk, wrote letters and articles, and Buisson remained their legislative advocate. By early 1906 Massé no longer pressed his proposal, for the controversy generated by the separation of church and state loomed larger on political agendas.[85]

In the functioning of the AIPDEN, male inspectors' views often predominated at national and regional meetings because, as a corps of more than 450, they constituted nearly three-fourths of potential members. Work loads and pay increases were the major concerns. The fact that some male members voiced reservations about the issues of equal pay for women educators and women's access to primary school inspection may well have contributed to a smaller presence of normal school directrices than directors. In 1907, 54 directors and 28 directrices were members. Five years later, when the full membership was 493 (out of a possible 647), only 32 of 86 directrices belonged, along with three primary inspectresses and three inspectresses of *écoles maternelles*.[86] Although the same credential was required for primary school inspection and normal school direction, differing professional interests evident before 1914 contributed to normal school leaders forming a separate association in late 1918.

The most prestigious professional representative body on which a normal school directrice could serve was the Conseil Supérieur de l'Instruction Publique (CSIP, Higher Council of Public Instruction), a "veritable chamber of notables" in education.[87] Whereas a directrice was automatically part of the departmental council of primary education, ministerial appointments

116   WOMEN AND THE POLITICS OF EDUCATION IN FRANCE

and elections determined membership on the CSIP, and only six of the fifty-seven CSIP seats were for primary education. Of the nearly 1,400 electors from primary education, just over a quarter were women: the directrices of normal schools and higher primary schools, teachers elected to departmental councils, and the small groups of inspectresses general and departmental inspectresses for *écoles maternelles*, and primary inspectresses. Kergomard, the first woman member, was not reelected in 1892; Saffroy was elected in 1896 while directrice of Fontenay-aux-Roses but as an inspectress in Paris after leaving Fontenay chose not to run again; and no woman won enough votes in 1900. Normal school directrice Eidenschenk was the next woman elected, running in 1904 while in Saint-Brieuc (Côtes-du-Nord), reelected while in Douai (Nord), and serving until 1924 when she neared retirement. The election in 1912 of Jeanne Déghilage, a pro-syndicalist teacher in Lille, gave the CSIP two women members.[88]

Inspector general Lamy, who evaluated Eidenschenk after her arrival in Douai, described her as a self-assured and strong personality with a "virilité d'esprit," characterizations that help explain her emergence as an influential leader of women educators for two decades. She acted with "natural authority" but lacked, Lamy thought, "the gift of communicating with words which warm from heart to heart." Many of her students evidently did not see that supposed deficiency, one at Douai later writing that she was like a mother with her daughters.[89] In 1903 Eidenschenk had campaigned unsuccessfully in a special CSIP election, drawing support from electors who saw her candidacy as a matter of fairness because women were nearly half of all personnel in primary education, including more than 55,000 *institutrices* (women teachers).[90]

Women educators' interests, Eidenschenk wrote, were not contrary to those of male colleagues but were "sometimes different." Announcing her next candidacy in 1904, she stated that her supporters, male and female, believed that a normal school directrice was "the most qualified to represent . . . the interests of all women personnel." She knew the needs and aspirations of the teachers she trained and remained their confidante. Recalling that she was an *institutrice* and a substitute in a higher primary school before admission to Fontenay, she had experienced "all the joys of the profession" and "all the miseries." Recently she had championed women educators' interests in the pedagogical press, including demands for equal pay. She also fully supported teachers' associations (*amicales*). As a representative on the CSIP of men and women working in all levels of primary education, Eidenschenk pledged that she would always act in accordance with "l'esprit résolument laïque, rationnel et démocratique" that had inspired the founders of republican primary education, Ferry, Bert, and her own "maître" Pécaut.[91]

La Fronde, not surprisingly, celebrated Eidenschenk's election as a "victory for feminism."[92] Her advocacy for equal pay and other issues of gender equity would intersect with feminist teachers' campaigning and also with that of feminist organizations pursuing a wide range of issues.

In the decade before 1914 Eidenschenk's emergence as a prominent advocate of women educators' interests was an important part of the evidence that many women's normal schools and their leaders were no longer so confined by the increasingly criticized model of the "couvent laïque." Normal school personnel and women teachers still wore the traditional long black dresses with high necklines, but their voices increasingly had a place in public discussion, albeit a place usually less prominent than that of male colleagues who led professional associations. In April 1911 the rector of Nancy gave directrice Géhin of Bar-le-Duc permission to speak in two towns at meetings organized by the Ligue pour la Défense de l'Enseignement public of the Meuse. Explaining how schools prepared students for their lives at work and in the home, she refused to engage in an explicitly political discussion when an adversary of public schools tried to provoke her. Her local republican defenders, reporting on the events, recognized that by speaking publicly she had exposed herself to attacks from enemies of the Republic.[93]

4

Directing Normal Schools
in *Petites Patries*

Brittany and the Vendée, Algeria

The highly centralized nature of French public education, a Napoleonic legacy extended by the Third Republic's reforms in curricular and personnel policies, did not necessarily exclude variations in the application of some policies from region to region.[1] Indeed, republican education officials encouraged teaching about the traditional *petites patries*. When presenting French history and geography in primary schools, teachers were thus encouraged to stimulate students' interest by discussing familiar local heroes or environmental features before presenting the national picture. Normal school personnel, in turn, alerted future teachers to such emphases.

In two areas known for their particularities, the Catholic West and Algeria, normal school directrices faced special challenges and conflicts. The seven Breton departments in the academy of Rennes, plus the adjacent Vendée department in the academy of Poitiers, had a tradition of royalist and Catholic opposition to national politics that dated from the Revolution of 1789 and fueled hostility to the Third Republic's secularization of public schools and separation of church and state. From the standpoint of republican leaders in Paris, much of the Catholic West looked like a region still to be won over to democratic political values.[2] Algeria, conquered by France between 1830 and 1848, was among the overseas territories subject to the much discussed *mission civilisatrice* (civilizing mission) but, unlike other parts of the French empire, had a unique status with its three administrative departments and sizable settler population. Through example and education, French officials sought to transmit the values of French civilization not only to the large Algerian population termed "indigènes" but also to European settlers from

---

Women and the Politics of Education in Third Republic France. Linda L. Clark, Oxford University Press.
© Oxford University Press 2023. DOI: 10.1093/oso/9780197632864.003.0005

DIRECTING NORMAL SCHOOLS IN *PETITES PATRIES* 119

other countries, notably Spain and Italy.[3] In some Breton departments and in Algeria, issues of language posed special problems for those who trained teachers because many students came from families where French was not the household language. Although normal school students knew enough French to qualify for admission, they might lack the mastery of it more common in other areas.

Discussing methods for teaching in Breton primary schools where children arrived with little or no familiarity with French, inspector general Irénée Carré recognized in 1888 that other regions also posed problems. Flemish remained in use in parts of the northeast, as did Basque in the Pyrénées. The Breton problem was more wide-ranging, however, because in virtually all of the Finistère department and about half of the departments of Morbihan and Côtes-du-Nord non-city dwellers routinely spoke a language unlike French and also were not accustomed to hearing sermons in French. Indeed, Carré remarked, many clergy feared that if French replaced Breton, their influence would decline greatly. To familiarize Breton schoolchildren with French as soon as possible, he recommended conducting classes entirely in French, a method likened to the way mothers introduced children to words. When he later addressed the teaching of French to indigènes in Algeria, Indochina, and other colonies, he drew upon recent practices in Breton schools but also recognized appreciable differences in contexts. In Algeria and Tunisia, he expected indigènes who learned French to continue to use Arabic as well.[4]

Official statistics on literacy during the 1880s further illustrate the challenges facing educators in Brittany, particularly educators of girls and women. In 1886, when about 90 percent of young men who were army conscripts could at least read French, about a quarter of those from Finistère and Côtes-du-Nord, and a third from Morbihan (ranked last among eighty-six departments) could not. Gender differences in literacy were reflected in the ability to sign a marriage register at a town hall (*mairie*): 86 percent of French men could sign in 1884, as compared to 78 percent of women. In the Breton departments highlighted by Carré, women's signing ranked last in Finistère (34 percent as compared to 77 percent of men) and Morbihan (women 41 percent, men 58 percent) and eightieth in the Côtes-du-Nord (women 52 percent, men 64 percent). Yet in two other Breton departments with traditions of effective Catholic teaching, Mayenne and Maine-et-Loire, women's signing rates (87 and 81 percent, respectively) exceeded the national average and were slightly above the men's rates.[5]

Establishing the Republican Normal School in the West

The timetable for opening women's normal schools in Brittany and the Vendée was indicative of the initial local resistance encountered when the government asked departmental general council to fund the facilities mandated by the Bert law of 1879. In 1881–82, when the Ferry laws were passed, laywomen were 57 percent of all women public schoolteachers in France, but in public schools in the seven Breton departments and the Vendée, all of which favored religious teachers, laywomen ranged from only 8 percent in Mayenne to 40 percent in Côtes-du-Nord.[6] The only Breton department to meet the Bert law's four-year deadline for compliance was the Loire-Inférieure, where a women's normal school opened in the port city of Nantes in 1883. By the end of that year, fifty-eight of the eighty-nine departments of France and Algeria had complied with the law.[7] When the last Breton school opened in 1887 in Laval (Mayenne), only five departments in France still lacked a women's normal school; three others shared a school with a neighboring department.

The first of the thirty-one directrices appointed in Brittany or the Vendée before 1914 was Clémence Moret, thirty-eight years old when she arrived in 1883 in Nantes, the region's largest city with a population of 125,000. Daughter of a cutler and a teacher, she had taught since 1861, first in public and private schools in the Yonne, Paul Bert's department, and in 1878 headed the first laicized girls' public school in Abbeville (Somme). She became the second directrice of the normal school in Amiens in 1879 and then opened the school in Dijon in 1880. When she requested the Nantes post, hoping that the maritime climate would benefit her sister's health, the rector of Dijon welcomed her departure because he wanted a better qualified directrice for the important Dijon school. Moret held only a *brevet supérieur* and had resisted the addition of professors holding the new credential. Rated by officials in 1879 as an "esprit libéral," Moret was also a Catholic likely to fit in well in Brittany. Of the twelve directrices assigned to the new Breton normal schools in the 1880s, Moret had one of the longest tenures, remaining for twenty-two years. At the outset, however, she reported not only the predictable regional resistance to *écoles laïques* but also her problems with adjusting to local personality traits, as she perceived them: a tendency to dissimulation, cold faces showing neither pleasure nor pain, and a penchant for quarrels and plotting.[8] Such characterizations were not unique; they figured often in reports from other directrices and inspectors.

DIRECTING NORMAL SCHOOLS IN *PETITES PATRIES* 121

Annual reviews of Moret's work by inspectors and rector Jules Jarry praised her successful launching of the Nantes normal school but sometimes noted her harsh criticism of others and domineering tendencies. She often complained about the poor preparation of students entering the school, a judgment Jarry confirmed in 1891 when he commended her for turning students, who arrived as children "à peine dégrossiers" (scarcely civilized) into serious teachers, "femmes de coeur" with a sense of professional duty. Because the Loire-Inférieure lacked a girls' higher primary school and post-primary *cours complémentaires* where students completing primary school at age thirteen could continue to learn and prepare for the normal school entrance exam, as they did in many departments, Moret was authorized to add a *cours complémentaire* to the *école annexe* in 1885. She was the "heart" (*âme*) of the school, Jarry wrote, and succeeded in a "difficult" milieu. Indeed, education minister Bourgeois, visiting the school in 1892, warned students that their task as teachers was harder in their *pays* than in others because of prejudices against the *école laïque*. Although the city of Nantes was supportive of the normal school, that was not true for many parts of the department, an inspector general reported in 1898.[9]

Moret's position in Nantes was more difficult after Jarry's death in 1900 because her religious practice became a public issue at a time when, after the divisive Dreyfus Affair, republican leaders resolved to complete the laicization of public schools in recalcitrant departments. Jarry, appointed rector of Rennes in 1873 under the monarchist Moral Order, subsequently worked to implant the republican school in a politically hostile area, but he also made compromises to avoid excessive conflict with local authorities. In 1901 the Loire-Inférieure's public schools had 429 lay women teachers, as compared to 114 nuns, but because nuns outnumbered lay women in private, and largely Catholic, schools by 682 to 46, they were more than 60 percent of the department's women teachers.[10] The socialist journal *Réveil social* denounced Moret in 1899 as an "old bigot" who allegedly compelled normal school students to engage in religious observances, but a brief investigation by departmental inspector Louis Larocque concluded simply that "this excellent directrice" needed a reminder to be prudent and reserved. A year later, however, another investigation was triggered when a socialist deputy and former teacher, Maximilien Carnaud of the Bouches-du-Rhône, reprinted the *Réveil* article in his *Bulletin des instituteurs et institutrices de France*.[11]

Moret then defended her right to religious practice and pointedly reminded authorities that many Breton parents wanted assurances that their

122   WOMEN AND THE POLITICS OF EDUCATION IN FRANCE

daughters had the same right while at the normal school. This time a new departmental inspector, Jacques Bourdel, was less sympathetic. He faulted her for not always distinguishing adequately between her "very legitimate" personal practice and expectations she set for students, adding that she had made the school into a "personal fief." Rector Raymond Thamin, a Dreyfusard, endorsed Bourdel's judgment, and an inspector general lamented that Moret had acquired "the habits and ideas of the region," allowing activities that made the normal school seem more like a convent. One young woman not admitted to the school's *école annexe* around 1900 long believed that the directrice, known for attending mass each morning, barred her because of her father's anticlerical views; she later entered the normal school in Rennes. After repeated official demands to moderate "her excesses in religious zeal," Moret evidently became more circumspect until retirement in 1905, but her reputation as a "dévote" lingered. Her successor Joséphine Escande, married and a mother, gave the school a more laic tone during the next two decades.[12]

Whereas Moret faced controversy at the end of her career, other directrices in Brittany encountered problems sooner when they launched a normal school or took charge of one recently established. Céline Mazier found an especially difficult situation in 1887 when she arrived in Laval (Mayenne) to open the last of the Breton normal schools. Like Moret she was an older directrice (born in 1849) whose training predated Fontenay-aux-Roses. Married and mother of two children, she had directed the normal school in Blois for seven years. Local republicans voiced concern soon after her arrival, fearing that because the ministry of finance had not yet reassigned her husband to a Mayenne post, his absence could compromise her image of respectability when she was already the target of so much clerical "malevolence" in a "backward" department. The Mayenne had no republican deputies or senators, and only half of the Laval normal school students admitted after the first entry examination came from the department.[13]

By 1890, unfortunately, the school's instructors and students were divided into two camps, for and against Mazier, and the conflict had local political ramifications. Republican city council members and the mayor and his wife backed Mazier, but departmental inspector Auguste Ditandy criticized her harshly, and the prefect was not helpful. More than one conclusion emerged from inspector general Carré's subsequent investigation. After initially agreeing with Ditandy, he then admitted to having too quickly accepted the judgment of someone who was not a strong republican. Nonetheless, he faulted Mazier for overplaying her republican views and called her a clever

DIRECTING NORMAL SCHOOLS IN *PETITES PATRIES* 123

and "dangerous" woman. The administrative resolution was to retire the conservative Ditandy and reassign Mazier to Toulouse, where she worked until retiring in 1909.[14]

Of the other five directrices who inaugurated Breton normal schools, three with Fontenay training—Marguerite Nivoley, Constance Robert, and Louise Sagnier—stayed for only a year or two before reassignment due to administrative orders or personal preferences. Élise Legros, also a Fontenaysienne, remained in Vannes (Morbihan) for four years, and seven more directrices would follow her before 1914, the school proving especially difficult to manage. Amélie Sage, nearly fifty when she opened the school in Saint-Brieuc (Côtes-du-Nord) in 1886 in a region known for "an esprit of systematic opposition," did stay until retirement in 1895, by which time her monitoring of school finances, problematic in her previous posts, was again judged deficient.[15]

In three Breton departments a second directrice played a more substantial role in stabilizing a normal school than the first. Élise Voinet, appointed to Angers (Maine-et-Loire) in 1888, two years after its opening, remained for twenty-six years. Like Constance Robert, her predecessor, she combatted hostility to the school. Her training during the 1870s in the Jura at the Lons-le-Saunier normal school, where strong Catholic traditions prevailed before the Bert law, was preparation for understanding the local religious culture. From a farming family, she had taught in public schools before becoming a normal school *maîtresse* and in 1884 entered Fontenay to prepare for professorial certification and, in 1887, for the directing credential. Inspectors soon credited her with winning acceptance of the school in a "pays archi-clérical," also commenting that her simple and discreet life gave no ammunition to critics of republican education. Rector Jarry remained concerned, however, that the backgrounds of many students could hurt the school's reputation because they were often from families with limited education and, he thought, sometimes dubious morality. The normal school functioned successfully in Angers, with a population of over 70,000 and from which many, if not most, students came, but graduates sometimes found it difficult to teach or gain acceptance in rural areas. As departmental inspector Fernand Robert lamented in 1901, *normaliennes* often sought transfers to schools in Angers as soon as possible.[16]

Similar comments about students' weaknesses and reluctance to stay in rural posts figured in the twenty-year record of Blanche Heigny, the second directrice of the normal school in Rennes (Ille-et-Vilaine). The daughter of

124   WOMEN AND THE POLITICS OF EDUCATION IN FRANCE

a teacher and wife of a disabled secondary school professor, she was already age forty-three when appointed in 1887 after benefiting from the Fontenay training for directrices. Jarry credited her with giving the school a good reputation and thereby attracting students in a department with many adversaries, but he also judged that students' deficiencies complicated professors' task. Students might have good intentions but lacked energy because of a presumably natural "mollesse," and their weak prior preparation still limited achievement in French composition in the late 1890s. Nonetheless, he deemed Rennes a "model" normal school in 1900, and various inspectors praised Heigny for exercising maternal authority with students and maintaining respect for the school. She retired in 1908.[17]

In Laval, Marie Simboiselle (later Mme Peltier) came into the contentious situation left by Mazier, but within a year, Jarry reported, her "tact" and "distinction" had won over the school's surveillance committee and local authorities, as well as professors and students. With the manners and bearing of a "femme du monde," she mingled easily in society in the small city of 33,000. Her marriage in 1893 to a philosophy professor probably helps explain why Jarry and departmental inspector Léopold Le Balle later remarked that her knowledge of philosophy was more extensive than that of most women.[18] To recruit better qualified students, she secured permission to add a *cours complémentaire* to the *école annexe*, as Moret had done in Nantes. By 1905 she had trained a majority of the department's lay women teachers. Yet during its first fifty years of existence, only 57 percent of the school's 757 students were from the Mayenne; the rest came from other normal schools' waiting lists, including 23 percent from other Breton departments. The numbers reflected not only the poor preparation of some applicants from the Mayenne but also continuing aversion to public education in a department with many congregational schools. Mme Peltier's death in 1911 cut short her twenty-one-year tenure in Laval, where she was remembered as "so distinguished, so *spirituelle*, so strictly fair."[19]

The long tenure of the early directrices in Nantes, Rennes, Angers, and Laval, each with only two or three directrices before 1914, was not the norm for the other three Breton normal schools—Quimper, Saint-Brieuc, Vannes—or for La Roche-sur-Yon in the Vendée. Quimper and Saint-Brieuc experienced six changes in leadership, and the other two schools, eight. Local controversies, conflicts among personnel, and personal preferences caused most of the turnover; retirement was the reason in only two cases.

École normale d'institutrices de Laval, c. 1900, Directrice Marie Simboiselle Peltier seated second row, fifth from right, with professors and students
© *Réseau Canopé – Le Musée National de l'Éducation. Rouen, 1979.36669.88*

The controversy that drew the most national attention to a Breton normal school occurred in 1897–98 in Vannes, then with its fourth directrice. It was not the first Vannes controversy in which religion figured prominently. The second directrice, Caroline Hoël, was accused of proselytizing for Protestantism in 1891, her third year there. She denied the allegation, stating that she always respected students' personal beliefs but would not permit them to make false claims, such as calling the St. Bartholomew's Day massacre of Protestants in 1572 a "pious work" or terming books on the Vatican Index "criminal." Although rector Jarry defended Hoël, there was a dearth of support not only from Catholics but also from some local republican notables, as inspector general Martel detected. Why, he asked, had Pécaut and Buisson sent a Protestant to this most Catholic of Breton departments? Her reassignment to Bourges in the academy of Paris did not end the Morbihan general council's hostility to the normal school. Inspector general Jean Métivier also reported that "in a blindly reactionary *pays*" the problems

126 WOMEN AND THE POLITICS OF EDUCATION IN FRANCE

facing Hoël's successor, Émilie Brocard, were compounded because the school attracted only students from the poorest classes. She restored respect for the school, according to Jarry, but soon requested reassignment and in 1895 left for Beauvais.[20]

The next controversy surrounding the Vannes normal school began in the press and reached the courtroom. On August 5 and 10, 1897, the conservative newspaper L'Arvor, subtitled a *journal catholique*, published articles denouncing students' misbehavior at the men's and women's normal schools. Some women students had been caught with letters from male students, and when groups from the two schools passed each other on walks on Thursdays or Sundays they allegedly exchanged knowing looks. Supposedly women students, when left unsupervised in the school's courtyard, were also seen smoking. L'Arvor attributed the recent expulsion of four young women to the failings of a school that did not base moral education on "Christ." After the republican *Avenir du Morbihan* counterattacked, the conservative *Courrier morbihannais* denounced women's normal schools and girls' secondary schools as contrary to religion. It also claimed that for girls the certificate of primary studies, obtained by examination at ages eleven to thirteen, was useless.[21]

Against this backdrop prefect Gustave Chadenier spoke at the Morbihan department's general council meeting on August 20, sorting out fact from fiction as he defended the normal schools from accusations by aristocratic members. Education officials also decided to counterattack to show support for teachers not only in Morbihan but also those feeling beleaguered elsewhere. Departmental inspector Joseph Aignan, with the ministry's approval, counseled each father or guardian of a woman student affected by L'Arvor's attack to bring an individual lawsuit for defamation, and thirty-six did so.[22]

At the civil tribunal in Vannes in 1898, the lawyer for L'Arvor argued that the leadership of the normal school directrice was the real target of its attack, not students. The attacks took a toll. Before a verdict was issued on June 23, directrice Angélina Petit, age forty-one, committed suicide by drowning, the only directrice driven to that act of desperation, which was publicized locally and nationally.[23] A graduate of Fontenay-aux-Roses and in her fourth directing post since 1884, Petit had been pleased to move from the Hautes-Alpes in 1895 to a school nearer to the Vendée where her family resided. In addition to the press attacks, she faced problems with some of her personnel in Vannes. Inspector Aignan provided support, and inspector general Jost, evaluating the normal school in March 1898, found that she judged personnel

DIRECTING NORMAL SCHOOLS IN *PETITES PATRIES*   127

fairly. Although Jost also advised that she should be "more calm and self-possessed," he did not think that the school's internal problems warranted moving her, particularly because "adversaries" of the school would interpret that in "the most deplorable way."[24]

After Petit's death, supporters in Vannes, described as "a large crowd" (*une foule nombreuse*), followed her coffin to the railroad station, from which it was transported to the Vendée for burial. The republican newspaper *Le Patriote de la Vendée*, reporting after her funeral on June 5 in the town of Triaize, pronounced that "clerical defamation" had killed her. At her funeral were the Vendée's chief departmental inspector, normal school directrice Legros and two professors, and a number of men and women teachers. A "friend of the family" who spoke at the funeral denounced the "fierce enemies" of public education who attacked women who were "without defenses" and perhaps lacked the temperament that enabled men better to withstand calumnies. Broadening his comments, he noted that men and women teachers were "constantly spied upon" but drew strength from their dignity, irreproachable conduct, and commitment to the important "mission" confided to them. Mlle Petit had commanded respect, he concluded, and deserved to rest in peace.[25]

In the end, the court vindicated the women students in Vannes, ordering the author of the offending articles and also the paper's publisher to pay 250 francs in damages to each of the thirty-five students, who were now permitted to place public notices of the judicial outcome.[26] A pedagogical review edited by Morbihan teachers, *L'Enseignement pratique*, celebrated the judgment, calling the "vile" attack on normal school students only part of the continuing campaign to benefit congregational teachers at the expense of lay teachers. In the Parisian press, André Balz, a frequent commentator on educational issues, saw the verdict as offering teachers new protection against defamation.[27] Predictably, *La Croix du Morbihan* reacted differently, alleging in the article "Les dollars de ces demoiselles" that administrative greed had driven the directrice to her death. It also added an antisemitic slur by linking *laïcité* in public schools to Jews, a common linkage during the Dreyfus Affair then raging. A more moderate and practical Catholic reaction came from the bishop of Vannes, who warned clergy that when they promoted Catholic schools their comments on public schools should respect legal limitations.[28]

To provide leadership to the beleaguered Vannes school as its students faced examinations for the *brevet supérieur* in 1898, the education ministry promptly appointed Marie Mahaut, a *répétitrice* at Fontenay since 1889 and

128   WOMEN AND THE POLITICS OF EDUCATION IN FRANCE

regarded as Pécaut's "right arm" before he retired. She stabilized the normal school, and her Catholic convictions and religious practice assuaged some local critics, but she did not wish to remain indefinitely. After her reassignment to Châteauroux in 1902, Amélie Landais led the school for the next six years.[29] From a family with more than one generation of men and women teachers, Landais was one of only three directrices of Breton schools born in the region. Unfortunately under Marie Buisson, named in 1908 to her first directing post, the school became embroiled in a "civil war," not hidden from students, as conflict developed between Buisson and certain professors. Her "mentalité peu laïque" also dismayed superiors at a time when bitterness over laicizing private school teaching ranks and the church-state separation lingered locally. Amélie Hui, resolutely *laïque* and a non-practicing Protestant, replaced Buisson, who was reassigned in 1913. As the eighth Vannes directrice, Hui would acquire the record for longevity in the long problematical post, staying until retirement in 1937.[30]

The Côtes-du-Nord department north of the Morbihan also witnessed controversy concerning its women's normal school in Saint-Brieuc, not only because of entrenched opposition to republican schooling but also because two directrices with strong republican views clashed with a more traditionalist and Catholic departmental inspector. Marie Thiébault, daughter of a tailor in Nancy, succeeded the founding directrice Sage in 1895 and experienced Brittany as an "outpost" (*pays d'avant-poste*) where the cause of public education was far from won. The depth of hostility to the normal school meant that many students arrived fearful of the moral consequences of exposure to its program, she reported. Students could, of course, leave the school to attend church, and no noticeable decline in their religious observance occurred during her tenure. Acutely aware of new Catholic private schools opened to compete with public schools, Thiébault spearheaded the creation of an alumnae association to support normal school graduates, as noted earlier.[31]

Thiébault's judgment and intelligence won rector Jarry's praise, but her dealings with departmental inspector Alexandre Nouet became troubled. Primary education director Bayet, after visiting Saint-Brieuc in 1897, reported to the minister that Thiébault, a "difficult, domineering, imperious, very authoritarian" woman, had annoyed the inspector and the rector. Inspector general Jost was more positive in 1898, citing letters from former students clearly attached to her and the school. Nouet, he added, obviously disliked her, did not support her, and accused her of lacking deference to him. In 1898 Thiébault had spoken to the prefect, boldly asking for his help because of the "bitter war" being waged against women teachers who were normal school graduates. The next evaluations by inspectors general also included praise, and in 1901 the new rector, Thamin, judged that the school functioned well and Thiébault behaved correctly with her superiors. Moved to a more prestigious post in Dijon in September 1902, she left as a local scandal surrounded her sister, abandoned by a husband doubtful of their child's paternity. The republican *Réveil des Côtes-du-Nord* regretted Thiébault's departure and praised her work, suggesting also that the department's academic administration and former prefect had not always adequately supported her. An infuriated Nouet then insisted on sending a copy of the *Réveil* article to the ministry in Paris, complaining in an attached letter that it was unfair to him and that a woman like Thiébault was bad for public education. Thiébault would serve in Dijon until 1921.[32]

Thiébault's successor in Saint-Brieuc was the strong-minded Albertine Eidenschenk, who arrived with her husband, named professor of German at the small city's lycée. Within six months of her arrival, inspector Nouet drew the rector's attention to the Eidenschenks' freethinking tendencies and accused the directrice of pressuring normal school students to shun church services. Only about a quarter of the eighty-eight students were attending services in May 1903, he reported, whereas previously "even under Thiébault's administration" all did so. Terming Mme Eidenschenk a "cold *sectaire*" and an "arriviste," he insisted that students' absence from church offended local religious sensibilities. Inspector general Leblanc's evaluation in June 1903 provided a different perspective for the ministry in Paris. Eidenschenk understood the meaning of "neutrality" in public education better than Nouet, he judged, and her morning "morale" lessons offered commonsense advice reminiscent of Pécaut's talks at Fontenay. He also reported that because Nouet and his wife attended the same parish church as normal school students, it was Nouet himself, not other citizens, who made students' churchgoing an issue. Their declining attendance was comparable, he noted, to a similar development in Troyes under a new directrice, Julia Mayaud, and in each case students evidently felt freer to make their own decisions.[33]

In deference to a request from Nouet, her immediate superior, Eidenschenk contacted students' parents to ask whether they wanted their daughters to attend church. Of the 86 responses received, 76 indicated that daughters could decide for themselves, 6 wanted no church attendance, and 4 did. That about twenty students whose parents did not dictate churchgoing continued

130 WOMEN AND THE POLITICS OF EDUCATION IN FRANCE

religious observance, while others chose not to, seemed to Eidenschenk to demonstrate that the normal school was succeeding with the goal of encouraging students to think for themselves. Nouet disagreed and denounced her to the rector for telling students about her consultation of parents, alleging also that some students might fear that classmates would ridicule their religious practices. He was further outraged when the prefect informed him that director Gasquet found his judgments of Eidenschenk too severe. A year later Eidenschenk's peers elected her to the prestigious Conseil Supérieur de l'Instruction Publique (CSIP). Inspector Nouet retired in October 1904.[34] Laurent Eidenschenk, in the meantime, was president of the local branch of the League of the Rights of Man and ran unsuccessfully on a republican and socialist list for the city council in 1904, his activism placing him in the company of other staunchly republican educators in the Côtes-du-Nord.[35] From Saint-Brieuc Mme Eidenschenk advanced in 1905 to Douai (Nord), a normal school with more than two hundred students.

Official statistics record the evidence of the church-state competition over girls' schooling that normal school directrices in Brittany and the Vendée regularly encountered and reported. For the school year 1901–02, two decades after the Ferry laws and fifteen years after the Goblet law, nuns' presence among women teachers in France's public primary schools had fallen to 9.7 percent, but in the seven Breton departments still ranged from 19 percent in Finistère to fully 57 percent in Mayenne; in the Vendée, 26 percent. The full story of Breton support for girls' Catholic education is told by adding the number of nuns teaching in the many private congregational schools (*écoles libres congréganistes*). In every Breton department and Vendée, religious teachers outnumbered lay women, ranging from 53 percent of women teachers in Finistère to 75 percent in Ille-et-Vilaine, the administrative center of the academy of Rennes. Nuns' representation in other Breton departments was 56 percent for Côtes-du-Nord; 62 percent, Morbihan; 62.5 percent, Loire-Inférieure; 72 percent, Mayenne; 73 percent, Maine-et-Loire; and in Vendèe, 61 percent. In all of France, nearly 44 percent of women teachers in primary schools, public and private, were nuns, a demonstration of the weight of a centuries-old tradition.[36]

The statistics on girls' enrollment in Breton schools complement those on religious women's preponderance as teachers. Thirteen percent of girls in French public primary schools in 1901 were still taught by nuns; combining enrollments in public and private schools put the national figure at 39 percent, an 11 percent drop since the Ferry laws but still a significant minority.

In Brittany and Vendée the percentage of girls taught by nuns in all types of primary schools ranged from 53 percent in Finistère to 78 percent in Ille-et-Vilaine. The comparable range in 1881 had been 61 percent for Finistère to 91 percent for Mayenne. In each of the eight departments in question, more girls in public schools in 1901 had lay teachers than in 1881, but enrollments in private schools had increased noticeably because the drive to laicize girls' public schools, furthered by normal school training for lay women, was countered by the opening of more private Catholic schools. In the Côtes-du-Nord, Finistère, Mayenne, and Morbihan, girls' enrollments in private congregational schools more than doubled between 1881 and 1901, and they also rose in the other four departments.[37] For all of France, the increase since 1881 of girls attending private congregational schools was less dramatic, at about 50 percent. In nonreligious private schools, enrollment had plummeted when public primary schools became free.[38]

Did the competition in the west between public schools and private Catholic schools make a difference in pupils' acquisition of the basic knowledge that primary schools should transmit? If parents wanted their children to obtain the certificate of primary studies (*certificat d'études primaires, c.e.p.*), a requirement for many public sector or office jobs but not for manual labor, then Catholic schools had an incentive to prepare students for the *c.e.p.* examination administered by public officials. In 1907, girls received 46 percent of primary certificates awarded in France, but all Breton departments and Vendée fell below the national average, five of them ranking among the bottom eight departments, with rates from 35 to 40 percent. The low numbers could signify less academic accomplishment or simply disinterest in a *c.e.p.*, or a combination of the two factors.[39]

The ability to sign a marriage register was a far less rigorous measurement of learning, but the increase in women's signing over the span of two decades indicated that schools, public and private, had furthered the acquisition of basic literacy in the Catholic West, even if not always to the same extent as in other regions. By 1905, 95.6 percent of French brides could sign the marriage register, an increase of more than 17 percent since 1884. In Breton departments and the Vendée, where women's signing in 1884 had ranged from 34 percent to nearly 87 percent, there was also marked improvement, with a new range of 71.7 to 98.7 percent. Four Breton departments, in fact, stood above the national average for women, but the Vendée and traditionally Breton-speaking departments—Morbihan, Finistère, Côtes-du-Nord—fell below it. The Morbihan ranked last at 71.7 percent, and Finistère was the

132   WOMEN AND THE POLITICS OF EDUCATION IN FRANCE

third lowest, 78.4 percent.[40] Despite lags, Brittany and the Vendée thus recorded important gains in girls' education as improvements in public schools since the Ferry laws spurred improvement in competing Catholic schools.

After 1901 a new push to secularize girls' education was furthered by more rigorous enforcement of the Goblet law of 1886 and by the Associations law of July 1, 1901, which removed the right of many congregations to teach. As a result, the next official statistics, compiled for 1906–07, indicated that most teachers in girls' public primary schools in Brittany were laywomen (90.4 percent), as they were in all of France (98.6 percent). No nuns remained in Vendée public schools. Of the 798 nuns still in France's public schools, just over half (431) were in Brittany.[41]

For private schools the 1906–07 statistics on teachers' identity were misleading and masked an important reality. The law of July 7, 1904, banned congregations from teaching in private schools, its sponsors hoping that in ten years private schools would have only lay personnel. Not anticipated, evidently, was the response of many nuns, who abandoned religious garb for civilian clothing but often remained what they truly were, religious teachers. For all of France the percentage of congregational teachers in girls' private schools dropped from 87 percent in 1901–02 to 16 percent in 1906–07. In Breton departments, nuns had been 94 to 98 percent of private school teachers, but in 1906–07, 14 to 51 percent. For the remainder of the Third Republic it became nearly impossible to gauge the presence of male and female religious in private schools from official statistics, and after World War I efforts to enforce the 1904 law declined greatly. What statistics did continue to record was the balance between public and private schools, as well as numbers of teachers. In three Breton departments in 1906—Ille-et-Vilaine, Loire-Inférieure, Maine-et-Loire—women teachers in private schools outnumbered public school counterparts and would continue to do so. Behind departmental trends were local social, political, and religious factors that perpetuated the public school-private school rivalry up to World War II and beyond it.[42]

The data on lay women teachers and girls' enrollments testify not only to resistance to secularizing girls' education in Brittany and Vendée but also to limits on the impact of normal schools and their directrices. Official evaluations of directrices typically included many positive comments, along with criticisms varying in severity, and also assessments of the reputation of directrices and normal schools in local communities. Yet a fine reputation in a department's administrative center, with populations ranging in 1901 from

DIRECTING NORMAL SCHOOLS IN *PETITES PATRIES* 133

133,000 in Nantes down to 19,400 in Quimper (Finistère) or 13,600 in La Roche-sur-Yon (Vendée), did not tell the full story about a normal school's standing elsewhere in a department and particularly in rural areas where lay women teachers and some male colleagues, whether normal school graduates or not, often experienced greater difficulty.

Directrice Peltier in Laval, for example, was well regarded in the town of 30,400, as noted above, but because of substantial resistance to lay women teachers in the Mayenne department, 72 percent of girls in public schools in 1901 still had congregational teachers and recruiting qualified normal school students remained difficult. Former Laval students reported hearing from older graduates about hostilities they faced, such as refusals to sell food to teachers.[43] The normal school in Rennes, a city of 75,000 in a department of 614,000, had no recruiting problems, but half of the girls in public schools in the Ille-et-Vilaine department had congregational teachers before the big push for laicization after 1901. In Nantes, directrice Escande was praised in 1911 for securing the cooperation of the "reactionary" general council of the Loire-Inférieure, where Catholics supported many private schools.[44]

The limits to building local support notwithstanding, the directrices and professors in normal schools trained more than 2,600 women teachers for Brittany and Vendée between 1883 and 1907. The attractiveness of a teaching career for women typically drew larger numbers of applicants, even as men's interest diminished. By 1912 in Finistère and Côtes-du-Nord the number of young women seeking admission was four or five times greater than could be accommodated.[45] Normal school graduates were also increasingly well-credentialed when they completed their studies, as success on the examination for the *brevet supérieur* indicated. Between 1903 and 1907 three Breton schools—Nantes, Angers, Saint-Brieuc—and La Roche-sur-Yon (Vendée) recorded passing rates greater than the national average of 92 percent for new graduates. Only for Quimper (Finistère) was it below 80 percent.[46] Teachers who had not attended normal schools and might hold only the *brevet élémentaire* could be tenured, but the advanced *brevet* was advantageous for gaining preferred postings and promotions.

Normal school graduates in Brittany and the Vendée, as in other departments, joined alumnae associations to maintain friendships and share teaching experiences. In the Ozoufs' survey of pre-1914 teachers, some respondents from the region indicated positive memories of a normal school or gratitude to specific directrices, including Eidenschenk, Maria Bouige, and Élise Labergère.[47] Like retired teachers elsewhere, some also reported

134   WOMEN AND THE POLITICS OF EDUCATION IN FRANCE

abandoning religious practice while at the normal school or after leaving it, sometimes stating that the clergy's hostility figured in their decision, particularly if public school teachers were denied sacraments.[48] Accounts of local hostility certainly concerned more than one part of France but were common in reports from Brittany, where some citizens hurled verbal insults, and sometimes objects, at a teacher or a school.[49] Mayors and their wives might also cause problems. Sent to open a new public school in 1902, a woman who was the only Protestant student at the Rennes normal school in the early 1890s encountered a mayor who told her that she would not succeed because the town of Paramé was French and Catholic. A teacher who replaced a nun in 1912 at one of the last schools laicized in the Maine-et-Loire heard the mayor denounce the "school without God." To attract students, this *libre-penseuse* (freethinker) decided to attend church and sit with her students. Her motivation was not unique, but some women indicated that they soon stopped attending church because listening to condemnations of public schools was painful.[50]

Not all Breton teachers recalled hostile encounters. A graduate of the Angers normal school in 1907 indicated that when she laicized a school in a small town, she was greeted as a phenomenon by a population accustomed to nuns, but she had no problems because she was in an area that leaned left politically. When a new private school opened, her school retained more than half of its students, even though big landowners pressured tenants to send their children to the private school, a common occurrence in parts of Brittany. An earlier graduate attributed a lack of incidents to having a post in Angers, and a 1911 graduate stated that by the time she began teaching the Maine-et-Loire was relatively calm. Still another woman, who left the Saint-Brieuc normal school in 1911, thought that she had simply been lucky to obtain posts in tranquil areas.[51]

The intense church-state competition over schooling, further fueled by the separation of church and state in 1905, prompted directrice Eidenschenk to publish a combative article "La Bretagne religieuse" in the *Annuaire de l'enseignement primaire* in 1906, a year after she left Saint-Brieuc for Douai. Her unflattering picture of the region was not unique; it resembled what many other officials said to explain the area's mounting resistance to the government's educational and religious policies. Brittany might be changing gradually because of republican newspapers, public schools, and also tourism, Eidenschenk wrote, but in popular religious traditions she found much that she deemed pre-Christian and superstitious. Identifying infanticide and drunkenness as some of the vices exhibited to excess in the region, she blamed the Catholic church for promoting inertia, lazy bodies and minds, and a lack of self-discipline. Like inspector Carré and many other commentators on Brittany, she cited clerical opposition to expanding the use of the French language. Her critique even included the judgment that Breton people were "morally inferior to French people as a whole."[52]

Yet Eidenschenk hoped for changes through the further implantation of the *école laïque*, which would "liberate this backward people from the dreams of another age" as children acquired "good habits of thought" and "self-control." In a more conciliatory tone, she concluded that the republican school could prosper not by warring against religion but by demonstrating its superiority to the opposing school, thereby laying a foundation to enable Brittany eventually to enter intellectually and morally into the "great French family."[53] Eidenschenk's voice carried weight when her article appeared in a widely consulted publication because she was now a representative of primary education on the CSIP.

Privately, if not publicly, other directrices and inspectors in Brittany and the Vendée echoed some of Eidenschenk's sentiments. Maria Bouige, her successor in Saint-Brieuc, complained about the difficult "character of Breton populations" and students needing discipline. Émilie Olanier, who followed Bouige, described some students as "rebels against habits of order and cleanliness." At the normal school in Quimper, Suzanne Pingaud struggled to gain the confidence of young Bretonnes who had, judged departmental inspector Bernard, the somewhat "savage" disposition "of their race."[54] Outside the normal school, of course, hostility to its *laïcite* remained. Directrice Jeanne Palanque, appointed to the Vendée in 1912, observed that nuns walking by the normal school "made the sign of the cross to exorcise the evil spirit."[55] The competition between public and Catholic schools would continue to engage the energies of directrices in the region in ensuing decades.

French Normal Schools in Algeria

If directrices like Eidenschenk experienced Brittany as a backward place unlike the rest of France, it is not surprising that some of the eighteen directrices assigned to the "petite patrie" of Algeria before 1914 had similar reactions. Jeanne Palanque, who arrived in Oran in 1907, later wrote, "it is still France and yet it is in Africa."[56] In Algeria, of course, directrices, like other French educators, represented the colonizer rather than the colonized. Their work thus constituted an aspect of French women's role in reinforcing western control in a colonial setting, a perspective emphasized in recent works on women's place in European colonial histories.[57] Although European women in Algeria were less likely to be employed than French counterparts, they engaged in a variety of activities, including teaching and nursing, as did French women in Indochina.[58]

The term *mission civilisatrice*, used repeatedly in French leaders' discussions of goals for the colonies, conveyed the assumption that indigenous cultures were lesser than that of the colonizer. The primary school in Algeria, declared the governor general in 1910, is "the foundation of our domination."[59] The French designated the Muslim majority in Algeria as "les indigènes" and long used the term "les algériens" to refer to Europeans born there or long-term residents. Because of the heterogeneity of the population in Algeria, the "civilizing mission" since the initial conquest in 1830 in fact encompassed other Europeans as well as indigènes. Algeria Jews acquired French citizenship in October 1870, a measure long resented by many European settlers, politicians among them, and an 1889 law facilitated the acquisition of French nationality for people born in Algeria to parents from Spain, Italy, and other European countries.[60] When the rector of Alger, Ernest de Salve, wrote to the education ministry about opening a women's normal school in 1875, he requested an experienced directrice who could offer future teachers "solid principles of education and conduct," which he termed "too rare in Algeria."[61]

Five normal schools functioned in Algeria by 1914. The two for men dated from 1865 in Algiers and 1878 in Constantine. The first one for women opened in 1875 in Miliana, a garrison town about 70 miles southwest of Algiers. In Oran the women's normal school opened in 1883 and that in Constantine in 1908. From the outset the men's schools enrolled a few indigènes, albeit soon in a separate section, and initially there was the same expectation for Miliana. Although the rector realized that customs and religion would keep many young Muslim women away from the school, he wanted to plan for their admission. Article 9 of the ministerial decree of 1875 detailing the organization of the school thus called for special provisions for "les élèves indigènes, israélites et musulmanes" with regard to diet and religious practice.[62] Yet according to various sources, no Muslim girls enrolled in an Algerian normal school before World War I, although very small numbers of Muslim women educated elsewhere did teach in public schools.[63]

A separate *cours normal* for young Muslim women, established in 1893, was short-lived.

What did an assignment in Algeria represent in the professional and personal lives of normal school directrices? They implemented the same curriculum as in France, but only in Algeria was Arabic the foreign language offered, and teachers from France who were certified in Arabic received a pay supplement. Personnel files provide indications of directrices' reactions to being sent to Algeria, the extent to which they faced political conflicts akin to those in France, and their perceptions of their role in a colonial society. The first directrice, Henriette Huet, opined that in a "young colony" with a population "of diverse and unequally cultivated races," it was even more necessary than in France to have well qualified women teaching girls and very young children. Indeed, education officials often stated that women teachers were France's best hope for reaching indigenous women, sheltered by custom and male relatives from contact with French men.[64] The *institutrice*, commented one governor general, was "a *missionnaire laïque* of French influence."[65] Yet the majority of women teachers in Algeria taught only European pupils, and throughout the colonial period the number of indigène girls attending schools was always less than that of indigène boys.

Sixteen of the eighteen normal school directrices in Algeria between 1875 and 1914 were born in France. When first appointed in Algeria, 11 were single, 3 widowed, and 4 married. Their ages ranged from 27 to 57, with an average age of 37. For two-thirds of them, Algeria meant their first promotion to direct a normal school. Their professional profiles mirrored the changes expected in the qualifications of normal school personnel once training became available at Fontenay-aux-Roses. For the Miliana school, opened four years before the Bert law, the education ministry initially selected women with teaching *brevets*. The first three directrices would not have met the criteria for appointment by the mid-1880s. Eleven directrices were Fontenay graduates, including most of those appointed to Oran, but not the two born in Algeria.[66]

The ministry of public instruction often found it difficult to persuade women to accept Algerian posts, typically viewed as assignments for beginners who were not offered any other posts. Directrices from France stayed, on average, only four years, although two did go on to posts in Tunisia. The two Algerian-born directrices had by far the longest tenure, each with more than twenty years. Because of the equally rapid turnover among normal school professors in Algeria, directrices were repeatedly

138 WOMEN AND THE POLITICS OF EDUCATION IN FRANCE

helping beginners gain experience.[67] Complaints about the climate and separation from families were common reasons for asking to leave. Occasionally an inspector also commented that a particular French woman did not like "les algériens," by which he meant European Algerians.[68]

The normal school students, as compared to the directrices and professors, were far more often born in Algeria or longterm residents.[69] Indeed, inspector general Félix Hémon lamented after visiting Algerian normal schools in 1905 that teaching French to students from families who spoke the *colons'* "mixed" language, a combination of French with the language of their origins, could be more difficult than teaching it to those who knew only a foreign language.[70] As in France, each normal school also had an *école annexe* where students gained practice in teaching, and in Oran the many Spanish children attending the *école annexe* often spoke French poorly and were, judged the departmental inspector, "rebelles à toute civilisation."[71]

The Miliana normal school's first decade was marked by various difficulties and controversies, sometimes related to the inadequacy of directrices or instructors, or to students' poor performance on examinations for *brevets*. The first directrice, Henriette Huet, appointed in 1875, was a fifty-seven-year-old widow familiar with public schools because of experience inspecting Algeria's *salles d'asile* (nursery schools) since 1860, but she soon angered local authorities by neglecting duties. Her replacement in January 1877 was Jenny Maillier, an army officer's widow from France who had a *brevet supérieur* but no experience in public education. Unable to assert authority effectively, particularly with two instructors who had hoped to succeed Huet, she was dismissed in November 1878. By then the school's enrollment, drawn from the three Algerian departments, had reached the initial target of twenty-four students, most of them Catholics but also three Protestants and one Israélite. Only in the *école annexe* was there a young Muslim girl trying to prepare for the normal school entry examination.[72]

The third Miliana directrice, Amélie Sage, age forty-one, fared better, although the rector had doubted that her experience teaching in her aunt's boarding school in Alger suited a normal school with students from modest backgrounds. Despite lacking public school teaching experience, she did understand economic necessity, her mother as a widow having taught in the Dordogne for fifteen years. Amélie and her sister, also a teacher, came to Algeria during the 1860s. In Miliana Sage improved discipline and enhanced the school's reputation, but she found deficiencies in students which she attributed to Algeria's "population flottante" (floating population). Families' frequent moves in search of better economic opportunities disrupted children's education, and that education was in primary schools with pupils who were not only French but also Italian, Spanish, Maltese, and "even indigène." Thus one of the normal school's important roles, she stated, was to counter threats to "our beautiful language" that different dialects and languages posed for pronunciation, spelling, and syntax. Although Sage's work with students was often commended, her financial oversight eventually proved deficient, and her advocacy of moving the school to Alger infuriated local officials.[73] In April 1884 she was reassigned to Saint-Étienne (Loire), but her leadership in Miliana continued to be discussed when Marie Matrat, an inspectress general of *écoles maternelles*, became the interim directrice, designated while already in Algeria on an inspection tour.

New and much publicized controversies erupted during Matrat's brief tenure, marked by her introduction of a more secular tone in the school. Because republicans often predominated on Algerian town councils, their conflicts with Catholics were less common than in some parts of France when public schools were laicized, but they did occur. Matrat complained about the many religious texts in the school library, the tradition of prayers and pilgrimages, and evident pressure on students to attend religious services. The six women teaching at the school were divided into a Catholic camp and a less religious camp (which included one Protestant), and many students and parents took sides. Thirty-two students signed a letter asking Matrat to excuse them from attending mass, and when she asked if they were certain of their parents' approval and not acting simply because of antipathy to certain professors, 31 reaffirmed their statement, thanking Matrat for ending the pressure to attend church and for better preparing them for examinations. The republican newspaper *Le petit colon algérien* published a letter from seven students who called themselves "[v]ictims of clerical intrigue" previously, and it praised Matrat's "anticlerical energy" directed against "Jésuitisme." Not all journals were as sympathetic.[74]

The press also took note when the directrice of the *école maternelle annexe*, Carmen Aucher, slapped the chief departmental inspector, Georges Lamy, at the normal school after he refused to make instructor Marie Secrétant sign a statement detailing her inappropriate remarks about Aucher. Secrétant had discussed salacious rumors concerning Aucher's private life while she and Matrat were riding in a coach to Miliana, and other passengers, some of them indigènes, could hear the conversation. Inspector Lamy subsequently told others in Miliana about Aucher's slap, presenting himself as the victim

140 WOMEN AND THE POLITICS OF EDUCATION IN FRANCE

of Matrat and Aucher, and the mayor of Miliana sent an account to *La Vigée algérienne*. In a context where public employees were expected to provide models of correct behavior, such public indiscretion was unacceptable, as was the publicity about problems inside the normal school. The ministry in Paris promptly replaced all the normal school personnel, the departmental inspector, and rector Gustave Boissière.[75]

Denise Guillot, appointed in August 1884 as Miliana's sixth directrice in nine years, replaced a second interim directrice, Ernestine Béridot, and had to face what the new rector, Charles Jeanmaire, termed "the most difficult conditions." She soon won praise for improving students' attitudes, repairing the school's reputation, and remedying many students' poor educational preparation. For Guillot, Algeria represented a welcome promotion. Then twenty-nine years old, this daughter of an *instituteur* in the Saône-et-Loire was an *institutrice* before becoming a *maîtresse* at the normal school in Mâcon, which she had attended. Certified as a professor in 1883, she then went to Fontenay for the course preparing directrices. North Africa suited her, and she remained in Miliana for seven years before going to Tunis where, until retirement in 1910, she directed the girls' secondary school which also served as a kind of normal school until 1912. For her accomplishments Guillot was among the first five directrices inducted into the Legion of Honor.[76] The next directrice, Marie Lafforgue, profited from Guillot's stabilization of the school and encountered few major difficulties, receiving largely positive evaluations until serious neurological problems lessened her ability to function and led to early retirement in 1899.[77]

The Oran normal school, like Miliana, also experienced a rapid turnover with the first directrices. Ernestine Béridot, trained at Fontenay, opened the school successfully in 1883 and gained departmental inspector Raphael Périé's praise for transforming students, said to need that in every respect. Pressed into temporary service in Miliana in June 1884, she was next assigned to open the normal school in Toulouse. Her replacement, professor Aurélie Lacroix, also a Fontenaysienne, was delegated temporarily because she lacked certification for directing, and she preferred a post in France once certified in 1885. Under its third directrice the Oran school also faced a controversy with political and religious dimensions, but with some dynamics different from those in Miliana in 1884. Hermance Guttron, a fifty-seven-year-old widow from the Yonne who held only teaching *brevets*, drew complaints in 1887 from some republicans and journalists disturbed by her Catholic religious practice. Rector Jeanmaire then intervened, indicating that she scrupulously

DIRECTING NORMAL SCHOOLS IN *PETITES PATRIES*   141

maintained religious neutrality in the school and that church attendance was not an official concern if she did not proselytize. In fact, the mothers of Protestant and Jewish students came to her defense when a hostile journalist demanded an investigation. Reacting to attacks by anticlerical republicans, the academic administration supported Guttron so as not to seem to yield to local political pressures.[78]

After Guttron retired in 1890 the next three Oran directrices, all Fontenaysiennes, also served briefly, albeit for different reasons. Marie Larivière provoked discord among instructors, which students noticed, and the rector could not resolve the difficulties. Albertine Patin, appointed in 1892 to her first directing post after five years as a *répétitrice* at Fontenay, had the challenge of restoring harmony and bringing the school up to the academic level achieved at Miliana under Guillot's leadership. Departmental inspector Laurent Eidenschenk judged her successful in both regards, and, as already noted, their marriage in 1894 necessitated her taking a leave because he was her immediate superior.[79] Marie-Thérèse Champomier, the next directrice, reluctantly accepted Oran as her first directing post and soon complained about its debilitating hot climate. Credited with helping students make noticeable progress in their command of French, she was happy to leave in February 1898 when rector Jeanmaire wanted the post to go to Louise Sahuc.[80]

No references to the antisemitic riots in Oran, Algiers, and other Algerian cities during the Dreyfus Affair figure in personnel files for directrices and professors in the normal schools, but for the girls' secondary school in Oran Jeanmaire came to the defense of its directrice, Cécile Fuchs, and two professors, They and the school were subjected to what he termed "the absurd war" waged by "antijuifs," members of the municipal council among them.[81]

For Louise Sarradet Sahuc, the first Algerian-born directrice, the Oran appointment was a reward for previously taking on a difficult assignment. Born in 1866, the daughter of a wheelwright in Béni-Mered near Blida, she had studied at the Miliana normal school and impressed directrice Guillot, who encouraged her ambitions. Guillot secured her appointment as a *maîtresse* at the school in 1886 and helped her prepare for professorial certification, obtained in 1888. Two years later she married the son of a prosperous landowner, the marriage presumably easing the financial burden of aiding her siblings. She then spent a year in France as a professor at the normal school in Foix (Ariège), directed by Lacroix, and prepared for the examination for directrices in 1891. She was resolutely *laïque*, having appreciated Matrat's

142 WOMEN AND THE POLITICS OF EDUCATION IN FRANCE

efforts in Miliana in 1884 and ably characterizing "l'esprit laïque" in an essay, previously cited, for the 1891 examination. Returning to the Miliana school, she also acquired a *brevet* in Arabic. Her professional credentials and familiarity with Algerian culture and language led Jeanmaire to recommend appointing her in 1895 as the directrice of a *cours normal* for young indigène women in the Kabylia, a mountainous region in the eastern part of the department of Alger.[82]

The *cours normal* in Taddert-ou-Fella, opened in 1893, had a troubled history that is a small part of the complex story of relations between the colonizer and the colonized. Intended to train young Muslim women for roles as *monitrices* in schools for very young indigène children, it functioned until 1897 in a region which the French especially favored for opening schools for indigènes because they believed that its Berber population was more receptive to French schooling than were many Arabs.[83] The training course was added to a primary school for indigène girls created in 1884 and mostly drawing girls from poor families or orphans. Soon regarded as a model school for indigènes, it received favorable publicity in *Le petit colon algérien* and the *Revue pédagogique*.[84] The historian Alfred Rambaud, an aide to Jules Ferry and later himself an education minister, featured the primary school and a photograph of its directrice, Louise Malaval, with students in articles in *L'Illustration* and *La Science illustrée* in 1891, when thirty-three girls were in residence. He praised this widow from the Aveyron for demonstrating what a French woman teacher could accomplish with girls of another race and religion, and he did not find it inappropriate that she assigned French first names to her students. Malaval believed that sewing and housekeeping skills which pupils also acquired at the school enhanced their marriage prospects and could help them earn a living.[85]

Rector Jeanmaire, unlike Rambaud, judged the creation of the Taddert-ou-Fella school "an error," albeit one well-intentioned, because its students, who sometimes earned a certificate of primary studies, risked becoming "déclassées," people without a place in either indigène or French society.[86] Throughout the colonial period the number of indigène girls attending schools was always much less than that of indigène boys, due in part to Muslim resistance to sending girls to school but also to French officials' decision to prioritize schools for Muslim boys. In 1893, only 1,407 Muslim girls attended school, as compared to 15,001 Muslim boys.[87] Many colonists opposed paying to build schools for indigènes, even when the state paid teachers' salaries, and they also feared that education would give indigènes

DIRECTING NORMAL SCHOOLS IN *PETITES PATRIES*   143

ideas likely to make them more difficult to control. Rambaud explained in 1892 why French policy prioritized educating indigène boys. Schools would encourage indigène men to embrace the benefits of French civilization, and then "the condition of the woman that we now seem to forget" could be addressed because indigène men would stop opposing girls' schools and indeed would demand them. Schooling could lead in turn to "all legal and moral emancipations" for indigène women.[88]

Despite Jeanmaire's misgivings, in 1893 Taddert-ou-Fella acquired a *cours normal* for training *monitrices indigènes* who could work under a French teacher's supervision, as male *moniteurs* did. Its creation came in the wake of the important decree of October 18, 1892, reorganizing indigène education, and soon after the men's normal school in Alger-Bouzaréa, already enrolling indigènes, added a division for training French men to teach indigènes. The 1892 curriculum for indigène schools emphasized practical subjects, as well as elementary education, and half of the instruction for girls covered sewing, needlework, and homemaking.[89] The credential already required for *moniteurs* and *monitrices* was the certificate for primary studies, not a *brevet*. In Taddert-ou-Fella the existing primary school, where pupils could board, became the *école annexe* for the *cours normal*. Mme Malaval was promoted to direct the course, and two recent Miliana graduates were appointed to teach. Both left after one year, faulted for poor rapport with students, and Malaval was dismissed in late 1895. A memoir dictated years later by Fadhma Mansour Amrouche, a Kabyle woman who had attended the primary school, recorded a pupil's impression of Malaval's sudden departure and the arrival of Sahuc, whom she found cold and distant, unlike Malaval. She did not know that Malaval's career ended because of an affair with a married administrator.[90]

Jeanmaire closed the school after Malaval's dismissal, but education minister Émile Combes soon ordered him to reopen and reform it. Sahuc's assignment was to rehabilitate its reputation with local leaders, French and indigène. She knew Arabic and would study the Kabyle language. Two years later, however, Rambaud, as minister, closed it, presumably because students often failed examinations for certification and because of a lack of special posts for those who passed.[91] Yet officials previously had celebrated several examples of successful Taddert-ou-Fella students, such as Mlle Fatma, a *monitrice* at an *école enfantine* (for pupils aged four to seven) who attracted attention in 1892 by insisting that, as an employee of the French state, she had the right to defy her father and marry the man she chose, an indigène teacher.[92] Statistics for the first three years of the *cours normal* training for *monitrices* indicate that enrollment ranged from seven to ten students, but only for 1893–94 is there a record of two students earning a certificate of primary studies. At least one of the *cours normal* students eventually had a noteworthy career. Yamina Larab, an orphan born in 1881, became a *monitrice* at an indigène school in 1897 and then, with a *brevet élémentaire* obtained in 1898 and later a certificate of professional aptitude, was appointed to other schools in the department of Alger. Inspector Hémon reported her presence at a public school in Miliana in 1905, citing a comment on her "entirely French" mentality.[93]

Sahuc's dossier records only administrative praise for her work in Taddert-ou-Fella, and although some students there found her unsympathetic, she did understand certain realities about women's lives in Kabylia. In a later statement on the region's unfortunate lack of girls' schools and a tradition of "paternal power" so "absolute" that fathers often set a price for daughters' marriages, she wrote that Kabyle women might not wear veils, but they were not "more independent" than Arab women.[94]

From the Oran normal school Sahuc went on to replace directrice Lafforgue in Miliana, closer to her husband's property in Affreville, and her tenure there from 1899 until retirement in 1925 set a record for longevity among directrices in Algeria. The Miliana normal school's remote location continued to dismay some inspectors general, but, as inspector Hémon opined in 1905, if anyone could save it, Sahuc could. In fact, as the growing European population in Algeria necessitated more teachers, she presided over the school's expansion to seventy-five students, garnering praise for training "excellent" teachers and exerting a good "moral influence" as "l'âme" of the school.[95] At least twenty-five teachers trained by Sahuc gained additional credentials and became professors in normal schools or higher primary schools, most of them staying in Algeria, but one, Jeanne Bergerat, completed her career as directrice of the important normal school in Paris.[96] Sahuc was also a founding member of the Miliana branch of the Ligue de l'Enseignement and part of its local council for twenty years. An Algerian deputy who later recommended her for the Legion of Honor, awarded in 1930, wrote that she had devoted her life to women's education in "an Algerian region denuded of all intellectual resources" and in Miliana was "almost venerated."[97]

While Sahuc's leadership provided continuity in Miliana after 1899, the Oran school had three more directrices, plus a professor directing

Louise Sarradet Sahuc, directrice, école normale d'institutrices de Miliana. *Courtesy of Claude Poitrenaud*

temporarily, before 1914. The warm climate initially appealed to Éva Allégret, a Fontenaysienne from the Isère, who requested Oran, her sixth directing post since 1884. Yet as she guided students and staff, she soon voiced frustration with many students' defective French and deplored first-year students' lack of curiosity and difficulty paying attention. She questioned their ability to master Arabic as well because many normal school graduates could not understand the speech of indigènes or make themselves understood. Thus

146 WOMEN AND THE POLITICS OF EDUCATION IN FRANCE

she recommended limiting normal school instruction in Arabic to conversation and translation and dropping a written component. Unsurprisingly, departmental inspector Grand reported in 1905 that Allégret, often critical of others, seemed to dislike [European] "Algerians" in general and her students in particular.[98]

Allégret was not the only woman educator from France to feel distant from the *colons* as well as from indigènes. A teacher from southern France reported in the Ozoufs' survey that she left a post in Algeria in 1916, after five years, because she could not adapt to the "European mentality" there.[99] Indeed, various opinion brokers in Algeria had for decades identified the European settler population as a "new" Latin race whose culture differentiated them from the French.[100]

The next directrice in Oran, Jeanne Palanque, was, wrote inspector Grand, the opposite of Allégret in personality. Appointed in 1907 after Allégret returned to France to launch the normal school in Nice, Palanque developed excellent relations with personnel, taught well, and was adored by students who previously disliked the school. Born in the Gard in 1868, she had a "meridional exuberance," an inspector in the Vendée later noted. With her husband Pierre, the *secrétaire* in the office of departmental education administration, she participated in the cultural life of Oran and grew accustomed to its differences from France. As Palanque later recalled, when she first went shopping in the French part of the city, separate from the "indigène" and Jewish quarters, she heard only Arabic and Spanish spoken and needed to ask young Arab boys "who spoke all languages" for interpretive help. The Arab, she decided, was characterized by "fatalism" and "laziness" overcome only when required to attend to the most pressing needs of life. She did not consider that such traits, common in Europeans' accounts, might represent a type of resistance on the part of the colonized. Among the French she found social relations "more friendly, less conventional than in the metropole."[101]

While in Oran, Palanque gave public lectures for the *université populaire* and wrote articles for *L'Instituteur républicain* on such topics as moral instruction and experiences serving on examination commissions. In the department's educational bulletin, she offered advice to teachers on goals for lessons in history and geography, emphasizing the importance of combining local and national content. They should develop students' love of this "petite patrie" with its sun and fertile soil but also inculcate love of France by noting that it gave Algeria liberal institutions, facilitated progress in agriculture and commerce, and provided security and schools.[102] At her next

DIRECTING NORMAL SCHOOLS IN *PETITES PATRIES*   147

post in the Vendée, where normal school graduates were often unhappy with assignments in rural schools, she referred to her work in Oran and Saint-Étienne to make the point that dedicated servants of the state should try to find positive features in their surroundings. She did that when she accepted Oran in order to obtain her first directing post, for which she waited six years after being credentialed, and her husband left his post in Saint-Étienne to accompany her. In 1911, when the Palanques asked to leave Oran, she asserted confidently, as she sought rector Édouard Ardaillon's support for a transfer, that she had done much to overcome weaknesses in the normal school identified by inspector Grand: students' academic performance had improved, the school enjoyed a good reputation in the city and department, and former students often returned to the school.[103]

By 1907 the Miliana and Oran normal schools had trained nearly 600 teachers, 45 percent of the 1,332 women teachers in public schools in the three Algerian departments. Completing the same courses as their counterparts in France, these teachers had also heard similar presentations of gender norms as they learned about expectations for women teachers.[104] Because laicization of schools was fairly rapid in Algeria, normal school graduates were in demand. The number of congregational teachers in girls' public schools declined from 14 percent in 1891 to 5 percent in 1901, and none remained in 1907.[105] Normal school students' ability to pass the *brevet supérieur* examination continued to lag, however, in comparison with counterparts in France. For the years 1903–07, when 92 percent of women normal school students in France obtained the advanced *brevet*, the passage rate for Miliana students was 78 percent and for Oran, 72 percent, figures comparable to the underperforming Breton departments of Finistère and Ille-et-Vilaine, then at 77 percent. In Algeria, as in Brittany, administrators long attributed such lags to poor French language skills and so were pleased when Oran students had unprecedented success in 1909, at the end of Palanque's second year, 20 of 22 students obtaining the *brevet supérieur*.[106]

The opening of the women's normal school in Constantine in 1908 responded to the need for more women teachers with better training as Algeria's European population continued to grow. By 1908 the Miliana school accommodated 75 students, the Oran school enrolled 50, and the new Constantine school would have 75 by 1910.[107] Juliette Vallet, the first Constantine directrice, was a Parisian from humble circumstances who had managed while a teacher for ten years to obtain the professorial credential

École normale d'institutrices de Miliana. *Postcard, Author's collection*

leading to a Miliana appointment in 1905. Sahuc recommended her for Constantine after she qualified as a directrice, and in 1908 she opened the normal school with two professors and part-time instructors for Arabic, music, and drawing. Sixty students from the department's higher primary and secondary schools sought admission and, as elsewhere, many were daughters of teachers, other public employees, small shopkeepers, and artisans. Vallet and the school were soon rated as successful. Jeanne Honot, a student from 1908 to 1911, later described her as a "personne de goût" (person with taste), adding that students also appreciated Mme Douvier, a professor whose lessons about Algeria and France's contribution to it were a "revelation."[108] In 1912 Vallet and her husband Ferdinand Pontal, a history professor at the city's lycée whom she married in 1909, decided to accept posts in the protectorate of Tunisia. She would direct the new normal school in Tunis—the only other women's normal school in a colonial setting before 1914, although the much older colony of Martinique had a *cours normal* attached to a girls' boarding school since 1883.[109]

Constantine's second directrice, Félicie Sposito Muraccioli, was Algerian-born, like Sahuc, and trained at Miliana from 1891 to 1894 under directrice Lafforgue. Like Pontal-Vallet, she was an experienced *institutrice*, having taught for eighteen years in primary schools in the department of Alger. At a time when most directrices had Fontenay training, neither Constantine

École normale d'institutrices de Constantine. *Postcard, Author's collection*

directrice had that background, nor did Sahuc. After long lamenting that Fontenay graduates were reluctant to accept Algerian posts or stay for a long time, administrators realized that Algerian-born appointees were more likely to remain until retirement. Two Constantine professors in 1912 were also Miliana graduates. What made Muraccioli's appointment most unusual, however, was her lack of normal school teaching experience. Thus inspector general Lamy judged in 1913 that she was poorly prepared and "dépaysée" (out of her element) in her new role, with the result that relations inside the school were akin to an armed peace, if not war. One of the four professors was a Fontenaysienne whose husband was a lycée professor, whereas Muraccioli's husband was an *instituteur*. Muraccioli soon managed to acquire a reputation for firmly asserting authority in the school, and she gained support from Constantine's longtime republican and antisemitic mayor, Émile Morinaud. But further conflicts with professors and *économes* marked her record until she retired in 1935.[110]

The striking omission in the dossiers of directrices of Algeria's normal schools, with the exception of Sahuc, is attention to the training of teachers for indigène girls. After the closure of the Taddert-ou-Fella *cours normal* in 1897, the next efforts to prepare teachers of indigène girls also were based outside normal schools. Whereas the men's normal school in Alger-Bouzaréa had special sections for training indigène men and men from France to teach

150   WOMEN AND THE POLITICS OF EDUCATION IN FRANCE

indigènes, the next limited effort to prepare women to teach indigène girls was focused on primary schools with indigène pupils. In 1905 special training was added at an indigène girls' school in Oran, directed by Louise Quetteville, and she and the program were transferred to Alger in 1909. Typically that program enrolled more Europeans than indigènes, admitting normal school graduates after their studies or soon after they started teaching.[111]

The special training was adapted to the curriculum of 1892 for indigène children, a separate track from that for European schools and lasting until 1948. For indigène girls, the curriculum emphasized traditional crafts and skills, and it drew on successful precedents, most notably that of Mme Luce's school in Algiers, opened in 1845. Such training, although less academic than schooling for European children, nonetheless gave indigène girls more familiarity with French language and customs and was a lure for their parents because skill in crafts provided a way to earn money.[112] Apart from the separate schools for indigènes, some European schools had special classes for indigènes, and some indigène pupils sat in classrooms with Europeans. By 1914, when most European children in Algeria attended school, only 5 percent of indigène children did so, and of the 47,193 indigène pupils, only 8.5 percent (3,989) were girls, nearly half of them in European schools taught by women who were often normal school graduates.[113]

In observations about schooling in the "petites patries" of Brittany and Algeria, French officials often commented on how they differed from much of France, and normal school directrices echoed such opinions. Brittany was the region that posed the greatest resistance to the laicizing project of the Third Republic, and the persistence of Breton dialects as the language used in many households before and after World War I added another complication.[114] In Algeria resistance to laicization was minimal, but enabling students from various cultural backgrounds to achieve mastery of French was often problematic in primary schools and sometimes even in normal schools. Commenting on the results of the examination for admission to the Miliana school in 1916, directrice Sahuc stated that the "most feeble" results were those for the French language; and professor Jéromine Cacciaguerra, born in Corsica and trained in Miliana, added that "in a country where our language is threatened by so many foreign influences, we must make more efforts to preserve it intact."[115]

Directrices and professors in Brittany recognized that religion and politics were the big sources of division with which they and their students needed to contend. In Algeria, recalled a woman teacher trained in Miliana from

DIRECTING NORMAL SCHOOLS IN *PETITES PATRIES* 151

1911 to 1914, ethnic divisions loomed large, and along with the close proximity of races, languages, religions, and different customs there were also hatreds.[116] Similarly, an earlier commentator, who was not unbiased, wrote that the French in Algeria were "a kind of aristocracy, which looks down on Spaniards, who scorn Italians, who in turn scorn the Maltese and Jews," adding that Arabs were "disdained and disdainful."[117] Just as normal schools and their directrices in France could not eliminate the dislike of the Republic and secular public education that persisted with segments of the population in regions like Brittany, so the normal schools and directrices in Algeria could not eliminate prejudices they should not condone as they tried to further a "mission civilisatrice."[118]

5

Approaches to Feminism

In March 1914 the feminist newspaper *La Française* informed readers that twenty-five directrices of normal schools and a number of professors had joined the Union Française pour le Suffrage des Femmes (UFSF), the largest French women's suffrage organization.[1] Founded in 1909, it claimed a membership of 12,000 by 1914 and 15,000 by 1915, far more than that of any older French suffrage group but much less than memberships in major women's suffrage groups in Great Britain or the United States.[2] Middle-class women and professional women were prominent in feminist ranks in most Western countries, and it is no surprise that normal school directrices and professors were among the women educators supporting various French campaigns for women's rights.[3] What led some normal school directrices to support women's suffrage, and how did the development of such support intersect with the history of French feminism, education, and politics after 1900?

Although the history of French feminist organizing to advocate equal rights for women dated from the efforts of Saint-Simonian women during the 1830s and then the founding of new associations in the late 1860s and 1870s, feminist activity intensified after 1900 and increasingly attracted attention.[4] Indeed, the term "feminism" (*féminisme*) had French origins.[5] But, as in other Western countries, not all French feminists espoused all of the same aims, and not all advocates of gender equality chose to call themselves feminists. Hubertine Auclert, who termed herself a feminist and championed women's suffrage in her newspaper *La Citoyenne* during the 1880s, could never gain a large following.[6] In 1889 and 1900 the international congresses on women's charities (*oeuvres*) and institutions drew more French women than the congresses specifically devoted to "women's rights" in the same years. Nonetheless, advocacy of equality for women in access to education and employment did figure prominently in the congresses featuring women's institutions.[7] The feminist newspaper *La Fronde*, published daily from December 1897 until August 1903 by an all-women staff, also embraced a wide range of women's issues but could not maintain its initial circulation of 50,000 for very long, and its average daily circulation of 12,000 did not cover

---

Women and the Politics of Education in Third Republic France. Linda L. Clark, Oxford University Press.
© Oxford University Press 2023. DOI: 10.1093/oso/9780197632864.003.0006

expenses.[8] Another important development was the founding in 1901 of the Conseil National des Femmes Françaises (CNFF, National Council of French Women), affiliated with the International Council of Women. In 1906 the CNFF added a section advocating women's suffrage, a sign that Auclert's demand finally seemed less radical.

The professional evaluations in the personnel files of normal school directrices often reported their involvement in organizations (*patronages*) that supported local primary schools through after-school programs or activities for recent graduates and working women, but they rarely mentioned feminist affiliations. Presumably such membership was considered a private matter, just as a religious affiliation was judged to be private, so long as there was no proselytizing in a normal school. On occasion, however, some inspectors complained when directrices addressed issues of gender equality, as in 1890 when Marie Winter in Charleville was criticized for talking too much about women's right to "émancipation" and "indépendance," or later, in 1908, when Emma Frugier, directrice in Angoulême, was faulted for spending too much time encouraging students to demand "independence and all of their rights" (*droits*). Yet in May 1914 when an inspector general mentioned being told that normal school professor Juliette Thimer, also in Angoulême, was a "féministe," he asked with seeming amusement, "is that a crime" (*est-ce un crime*)?[9]

For evidence of advocacy for women's rights among women educators— including normal school directrices and professors—pedagogical journals, normal school alumnae bulletins, and feminist publications are better sources than the ministry of public instruction's official records. In particular, these publications record the development of a campaign for equal pay for women primary schoolteachers and also for women staffing higher primary schools and normal schools. Encountering resistance to their demand for equal pay could readily lead women educators to see a link between the perpetuation of pay inequities and their lack of voting rights.

Women Educators and Feminist Allies: Parallel and Intersecting Campaigns

Normal school directrices' concerns with issues of gender equality had first been aroused by discussions of women's role on departmental primary education councils and debates about whether women should inspect primary

154 WOMEN AND THE POLITICS OF EDUCATION IN FRANCE

schools. Then came the major question of equal pay. Republican politicians repeatedly stressed the importance of educating France's future wives and mothers, as did Pécaut and other professors at Fontenay-aux-Roses when they sought to instill professional pride in the future normal school directrices and professors who would train the Republic's women teachers. Unsurprisingly, some women educators would ask why, if their role was so crucial, they did not receive the same pay as male colleagues. At the time of the Ferry reforms, Paul Bert had advocated equal pay for women teachers, but legislative opponents prevailed, insisting on limiting budgetary outlays. Pay inequity was among the issues highlighted by inspectress general Pauline Kergomard during and after her service on the Conseil Supérieur de l'Instruction Publique (CSIP), and normal school directrice Albertine Eidenschenk also made it prominent when she ran for the CSIP in 1903 and 1904, vowing to be the advocate for the more than 50,000 women in primary education.[10]

After 1900, primary schoolteachers themselves, not higher-ranking women educators, took much of the leadership in efforts to mobilize both women and men colleagues in support of equal pay. When the teachers' association (*amicale*) in the Seine-et-Oise asked other *amicales* and normal school alumni associations to support a petition in 1902 for pay increases and equal pay for men and women, Eidenschenk, then directrice in Chambéry (Savoie), persuaded her school's alumnae association to add to its endorsement a demand for equal pay for women normal school personnel.[11] In 1903, as teachers' *amicales*, led largely by men, pushed aggressively for higher pay, Marie Guérin, a primary schoolteacher (*institutrice*) in the Meurthe-et-Moselle, founded a local study group for women teachers, urging them not to remain indifferent to feminist groups seeking women's "emancipation."[12] Her dismay that the April 1905 law raising salaries did not establish equal pay for all ranks prompted her to discuss the issue with like-minded women teachers at the national congress of *amicales* in Lille in August, also attended by Marguerite Bodin, a teacher on the Yonne department's education council and soon an important ally. The congress's resolutions on coeducation, favored for primary schools and even normal schools, also included the assertion that men and women teachers should have equal pay because they had the same duties.[13]

For the next *amicales*' congress in Clermont-Ferrand in 1907, Guérin and Bodin arranged a special meeting for women teachers and encouraged the formation of feminist teachers' groups in other departments. Henri Murgier, an *amicale* leader in the Seine-et-Oise and member of the CSIP, attended their meeting and urged women to take a stand on equal pay when they voted in December for representatives on their department's education council. He recommended that on the first ballot they write in "equal pay" ("égalité des traitements des instituteurs et des institutrices") rather than vote for candidates, whom they could choose on a second ballot. Although teachers in many departments evidently did not learn of this recommendation, were confused by it, or chose to ignore it, feminist teachers celebrated making their voices heard in some departments and thereby drawing the attention of the department's prefect, who had to report election results to the education ministry in Paris. In the Basses-Pyrénées, 308 out of 504 women teachers voted for "equal pay," but with the result that only a minority of votes on the first ballot were then counted to select two women to the council. In fact, there were actually 408 votes for equal pay because one winner, a feminist whose own vote was for equal pay, won a seat because a hundred voters had written her name next to the equal pay wording. In four other departments in southern France, a majority of women teachers also voted for equal pay, and six more recorded significant support.[14]

By 1908 Guérin's group, based in Laxou-lès-Nancy since 1906, had two hundred members, and she and her younger brother Paul, also a teacher, pressed ahead with organizational efforts, working with allies in other departments to found the Fédération Féministe Universitaire (FFU), an umbrella organization for departmental feminist groups (*groupes féministes universitaires*, GFU).[15] The FFU statutes, formally approved at a meeting of about one hundred women teachers in Nancy in August 1909 on the day before the opening of the *amicales'* national congress, announced the big goal of working "to improve the condition of women in general and women in primary teaching in particular."[16] By then the FFU had also launched a journal, boldly titled *L'Action féministe*. Accused by some colleagues, male and female, of "separatism" that sowed division and selfishly ignored interests shared by men and women, FFU leaders pointed to the requirement that GFU members belong to their department's *amicale*, but they also insisted that issues of equality for women teachers required special attention. At the Nancy congress, the FFU won support for equal pay from a majority of the delegates, as is further recounted below.[17] By 1909 the relationship of men and women teachers had gradually evolved "from conflict to cooperation" as many male teachers realized that equal pay was less a threat to their own status and more a matter of collective self-interest.[18] Nonetheless, *L'Action féministe* would report that

156 WOMEN AND THE POLITICS OF EDUCATION IN FRANCE

some male teachers pressured their political representatives to oppose equal pay. The FFU leaders thus saw a compelling reason to persist with their own campaigning, and in 1911 Guérin, as FFU general secretary, reported that it had four thousand members in fifty departments.[19]

The feminist teachers' organizing was an important part of the growing feminist pressure for reform in many aspects of French law and society. The Conseil National des Femmes Françaises (CNFF), launched in 1901 with 35 affiliated groups, claimed at least 125 affiliates by 1914. Through its issue-oriented sections the CNFF advocated more educational and employment opportunities for women; legal reforms to expand the rights of women, married and unmarried; assistance, public and private, for the needy and unfortunate; and an end to legalized prostitution and what contemporaries called the "white slave trade." Although the agendas of many of the CNFF's affiliated societies were charitable or philanthropic, several older feminist groups were among the first affiliates: Amélioration (Société pour l'Amélioration du Sort de la Femme et la Revendication de ses Droits); Solidarité des Femmes; and the Ligue Française pour le Droit des Femmes (LFDF), which embraced women's suffrage by 1900. Hubertine Auclert's Suffrage des Femmes joined in 1906, as did the UFSF soon after its founding in 1909, when it also joined the International Woman Suffrage Alliance (IWSA). Yet because not all CNFF members were comfortable with the term "feminist," the CNFF cautiously titled its newsletter, started in 1909, *L'Action féminine*. As of 1912, when the CNFF had 115 affiliates, 8 were focused on feminism and 12 on education.[20]

The FFU joined the CNFF in 1909, although not without some controversy and division of opinion among teachers.[21] Against a backdrop of increasing interest in and support for socialism, some teachers, like Marie Vidal in Marseille, argued that their associations should identify closely with labor unions (*syndicats*) and shun the CNFF because of the "bourgeois" social backgrounds of many of its leaders. This was the argument that many European socialists, male and female, routinely employed to deter working-class women from supporting "bourgeois feminism."[22] FFU leaders insisted, however, that alliances with other women's groups were not incompatible with sympathy for the working classes from which many teachers came. In the *Revue de l'enseignement primaire*, a progressive pedagogical journal, Lucie Bouvrain, secretary of the Ardèche GFU, defended the sincerity of the CNFF's efforts to help all women, including women workers, and firmly disputed Vidal's claim that the CNFF expected teachers to spread the ideas of big capitalists like the Rothschilds. Paul Guérin cited the importance of the CNFF's role in persuading the Ligue de l'Enseignement to endorse the FFU's demand for equal pay.[23]

From the standpoint of CNFF leaders, feminist teachers' support was clearly welcome, as secretary general Ghénia Avril de Sainte-Croix indicated in 1910. Marguerite Pichon-Landry, a CNFF secretary and vice president of its legislative section, emphasized in *L'Action féminine* that thousands of teachers could help spread the feminist message from Paris to provincial France, where indifference to feminism was proving hard to overcome. Furthermore, she added, feminists already owed a great deal to women teachers: they had demonstrated women's intellectual ability and also shown that women could successfully combine professional and familial duties.[24]

Fontenay-aux-Roses graduates who staffed normal schools and higher primary schools could learn about feminist goals in their alumnae association's *Bulletin*. Already in 1899 professor Rachel Albert, who had studied in England for two years, cited the importance of feminist organizing there.[25] The multifaceted CNFF program was also presented. When Kergomard, who had chronicled educational issues in *La Fronde*, took charge of the CNFF education section, she focused not only on equal pay but also on expanding women's access to school inspection, the latter issue of special interest to two Fontenay association leaders who moved from directing provincial normal schools to inspection posts in the Paris area. Marguerite Ginier, after eighteen years as directrice of four normal schools, became an *inspectrice primaire* in Paris in 1904; and Eugénie Kieffer, also with eighteen years of experience in three schools, became the *inspectrice primaire* in Versailles in 1905. Only four women were then in the corps of 450 primary inspectors, all four assigned to the Seine or Seine-et-Oise.[26]

In the Fontenay *Bulletin* of January 1906, under the heading "Féminisme," the association president Marie Mahaut, directrice of the Indre normal school, refuted arguments still used to bar women from primary school inspection. Kieffer, the association treasurer, then reported on Kergomard's CNFF advocacy and invited readers to submit their views about the current functioning of "inspection féminine" and their reactions to the "masculine opinion that the role was 'too hard' for women." Should women be allowed to inspect normal schools or higher primary schools, she also asked. For readers unfamiliar with the CNFF, Kieffer identified it as the French branch of the International Council of Women (ICW), founded in the United States in 1888 to bring together "all the associations of women working for the

158 WOMEN AND THE POLITICS OF EDUCATION IN FRANCE

well-being of the community" and as such taking no specific religious or political position.[27]

Kieffer again publicized the CNFF while president of the Fontenay association from 1908 to 1911, providing a brief history of its goals and accomplishments, and highlighting its addition of a section promoting women's suffrage, "the reform which is the base of all feminine claims and on which the fate of such claims depends." At the alumnae group's meeting in 1910, her proposal that it become a CNFF affiliate received unanimous approval, as did paying 200 francs for the status of "perpetual member." As the association's vice president after Ginier became president, Kieffer continued to attend the CNFF education section's monthly meetings and reported on CNFF planning for the international women's congress slated for 1913.[28] The alumnae associations of the normal schools in Rouen and Lyon, following Fontenay's lead, also affiliated with the CNFF. Alcidie Menat, the Rouen directrice and a Fontenaysienne, favored the affiliation, and it is likely that in Lyon Kergomard's daughter-in-law, head of the local CNFF branch and wife of the director of the men's normal school, encouraged the decision.[29]

The Union Française pour le Suffrage des Femmes (UFSF), founded in 1909, also received attention in both the Fontenay *Bulletin* and *Action féministe*. Fontenaysiennes who attended UFSF meetings in Paris alerted readers in 1911 to the existence of this "modest" Parisian group dedicated to advocating "through legal means" women's right to vote in local elections. Aline Martin, one of the attendees, later recalled that she and fellow student Aline Zeller were among the "pionnières" of the UFSF.[30] The support for the UFSF provided by normal school personnel and schoolteachers is detailed below.

Normal school directrices and professors could, of course, follow the progress of feminist efforts in many publications. The Parisian press routinely reported on feminist congresses and some smaller meetings, and local papers often provided coverage when feminist speakers visited provincial towns. Drawing on the widespread use of the term *femme nouvelle* (new woman) to characterize women with modern interests, attitudes, and professional pursuits, Léa Bérard, a secondary school professor in Montpellier, started a bimonthly magazine with that name in 1904, hoping to attract women educators and their former students. *La Femme nouvelle* addressed a variety of literary, cultural, and social topics and also included information on professional examinations and promotions. Although women from secondary schools predominated on its editorial board, normal school directrice Eidenschenk soon joined it, her election to the CSIP giving her a national reputation among women educators. At least fourteen directrices ordered subscriptions for their normal school. Eidenschenk also contributed articles on "la femme nouvelle" and another with a more feminist focus, cited below. Bérard's short-lived review was unable to compete, however, with the more popular and glossy publications *Fémina* and *La Vie heureuse*, which Rachel Mesch has termed inventors of "the modern woman."[31]

The feminist teachers' campaign for equal pay inevitably involved directrice Eidenschenk, the only woman representing primary education on the CSIP. In July 1906, in response to a request from the Chamber of Deputies, the government created an extraparliamentary commission to review the salaries of teaching personnel. Because primary teachers' pay was raised in 1905, the fifty-three-member commission focused largely on secondary education. Nonetheless, it heard testimony in February 1907 from the secretary of the federation of teachers' *amicales*, the leader of the group representing teachers on departmental education councils, and also Eidenschenk. She asked the commission to endorse the principle of equal pay for men and women of all ranks, arguing that an endorsement would have "considerable social significance" because "it would be official proof . . . for private employers" that the government did not approve of using women's "legal inferiority" to limit their salaries. In other words, failure to accept the principle of "à travail égal, salaire égal" (equal pay for equal work) would set a poor example for the private sector. She also pointed out that while personnel of men's normal schools received extra compensation for monitoring students at night, women normal school personnel did not.[32]

The commission's discussion of Eidenschenk's recommendations led to a somewhat tumultuous session on March 7, particularly because the director of secondary education judged the principle of equal pay impractical in light of the differences in qualifications expected of men and women teaching in secondary schools. Yet Louis Liard, vice-rector of the academy of Paris and vice president of the commission, secured a majority vote (15 to 4, with 19 abstentions) in favor of equal pay for personnel with the same rank and qualifications: "à égalité de grades ou de titres de capacité, les femmes auront, dans les mêmes fonctions, les mêmes traitements que les hommes." A statement of principle was not, of course, the same thing as legislative action, but Eidenschenk believed that this new official recognition of a "right" (*droit*) to equal pay would "sooner or later" result in action to deliver on it.[33] Advocates of equal pay frequently cited the commission's landmark statement as they continued their campaign.

While achieving equal pay for women at all levels of primary education long remained elusive, Eidenschenk had more success addressing women normal school professors' complaints about their role in surveillance of students, which included nighttime hours and for which they, unlike male colleagues, received no extra pay. In her report to the ministry of public instruction on the issue, Eidenschenk drew an analogy between the unfair treatment of women professors and practices among "certain people we call barbaric, because they place the heaviest burdens on the weakest."[34] The surveillance requirements, a cause of tension between directrices and professors, and also among professors, were modified by a decree of December 23, 1909, that incorporated CSIP recommendations which Eidenschenk had helped shape. Minister Gaston Doumergue's instructions to rectors obliged to monitor implementation of the new policy called it a remedy for an "inequality" between the men's and women's schools overlooked previously when more women professors were young and single, lived in the normal school, and presumably appreciated receiving room and board at reasonable cost.[35] Although nighttime surveillance ceased to be obligatory for professors, the distribution of other surveillance duties could still cause disputes, as Eidenschenk conceded in 1912.[36]

During 1909 Eidenschenk also continued to support the FFU's intensified campaign for equal pay. In a letter addressed to all women teachers, professors, and directrices in March, Marie Guérin and Pauline Rebour, a higher primary school professor in Le Havre, urged colleagues to write to deputies and senators, and they provided a model letter citing recent FFU efforts and goals for the next education budgets. The *Journal des Instituteurs* and the *Revue de l'enseignement primaire*, which sometimes chided women teachers for their passivity with regard to professional issues, published the full text of the appeal. Then on March 31 Eidenschenk arranged to take an FFU delegation to meet with minister Doumergue, FFU leaders having previously spoken to Gasquet, director of primary education. The ministerial meeting was hailed as an important sign of "official" recognition of the FFU's existence.[37]

To show their determination in advance of the *amicales'* national congress in August 1909, Guérin and Rebour, joined by Eidenschenk, drew up a slightly revised letter for teachers to send to legislators representing their localities.[38] The CNFF, represented by Maria Vérone of its LFDF affiliate, also persuaded the annual congress of the influential League of the Rights of Man to support the principle of equal pay for equal work for teachers and other women employed by the state.[39] At the *amicales'* congress in Nancy, the FFU held an organizational meeting for about a hundred teachers, and the full congress, attended by 1,500, heard presentations by Paul Guérin and feminist teachers, who cited Eidenschenk's widely publicized extraparliamentary commission testimony. After some stormy debates, the official delegates passed a resolution to prioritize equal pay by placing it at the top of all lists of the Federation of *Amicales'* demands, hoping thereby to put additional pressure on the government. The lengthy report on the congress, published in *L'Action féministe* by Cécile Panis, FFU assistant secretary, included an appreciation of Eidenschenk as "one of the most authoritative among us."[40]

For the next four years the campaign for equal pay, pursued in tandem with the *amicales'* campaign for higher pay for all teachers, was marked by moments of hope and disappointment. Buisson, the former administrative director of primary education and a Radical republican deputy since 1902, persuaded a majority in the Chamber of Deputies in January 1910 to ask that equal pay for primary teachers be part of the 1911 budget, but the government resisted.[41] The next Chamber, elected in 1910, considered pay increases, but when it raised the salaries of normal school personnel in July 1911, it maintained a gap between men's and women's pay.[42] Eventually in December 1912 the Chamber's budget commission endorsed an equal pay resolution for which the CNFF and FFU had lobbied, and once again the FFU and supporters in *amicales* intensified efforts to persuade legislators. So did associations representing normal school, higher primary school, and primary inspection personnel, whose leaders met in Paris in January 1913, a meeting also attended by Eidenschenk and another CSIP member, and by the supportive deputy Louis Marin. Inspectress Ginier, representing the Fontenay association, chaired the meeting and forwarded its equal pay resolution to Buisson.[43] The legislature did vote in June 1913 to raise all primary teachers' pay gradually over a period of four years, but women teachers were asked to accept a reduction of the disparity between men's and women's pay from 200 to 100 francs for those on the upper four tiers of the pay scale. Disappointed FFU leaders, like normal school colleagues, then prepared to continue the battle for pay equity, not knowing that the outbreak of war in 1914 would delay action until 1919.[44]

Normal School Directrices, Feminism, and Women's Suffrage

Eidenschenk's advocacy of equal pay for equal work, like her previously cited labeling of the Napoleonic code a "monument of injustice" and her call to educate women for their own benefit and not just to serve others, echoed the convictions and demands of many women in feminist organizations. In "La Femme française et la République," published in *La Femme nouvelle* in 1905 and utilized in *Petits et grands secrets de bonheur* (1907), Eidenschenk complained that old prejudices kept republican leaders from doing everything necessary to remedy the "inferior" status of women, married or single.[45]

Because of Eidenschenk's strong statements and public advocacy, it may seem surprising that she stated in April 1909, "I am not, properly speaking a feminist" (je ne suis pas, à proprement parler, féministe). Writing about "some ideas on feminism" in the widely read *Manuel général de l'instruction primaire*, she was replying to a higher primary school professor, Jeanne Roger-Lévy, who argued that bringing women into public life, if they gained the right to vote, would lower the moral level of society. Roger-Lévy's equation of public life with political life did not, of course, consider broader notions of women's role in public life, which could well include the work of republican women teachers like herself. Eidenschenk, in rebuttal, cited current examples of the valuable participation of enfranchised American and Australian women in public life, adding that many French women already devoted themselves to important efforts to improve society.[46] She did not explain why she resisted calling herself a feminist, but her thinking about feminism would continue to evolve.

Within two years Eidenschenk was more openly a feminist. Writing on "féminisme" in *L'Action féministe* in March 1911, she urged teachers in the FFU to recognize that the injustice they experienced with unequal pay was but one example of how women were generally regarded as, and treated as, "inferior beings" (*êtres inférieurs*). Women teachers should therefore see their "cause" as part of a much larger effort to help all women and children. Thus she advised them to make contact with other feminist groups, such as the CNFF, UFSF, and the Ligue contre le Sweating System. They should work for "*le droit de suffrage* complet" for women because justice could be secured only when women had the vote. Recognizing that feminism was still not

APPROACHES TO FEMINISM   163

well regarded in some social circles, Eidenschenk assured teachers that advocacy of women's suffrage did not make them revolutionary or dangerous. That said, she also asked them to take an interest in issues of behavior and *moeurs* (social customs) that affected society negatively. In particular, she cited the work of the International Council of Women and the International Abolitionist Federation to halt the traffic in women (*la traite des blanches*). Practical steps already taken by many teachers could further heighten awareness of feminist and social issues: engagement with associations of former students, support for *patronages*, and lectures for adult women. Eidenschenk also wanted women teaching in higher primary schools and normal schools to join with *institutrices* in such projects.[47]

By the time that Eidenschenk urged teachers in the FFU to advocate women's suffrage, some already did, despite pressure from other colleagues, male and female, to focus only on professional issues. Marie Guérin would invite Cécile Brunschvicg from the UFSF and Marie Bonnevial from the LFDF and CNFF to attend the FFU's meeting for women teachers in Nantes in August 1911, coinciding with the *amicales'* national congress.[48]

Asking teachers to combine their push for professional equality with efforts to alleviate social problems typified the mix of issues found in many French feminist programs, notably that of the CNFF, and was consistent with normal school directrices' mission to train teachers who made students aware of their duties to family and society as well as of their rights. As Eidenschenk, like other women educators, became more vocal about the importance of women's suffrage shortly before 1914, she also wrote a series of fifteen more traditional articles for the *Manuel général de l'instruction primaire*, "Pour nos filles" (For our daughters), presenting topics that would help teachers make girls' education "truly a preparation for life" after school. Through their lessons and actions, teachers could try to combat problems like alcoholism, slums, and pornography and thus enable girls who would become wives and mothers to keep these scourges away from their homes. She also advised teachers to attach "less importance to instruction not in contact with the realities of life."[49]

While Eidenschenk and other women educators were finding allies in the CNFF, LFDF, and UFSF, deputy Buisson, the champion of pay equity, was also leading an effort in the Chamber to give women the right to vote in local and departmental elections, a first step toward full political equality. His lengthy report on women's legal and political rights in France and other countries,

164   WOMEN AND THE POLITICS OF EDUCATION IN FRANCE

issued in 1910, was soon published and widely circulated. Treating France as a laggard in enhancing women's rights, as Buisson did, became common in feminist argumentation.[50]

By 1910 the respectable and largely middle-class leaders of the major feminist groups had managed to lessen, although certainly not dispel, the idea that feminism was a radical undertaking. After the death of Protestant philanthropist Sarah Monod, the first president of the CNFF, Protestant Julie Siegried, wife of a prominent businessman and deputy from Le Havre, succeeded her and worked closely with Marguerite Pichon-Landry, whose husband was the secretary of Raymond Poincaré, president of the Republic as of February 1913. Cécile Brunschvicg, secretary of the CNFF's labor section and secretary general of the UFSF, was from an assimilated Jewish background, the daughter of an industrialist and wife of an eminent philosophy professor. The president of the UFSF in 1914 was Marguerite DeWitt-Schlumberger, also Protestant, a mother of six and wife of a prosperous businessman. More humble origins and leftist, though still republican, political leanings characterized LFDF leaders: president Marie Bonnevial was a blacksmith's daughter, and secretary general Maria Vérone was the daughter of an accountant active in freethinking circles. Catholic women typically remained suspicious of women's organizations with prominent members from religious minorities or with views that were often anticlerical, and so flocked to the politically conservative and anti-suffragist Ligue Patriotique des Françaises.[51]

The tenth international congress on women's charities and institutions, held in Paris in June 1913, put the full array of CNFF and ICW interests on display. Official approval of the congress, reportedly attended by a thousand people, was evident as vice-rector Liard allowed the use of the Sorbonne amphitheatre and Louis-Lucien Klotz, minister of the interior, addressed the opening session and thanked women for their contributions to social reforms. The sections into which deliberations at the congress were divided reflected the CNFF's organization: Assistance; Hygiene; Education; Legislation: Work; Science, Arts, and Letters: Peace; and Suffrage—the latter presided over by lawyer Maria Vérone of the LFDF.

Normal school personnel contributed reports, summarized and quoted by inspectress general Kergomard who presided at the education section. In addition to the submissions by directrices Varlet from Lyon and Martin from Nîmes, there was one by professor Marie Soboul, also from Nîmes, who discussed the importance of scientific learning as a corrective to mystical and magical thinking. Aimée Fiévet, a Fontenay graduate and directrice of the most prominent girls' higher primary school in Paris, served as *rapporteur* for the sciences, arts, and letters section which featured reports from educators in nine countries on women's access to higher levels of education and professional careers. For French primary education Fiévet cited submissions by inspectress Kieffer and three normal school professors: Émilie Miroux of Douai, where Eidenschenk was the directrice; Jeanne Nazon of Albi; and Joséphine Zgraggen of Beauvais. Access to careers and differences between men's and women's salaries were central topics, and inequities in France were treated in detail.[52]

The many resolutions approved by the women's congress included calls for equal pay for men and women educators with identical qualifications and women's access to the inspection of girls' schools at all levels. Reporting on the congress in the pedagogical journal *Le Volume*, former normal school directrice Louise Sagnier told women teachers that its proceedings demonstrated that teachers were not alone in their struggles and that feminist leaders well understood their concerns, as she herself had learned by attending feminist meetings. Leaders like Lady Aberdeen of the ICW and Mme Siegfried of the CNFF were privileged women, she wrote, but they were dedicated to helping other women in France and internationally.[53]

Similarly, Eidenschenk reemphasized the importance and respectability of the CNFF and UFSF when she responded to primary school inspector Émile Bugnon's request for comments on a draft of his article about discord between public school teachers and the nation. He had already expressed alarm about the growing political militancy of some men in teachers' *amicales* and, particularly, of leaders of the technically illegal teachers' *syndicats* which advocated ties with workers' unions, legal in the private sector since 1884. In *La Grande revue/Pages libres* in April 1914 Bugnon criticized women in the FFU for combining demands for pay equity with "manifestations of a political nature," as evidenced by the FFU congress in Bordeaux in August 1913.[54]

Lengthy excerpts from Eidenschenk's comments on Bugnon's manuscript appeared in a footnote. Sharing his concern about the dangers of discord between teachers and the larger society, she added that "feminism in general, and feminism in education in particular, have nothing to gain from *militant* methods, [of] the English suffragette genre," tactics that would harm feminism in France. But then she stated, "I have urged women teachers to become *militantes*" in a way that Bugnon might well approve. In *L'Action féministe* she had asked teachers to combine efforts to improve their material situation with

166   WOMEN AND THE POLITICS OF EDUCATION IN FRANCE

those of organizations working to help "other women victims of injustices still more painful." The CNFF, she told Bugnon, was a "moderate, serious," association, "skillfully directed by women of high intellectual and moral value"; the UFSF was "admirable for [its] elevated and generous positions." Women who joined such organizations to make claims for their rights did so, she asserted, "to better fulfill their duties as women and mothers." Yet she added a caution: a woman teacher should not become "une militante féministe" in her village because she would alienate part of the population, as some militant male teachers had done.[55]

Eidenschenk also strongly supported the UFSF in March 1914 with a letter to normal school directrices and professors which urged them to join the UFSF, whose statutes she attached. Her letter, reprinted in *La Française*, Jane Misme's weekly feminist newspaper, recognized that some normal school colleagues were already members, but to persuade those who were not, she first disputed arguments against women's suffrage. Women satisfied with their current status should realize, she wrote, that millions of women suffered from harsh laws relegating them to an inferior moral and economic status harmful to the nation. To the common objection that women were not ready to vote because they were too ignorant or too frivolous, she countered that the UFSF was actively engaged in women's political education, and she pointed to the positive results of women's voting in New Zealand, some American states, Norway, and Finland. With the vote women could support measures to improve social hygiene and public assistance and attack social ills like alcoholism and debauchery. Accordingly, Eidenschenk asked colleagues to join a local UFSF group or to help establish one where none existed, thereby bringing to the cause their students and teachers who were their former students. Her arguments about how women voting would benefit society were not unusual for feminists before 1914, but they were an unusually strong public statement for a woman highly placed in educational ranks. Her department, the Nord, had a central UFSF group based in Lille and sections in seven other cities or towns, including Douai, where she took a leading role.[56]

DeWitt-Schlumberger and Brunschvicg thanked Eidenschenk in *La Française* for her initiative with normal schools and emphasized that the civic instruction in school curricula provided excellent preparation for young women to assume "their social role as women and *citoyennes*." Already, as noted above, twenty-five directrices and a number of professors had joined UFSF departmental groups, bringing what the UFSF leaders recognized as valuable "force and moral support." Along with "new rights" for women would come "new duties," in preparation for which the USFS expected normal school personnel to bring to bear the force of their "intellect" and "moral authority."[57]

By the time that Eidenschenk sent her appeal to normal school colleagues, many teachers, with or without normal school training, were already UFSF members, as were some normal school personnel. One of the UFSF's largest affiliated societies was the Fédération Féministe du Sud-Est (FFSE), founded in 1911 to bring together GFU teachers in ten southeastern departments and women in local feminist organizations. Numbering 2,800 by June 1912 and 5,000 by 1914, the FFSE was led by secretary general Venise Pellat-Finet, a teacher in Pont-Évêque in the Isère. An estimated 75 percent of the 12,000 UFSF members in early 1914 lived outside Paris, and teachers were a big part of the membership in provincial departments. In some cases, as UFSF leaders acknowledged, a normal school directrice played a crucial role in founding a departmental group or securing members. Some secondary school professors, such as Léa Bérard in Montpellier, also became local leaders. Because primary schoolteachers' interest in feminist and suffrage organizing was often an extension of their earlier and still ongoing campaign for equal pay, activist teachers asked normal school directrices to encourage students to join a GFU and an *amicale* upon graduation. The FFU forged links with the UFSF, and Jeanne Méo, a teacher in a Paris suburb and Guérin's successor as FFU secretary general in 1913, joined the UFSF central committee.[58]

Who among normal school directrices, apart from Eidenschenk, joined the UFSF by early 1914? Cécile Chaudron, the directrice in Troyes, spurred the organizing of a group in the Aube department in 1912, an effort reported in the UFSF *Bulletin* and *La Française*. In light of the attacks that she endured in Lons-le-Saunier before reassignment to Troyes, her interest in feminism is not surprising, and her activity as a local feminist leader points to her managing to overcome the hesitancy reported by inspectors after her unpleasant experience in the Jura. Chaudron welcomed Brunschvicg to Troyes in November 1912 when, as part of a UFSF promotional tour, Brunschvicg spoke to an audience of six hundred about women's "social role" and demonstrated, Chaudron reported, "strong feminist convictions" and powers of persuasion. The talk, summarized by Chaudron in *La Française*, again exemplified the familiar French and continental European feminist advocacy of "equality in difference" highlighted by Karen Offen. Because women

168   WOMEN AND THE POLITICS OF EDUCATION IN FRANCE

and men were presumed to have different natures, women, if enfranchised, could make distinctive contributions to society, contributions as valuable as those benefiting their families. Thus Brunschvicg urged support for the Dussaussoy bill to give women the vote in local elections, a first step toward securing the vote in national elections.[59]

Subsequently Chaudron chaired local meetings and headed the Aube UFSF group's executive committee of twenty members, half of them teachers. The leader of the normal school alumnae association, Mme Dechance, was a UFSF supporter. By 1914 the Aube group's membership reached 159, and in June Chaudron persuaded Buisson, head of the parliamentary commission on electoral reform, to speak in Troyes. The timing was opportune because in late April, when public attention was focused on the upcoming legislative elections, Le Journal, a major Paris newspaper, had conducted a poll asking women whether they wanted the right to vote, and nearly 506,000 responded that they did. That total included some three hundred submissions gathered by the Aube UFSF chapter.[60] Signs of mounting enthusiasm for women's suffrage encouraged Chaudron and other French feminists until the outbreak of war in August 1914 halted further legislative consideration of it. What is notable here is the public engagement of normal school directrices like Chaudron, perhaps emboldened by Eidenschenk, in the feminist campaign to secure political rights and other reforms in women's status in law and society.

Directrice Émilie Flayol, a merchant's daughter trained at Fontenay from 1894 to 1896, also joined the UFSF in 1912. A supporter of the Groupe féministe universitaire of the Eure while a professor at the normal school in Évreux, she assumed her first directing post in 1909, at the age of thirty-six, in the southeastern department of Ardèche and soon joined its GFU as member 198 on a list of 200. Many women teachers also belonged to the Ardèche amicale, which had 900 members by 1906.[61] Flayol's independent nature quickly drew criticism from administrative superiors, even as they appreciated her strong commitment to laic education. Rector Petit-Dutaillis complained in 1911 that she seemed to regard the normal school as "autonomous" and preferred to share leadership of it with her personnel rather than her "chefs" (superiors). To conform to expectations for a directrice, he wrote, she should give up smoking cigarettes and walk instead of riding a bicycle. Indeed, reported an inspector general in 1912, Flayol often took long bicycle rides alone and lacked the "reserve" expected of women teachers and educators of women teachers. Departmental inspector Jacques Molitor recognized in 1913, however, that she was the "soul" (*âme*) of the school's alumnae association, a valuable support for public education.[62]

The catalyst for UFSF organizing in the Ardèche was Cécile Brunschvicg's visit in 1912 to Annonay, Tournon, and Privas, the site of the normal school. By May 1913, the Ardèche had 254 UFSF members, including 88 in Privas, where Flayol encouraged participation. The secretary of the Annonay UFSF group was Lucie Bouvrain, head of the Ardèche GFU, which also belonged to the FFSE, a UFSF affiliate. By 1914, four Ardèche towns had UFSF groups, and two others had "delegates." Flayol shared the role of secretary for the Privas group with the wife of primary inspector Paul Liquier.[63] Feminists were elated when the Ardèche general council voted unanimously in May 1914 in favor of a suffrage resolution, the tenth departmental general council to do so.[64] It was not Flayol's activity with the respectable UFSF that drew criticism in annual evaluations but rather her sympathy with the "syndicalisme primaire" allying teachers with labor unions and calls for direct action. Administrators who detected attempts to turn the two Ardèche normal schools into "parishes of syndicalism" noted with relief in 1914 that Flayol had become more prudent.[65]

In the Charente department in western France an energetic young normal school professor, Juliette Thimer, and an older directrice, Emma Frugier, known for independent leanings, began organizing a UFSF group in December 1912 after a talk by Pichon-Landry. When Brunschvicg visited Angoulême in January 1914 while on a regional speaking tour, Frugier, professors, and eighty students greeted her at the normal school and listened to a talk on women's suffrage. Students' responses convinced Brunschvicg that "all were ready to share our convictions" and provide support, and the encounter confirmed her view "of what strength these normal schools could bring us, and how much we need to win over to our ideals those who direct them and hold in their hands the women educators of the country." She characterized Frugier, the directrice since 1884, as "intelligent and distinguished," and a "militante" who trained feminist teachers for the Charente and also exerted influence beyond it because of the school's fourth-year program preparing normal school graduates for the Fontenay entry examination. At least eight women trained in Angoulême were studying at Fontenay and would later hold positions throughout France.[66]

Brunschvicg also praised the thirty-year-old Thimer, secretary of the local UFSF group, as "une vaillante, une ardente, une précieuse suffragiste" who publicized the cause in the press and reached the countryside through

170   WOMEN AND THE POLITICS OF EDUCATION IN FRANCE

contacts with teachers. In June 1913 Thimer had helped draw more than four hundred people to a talk by Marguerite Clément, a professor at the lycée of Versailles and frequent UFSF speaker. Because Thimer reported that some people in Angoulême still found a woman speaking in public to be a novelty, it was no surprise that Brunschvicg commented in 1914 that the local bourgeoisie had not yet embraced the UFSF.[67] Like Flayol in the Ardèche, Thimer also participatd in her department's GFU, one of the first five groups to join the Fédération Féministe du Sud-Ouest (FFSO), modeled on the FFSE and proposed by GFU teachers in the Gironde department in 1913–14.[68]

For Frugier and Thimer there is also evidence to confirm feminist leaders' belief that normal school directrices and professors influenced the ideas about women's roles in society that their students would bring to their work as teachers. A woman trained in Angoulême from 1910 to 1913 later remembered Thimer as an "ardent feminist" who persuaded many students.[69] Testimony to students' respect for Frugier, although it did not include comments on her feminism, was evident in 1920 when nearly 120 current and former students signed letters to the rector praising her and requesting Legion of Honor recognition for her as she neared retirement. Former student Renée Lebel recalled in *La Française* that Frugier spoke persuasively about social injustices and advocated women's rights. Frugier had prepared students for a talk by Brunschvicg by telling them that they would hear "une femme de grand coeur."[70]

Normal school students' presence at Brunschvicg's talk in Angoulême is but one illustration of how respectable feminism had come to seem in many, if not all, quarters by 1914. Talks by anyone from outside the school required authorization from the chief departmental inspector. A decade earlier, a lecture on "feminism" delivered by a higher primary school professor, Pauline Rebour, at the Rouen city hall, under the auspices of the local branch of the Ligue de l'Enseignement, had prompted inspector general Duplan to tell her to keep feminist issues out of the classroom and not involve students—even as he admitted that the content of her public talk did not exceed what was permissible for a state employee.[71]

By 1913, reports in *La Française* on UFSF organizing often noted normal school students' attendance at feminists' presentations. Thus the announcement of a new UFSF group formed in Alençon in February 1913 mentioned normal school students in the audience at a recent talk, adding that through them the UFSF hoped to increase support in the Orne department. The LFDF also sought recruits at normal schools, as in December 1912 when Vérone spoke in Chartres and directrice Bonnefon encouraged the audience of students, professors, and local teachers to form an LFDF group. In Valence, where the Drôme prefect's wife was the UFSF group's honorary president and directrice Joséphine Desvignes a member, students from the men's and women's normal schools, along with their directors and professors, attended a talk in May 1913, as did many local teachers. In the Breton department of Finistère, a talk on women's suffrage in Quimper in June drew more than five hundred, including normal school students and professors, accompanied by directrice Suzanne Pingaud, a former colleague of Frugier in Angoulême. Also attending were teachers and the chief departmental inspector with his family. Another supportive departmental inspector, Henri Havard in the Bouches-du-Rhône, allowed teachers in Marseille to leave their schools at 4 p.m. on March 14, 1913, to hear DeWitt-Schlumberger and Brunschvicg speak to an audience of five hundred, including the prefect. Havard also became an honorary member of the Marseille UFSF committee. In the Vienne department, the UFSF group president was Mme Cavalier, wife of the rector of the academy of Poitiers, which included eight departments.[72]

When Brunschvicg alluded in 1914 to Fontenay graduates' likely influence throughout France, she had already spoken to Fontenay alumnae and students on various occasions, as well as to students at the *école normale supérieure* in Sèvres that trained women secondary school professors. By 1912, Fontenay directrice Dejean de la Bâtie was one of fifteen honorary members of the UFSF central committee, which also then included deputies Buisson and Marin and six other men.[73] Speaking to Fontenay alumnae in August 1911, Brunschvicg had combined a familiar emphasis on the UFSF's commitment to remedying economic and legal injustices facing women with insistence that winning the vote would better enable women to serve France. For evidence, she cited the benefits to society now apparent where women did vote: New Zealand, Australia, Scandinavia, and some American states. She also stressed that the UFSF would not imitate the "violence" evident in some English suffrage activity, even though she admired the dedication of English women who gave their time and money to try to "conquer their rights." Half of the UFSF's current supporters were in public education, Brunschvicg reported, and she urged her audience to help the UFSF individually and in groups.[74]

Inspectress Ginier, the Fontenay association's president, strongly supported the UFSF and had attracted considerable attention with her combative article in the *Revue pédagogique* in which she linked male educators'

172 WOMEN AND THE POLITICS OF EDUCATION IN FRANCE

successful resistance to appointing more women school inspectors with the reality that women, lacking the vote, could not influence politicians as effectively as men. Her colleague, inspectress Lucie Saffroy, the former Fontenay directrice, voiced similar concerns in meetings of the LFDF, also joined by Marthe Janin, who had become the directrice of a higher primary school in Paris.[75]

Brunschvicg's recruiting trip to southwestern France in January 1914, cited above, took her from Angoulême to Bordeaux, which had a UFSF group with more than two hundred members, and then farther south to the Landes department, where, with assistance from the well-established UFSF group in Pau in the neighboring Basses-Pyrénées, primary school inspector Gabriel Périères organized a meeting in Mont-de-Marsan that led to the creation of a twenty-member committee. It included teachers and Périères's wife Émilie, a professor at the normal school, who became the secretary. The Périères, also supporters of the regional FFSO, would continue suffrage activity after World War I when Mme Périères became the normal school directrice in the Tarn department.[76] Brunschvicg's southwestern tour ended with stops in the Charente-Inférieure, where the UFSF had a base in two towns, and then the Deux-Sèvres, which had two groups but none in Niort, the department's administrative center and site of the normal school. Mayor Cibiel of Niort presided at her talk on "women's social action," which the local chapter of the League of the Rights of Man also supported. A group with fifty members then formed, led by an eleven-member committee including lycée professor Louise Quioc as president, normal school directrice Amélie Landais, normal school professor Adrienne Veveaud, two *institutrices*, and a woman pharmacist. For help with creating the Niort group Brunschvicg thanked Juliette Thimer, an alumna of the Niort normal school and teacher in the Deux-Sèvres before appointment to the normal school in Angoulême.[77]

The Basses-Pyrénées UFSF group that assisted Brunschvicg's recruiting in Mont-de-Marsan was one of the largest branches outside the Paris area, where there were at least 2,700 members, or Lyon, which claimed 1,000. The main departmental group based in Pau since 1912, a group in Orthez, and sections in Bayonne-Biarritz and Oloron counted at least 345 members by 1913, all led by teachers in the FFU.[78] Adéle Dollé, directrice of the normal school in Pau since 1887, joined the UFSF in 1912, as did her husband, a higher primary school professor and an outspoken leader of the department's *amicale* for teachers, sometimes to the chagrin of his administrative superiors. Directrice Dollé, one teacher later remembered, was one of three courageous local women who spoke out in favor of equal pay for women before 1914. The other two cited were Mlle Privat, head of the UFSF section in Biarritz, and Mme Ladousse, head of the Oloron section and a member of the departmental education council.[79] In sum, the Basses-Pyrénées well exemplified the strong connection between activist teachers and feminist organizations in provincial France.

Women Educators and the UFSF Campaign In 1914: An Assessment

The first UFSF *Bulletin* for 1914 provided a detailed organizational list that further confirms the significance of women educators' support. There were 31 members on the Paris-based UFSF central committee and 186 leaders of 77 departmental groups and sections, 10 of them also on the central committee. Of the 207 individuals named, 193 were women and 14 men, with occupations sometimes listed. Over half (102) of the women can be identified as educators, either from the UFSF list or other sources. The eight officers on the central committee included the socially prominent DeWitt-Schlumberger, Brunschvicg, and Pichon-Landry, and as vice presidents, two feminist publicists, Misme who founded *La Française* in 1906 and Marie-Louise Le Verrier, editor of the French edition of *Jus Suffragi*, the IWSA bulletin. Veteran feminist Eliska Vincent, listed as honorary UFSF president, had died recently.[80]

Some familiar figures in French feminism since 1900, if not earlier, were also central committee members: author Marie Chéliga; Amélie Hammer, president of the Union Fraternelle des Femmes, founded in 1901; Blanche Cremnitz, known for articles in *La Fronde* signed with the pseudonym Parrhisia. Lawyers Maria Vérone and Suzanne Grinberg served as legal advisers, their professional credentials evidence of women's entry into previously all-male professions, as was the medical degree of Lasthénie Thuillier-Landry, one of two secretaries, the other her sister Marguerite. The central committee also included five educators. Apart from the professional women, writers, and 102 educators already noted, only 10 other women on the large list had identifiable occupations. They include author Marie-Louise Compain, also on the central committee; journalist Alice La Mazière, secretary for the group in the third arrondissement of Paris; and Mme d'Ardenne de Tizac, better known by her pseudonym Andrée Viollis, secretary for the

174   WOMEN AND THE POLITICS OF EDUCATION IN FRANCE

eighth arrondissement. Marie Le Gac-Salonne, a Breton feminist who had used pseudonyms to sign articles on women's issues in various provincial newspapers since 1906, was secretary of the group in Morlaix (Finistère) and delegate for the Côtes-du-Nord department.[81]

Normal schools were represented on the UFSF list of departmental leaders in March 1914 by four directrices, five professors, and two others with teaching roles. The directrices were Eidenschenk, Chaudron, Flayol, and Camille Modrin from Châteauroux. Modrin was a "delegate" because the Indre department lacked the twenty-five-member minimum for a group. Although the Indre had a strong teachers' organization, its second Indre "delegate," Cécile Panis, an FFU officer, lacked the time to continue UFSF organizing alone and so persuaded Modrin and professor Jeanne Castaing (a future directrice) to help.[82] The professors identified as leaders were Thimer, Périères, Sarah Goron (Ariège), Marie-Antoinette Souliat (Nièvre), and Joséphine Zgraggen (Oise). All four directrices were Fontenaysiennes, as were Zgraggen, Périères, and Goron (the latter two, directrices after 1919). The other women who taught or had taught in normal schools were Camille Fontvieille-Moller, vice president of the Haute-Savoie group in Annécy and an art teacher at both the normal school and girls' lycèe; and Louise Bernard, secretary of the Vaucluse group and for eighteen years directrice of the *école maternelle annexe* in the Basses-Alpes. After retiring to Avignon, Bernard started the Vaucluse group almost single-handedly.[83]

If departmental normal schools stood near the summit of primary education, just below the two *écoles normales supérieures* training men and women for departmental normal school posts, the higher primary schools (*écoles primaires supérieures*) occupied the echelon just beneath them. Ten women from higher primary schools were local UFSF leaders in 1914: 4 directrices and 6 professors, 6 of them Fontenaysiennes. Two directrices and a professor taught in the Nord department, professor Alice Jumau in Lille having studied at Fontenay when Eidenschenk was a *répétitrice* there. The other higher primary directrices came from the Ardèche and Haute-Savoie, departments with teachers active in the FFSE, as was also true for the Drôme, where professor Marguerite Verguet presided over a UFSF group of nearly four hundred, three-fourths of them teachers. Two other professors, from Belfort and Alençon, were Fontenay graduates under the age of thirty, and a third Fontenaysienne, teaching in Tours, was thirty-one.[84]

The most prominent higher primary school professor in the UFSF was Pauline Rebour, a founder of the Société Féministe of Le Havre and an associate of Julie Siegfried, founder of the CNFF branch in Le Havre and second CNFF president. Rebour wrote numerous articles for the FFU's *Action féministe* and helped launch a GFU for higher primary school personnel. In the pedagogical review *École nouvelle* she often contributed a "Chronique féministe." A former *institutrice* who obtained professorial certification in 1903, she had a talent for public speaking and, as a young professor in Rouen, did not shy away from controversial topics. While at her next post, the normal school in the Orne, she and her husband Raoul, also a normal school professor, attended syndicalist meetings, participation that directrice Gaudefroy and the rector considered troubling. She was appointed in 1907 to the higher primary school in Le Havre where she continued with feminist advocacy, soon criticized by the departmental inspector as an unnecessary diversion from professional duties. The Rebours' move to the Paris area in 1912 briefly necessitated a professional step downward when she was assigned to a *cours complémentaire* in a primary school, but in 1913 she obtained a higher primary post in Paris.[85]

Relocation also placed Rebour close to the center of feminist activity: in 1914 she was one of five educators on the UFSF central committee, secretary of the Paris group headed by UFSF president DeWitt-Schlumberger, and delegate for a suburb. The other educators on the thirty-one-member central committee were secondary school professors Clément (cited above) and Mme Cépède (retired); primary schoolteacher Marguerite Martin, representing a committee of socialist women; and an inspectress of *écoles maternelles*, Jeanne Girard, greatly influenced by inspectress general Kergomard.[86]

All told, by March 1914 the UFSF's 102 local and national leaders employed in education included 11 women from normal schools, 10 from higher primary schools, 2 inspectresses of *écoles maternelles*, another 22 from secondary schools (lycées or collèges) in 16 departments, 3 from vocational schools, and a head of a laic private school in Brittany. In addition, at least 14 women not listed as employed had ties to the educational hierarchy through husbands who were professors, inspectors, or, in one case, a rector. Yet the largest contingent among these educators active in the UFSF consisted of 53 *institutrices* from primary schools in 31 departments. Without them, there would have been no UFSF leadership in 11 departments. Their presence in UFSF ranks is testimony to the independent judgment and professional pride that normal school directrices encouraged students to develop. Personal and professional experiences beyond the normal school also contributed, of course, to the embrace of feminist convictions, and not all *institutrices* among the local UFSF leaders had attended a normal school. Indeed, although many more women teachers in 1914 had normal school training than in the 1880s and 1890s, almost half of all teachers were not normal school graduates.[87]

Leaders and members of the FFU assumed an important role in local organizing for women's suffrage. Marie Guérin, the FFU founder and honorary president in 1914, was one of two UFSF delegates for the Meurthe-et-Moselle department. Others were active in Paris and its suburbs. Jeanne Méo, the second FFU secretary general and alumna of the normal school in Alençon, headed the UFSF group in the suburb of Levallois-Perret; and Marthe Pichorel, FFU treasurer and active socialist, led the group in Sceaux. Rebour, founder of the FFU group for higher primary schools, was the delegate for Coubevoie and Puteaux. The FFU assistant secretary, Marthe Bigot, a graduate of the Seine normal school, led the UFSF group in the twelfth arrondissement of Paris, and another Seine alumna, Marie Grimmer, did so in the ninth and tenth arrondissements. Beyond Paris, assistant FFU secretary Panis campaigned in the Indre department, and Bouvrain led the UFSF group in Annonay (Ardèche). In the Isère, Pellat-Finet, head of the affiliated FFSE, figured on the UFSF list led by Estelle Bouchet, departmental inspectress of *écoles maternelles*. Teacher Marie Guillot, founder of the Sociétè Féministe in the Saône-et-Loire, affiliated her group with both the FFSE and UFSF.[88] Like middle-class feminists, FFU teachers such as Bigot frequently presented their advocacy as more than self-serving, calling the vote a tool for remedying the "totality of feminine misery."[89]

Teachers campaigning for women's suffrage in some departments might find the effort more daunting than it was in the Paris area or other large cities like Lyon and Marseille. One of the two UFSF delegates for the Dordogne in 1914 was a young teacher who later recalled that women working for "emancipation" were a small minority often subjected to ridicule. At the normal school in Périgueux from 1909 to 1912 she learned to regard teaching as an "apostolate," she reported, and she also became a "féministe" and pacifist. She admired an older colleague in the GFU, Suzanne Lacore, who had studied at the Périgueux normal school during the 1890s, became an active socialist, and in 1936 would be one of the first three women undersecretaries in a cabinet.[90] Other testimony linking the normal school to exposure to feminism came from Léonie Sourd, a GFU member and syndicalist who reported in *L'Action féministe* that classmates enthusiastically discussed feminism in the

APPROACHES TO FEMINISM   177

school courtyard in Chambéry (Savoie) when she was a student from 1906 to 1909. Similarly, a teacher in the Vienne department traced her feminist and suffragist views to her experience at the normal school in Poitiers from 1909 to 1912, and another recounted a similar experience in Angoulême.[91]

The substantial involvement of women educators in the UFSF was routinely reported in *La Française* and other publications, and such accounts, like Brunschvicg's records, supplement the information on participation by normal school personnel provided on the 1914 organizational list. Nancy Perseil, directrice of the normal school in Melun, was an honorary member of the committee guiding a new group in the Seine-et-Marne in 1913, and before its formation the school's alumnae association *Bulletin* featured articles on feminism by an association officer and by Buisson.[92] Juliette Marie, as directrice of the normal school in Moulins, helped launch the Allier department group, an action consistent with her views on the equality of men and women expressed in the textbook for girls' schools that she coedited.[93] Directrice Sophie Schreck, vice president of the Calvados group, presided in February 1914 at a meeting in Caen attended by four hundred people. In the Yonne, directrice Hélène Odoul became president of the department's group when it reorganized in March 1914, and professor Marie Py joined its executive committee. In July 1914, directrice Pingaud agreed to head the group in Quimper (Finistère).[94]

Across the Mediterranean in Algiers, law professor Paul Gemähling and his wife Marguerite were "delegates" when the early 1914 UFSF list was compiled. Then in April the formal organization of a group was completed at a meeting where mayor Charles Galland presided. Of the 250 members soon recorded, 180 were in Algiers. In other cities, including Constantine, active delegates were recruiting members. Louise Sahuc, directrice of the normal school in Miliana, joined the new Algerian UFSF committee whose president was a woman doctor. Berthe Charoy, a former Miliana professor now at the higher primary school in Algiers, also served on the committee. That the rector of Algiers, Édouard Ardaillon, and mayor Galland accepted honorary membership testified to the group's respectability.[95]

Normal school directrices also helped start UFSF groups in two other departments not represented on the early 1914 organizational list. In Limoges (Haute-Vienne) in late June a group was formed after a lecture by Mme Le Verrier, attended by five hundred people, including students from both normal schools and from secondary schools. A city councilor, M. Hébras, presided. Before the lecture, a group of 50 already had been

178   WOMEN AND THE POLITICS OF EDUCATION IN FRANCE

started and another 55 joined thereafter. Reporting in *La Française* on progress in Limoges, Angoulême professor Thimer credited Alix Rambault, the recently retired normal school directrice, with preparing the way for the new group, headed by a committee that included the current directrice, Marie Bordas, and normal school professors Juliette Château and Modeste Bézier; Mlles Lorin and Tallon, collège professors; and M. Hébras and a lawyer. Thimer also cited the support of departmental inspector Jacques Crévelier.[96] In Perpignan, normal school directrice Annette Bringuier took much of the initiative in the founding in July 1914 of the departmental group for the Pyrénées-Orientales. Speaking to about a hundred people at the school, which she had headed since 1909, she discussed the feminist movement and reasons why votes for women were a matter of justice and certain to benefit the nation. With the adoption of UFSF regulations, a group with 150 members was established, led by a committee of 30.[97]

By the time that the groups in Limoges and Perpignan were organized, the UFSF had held its annual congress in Lyon on May 31 and June 1, attended by several hundred people. Coverage of the proceedings in *La Française* and *Action féministe* reflected current optimism about prospects for women gaining the local vote, optimism fueled by the much publicized results of *Le Journal*'s poll as well as by endorsements from seventeen departments' general councils.[98] Along with reports on UFSF membership and local groups' activity, two major topics figured on the agenda: whether the UFSF should express opinions about current economic conflicts, and the status of civic education for women. The second issue was timely because opponents of women's suffrage often argued that women were not yet ready to vote because they knew little about the functioning of government or public affairs. Hence Jane Misme asked, in advance of the congress, whether civic education was really given in girls' primary and secondary schools, whether teachers believed that the principle of the civil and political equality of the sexes should be introduced in schools, whether there were examples of the principle already being taught, and whether any textbooks stated it.

L'Action féministe publicized Misme's questions and encouraged teachers to respond, Pauline Rebour remarking that teachers could strongly affirm that women's civic education was "not neglected and is our work." Indeed, women teachers at the FFU congress in Bordeaux in August 1913 had passed a suffrage resolution prefaced by statements about girls' education, including the point that the curriculum for boys' and girls' schools, identical for "national history, political and economic geography and even civic instruction,"

APPROACHES TO FEMINISM   179

seemed to anticipate that "girls should one day participate in the running of public affairs." After the UFSF congress, Rebour reported that "When we affirmed that schools already provide this education, we encountered some incredulity."[99] Although the UFSF had recruited many women educators, the force of antifeminist assertions that women were unprepared to vote evidently left distorted impressions, even among feminists, about what public schools offered in civic instruction or history lessons with obvious political content.[100]

At the Lyon congress, after UFSF members heard that laws, regulations, curricula, and some examinations indeed mandated civic education for girls and young women, they adopted several resolutions to bolster it, some suggested by Rebour. They asked for including questions about civic education on all primary and secondary school examinations; and they urged teachers to shun textbooks for history, moral instructions, or reading with "antifeminist" content and to tell pedagogical journals not to publish sample lessons drawn from texts conveying women's intellectual or social inferiority. In addition, the congress resolved to intensify "feminist propaganda" with educators in normal and higher normal schools so that future teachers and professors being trained would truly prepare "citoyennes" able to understand and fulfill the civic role feminists claimed for them.[101] With such resolutions the UFSF congress echoed the message of Denise Billotey, directrice of the Seine normal school, who had told members of the Ligue de l'Enseignement in late March that the education of women by women would surely overcome resistance to "our emancipation."[102]

Women teachers in public schools certainly presented lessons on French political history and the functioning of government, but their own interest in contemporary politics and feminism admittedly varied. The commitment of several thousand women teachers in the FFU, as well as those in the UFSF, to a feminist reform agenda did not mean that most women teachers shared feminists' convictions. Nonetheless, the support for equal pay by teachers' *amicales* with much larger memberships—97,000 of the 124,000 men and women primary schoolteachers in 1911—does suggest that more women teachers were sympathetic to the broader FFU program for equality than just the four thousand or more who actually joined it and embraced its "feminist" label.[103] In 1911 the new edition of Buisson's pedagogical dictionary, a standard reference work, included a paragraph on "féminisme" in the entry on "woman" (*femme*), defining feminism broadly as demands for women's civil and political equality and indicating that "féminisme universitaire"

180 WOMEN AND THE POLITICS OF EDUCATION IN FRANCE

referred specifically to demands for equal access to programs of study and "equal pay for equal work."[104] Commentators continued to report, however, that some "antifeminist" men in *amicales* remained hostile to women's claims for professional equality and mocked male, as well as female, colleagues who called themselves feminists.[105]

The desire of many women teachers for equal pay notwithstanding, the Ozoufs' survey of pre-1914 teachers' attitudes has indications of many women teachers' indifference to politics, even as they routinely gave lessons on government, local, departmental, and national. Asked in the early 1960s about their interest in politics before 1914, 60 percent of 1,029 men but only 35 percent of 1,060 women said that they had been interested or somewhat interested, some women explaining that their interest then was minimal because women could not vote. When these teachers were also asked to describe political interests in later years, men's level of interest did not change, and women's interest rose only slightly, to 39 percent. Yet of the much smaller number of teachers replying to a question about reactions to social changes such as women's access to new occupations, a majority of women, but not men, were favorable.[106]

That normal school directrices and professors sometimes joined the UFSF is evidence that educators of future teachers had, in fact, often absorbed messages from the moderate feminists' program. So were publications like directrice Eidenschenk's *Petits et grands secrets de bonheur* (1907), written for teachers and future teachers, or the primary school textbook *La jeune française* (1910), coedited by directrice Juliette Marie and inspector Alcide Lemoine. Their preface to two hundred short readings chosen to further girls' intellectual, moral, and social education did not mention women's suffrage but did assert that woman is "the equal of man" and that the "modern" woman was more aware of her "rights" as well as her duties. The idea of the equality of the sexes also figured in their presentation of an excerpt from a talk on women's current situation delivered by the eminent historian Ernest Lavisse at a public school's prize ceremony. Beneath the excerpt, they first highlighted the word "doctoresse" for a vocabulary lesson. Lavisse had told pupils that "the majority of girls, like most boys, must earn a living," but he warned that girls might find this harder because most would not enter professions as "doctoresses" now did. Then they took up the bigger ideas in Lavisse's text, asking students to consider what kind of "prejudice" against women had long prevailed and to explain the statement "boys and girls are equal in humanity."[107]

APPROACHES TO FEMINISM 181

Young women entering Fontenay-aux-Roses in 1913 to prepare to become normal school professors would find a question on their certifying examination three years later that asked for a critical discussion of a contemporary philosopher's statement that "civic virtue" is not "feminine."[108] The question raised the fundamental issue of presumed differences between masculine and feminine qualities and the relationship of such differences to roles in society. Fontenaysiennes of the 1880s had encountered notions of "equality in difference" in the teachings of Marion, Compayré, and Pécaut, among others. Over time, and especially after 1900, Fontenay graduates like Eidenschenk, Frugier, or Ginier—born between 1855 and 1864—began offering feminist adaptations of that teaching. Without questioning the importance of women's domestic and maternal roles, or women teachers' mission to help prepare students for such roles, they nonetheless argued that differences did not justify women's continued exclusion from prestigious professional opportunities or political rights. Their ties to the UFSF made that commitment visible.

Two of the young Fontenaysiennes taking the examination for professorial certification in 1916 were born in 1891 and 1893. Both asserted that women indeed had "civic virtue" but had different social roles from those of men, Henriette Sourgen remarking that women seemed to be guided more by "sentiment," men more by "abstraction." Both believed that women should extend their interests beyond the home and know about political and national issues, in part so that they could share their understanding with a husband or children. But unlike a number of the older normal school directrices and professors, neither thought that women as a group were yet sufficiently educated to exercise the right to vote, although they did not rule it out in the future.[109] Was their caution due to a desire to satisfy the expectations of examiners, or did they still lack the experiences, professional and personal, that had won directrices like Eidenschenk over to the cause of women's suffrage?

After the outbreak of war in August 1914, the once frequent reports in *La Française* and *L'Action féministe* on women educators' support for feminists' agenda, including women's suffrage and changes in the civil code, became rare. Because of interruptions in publication, neither journal reported on the success of the demonstration of support for women's suffrage in Paris on July 5, organized by the LFDF and UFSF, now with memberships of 1,000 and 12,000, respectively. Some daily newspapers covered the massive rally and orderly march that drew five to six thousand people and commemorated the

182 WOMEN AND THE POLITICS OF EDUCATION IN FRANCE

Marquis de Condorcet, champion of women's rights and education during the French Revolution. By the time that *La Française* and *L'Action féministe* reappeared in November 1914, millions of men had been called up to fight Germany and Austria-Hungary, and parts of northeastern France were under German military occupation. The feminist journals then featured women's substantial contributions to the war effort as workers or unpaid volunteers. In France, as in other belligerent countries, the beginning of the war halted the suffrage campaign.[110] For normal school directrices, the war and its long aftermath posed new challenges.

6

Old Issues, New Challenges

From World War I to World War II

The German declaration of war on France on August 3, 1914, quickly affected planning for the *rentrée*, the start of the school year in October. As more than half of all male teachers and many professors and inspectors obeyed orders to report for military service, education administrators implemented plans for temporary replacements. In due course, many women, sometimes with limited qualifications, became substitute teachers, and some retired men and women teachers returned to work. Third-year students at women's normal schools also began staffing empty classrooms, and their male counterparts were mobilized. In advance of the order for military mobilizations, the government had anticipated the requisitioning of normal schools, among other public facilities, and the large numbers of casualties during the first weeks of combat meant that dormitories soon became military hospitals or billets. Departmental education officials, in turn, had to relocate classrooms for normal school students and find alternative housing.

For most normal school directrices "la Grande Guerre" (the Great War)—so dubbed by the autumn of 1914 because of its scale—complicated their work and added extra duties, particularly if they and professors also assisted with hospital tasks. Women educators' contribution to the war effort was, of course, just one part of the story of how many thousands of women assumed new roles in offices and factories or replaced men on farms and in small businesses.[1] Already 38 percent of the labor force in 1911, women were about 46 percent of all workers in 1918. The wartime "upheaval . . . of civilization," opined feminist Jane Misme, "was producing the equality of women with men on a vast terrain."[2]

Not only the Great War but also its extended aftermath brought new challenges for normal school directrices. As older directrices retired, new appointees replaced them. Prewar concerns about appropriate curricula and the normal school's relationship to the larger community again loomed large, and controversies over *laïcité* continued. Interest in feminist campaigns for

Women and the Politics of Education in Third Republic France. Linda L. Clark, Oxford University Press.
© Oxford University Press 2023. DOI: 10.1093/oso/9780197632864.003.0007

184 WOMEN AND THE POLITICS OF EDUCATION IN FRANCE

women's suffrage also revived as French women learned of women gaining the right to vote in Great Britain, the new German republic, and the United States. The Third Republic itself would face new challenges from a more assertive political Left, inspired by the Russian Revolution of 1917, and from antidemocratic organizations on the Right, impressed by the emergence elsewhere of new authoritarian and dictatorial leaders, such as Benito Mussolini in Italy in 1922. Because France suffered a loss of manpower proportionately greater than that of any other major belligerent in the Great War, many educators embraced pacifism and hoped that the new League of Nations, based in Geneva, could prevent future wars. Of the 28,309 male teachers mobilized, more than 7,400 had died.[3] The catastrophe of a Second World War would bring the Third Republic to an end in 1940, and the collaborationist Vichy regime that replaced it soon attacked the very existence of normal schools.

World War I, 1914–1918

In early August 1914 directrice Marie Dosser fled from the normal school in Laon in northeastern France, subsequently reopening it in Château-Thierry in the southwestern part of the Aisne department. From there she would flee again in 1918 as battle lines changed. The Aisne and the other four departments in the academy of Lille experienced massive material damage during the war, and rector Georges Lyon soon became a "veritable minister of public instruction in the occupied territories" as communications with Paris were severed.[4] When the evacuation of Charleville (Ardennes) was ordered in late August, directrice Blanche Maucourant took refuge in the Gard, teaching in a boys' lycée until July 1915 when she rejoined a remnant of her school in the Aube department. The Ardennes was the only department completely occupied by the German military throughout the war. Maucourant was reassigned in September 1915 to the normal school in Châlons (Marne), replacing a retired directrice. In the Pas-de-Calais, Juliette Marie, directrice in Arras, remained at her post in August 1914 until German bombing forced her to leave. She salvaged many records, but the destruction of the school led her to refuge in central France until she received orders to reopen it in Berck-Plage on the English Channel. Instead of the 115 students expected in 1914, she supervised only 76 in 1915, many students having stayed in the occupied region. A new normal school in Arras did not open until 1925. The German occupation of Amiens in the Somme department, close to the front lines, was brief, and thereafter directrice Marie Marsy and her staff helped organize a hospital on the school's premises, the return of students delayed until May 1915. Albertine Eidenschenk remained at the Nord department's school in Douai, where the German occupation began on August 31; she stayed until early 1918, by which time the school was closed.[5]

In the Fontenay-aux-Roses *Bulletin* Eidenschenk later recounted the nature of life in occupied Douai and her efforts to keep the normal school functioning on a limited basis in alternate locations. The German army requisitioned the school in October 1914, and for the next six months she and her staff assisted with nursing the injured, British and French soldiers among them. Most primary schools in Douai, like the normal schools, did not function during the autumn of 1914, when there was still hope that the German occupation would be brief, but most reopened by early 1915. Eidenschenk found only a dozen former and recently admitted normal school students still in Douai, and in April she and her personnel were ordered to leave the school. She then arranged to hold classes elsewhere, and in October 1915 started the new school year with 29 students, a huge decrease from previous enrollments of around 200. The war also separated Eidenschenk from her family: her husband, a captain, volunteered at age sixty-four to serve the army as a translator of German; her son was also in the army; and her daughter, a normal school student, eventually left Douai, as did many classmates. Like the rest of the city's population, Eidenschenk experienced food shortages, rationing, curfews, and the need for a pass to go beyond a restricted area. One act of resistance that she allowed for students was ending lessons in singing with the "Marseillaise," sometimes in a low voice if German authorities seemed particularly watchful. The skeletal operation of her school in cramped quarters continued until February 1917, when the German command ordered the closure of schools. Eidenschenk's attempt to continue operating surreptitiously was soon denounced, and she left for Paris in early 1918, receiving a medical authorization to depart and three months of leave for health. Like Juliette Marie, she later received Legion of Honor recognition for her wartime service.[6]

In most parts of France, the military requisition of normal schools was the typical reason for relocating staff and students. This happened quickly in three other eastern departments in the academy of Nancy. The Meurthe-et-Moselle school in Nancy was partly converted to a hospital in August 1914, and directrice Rose Évard received orders in 1915 to move the school to Vittel

186 WOMEN AND THE POLITICS OF EDUCATION IN FRANCE

in the Vosges, where the normal schools of Épinal (Vosges) and Bar-le-Duc (Meuse) were also relocated. Jeanne Grunfelder, the Bar-le-Duc directrice, became a temporary primary school inspector in the Vosges until 1917 when she replaced Évard as directrice of the Nancy school. The Épinal directrice, Blanche Valin, also assumed some inspection duties until her school could return to Épinal in October 1917. Nancy Perseil, directrice in the Seine-et-Marne, had to move her school from Melun to a site in Paris in late 1915 after it was requisitioned for training temporary medical personnel. The number of students Perseil then supervised—180—was more than double the number that she previously directed because some of the students from the Nord and Marne departments had come to Melun. The move separated Perseil from her husband, a higher primary school professor in Melun, until Easter 1918.[7] Elsewhere in France, wartime relocation for many directrices usually meant moving to a different site in the same city or town, although some normal schools continued to share space with a hospital.

Inspectors and rectors frequently praised the contribution of directrices who helped with hospital administration while they also worked with students. In some instances, however, conflicts occurred, as in Lyon where Marie Varlet had difficulties with women in the Red Cross organization, the Femmes de France, who volunteered in the hospital and contested her authority. An inspector general did not attribute the problems primarily to her, but Varlet finally decided to relinquish her hospital role. The rector of Clermont-Ferrand similarly defended directrice Blanche Échard in Moulins, stating that she did not deserve the hostility of the local Red Cross committee of the Dames de France. In Nîmes, Red Cross women simply rejected the help offered by directrice Marguerite Foulet-Martin and her personnel, who instead aided other war-related organizations assisting soldiers on leave and families of prisoners of war. Anne-Marie Grauvogel and professor Thérèse Sclafert had to resign as administrators of the hospital in the normal school in Grenoble after conflicts with civilian and military authorities, compounded by their difficulty in sharing authority with the normal school doctor in charge of the medical service.[8]

Whether a normal school was fully or only partially turned into a hospital, directrices had new responsibilities beyond its walls. Although classes were sometimes taught in the school's *école annexe* or even in a room in the directrice's own school apartment if she still resided there, often she had to find and negotiate for suitable space elsewhere. Girls' higher primary and secondary schools frequently shared facilities with a normal school, and some prefectures offered a room to accommodate a class. Often, however, departments had to rent rooms in privately owned buildings. Complaints about normal schools' inadequate science laboratories were common before 1914, and many wartime substitutes were more deficient. Students whose families did not reside locally needed housing, and directrices needed to determine that families or facilities willing to house them met the expected moral standards. In addition, because many students about to enter their third year of study were instead pressed into service as temporary teachers, directrices also visited primary schools to evaluate students' pedagogy and offer advice and support.

The very fact that many normal schools functioned in alternate locations meant that they were less convent-like than before the war. Long black dresses for students and normal school staff were still required for activities outside the school, but some directrices were fussier than others about students' clothing. Students at the relocated Vosges normal school later recalled directrice Valin's insistence that not the slightest bit of throat should be exposed when they left the school for supervised walks, and so they wore a "guimpe," a kind of wimple without a head covering.[9] Some other directrices, such as Eidenschenk, eighteen years older than Valin, were less strict. Recognition of the less cloistered wartime experience of young women students likely influenced the education ministry's decision to relax some disciplinary aspects of women's normal schools in 1920.

Noteworthy observations about the impact of the war on social relations also appeared in evaluations of some directrices. When Jeanne Palanque started the hospital in the normal school in the Vendée, she secured assistance from both lay teachers and the Soeurs de la Miséricorde—a change from the nuns' prewar hostility to the school. As prefect Fernand Tarif noted approvingly, Palanque, professors, and students received many letters from soldiers grateful for the care they received.[10] In the Charente the wartime housing of Angoulême normal school students in a villa owned by a bourgeois family prompted an inspector general to comment in his assessment of directrice Emma Frugier in 1919 that the family no doubt had once believed that providing space to future lay teachers was as dangerous as housing "the devil." Students had coped with classes held in a room where the only table was a billiards table, and the family came to recognize and praise their merits.[11]

Directrices and future directrices assigned to temporary inspection of primary schools also experienced new contact with a larger public. Before 1914

188   WOMEN AND THE POLITICS OF EDUCATION IN FRANCE

no women inspected primary schools in departments other than the Seine and Seine-et-Oise, but wartime necessity eventually overcame previous objections to women in provincial inspection posts, particularly because, as of 1917, 180 of 444 primary inspectors served with the military, and 32 had died.[12] Nonetheless, directrice Cécile Chaudron's use of a bicycle to inspect schools in the Aube department led an inspector general to remark in May 1917 that in normal times he would disapprove of such transport for women. Hélène Odoul, directrice in the Yonne, rode with a milkman in a horse-drawn cart to visit schools in Auxerre. Eidenschenk, while waiting to return to the Nord, was assigned to inspect girls' schools and écoles maternelles in the Landes department in southwestern France.[13]

Temporary inspection assignments also went to women who held the credential required for both normal school directing and inspection and were awaiting regular appointments. They set the precedent for primary school inspectresses in departments in the mountainous Savoie, Haute-Savoie, and Hautes-Alpes; the remote Ardèche, Gers, Landes, Lot, and Lozère in the south; the western departments of Morbihan in Brittany, the Deux-Sèvres, and Sarthe; and across the Mediterranean in Alger. Twenty wartime inspectresses subsequently became directrices.[14] After 1918, more primary inspectresses served outside the Paris area, although their numbers remained limited.[15] In addition, postwar education officials often recommended a small role in local school inspection for directrices able to spend time away from duties in the normal school, recognizing that directrices thereby gained insights useful for preparing their students for the realities of the public school and its surrounding community. In 1928 at least twenty-six normal school directrices, as well as thirty-six directeurs, did such inspections.[16]

New Directrices, 1914–1939: A Collective Profile

The demands placed upon women educators during the Great War caused some normal school directrices nearing retirement to work longer than once anticipated, but in due course many new directrices were appointed. Of the 10 directrices, plus Fontenay directrice Dejean de la Bâtie, who retired during the war, 9 were appointees from the 1880s, 4 of them remaining until October 1918, when an end to the conflict seemed near. These retirements plus one death and several reassignments to inspection posts created openings for the wartime appointment of 15 new directrices. Although some older directrices stayed on to see that their schools functioned well in peacetime, 10 more veterans from the 1880s retired by the end of 1921, and the last 7 directrices from the 1880s retired by 1927. By 1929 so had all appointees of the 1890s and 14 named after 1900. Rose Évard, named in 1887, did work until 1930, but since 1917 she was one of four inspectresses general of *écoles maternelles* whose retirement age was seventy. In 1940 only four pre-1914 directrices remained, all appointed after 1910. By the time of retirement or soon after, many prewar directrices were rewarded with Legion of Honor recognition. Indeed, the postwar French state more often bestowed this distinction on its women civil servants, including educators: only 8 directrices were so recognized before 1914, but after 1918 another 40 prewar directrices were *chevaliers* of the Legion.[17]

As of 1929, 80 new directrices had been appointed—15 during the war and 65 since 1919. Another 40 assumed the position during the 1930s. How did their profiles, personal and professional, compare with those of predecessors? Born in sixty-one different departments, plus Morocco, the directrices continued to represent much of France. Six were from the Seine, 4 from the Bouches-du-Rhône, and 3 each from the Alpes-Maritimes, Nord, and Corsica. Only 4 came from a Breton department or the Vendée. Their family backgrounds, middle-class or more modest, resembled those of earlier generations and again included a large number of parents employed in education or other public services. Thirty-three fathers worked in public education (25 as *instituteurs*) and 24 in other public functions, including the police and the military. At least 25 fathers were artisans or workers, 9 were employees, 8 were in commerce, and 10 in agriculture. Among their mothers, 45 percent (54) had occupations that can be identified, as compared to 32 percent of prewar directrices' mothers. Nearly three-fifths of the employed mothers (31) were in public education, including 25 *institutrices* (20 of them wives of *instituteurs*). Jeanne Dollé, appointed in 1928, had followed the path of her mother Adèle Tourret Dollé, long the directrice in Pau. Five working-class mothers were unmarried when their daughters were born, four of them later marrying.[18]

Most of the 120 directrices appointed from late 1914 to 1939 (87 percent) received their initial training for teaching at a departmental normal school, which 85 of the 105 *normaliennes* had entered before the war. The others were graduates of higher primary schools or secondary schools. Far

190 WOMEN AND THE POLITICS OF EDUCATION IN FRANCE

fewer of the directrices of the 1880s, born before the Third Republic, had been able to attend a normal school, let alone a republican normal school like those they would help create. The post-1914 cohort of directrices attended 52 different normal schools, the tally headed by 5 from Aix and 4 each from Paris, Auxerre, Bordeaux, and Pau. Fifty-one future directrices also went on from the three-year normal school program to a special fourth-year option in letters or sciences provided at ten of the largest normal schools to prepare ambitious young women for the entry *concours* for Fontenay-aux-Roses. Directrice Aglaë Bancilhon, before retiring in 1920, had supervised this advanced training in Aix for 8 of the post-1914 directrices, as did Frugier for 7 in Angoulême and Varlet for 6 in Lyon.

Two-thirds of the 120 new directrices prepared for professorial certification at Fontenay, 49 of them completing or entering its program before 1914, as 31 more did later. Another 11 women credentialed as normal school professors without attending Fontenay benefited from its special preparation for directrices that Anne-Marie Grauvogel, Dejean de la Bâtie's successor, revived in 1921. Of the 29 directrices who lacked Fontenay ties but gained necessary credentials after other preparation, including study at universities, 27 had first taught in primary schools, 5 of them for more than ten years. Mme Bernarde Poujade spent twenty-four years as an *institutrice* in the Tarn-et-Garonne but eventually pursued studies at the University of Toulouse, receiving both a university degree (*licence*) and the credential for normal school professors in 1931, and thereafter advancing to a higher primary school and, at the age of forty-seven, to directing the normal school in the Vosges.

Most directrices did not wait as long as Poujade for their first directing assignment. Although the women in the post-1914 cohort ranged in age from 30 to 49 when first appointed, the average age for a new directrice was 36, slightly older than predecessors named between 1901 and 1914 but noticeably older than many of the young Fontenaysiennes of the 1880s, who often became directrices while in their twenties. Over time, significant experience as professors in normal schools or higher primary schools was increasingly expected of directrices. The minimum age for directrices remained at thirty, and as of 1930 new directrices were "delegated" for two years before being tenured in the post.

Marriage was also more common for directrices named after 1914 than for the pioneering directrices of the 1880s, although not more so than for those appointed after 1900. Fifty-one (43 percent) of the wartime and postwar appointees would marry, and in light of the average age of thirty-six for the first directing assignment, it is unsurprising that 36 were married when they became directrices. Three-quarters of directrices' husbands were in public education (36, or 38 with second marriages), 32 of them as inspectors (9) or professors (23) in higher primary, normal, or secondary schools and thus of higher status than 6 *instituteurs*. Five husbands were higher-ranking civil servants or professional men in medicine or law, and only 3 engaged in commercial activities. The married directrices, like earlier counterparts, often gained higher status than their parents through their own professional achievement and maintained that status with marriage.

Of the 35 directrices who were mothers, 25 had one or two children, rather than the *famille nombreuse* regularly advocated by natalist politicians whose preoccupation with increasing the birthrate intensified after the massive wartime loss of lives.[19] For both sexes the normal school curriculum included teaching about the duties of family members, and the higher primary school curriculum for moral instruction included "the duty to found a family." For young women the curriculum for normal and higher primary schools had prescribed *puériculture* (infant care) since 1905.[20] Yet as national census records revealed, many postwar couples limited family size. Heading a normal school was a demanding job and may well have influenced directrices' personal decisions. Blanche Gambey and Hélène Collet who had five children, and Marie Hugonnier-Ginet and Germaine Salducci who had four, were exceptional cases.

Like most directrices appointed before 1914, the later contingent worked until retirement, most often in normal schools. Two-thirds (75) of the 113 women alive at retirement age ended their careers as directrices. Twenty-seven others retired from posts in school inspection: 17 as primary inspectresses, 3 as inspectresses general of *écoles maternelles*, and 7 as inspectresses general of public instruction, the latter title not accorded to women until after World War II. Seven directrices moved to higher primary schools before 1940, 4 of them ending careers in collèges or lycées, as did 4 other pre-1940 directrices, because of policy and institutional changes made by the Vichy regime and the postwar Fourth Republic. With the exception of a directrice in Oran, another in Algiers, and an inspectress in the protectorate of Morocco, careers were completed in metropolitan France.[21]

Curricular Changes and Pedagogical Debates

Whether appointed before or after 1914, all normal school directrices had to implement the curricular changes introduced in August 1920 and the modifications of rules that had governed student life since the 1880s. Paul Lapie, director of primary education since May 1914, championed the changes, which addressed prewar demands for better connecting normal schools to the society beyond their walls. Son of an *instituteur* from the Marne, Lapie also hoped to enhance the academic reputation of normal schools. Critics of the 1905 curricular revision had complained that students learned less because much subject matter was crammed into the first two years so that professional preparation could be the third-year focus. The 1920 reform, approved by education minister André Honnorat, added more coursework in "letters" and "sciences" to the third year but also required that in each year students spend more time in actual primary school classes, either in the *école annexe* or in town, first as observers and later as apprentice teachers supervised by normal school professors or *école annexe* teachers. For the natural and physical sciences, Lapie wanted more emphasis on methods and philosophy, and he approved the inclusion of evolutionary theory, recognizing both Darwinian natural selection and Lamarck's environmental emphasis. The theoretical material was part of a third-year course on "general principles of science and *morale*" that included a philosophical component, ranging from Plato to Descartes to Bergson, which directrices found challenging but welcome.[22]

Certain differences between the courses for men and women were maintained in the new curriculum. Although instruction in mathematics and sciences would be nearly identical for men and women for the first two years, one part of the third year would differ, Lapie stated, because of "the difference which exists between the social functions of the *instituteur* and those of the *institutrice*." Instruction for women on applying science to "domestic economy" and child care was moved to the third year, and while the men's program featured four hours of "manual and agricultural works" (*travaux manuels et agricoles*), the women's program specified four hours for "housework" (*travaux ménagers*).[23]

The most novel part of the new curriculum was the introduction of sociology for one hour a week in the second-year program, the teaching of it to begin in October 1921 after normal school directors and directrices, responsible for the course, were prepared to offer it. Sociology was not a subject then taught in secondary schools, and critics soon challenged its introduction in normal schools. Under "Notions of sociology applied to *morale* and education," the new program listed four broad categories: economic; domestic (types of families); political; and religion, art, and science. Like earlier controversies over *laïcité*, lessons on the evolution of religion and comparative religious practices and beliefs generated protests, particularly as they were coupled with an item in political sociology regarding the "progressive separation of religious society from political society." There was also concern, heightened by the Communist victory in the Russian Revolution as well as by the appeal of socialism to many teachers, that economic sociology might become an invitation to embrace Marxist views of historical materialism because the program specified considering the "influence of economic transformations on institutions, customs, ideas." Lapie strongly disputed that charge.[24] The most serious challenge for Lapie came from Léon Bérard, education minister from 1921 to 1924 and a traditionalist on curricular matters. Bérard tried to remove sociology from the normal schools but failed because of hesitation by the Higher Council of Public Instruction (CSIP) and then the victory of the republican left, the Cartel des Gauches led by Édouard Herriot, in the spring 1924 elections.[25]

Evidently less disputed were topics in the sociology curriculum concerning women. "Domestic sociology" included not only the "reciprocal relations of spouses" but also the "progressive enhancement of the dignity of the woman." "Political sociology" had an item on "women's accession to political life."[26] Professor André Hesse and normal school director Auguste Gleyze, authors of the most successful manual for sociology instruction in interwar normal schools, soon presented strong statements about women's rights and women's changing place in contemporary society. Criticizing the requirement of wifely obedience in article 213 of the civil code, they wrote, "Nothing any longer justifies male hegemony in conjugal society," where "increasingly equality exists between wife and husband." In italics they added, "The wife who works liberates herself."[27] While Lapie's instructions reminded teachers of differences between men's and women's social roles, Hesse and Gleyze presented egalitarian arguments that went well beyond the views on "equality" in "difference" presented to Fontenaysiennes in the 1880s by Marion and Compayré, who regarded husbands' leadership in marriage as natural.

The political sociology section of Hesse and Gleyze's textbook discussed the characteristics of a "nation," types of government, and international

194 WOMEN AND THE POLITICS OF EDUCATION IN FRANCE

relations. Their chapter on "the state and individuals" devoted a lengthy paragraph to women's suffrage and concluded, "Suffrage is universal only if woman participates in it." First published in 1922 when it seemed that the Chamber's strong endorsement of women's suffrage in 1919 might still win approval in the Senate, the textbook retained advocacy of women's suffrage in later editions, including the eighth in 1938.[23]

More than one inspector's observations on a directrice's teaching of sociology cited the use of Hesse and Gleyze's book and noted students' special interest in discussions of the evolution of women's roles and women's rights. In 1926, for example, Marie Privat's students in Bourges brought many personal observations into a "very lively discussion" of the impact of women's employment on families.[29] One inspector general expressed dismay, however, that the notebooks of students of directrice Émilie Périères in Albi in 1928 contained statements about women teachers' important role in political matters because, in his opinion, teachers had far more important concerns.[30] Nonetheless, the curricular component that went beyond past emphasis on women's roles as wife and mother was evidence of changes in some mentalities, and a number of directrices like Périères maintained involvement in women's suffrage activity, as noted below.

Lapie's reform of normal schools also entailed changes in their internal organization, designed to lessen their reputation as *couvents laïques*. In his instructions for implementing the section of the decree concerning order and discipline in normal schools, he recommended a "liberal" system, stating that students should not be treated as children but rather as individuals able to govern themselves, under the watch of professors and directors. Previously male students could go by themselves to church on Sunday, but women students had to be escorted. The August 1920 decree eliminated that required supervision, allowing women students to organize this themselves, albeit "under the control of the directrice" who could punish students who used leaving to attend church for different purposes. Although women students still could not leave school for other reasons on Sundays and holidays unless their parents made a request or named another person to chaperone them, the directrice could authorize individual *sorties* (outings).[31]

Lapie also abolished the 1887 requirement that all students, men or women, wear a "uniform" when outside the normal school for walks or excursions. Students were to be reminded, however, that their appearance and conduct were "exterior" signs of a good education. The goal of eliminating certain "material constraints," wrote Lapie, was to make life in a

OLD ISSUES, NEW CHALLENGES   195

normal school more like life in "ordinary society." If students were to be able to direct the conduct of their future pupils, they should no longer "be led" but instead habituated to conduct themselves properly, even if advice from their "elders" remained "indispensable." Monitoring students' correspondence would also continue. Appropriately, then, Lapie concluded this section of his instructions by stating, "This [new] liberty is not anarchy." Within and outside the normal school, students should observe the norms of politeness expected in "civilized societies." Those whose conduct troubled the necessary "order" in normal school could be excluded.[32]

What the new instructions on the normal school's "interior regime" and "discipline" meant in practice varied from school to school, but their significance often figured in reminiscences by former students, professors, and directrices. Certainly students and their instructors were aware of changes in women's dress, hairstyles, and public conduct that many commentators observed during the 1920s, often pointing to the Great War as a catalyst for such changes.[33] Directrice Yvonne Omnès, who grew up in a normal school environment, well understood how Lapie's policies liberalized the school experience of the 1920s. Her mother had been a professor at the normal schools of Quimper, La Roche-sur-Yon, and Alençon, and she was a student in Alençon from 1905 to 1908. Her career took her from a primary school to higher primary schools, a normal school professorship, and then, after the Fontenay year for preparing directrices, to heading the normal school in La Roche-sur-Yon (Vendéé) from 1924 to 1940. A student who entered the school in 1921 heard about previous practices from third-year students and later recalled how the school was "modernized." The "old traditions were losing their value; bold people were introducing us to life at the same time as to books, the 'exterior' reached us."[34] Whereas Omnès's predecessor in the Vendée, Jeanne Renault, altered the dress code soon after Lapie's pronouncements, that did not happen in the normal school in Rumilly (Haute-Savoie) until a younger directrice, Thérèse Mathieu, replaced Caroline Vincent (born in 1875) in 1924.[35]

As that Rumilly example indicates, not only changes in official policy but also changes in personnel influenced students' perceptions at the time and later. A student at the Épinal normal school (Vosges) recalled the difference between the stern and very religious directrice Blanche Valin and her successor in 1919, Louise Gaillard, a young mother who created a "more calm, more humane" atmosphere. Under Gaillard's "liberal" direction (1919–31), students visited cultural institutions more often and heard more guest

École normale d'institutrices de Beauvais, first year students, 1930. © *Réseau Canopé – Le Musée National de l'Éducation, Rouen, 1978.01056.20*

lecturers. On Sunday mornings she gathered students who did not attend church and read from her favorite authors. Photos in a book about the men's and women's normal schools in the Vosges show a contrast between 1918, when first-year students and professors wore long dark dresses, unadorned except for a white collar, and 1928 when third-year students and the staff wore shorter dresses, of various colors—dresses that did not hide the legs of directrices and professors seated in the front row.[36] Similar changes are shown in photos of the directrice and professors in Saint-Germain-en-Laye in 1929 and of students in Beauvais in 1930.

In conservative Brittany, students in Laval (Mayenne) appreciated the liberalization occurring after an authoritarian directrice, Delphine Combe, retired in 1925 and was replaced by the well-liked Antoinette Espiau, who permitted changes that students saw as "revolutionary." They were allowed more freedom in dress and could cut their hair, go into the school's park alone, and have private conversations.[37] The Lyon normal school offers a third example of students' appreciation of changes after a directrice, Varlet, retired in 1923. Marie Bordas, a directrice since 1907 and mother of four, relaxed the school's atmosphere, saw to the improvement of food, permitted

École normale d'institutrices de Saint-Germain-en-Laye, Directrice and professors, 1929. © *Réseau Canopé – Le Musée National de l'Éducation, Rouen, 1978.01291.17*

students to visit parents on Thursdays when there were no classes, and was soon appreciated as a "*mère de famille* ... smiling and understanding."[38]

If young students liked the more relaxed but still disciplined atmosphere of their normal school during the 1920s, senior inspectors were sometimes taken aback, as were older directrices. When Juliette Marie retired in 1930 from the large Arras school that she had led since 1914, she praised students assembled in her honor for dedication to their work and respect for the school, but she also admitted to complaining sometimes that recent students were "less serious" and "less docile" than predecessors. Attributing such changes partly to unfavorable circumstances since the war, a "cataclysm unparalleled in the history of humanity," she hoped that something like the previous equilibrium would return.[39] Former Fontenay-aux-Roses students would report in the history published for its centennial that the interwar directrice, Grauvogel (born in 1868), "seemed jealous of the charm" of young women students and often criticized short hair styles, leaving many of them with "rather bad memories" of her.[40]

An inspector general assessing the normal school in Limoges in 1925, then directed by Marthe Billot-Kay (born in 1883), was pleased to find "one

198 WOMEN AND THE POLITICS OF EDUCATION IN FRANCE

of the rare normal schools" where he did not see any bobbed hair cut "à la garçonne" or any trace of "the modern silhouette" in students' dress.[41] On the other hand, inspector general Charles L'Hôpital reported after visiting the normal school in the Aisne in 1926 that the young directrice Cécile François, born in 1894 and recently married to a normal school professor, had short hair and wore a short skirt, an appearance he found surprising for a directrice. Also faulting her for the school library's lack of classic works and an excess of books by unimportant recent authors, he did concede that she was intelligent and cultivated but then wrote an only partly favorable concluding statement.[42] Certainly Mme François did not fit the long familiar image of a directrice with long hair pinned up in a bun. Her appearance in 1926 was unlike that of Blanche Maucourant, the Bordeaux directrice in 1917, later described by a former student as a tall and thin woman, dressed in black, grave and serene, "a perfect image of a normal school directrice as one then conceived it."[43]

Like many other interwar educators, normal school personnel also engaged in discussions of curriculum and pedagogy in their professional organizations and in publications. Six directrices contributed articles to the *Manuel général de l'instruction primaire*, ten wrote articles for *L'École et la vie* (the continuation of *Le Volume*), and several coauthored textbooks. Some also joined debates on alternate educational structures and practices. The Groupe Français de l'Éducation Nouvelle, formed in 1921 and affiliated with the similarly named international organization, proposed innovations to make classes more child-centered and individually paced, somewhat on the order of John Dewey's "progressive education" proposals in the United States. Adherents drew inspiration from the program of the *écoles maternelles*, less rigid than that of primary schools, and the newer Montessori schools in Italy and elsewhere. Directrice Émilie Flayol, author of a short book on Maria Montessori's methods, became a major advocate for "new education," encouraging students at the La Rochelle normal school to participate actively in making decisions about the school's "everyday life and discipline." In retirement after 1928 she was secretary general of the French "new education" group, continued to give lectures and publish articles promoting it, and wrote a book on Ovide Decroly, the Belgian doctor whose ideas about children's "biosocial needs" influenced the international organization.[44] At the annual meeting of the French group in Tours in March 1932, directrice Gaillard, introduced by the chief departmental inspector, reported on bringing "the active method to the traditional school," namely the *école annexe* of the Épinal normal school which she led before appointment to Tours.[45]

In the Fontenay *Bulletin* inspectress general Marguerite Angles, briefly a directrice, also reported sympathetically on the international congress on *éducation nouvelle* held in July 1932 in Nice, where 400 French educators were among 1,700 attendees. Yet Angles also acknowledged that many skeptical educators thought that the movement was in conflict with French education's traditional emphasis on rationalism. Indeed, primary inspectress Fernande Seclet-Riou, a strong supporter of "l'école nouvelle" since the 1930s, later conceded in an obituary on Flayol that the movement initially had been too idealistic because it did not adequately recognize the impact of the social milieu on children's behavior or understand that exalting children's "spontaneity" could lead to a "defiance" of adults that was contrary to reason.[46]

The most important discussion of reorganizing French public education after World War I used the rubric of "l'école unique" and sought to remedy the old structural divide between primary and secondary education that was often more a matter of social class than of age. An immediate goal was to make it easier for bright students in primary schools to move into secondary schools. Secondary schools were not free and had their own elementary classes, favored by parents who did not want their children mingling with children of "le peuple" in a primary school. As of 1926 such elementary classes, then enrolling about 22,500 pupils, were required to follow the same curriculum as primary schools, a first step toward the larger goal of a single system of public education. Flayol became an advocate, as did directrice Périères, one of six authors of a reader published in 1929 for the *école unique*.[47] In the late 1920s the government also began removing fees for secondary schools, one grade at a time, and under the Popular Front government of 1936, education minister Jean Zay called for creating orientation classes to facilitate pupils' ability to transfer from primary to secondary schools.[48] The goal of creating a single ("unique") system of public education of course raised the important question of what role higher primary schools and normal schools would have if the brightest primary school pupils headed instead to lycées and collèges.

Under the government of the Cartel des Gauches, which protected Lapie's curricular reforms, an important change in policy also affected educators' professional organizations, including those of normal school personnel. An official directive to all ministers in September 1924 called for

200   WOMEN AND THE POLITICS OF EDUCATION IN FRANCE

cooperation with representatives of *fonctionnaires* (public employees), in effect acknowledging the existence of their *syndicats* (labor unions). During the 1920s postal service workers and teachers were among the big groups of public employees pressing for recognition. The teachers' main national organization, the Fédération Nationale des Amicales des Instituteurs, claimed the title Syndicat National des Instituteurs (SNI) for its 80,000 members in 1920, and after 1924 affiliated with the large Confédération Générale du Travail (CGT, General Confederation of Labor). Teachers who leaned farther left—and often favored the new French Communist party that split from the Socialists in December 1920—maintained a separate organization until 1935 when they combined with the SNI. André Delmas, SNI secretary general from 1932 to 1940, well captured the attitudes of many SNI members when he compared teachers in the generation of 1885, focused on supporting the new secular republic, with the interwar generation, still committed to democracy but also wanting to tackle "social inequality." Whether public employees, including teachers, had a right to strike remained a much contested issue and thus a major reason why no law formalized the 1924 change in policy until October 1946.[49]

Most normal school directors and directrices belonged to the prewar association founded by primary school inspectors but in late 1918 split from it to create their own association, citing differences in professional interests. In 1929 most of them voted to make their association a *syndicat* tied to the Fédération Générale de l'Enseignement and the CGT. Men still dominated the leadership of the postwar organizations, but some directrices were elected as officers or members of a central committee. Juliette Marie was the association's vice president from 1918 to 1925; Marie Privat was the secretary and then a central committee member from 1920 to 1925; and Emma Brugalières of Cahors became treasurer in 1923, replacing Marie-Louise Renaudet of Angers. Although a few men and women resigned from the professional group after the 1929 vote, the *syndicat* reported a membership of 166 (83 men, 83 women) in June 1930, 92 percent of all directors and directrices. For the 1934 elections to an enlarged Higher Council of Public Instruction (CSIP), the *syndicat* endorsed Yvonne Fabre, a secretary of the old association and member of the current central council. She was the first directrice on the CSIP since Eidenschenk's departure a decade earlier but not the only woman member.[50] Convinced of the value of labor organizations, a topic in lessons on economic sociology, some directrices made the SNI journal *L'École libératrice* available to students and encouraged them to

Directrices and Public Issues

The commitment to defending *laïcité* in public education remained prominent on the republican agenda after World War I. Yet there was noticeable disinterest in enforcing the controversial law of 1904 banning members of religious orders from teaching in private schools. Officials recognized that many nuns simply stopped wearing their habits and continued teaching, and in August 1914 the government halted enforcement of the 1904 law for the duration of the war. After 1918, other concerns loomed larger, including planning for and financing the extensive postwar reconstruction of devastated areas in northeastern France, the costs of which German reparations would only partly cover. Traditional republicans were also alarmed by the threat posed by the new French Communist party, founded in 1920. A new level of labor militancy, including that of public employees, added to existing divisions. Moreover, the rejoining of Alsace-Lorraine to France after forty-eight years of German control posed the problems of inspiring new loyalty to France and reckoning with the related issue of language in a largely German-speaking area where a movement for regional autonomy would develop. For education, the region presented special concerns because the republican legislation of 1879–86 did not apply in the three reunited departments, regulated by the Falloux law of 1850 before coming under German control in 1871. German schooling was organized along confessional lines, as with the Falloux law, and immediately discarding previous policy seemed unwise.[52]

Directrices' commitment to *laïcité* and their presentation of its significance to France's future teachers continued to figure in inspectors' reports after 1914. A directrice's Catholicism was sometimes noted but, as previously, education officials typically judged religious practice unproblematic if she maintained religious neutrality inside the normal school. In two instances, however, Catholic directrices were removed and transferred to different functions because of controversy about their religiosity. The first instance occurred during the war in the Aveyron department after Marie-Louise Buisson, directrice in Rodez since 1913, married the men's normal school director, widower Jacques Combes. An investigation was triggered by

202 WOMEN AND THE POLITICS OF EDUCATION IN FRANCE

her extended conflict with two professors and teachers in the *école annexe* over the question of whether moral instruction should be grounded in religion. Her approval of a student's practice lesson stating the necessity of a religious basis prompted the professors to lodge a complaint.[53]

The inspectors investigating the conflict contrasted Combes's conduct with that of her predecessor, a practicing Catholic who avoided such problems. An "agitated and aggressive temperament" was intensified, they opined, by her recent marriage, termed a "fusion of two clericalisms" by inspector general Jules Gal. Mme Combes was "a slave of narrow dogmatism," dangerous in public education, he wrote, and rector Jacques Cavalier of Toulouse agreed that her religious zeal surpassed the most benevolent interpretation of respect for neutrality. Cavalier recommended her transfer to a higher primary school without a boarding facility, and in August 1918 both Combes were reassigned to Chaumont (Haute-Marne), she as directrice of the higher primary school and he as an inspector. After the Catholic press criticized their transfer, departmental inspector Oscar Auriac reminded a representative of Catholic educators that practicing Catholics headed a majority of girls' public schools in the Aveyron, adding that attending mass was not the reason for moving the Combes.[54]

The second Catholic directrice unhappy to be relocated was Blanche Valin, in charge of the normal school in Blois in the Loir-et-Cher, her department of origin, after she left Épinal in 1920. Departmental inspector Bernard soon noted that she tried to be a "director of conscience" for students, later reporting that her beliefs and especially her religious practice were much discussed and alarming to republican officials and educators who feared an increase in the number of Davidées (Catholic women teachers challenging *laïcité*) in public education. The department's general council voted a unanimous protest against Valin in 1923 and planned to withhold credits for expanding the normal school as long as she remained. Her students looked like "little nuns," one inspector general complained, and Bernard opined that she believed that she alone knew "the truth." Instead of her dogmatism, Bernard wrote, students needed a directrice who encouraged a free examination of ideas.[55]

Valin was reassigned in 1924 to inspect schools in Bordeaux. Her formal protest, encouraged by a Catholic teachers' organization, the Union Nationale des Membres de l'Enseignement Public, was finally reviewed in 1927 by the Comité Consultatif de l'Enseignement Public, which concluded unanimously that her actions were incompatible with a normal school directrice's obligation to maintain religious neutrality. The Committee also found that she had lied sometimes about reasons for absences from the school if she was attending religious retreats. In 1929, however, Valin returned to directing a normal school, Sélestat in the Bas-Rhin, designated for Catholic students in Alsace. The department's other women's normal school in Strasbourg was for Protestants. Valin's opinions were in harmony with the Alsatian milieu and, judged inspector general Fernand Gazin in 1931, probably excessively so. Nonetheless the "profoundly mystical" Valin did agree to suppress the collective communion that dated from the years of German control and obligatory religious practice.[56]

Valin was the third directrice for Sélestat, appointed after the death of Hélène Bigey. Blanche Gambey, in 1919 the first directrice, had been reassigned after three years because of conflict involving religion, but in this case she was the target of "violent attacks" by hostile Catholics. Although she won support from most, but not all, professors and teachers in the normal school, which also had two-year preparatory classes, she clashed with the school's *aumônier* (chaplain), who tried to influence students through the confessional. Unlike normal schools in other French departments, those in Alsace had chaplains because of the Falloux law. Gambey also encountered difficulty with the nuns who ran the enterprise supplying food to the school, particularly when she tried to introduce more typically French dishes. In a psychology class on the topic of perception, she reportedly suggested that psychologists would consider the visions of St. Theresa of Avila and St. Francis of Assisi to be hallucinations. Local Catholic leaders demanded Gambey's departure in 1922, as did the rector of Strasbourg, Sébastien Charléty, who wanted to calm the situation but admitted that she had not violated the status of a confessional school.[57] For the normal school in Metz (Moselle department), opened in 1928, the education ministry selected Germaine Martin, a practicing Catholic previously assigned to Miliana (Alger), where she had often displayed copies of religious art.[58]

At the normal school for Protestants in Strasbourg, Blanche Maucourant, the first directrice, was from a Catholic background but encountered no serious problems. She requested the post, she explained, because she wanted to help bring the republican ideals of Ferry and Pécaut to the region. In August 1919, she organized a special program, held at the Seine-et-Oise normal school, to give 110 Alsatian women teachers familiarity with French history, culture, and especially language.[59] Such programs for Alsatian teachers and normal school students continued, and by 1932, 3,200 teachers also had spent up to a year working with a teacher in another French department. To further the replacement of German by French, the education ministry assigned about 1,500 teachers from other departments to the Bas-Rhin, Haut-Rhin, and Moselle. Alsatian primary school students would first learn French and later receive instruction in German.[60]

When Maucourant became an inspectress general of *écoles maternelles* in 1931, the administration sought a Protestant replacement, but the first choice, Amélie Hui, declined, explaining that she no longer had a religious affiliation and would be uncomfortable working with a Protestant chaplain.[61] Jeanne Dollé accepted the post. The Strasbourg school, like the region's Catholic normal schools, had to include religion on the entry examination for prospective students, a requirement drawing national attention in 1932 when the mayor of Guebwiller asked whether his daughter could be excused from that part of the exam because she had no religious affiliation. No, the rector replied, that segment was obligatory.[62] The normal schools of Sélestat and Strasbourg had no Jewish students when France assumed control, and the religious component was a barrier for Jewish students, who faced no such test for the laic normal schools in other French departments.[63] The attempt of the Cartel des Gauches to introduce the laic laws in Alsace had sparked massive protests by Catholics, who demonstrated in Strasbourg and Mulhouse in July 1924 and kept children home from school on March 16, 1925, to protest the creation of inter-confessional schools if municipalities requested them. Since then governments had not tried to alter the region's educational status quo. Only a small minority of municipalities asked for religiously mixed public schools, and most Alsatian parents did not request excusing children from religious instruction.[64]

Apart from the exceptional situation in Alsace, republican officials remained committed to *laïcité* in public schools. Thus the Davidées, cited in Valin's file, were watched closely for signs of influence on women's normal schools and teachers. Their name came from René Bazin's novel *Davidée Birot* (1912), the story of a young teacher's struggle to overcome her normal school professor's insistence that moral instruction did not require a religious basis. The first group of teachers to identify with the heroine's embrace of Catholic spirituality emerged in the Basses-Alpes. They held their first retreat in 1916, also attended by ten teachers from the Drôme, and soon had a monthly bulletin, *Aux Davidées*.[65] Republican and socialist critics, such as syndicalist Marceau Pivert, insisted that they objected not to the Davidées' religious practice but to bringing into classrooms views inconsistent with the official curriculum. For example, one issue of *Aux Davidées* advised teachers to mention God as the creator and first cause in science and geography lessons about the origins of the earth and life. By 1930, according to one estimate, the Davidées numbered perhaps eight thousand and included recruits in secondary schools.[66]

Vigilant normal school directrices thus watched for signs of support for the Davidées, particularly active in the southeast. In the Basses-Alpes, reported the departmental inspector in 1929, directrice Suzanne Paul helped students develop an "esprit critique" that should deflect them from "extremist" groups like the Davidées. Directrice Berthe Parayre in Aix, another center of Davidées' organizing, indicated in 1931 that only two of one hundred current students openly supported them, but she had heard that some graduates were entering religious orders. In Valence (Drôme), reported the rector of Grenoble, Antoinette Cuminal stopped a professor at the girls' collège from proselytizing among normal school students. Farther north in Besançon, directrice Échard combated efforts to form a group in her school, and in the neighboring Jura, directrice Alphonsine Sélince worked to limit the influence of a lycée professor trying to draw normal school students to the Davidées. Unsurprisingly, directrice Omnès in the very Catholic Vendée also reported reprimanding a student whose proselytizing upset the calm in the normal school. In conservative Normandy, the Catholic press attacked directrice Thérèse Hue in Alençon for her laic views and sharp critique of Davidées.[67]

While the Davidées tried to win over women in public education, supporters of Catholic private schools continued the familiar combat against public schools, especially in western France. Interwar governments, in turn, supported *laïcité* but often ignored the ban on religious teachers in private schools. In Brittany and the West, as Jean Peneff noted, a "civil war" of words was raging again by 1925 when an estimated 80,000 people in the Loire-Inférieure gathered to hear General Édouard de Castelnau, founder of the Fédération Nationale Catholique, call for ending the laic laws. A majority of pupils in four Breton departments then attended private primary schools, and the Vendée and the other three Breton departments were among the next six departments with the highest private school enrollments. For all of France the statistic for pupils' enrollment in private schools was 19 percent.[68]

In Brittany, normal school directrices continued to work to protect public schooling and the Republic itself by emphasizing the values of democracy

206   WOMEN AND THE POLITICS OF EDUCATION IN FRANCE

and *laïcité* as they trained future teachers. Eugénie Morel, in Saint-Brieuc from 1914 to 1925, won officials' praise for her influence in a milieu where teachers had to be on guard against "mystical" tendencies, and she was similarly appreciated in her next Breton post in Rennes. In Vannes, Amélie Hui regularly tried to promote tolerance by alerting students to the importance of loyalty to the "État laïque," part of the curriculum on professional values. Berthe Fassou's leadership in Quimper from 1926 to 1933 was pronounced a success in a "difficult, agitated" milieu. After Amélie Beunot arrived in Vannes, her first directing post, to replace Hui who retired, she had to deal with two fervent Catholic professors' proselytizing with students. The inspector general reviewing her work in 1939 recognized her efforts in a school where "l'état laïque" had become troubled, but he also reported that she somewhat upset "la pudeur bretonne" (Breton sense of propriety) and would likely do better in the southwest, where the population's "psychology" was more like hers.[69] Not only in Brittany but also elsewhere in France in the later 1930s, as political tensions mounted, inspectors more frequently added comments on directrices' support of *laïcité* to evaluations of pedagogical and administrative competence.

Different issues of religion, as well as ethnicity and language, complicated the functioning of public education in the three departments of colonial Algeria. The longstanding challenges for French teachers in classrooms with pupils from various ethnic backgrounds continued, as a 1908 graduate of the Vendée normal school reported from Oran in 1934, noting how hard it was "to transform into *petits Français les petits vagabonds Espagnols, Arabes, Italiens, Maltais* who prefer the street and sunshine to school."[70] Unlike young Muslim men long able to enroll in a section of the men's normal school in Alger, only a handful of young Muslim women entered a normal school after World War I. The example of Nafissa Sid-Cara, whose father was a teacher, would eventually become noteworthy. She entered the normal school in Constantine in 1928, taught *indigène* girls, and later became the first Muslim woman in a French cabinet, appointed during the early Fifth Republic in 1959, as the Algerian War raged. She remembered that directrice Félicie Muraccioli welcomed her "in an appropriate environment" and had confidence in her, and she believed that Muraccioli wanted to demonstrate that an *indigène* woman could teach effectively and thereby honor the work of France in Algeria.[71] Nonetheless, the schooling of Muslim children still lagged far behind that of Europeans and was far more limited for girls than boys.[72]

OLD ISSUES, NEW CHALLENGES   207

The hostility of much of the European population in Algeria to the designation of indigenous Jews as French, always present since 1870, remained problematic as well. Indeed, republican politicians in Algeria were often antisemitic, but officials from France had to work with them. Directrice Muraccioli and teachers in the normal school's *école d'application* supported an after-school *patronage*, competing with one run by Catholics, and needed the backing of Émile Morinaud, an antisemitic deputy, longtime mayor of Constantine, and undersecretary for physical education in two French cabinets between 1930 and 1932. In Oran in 1929, when normal school directrice Georgette Raynaud, appointed in 1922, planned to marry a Jewish businessman, she anticipated the need to resign because the city government was notoriously antisemitic. City council members reassured her, however, and she remained. For a time education officials closely monitored her situation, an inspector general reporting in November 1930 that her marriage had not led to any public incidents. The departmental inspector also confirmed in 1931 that there was no reduction of her authority in either the school or the city. Her position, like that of two Jewish directrices in France, would change under the Vichy regime.[73]

As directrices defended the Republic and its secular policies, those who were feminists continued to argue that the right to vote would enhance women's advocacy for other important social reforms. Feminists had put campaigning on hold during the war, and postwar local organizing often required efforts to revive older groups or create new ones. Some directrices shared in the widespread expectations for success after the Chamber of Deputies, by a vote of 329 to 95, passed a bill to enfranchise women in May 1919. Thus Émilie Flayol, the prewar secretary of the UFSF group in Privas (Ardèche), informed UFSF secretary general Cécile Brunschvicg in December 1919 that she hoped to start a group in her new post, La Rochelle (Charente-Inférieure), which lacked one. Bemoaning the apparent waning of interest in suffrage in Privas, she soon reported, as secretary of a La Rochelle group, a membership of 150.[74]

Brunschvicg, of course, had resumed contact with local UFSF leaders, including previously supportive directrices like Annette Bringuier in Perpignan. Émilie Périères, secretary of the Landes group in 1914, would lead a new one in the Tarn when she was promoted to directrice.[75] Sarah Goron, also a prewar leader as a professor in Foix, maintained involvement as that school's directrice in 1926. Not all prewar supporters returned to the cause, however. Sophie Schreck, the former vice president in Caen, cited her

208   WOMEN AND THE POLITICS OF EDUCATION IN FRANCE

poor health, the burdens of her job, and imminent retirement to explain why she could not be active in 1923. When Brunschvicg tried to recruit the new directrice in Quimper, Jeanne Huber-Fortin, to revive a group whose prewar president, directrice Suzanne Pingaud, had retired, Huber-Fortin replied that in a Breton milieu unfavorable to the suffragist cause and where public education had many determined enemies she, as directrice, could not assume a "militant" position if she wished to avoid local distrust.[76]

The Senate's refusal to debate the Chamber's suffrage bill in 1922 dismayed feminists but also left many resolved to continue building their organizations and to press legislators to act. Because republican opponents still argued that women's suffrage could heighten a "clerical peril," presumably because Catholic women would vote as priests instructed them and thereby endanger the Republic's survival, La Française was pleased to report in June 1923 that a prominent moderate republican, Pierre Flandin, refuted that major argument in a recent speech.[77] Anti-suffrage claims about women and the "clerical peril" persisted, however. The UFSF, which had 12–14,000 members in 1914, drew 100,000 by 1929 and boosted the number of its groups and sections from 80 in 1923 to more than 150 in 1926 and 200 in 1927. The smaller LFDF reportedly grew from 1,000 to 25,000. Moreover, the Conseil National des Femmes Françaises (CNFF), the umbrella organization for charitable, professional, and feminist groups, saw membership increase from 100,000 in 1914 to 250,000 by 1932.[78]

A Catholic suffrage organization, the Union Nationale pour le Vote des Femmes (UNVF), founded in 1920, had only a few thousand members in 1926 but claimed 100,000 by the late 1930s. Complaining that the older suffrage groups' advocacy of equality between the sexes was excessive, the UNVF refused in 1929 to participate in an Estates General of Feminism organized by the CNFF and UFSF to draw public attention to women's issues. Although the secular feminist groups announced growing memberships, their numbers did not match the one million claimed by the Catholic and non-feminist Ligue Patriotique des Françaises, dating from 1902.[79] Whether or not women identified themselves as feminists, their participation in numerous associations dedicated to philanthropy, social reform, and even politics remained wide-ranging and impressive during the interwar years.[80]

Reports that normal school directrices and professors, like primary school teachers and secondary professors, supported women's suffrage and other feminist goals continued to appear frequently in La Française, edited by Brunschvicg since 1926. Local UFSF leaders sent her information about their groups' activities and lists of members. Some normal school alumnae bulletins also recorded directrices' feminist views. At least 18 directrices named before 1914 belonged to interwar UFSF groups, and at least 6 were officers. Marie-Eugénie Prieur-Lacroix, directrice in the Corrèze since 1890, delayed active involvement until she retired in 1923, after which she and her sister, a retired teacher, started a group in Tulle, persuading many of their former students to join. In 1929 she also enlisted the support of the department's association of war widows, thereby adding 1,400 members.[81] Lucie Saffroy, in retirement, was a vice president and then member of the LFDF central committee from 1920 to 1926, and Marthe Janin remained an honorary member of the central committee until her death in 1935. Among directrices appointed during and after the war, at least 36 (30 percent) were UFSF members, 17 of them also serving as officers or on local coordinating committees. At least two gave support to the LFDF: Marguerite Jacquot, honorary president in Le Mans, and Jeanne Chauvin in Amiens, where normal school professor Huguette Lallemant was the local group's president. Seven others spoke favorably about feminism to their students, normal school alumnae associations, or local women's groups. About half of interwar directrices can thus be linked to feminist views and organizations, and there may well have been others for whom records about feminist leanings are lacking.[82]

How might directrices convey a feminist message? Lessons on women's roles in the family and society, part of the sociology course, could easily prompt discussion of votes for women and other legal issues, particularly with the use of Hesse and Gleyze's popular textbook. Just as maintaining neutrality dictated that educators should not use the classroom to advocate support for a particular religion or political party, so they needed to take care about discussing feminist organizations. Meetings of normal school alumnae associations (*amicales*) were a different matter. In Blois, directrice Anaïs Berthelet spoke to alumnae in 1927 about "féminisme," noting that some newspapers and reviews regularly distorted and ridiculed it. "We are all feminists, even without knowing it," she asserted, "because we all care about society, we all want to develop our judgment and critical intelligence and that of our students, and that is the basis of feminism." Feminists wanted women to have the rights that they were fully capable of exercising, she stated. Mme Guichard, the *amicale* president, then urged fellow teachers to join the local UFSF group.[83]

210 WOMEN AND THE POLITICS OF EDUCATION IN FRANCE

On some occasions, alumnae associations invited students, or at least third-year students, to attend functions, as in 1925 in Saint-Brieuc for the farewell dinner for Eugénie Morel, just appointed directrice in Rennes. She had been president of the local UFSF group, whose members included other women from the normal school as well as the men's normal school director, Max Hébert. At the dinner she spoke about civic and social education for women and recommended reading *La Française*.[84] Talks by prominent suffrage leaders also attracted attendees from normal schools. In 1928 directrice Bringuier's students in Perpignan responded enthusiastically to Brunschvicg, giving her a standing ovation.[85]

The newsletters of alumnae associations also sometimes published articles on feminism, reports on local lectures by feminists, and notices about the UFSF and LFDF. In Poitiers, directrice Yvonne Fabre, who arrived in 1924, encouraged the start of an alumnae association with a "Bulletin" that included a "Tribune libre" for opinion pieces about women's status in society. The third issue in 1927 featured two teachers discussing their support for feminism, and later articles advocated women's suffrage and removal of legal disabilities affecting married women. In 1928 the *amicale* sent a demand for women's suffrage to all of the Vienne's legislators and legislative candidates, and it asked teachers' *syndicats* to take similar action in each department. Five years later the newsletter reported that directrice Marguerite Chardon, Fabre's successor, was president of the Poitiers UFSF group of 200, noting that the UFSF welcomed members from all political and religious persuasions.[86] Similarly, the alumnae bulletin of the Haute-Savoie normal school offered articles on feminism and suffrage during the 1930s.[87]

Students also contributed to some alumnae association newsletters. Their reports on student performances at the normal school or trips taken at the end of the third year of study were common; their opinion pieces on feminist topics appeared less often. A second-year student at the normal school in Mende (Lozère) reported in 1932 on a well-attended talk by a young woman lawyer whose arguments for women's suffrage effectively demolished those of opponents. Although the subject was not "unknown" to students, she wrote, they enjoyed attending the event outside the school, presided over by the mayor, and they hoped that the speaker had made "conversions" among men in the audience.[88] Jeanne Ithurbide, previously active in the UFSF in Angoulême, was then the directrice in Mende. At another southcentral normal school, Cahors in the Lot, an older directrice, Emma Brugalières, president of the local UFSF group, was the titular editor and administrator of a newsletter started by third-year students. In twenty issues published between 1930 and 1932 they reported on recently published books; school events like a trip to Paris for the colonial exposition of 1931; and local lectures by feminists Germaine Malaterre-Sellier, Brunschvicg, and Marcelle Capy, and the author Colette.[89]

Under the title "What Does Youth Want?" directrice Suzanne Paul presented her normal school students' opinions about important current issues, including feminism, in 1934. Her three articles in the *Manuel général de l'instruction primaire*, still widely read by teachers, drew on essays written by students in Digne (Basses-Alpes) for their sociology class. Paul had asked them to discuss their aspirations and fears and to indicate whether they were content with the place reserved for them in the family, schools, and society. Lively class discussions took place. Students did not show "a violent desire for reform," Paul reported, but they did hope for changes and were eager to become part of society and make an impact on it. Many envisioned a society where all could enjoy an adequate standard of living, and some from modest backgrounds criticized capitalism and called for redistribution of wealth, although they did not call themselves "communistes." Those from farming families who owned some land and a house were "more conservative" and defended their heritage. Also "resolutely feminist," these young women wanted the vote and an end to legal restrictions on married women. Senators opposed to women's suffrage were "old and backward," one student wrote. Students also viewed women's inexperience in politics not as an "inferiority" but as a guarantee of their sincerity and unselfish motives, which could help revive faith in the Republic. Eager to follow national and international events and to understand the policies advocated by major political parties, students read newspapers, attended lectures, and were no longer "séminaristes" isolated from a larger world, Paul concluded.[90]

In early 1936, nineteen months after Paul's articles appeared, directrice Ithurbide, now in Bourges, assessed the prospects for "feminism and suffrage" in *La Française* and was less certain than Paul about young women's interest. As a student at the normal school in Angoulême from 1912 to 1916, she had encountered directrice Frugier and professor Thimer, both feminists, and when she returned to the school in 1922 as a professor, she became an officer in the reconstituted UFSF group that included Frugier, then retired, as vice president. Fifteen years ago, she commented, the vote for women seemed "revolutionary," at least in provincial settings where it was perceived as an aspect of a scandalous "modernism" and contrary to women's natural domestic

212   WOMEN AND THE POLITICS OF EDUCATION IN FRANCE

vocation. Public opinion, she believed, now saw women's suffrage as less dangerous, although it was not yet a reality in France and still faced a "masculine egotism" resistant to full equality for women. In effect, she opined, the French feminist movement seemed to have surpassed its goal without reaching it. Women now engaged in a wider range of professional and social roles than previously, but many women leading more active lives, especially younger women, apparently saw the vote as less important for their interests.[91]

Such views, Ithurbide remarked, were also indicative of declining respect for the parliamentary system in some political quarters. Furthermore, when women did join political parties, loyalty to a party might outweigh support for feminism. She named no specific party but was voicing the kind of critique often made of Socialist and Communist women who insisted that the class struggle took primacy over women's issues, and also of women who joined the leading republican party, the Radicals, once membership was open to women in 1924. Although many men in the Radical party opposed votes for women, Brunschvicg and some other moderate feminists had joined it in the hope of winning over more men to their cause, their decision also drawing feminist criticism. Many women remained confused about the question of suffrage, Ithurbide concluded, but were still likely to follow the upcoming elections in 1936 closely. Her own hope was for a "feminine front" focused on peace and social renovation, not party slogans.[92]

The election alluded to by Ithurbide occurred against the backdrop of a decade marked by economic crisis, mounting concerns about threats to international peace posed by dictators Adolf Hitler in Germany and Mussolini in Italy, and the growth in France of rightwing movements hostile to the Third Republic. In reaction to the massive rightwing demonstrations and street riots against the Republic on February 6, 1934, the CGT called for a one-day strike on February 12, in which thousands of teachers (but almost no normal school directors or directrices) participated.[93] To defend the Republic, Radicals, Socialists, and Communists formed an unprecedented political coalition, the Popular Front, which won the bitterly fought election of 1936. Socialists and Radicals then formed a cabinet, with the backing of Communists, who did not join it. Léon Blum became France's first Socialist, and also first Jewish, premier. Antisemites who had already churned up hostility to the arrival of Jewish refugees from Nazi Germany alleged that Blum's religious identity made him un-French. Faced with massive strikes by workers suffering from the Depression of the 1930s, Blum in June 1936 announced major innovations in economic and social policy,

OLD ISSUES, NEW CHALLENGES 213

sometimes termed a French "New Deal": a forty-hour work week, paid vacations, and government involvement in collective bargaining. In August the age for completing compulsory schooling was extended from thirteen to fourteen.[94]

Blum also took the unprecedented step of appointing three women undersecretaries in the Popular Front ministries of education and health. Their appointments were heralded in the general press and in women educators' publications. Jeanne Hirtz, directrice in the Haute-Saône and an officer in the local UFSF group, called the "trois femmes au ministère" a new triumph for "la cause féminine," reminding readers of her school's alumnae *Bulletin* that Brunschvicg, undersecretary in the education ministry, had twice spoken in Vesoul. As president of the Fontenay alumnae association since 1933, Hirtz invited Brunschvicg to speak at its May 1937 meeting, and she reported in the Fontenay *Bulletin* that Brunschvicg's advocacy for children's welfare and appointment of more women to administrative posts well illustrated the value of having a woman placed in the corridors of power. Yet women's suffrage did not advance under the Popular Front, the resistance of many Radical republicans again blocking action.[95] Directrice Morel remained hopeful, however, telling a large audience celebrating the Rennes normal school's fifty years of existence in May 1937 that it was not "too daring" for women to seek "full civic rights" and want to play "an equal role" with men in public life.[96] The collapse of Blum's government in June 1937 ended the tenure of Brunschvicg and undersecretary of health Suzanne Lacore, a retired teacher and Socialist; Irène Joliot-Curie had resigned in 1936. Brunschvicg's inclusion in the cabinet was recognition of her prominence in advocating women's rights, but by 1936 many UFSF local groups reported declining memberships.[97]

By the time that Blum took office in June 1936, public awareness of threats to the preservation of peace in Europe and beyond had heightened. In the wake of the bloodletting of the Great War, many French citizens, like citizens of other countries, hoped that the postwar League of Nations could prevent future wars, and many embraced pacifism, represented by sometimes competing organizations. Most French educators shared such hopes, as did most feminists.[98] The Fontenay *Bulletin* featured articles urging support for the League of Nations by inspectress general Angles and, like departmental normal school alumnae bulletins, publicized the pacifist group founded in 1928 by retired directrice Eidenschenk, whose only son was killed in combat in 1916.[99]

214 WOMEN AND THE POLITICS OF EDUCATION IN FRANCE

As president of the Ligue Internationale des Mères et des Éducatrices pour la Paix (LIMEP, League of Mothers and Women Educators for Peace), Eidenschenk sent circulars to all normal school directrices, asking them to encourage professors and students to join the Ligue. An LIMEP flier mailed with the December 1931 issue of the Fontenay *Bulletin*—which also featured Eidenschenk's article on the LIMEP and hopes for disarmament— soon provoked controversy. One journalist complained that the LIMEP exemplified the pacifist illusions of many teachers in the SNI. Minister of air Paul Painlevé wrote to Fontenay directrice Grauvogel to chastise her for the "anti-French" project, prompting her reply that she did not control the alumnae *Bulletin*.[100] In the aftermath, Eidenschenk resigned as president of the Fontenay association. Forging links with the Ligue Internationale des Femmes pour la Paix et la Liberté, Eidenschenk claimed 65,000 members for the LIMEP in 1932 and 100,000 in 1938. In May 1936 she joined representatives of other peace organizations speaking at a "day of peace" in Arras where many World War I soldiers were buried in cemeteries.[101]

The normal school directrices active in the LIMEP included Marcelle Dudon in Nice, who spoke on "Peace through Education" at the southeastern UFSF conference in 1930 and continued public advocacy of pacifism and feminism after retiring in 1931. Similarly, Jeanne Palanque represented the LIMEP after she retired from the normal school in Aix and moved to the Gard.[102] In the Basses-Alpes, Suzanne Paul informed alumnae about LIMEP goals and offered to collect membership forms, action complementing her article in the *Manuel Général* urging teachers to convey the necessity of international cooperation to maintain peace to schoolchildren.[103] The normal school alumnae bulletins for Clermont-Ferrand, Orléans, and Rennes were also among those publicizing the LIMEP.[104] Directrice Marthe Flamant in Laon, an LIMEP member, drew the ire of a local newspaper by attending a pacifist meeting in 1933, the *Tablettes de l'Aisne* dubbing her "a canteen woman for the Germans." Although the attack infuriated the departmental branch of the SNI, the prefect complained to the education ministry that being seen at such public gatherings was problematic for a directrice.[105]

Anxieties about the deepening political divisions in France coexisted with fears caused by major international crises: Mussolini's conquest of Ethiopia in 1935, ignoring condemnation by the League of Nations; Hitler's remilitarization of the Rhineland in 1936, defying the Treaty of Versailles, and annexation of Austria in March 1938; and the ongoing civil war in Spain, launched in July 1936 by a military rebellion against the republican government. Directrice Ithurbide's comment in 1936 about declining respect for the parliamentary system mirrored many educators' concerns. In editions of Hesse and Gleyze's sociology textbook in the later 1930s an appendix cited "events that have disrupted economic and political life" and warned that fascism, Hitlerism, and Communism did not respect individual liberties as democracies did.[106]

After the disturbing rightwing actions in February 1934, teachers and normal school directrices were among the republican and Socialist women who joined the new Action Démocratique et Laïque des Femmes (ADLF, Women's Democratic and Laic Action), founded by secondary school professor Marguerite Schwab, a member of the CSIP and active in the Radical party and UFSF. *La Française* presented it in March 1934 as a group of "feminists of the left," an indication of some members' Socialist sympathies. The ADLF's primary goal was to bolster support for the beleaguered Republic, but feminist arguments also figured in attempts to enlist women's participation. In February 1935 Schwab, ADLF president, asked premier Flandin to urge reluctant senators to support women's suffrage.[107] She and Pauline Rebour, ADLF secretary general and veteran feminist, made similar approaches to Popular Front leaders. Membership in the ADLF probably never reached more than a few thousand, according to reports in its newsletter. Among the normal school directrices supporting it were the pre-1914 appointees Hui, founder of a section in Vannes, and Stolzenberg, president of the Montpellier group; former directrices Évard and Géraud, who became inspectresses general of *écoles maternelles*; and interwar colleagues Cuminal (Privas), Jeanne Fraysse-Auriol (Paris), François (Charleville), Gaillard (Tours), Hue (Alençon), Poujade (Épinal), Marie Soboul (Nîmes), Henriette Sourgen (Bordeaux), and inspectress general Angles.[108]

Directrice Soboul emphasized the ADLF's commitment to women's rights and more civic education for the exercise of those rights when she addressed its Gard section in November 1935. Because antidemocratic groups had mounted aggressive efforts to attract women, it was imperative, she warned, that women learn more about the functioning of government, society, and the economy. The ADLF, she stated, tried to strike a balance between "antisocial individualism" and the good of the larger society as it alerted women to the dangers of the fascist "mystique of a collective national spirit, the dangerous use of collective enthusiasm." Alumnae of the Nîmes normal school could read the text of Soboul's talk in their *Bulletin*.[109]

216   WOMEN AND THE POLITICS OF EDUCATION IN FRANCE

The ADLF newsletter detailed departmental sections' activities, citing normal school directrices' role in recruiting members and service as national or local officers. Directrice Gaillard, president of the group in Tours, echoed Soboul's concerns when she reported in 1937 that in a "city very restless since 1934" her group was competing with other organizations for members, and she singled out the women's section of the Parti Social Français (PSF) as an antidemocratic, anti-laic organization that used the appeal of its social services to influence women.[110] Her characterization of the PSF, the successor of the rightwing veterans' group Croix de Feu, was appropriate, for its women's section attracted far more members than the women's groups of any other political party, reportedly reaching more than 100,000 by 1939.[111] The ADLF newsletter also indicated the range of issues addressed at its annual meetings, publishing Gaillard's report on young women's civic education prepared for the December 1936 meeting, a summation of directrice François's report in 1937 on children's status in democracies, and directrice Sourgen's recommendations on social work education in 1938.[112]

How realistic were educators' hopes for maintaining peace in Europe by the late 1930s? After Hitler made demands on Czechoslovakia in 1938, heightening the possibility of war, the Ligue des Femmes pour la Paix circulated a petition in early September opposing another "massacre of our sons, our companions, our brothers." Eidenschenk, acting for the LIMEP, was among the first signers.[113] War was averted on September 30 at the Munich conference, the high point of the appeasement policy favored by British prime minister Neville Chamberlain and seconded by French premier Édouard Daladier. In retrospect, historians have typically judged as naïve the British-French acceptance of Hitler's assurances that he would make no more demands after Munich. Yet at the time, many citizens haunted by memories of the Great War felt relief.

In that context, it is understandable that leaders of the Poitiers normal school's alumnae association, of which directrice Chardon was an honorary member, sent Daladier a letter in October 1938 to applaud the preservation of peace.[114] The ADLF newsletter had featured Gaillard's talk at the Congrès national de la paix in Tours in May 1938, and soon after Munich, Schwab asked her to write about reactions to the pact with Hitler. Citing her anxieties before the pact was concluded, Gaillard reported that students and their parents now celebrated the maintenance of peace. Although she admitted to wondering whether the pact was honorable, she consoled herself by remembering that a war would be worse than anything else.[115] Historian

Antoine Prost, commenting on interwar educators' pacifism, aptly described it as "a kind of desperate rationalism," a rejection of violence to the point of no longer seeing where it actually was.[116]

Hopes for maintaining peace were dashed on September 3, 1939 when, in reaction to Nazi Germany's invasion of Poland on September 1, France and Great Britain declared war on Germany. The war necessarily disrupted the start of the school year, and normal schools in border areas were relocated. In the wake of the French defeat and armistice in June 1940, a majority of legislators voted in July to end the Third Republic and approved a new government led by Marshal Philippe Pétain, who had replaced Paul Reynaud as premier. Pétain's collaborationist regime, headquartered in Vichy in southcentral France, soon announced new plans for public education, including the normal schools. Once implemented, the Vichy's regime's policies would disrupt the careers of many normal school directrices who had believed in and loyally defended the Third Republic.

Epilogue

Beyond the Third Republic

After Nazi Germany's defeat of France in 1940, the French public sought explanations, and the collaborationist Vichy regime selectively provided them. Instead of faulting military leaders for poor planning for the use of equipment and manpower, Vichy claimed that republican and leftist politicians and also the Third Republic's teachers had demoralized the country and sapped the will to fight.[1] Yet the fact that 26,000 male teachers were among the soldiers quickly mobilized in 1939 indicates that their prewar pacifism did not diminish their patriotism.[2] Nonetheless, as Marshal Philippe Pétain and Pierre Laval, the first Vichy premier, began ushering in an authoritarian "national revolution" committed to "work, family, country" rather than the Republic's "liberty, equality, fraternity," they made changing primary education a major goal. The realities of German occupation of more than half of France limited Vichy's freedom of action from the start, but the French administration headquartered in the southcentral resort town of Vichy continued to function in both the occupied northern zone and unoccupied southern zone. Retired directrice Albertine Eidenschenk, shortly before her death in 1942, would privately characterize Vichy as a "bastard of the old regime and [the] 2 December" coup of 1851 by Louis Napoleon Bonaparte.[3]

Changes in the training of teachers were central to Vichy's educational policy, which also included rescinding the 1904 law barring members of religious orders from teaching in private schools and, to deemphasize *laïcité*, reintroducing the teaching of "duties to God" in primary and higher primary schools. Because Vichy leaders regarded the Third Republic's normal schools as incubators of leftwing and antipatriotic sentiments, the decree-law of September 19, 1940, announced their suppression, effective as of October 1941. Instead, teachers' academic preparation would be in secondary schools and lead to the baccalauréat. Their pedagogical training would occur in a

EPILOGUE   219

ten-month program that included courses offered in sixty-six *instituts de formation professionnelle* (IFP) where some, but not all, of the former normal school personnel continued to work. The restructured training for primary school teachers somewhat resembled the previous plans of supporters of an *école unique* and Popular Front education minister Jean Zay, but without their egalitarian emphasis. Zay had wanted to give primary school teachers more access to the "culture générale" prized for the secondary school system and thus improve their status; Vichy wished to insulate future teachers from republican and socialist notions and emphasized conservative values.[4] Unsurprisingly, Vichy also dissolved the teachers' national *syndicat*, one of the professional associations of civil servants targeted by the law of October 15, 1940.

The closing of normal schools in 1941 affected the careers of their directors and professors, male and female. Some received other appointments, usually in school inspection or in higher primary schools, which Vichy retitled "collèges modernes" in 1941. Those who were Jewish, like Jews in other areas of public administration, were removed under the terms of the law of October 3, 1940. The law of October 11, 1940, concerning women's work, presented as a measure to combat unemployment, called for retiring all women civil servants at the age of fifty and all married women civil servants whose husbands' income was adequate to support a family. It was a policy in keeping with Vichy's emphasis on the traditional primacy of women's domestic roles.[5] Among the 2,500 educators affected by Vichy's policies of removal for political and religious reasons and by its early retirements were some 350 women educators in normal schools.[6]

How did the 89 normal school directrices serving in 1939 fare under Vichy? The 2 Jewish directrices were retired, as were 27 other directrices ranging in age from fifty to fifty-nine. The directrice in Oran, Georgette Tubiana, born in 1888, would later insist that her early retirement was also linked to her husband's Jewish identity. Another 24 directrices, all under age fifty, were reassigned to higher primary schools or primary school inspection, and 4 were promoted to the rank of inspectress general of *écoles maternelles*. Most of the 32 veteran directrices named to head the new institutes of professional formation (IFP) in 1941 were under age fifty. but 6 were older.[7]

Those six exceptions help explain why, after the war, Marguerite Moitessier, the Rouen normal school directrice forced to retire at age

220 WOMEN AND THE POLITICS OF EDUCATION IN FRANCE

fifty-three, would contend, as she sought to extend a new date for retirement in 1948, that Vichy had used its women's work law to remove personnel hostile to the regime. Political concerns also affected Vichy decisions about some reassignments for younger directrices. As officials in early 1941 considered a new role for Thérèse Hue, an outspoken defender of the Republic and *laïcité* in a Norman department, the rector (another official later revoked) tried to ensure that she received a new post by arguing that the main critique of her conduct would apply to many educators who had made controversial remarks during the last ten years. Hue became the directrice of a higher primary school, soon redesignated a collège moderne, in a different department but after the war returned to Alençon. In Angoulême the prefect defended Mathilde Mir when critics cited her previous aiding of republican refugees from the Spanish Civil War, noting that his predecessor had asked her to help them. He also admitted that her strong personality had made enemies. In 1942 she became a primary school inspectress elsewhere in the Charente.[8]

Hue and Mir were not the only directrices denounced to Vichy authorities. At the normal school in Nantes, a professor who had married a pro-Hitler German businessman before the war denounced Yvonne Bar, the directrice since 1931. Bar was reassigned in early 1941 to head the normal school in the Sarthe, and after its closing became the directrice of a collège in the Seine department. In Rodez (Aveyron) directrice Emma Météraud and her husband, a normal school professor, were both denounced for leftwing sympathies but in late 1940 still had support from the prefect and rector. After the normal schools closed, Emma Météraud directed a collège in Toulon. Inès Magnat was also denounced for Communist sympathies, even if not a party member, but the allegation did not end her direction of the new pedagogical institute (IFP) in Nîmes. Similarly, statements criticizing the closure of normal schools made by Lucie Malivert while directrice in Châteauroux did not prevent her from heading the IFP in Caen.[9]

In the personnel files of directrices serving in 1939–40, there is documentation for just one case of a directrice expressing support for the Vichy regime. This directrice, born in 1884 and retired from her post in Tarbes under the women's work law in 1941, praised Vichy's attitude toward religion, claiming that previously her religious practice had required an exercise of courage.[10] After the liberation of France in 1944, only two directrices of Vichy's professional institutes were compelled to undetgo a review of their political stances during the war, and neither was dismissed.[11]

EPILOGUE   221

Evidence of some directrices' support for the resistance against the Nazi occupation and the Vichy regime was added to personnel files after the war and also figured in various testimonials. Mathilde Mir took advantage of the travel authorized for her work as a school inspectress based in Cognac (Charente) to convey messages on behalf of the Organisation Civile et Militaire (O.C.M.) and to recruit teachers for resistance efforts. In late August 1944 she narrowly missed being arrested and executed by the Milice, Vichy's fascist paramilitary force.[12] Whereas Mir was active in the Vichy zone, Cécile François, directrice of the IFP in Arras, worked in the northeast under German occupation. She supported the activities of her husband Raoul, a former professor who led a regional group tied to the O.C.M. until his arrest in 1943 and execution in April 1944.[13] The husbands of two other directrices died in Germany after being deported: Raymond Brulé, a businessman and resistance leader whose wife Hélène inspected schools in the Manche department, where she had previously headed the normal school; and Charles Grandjeat, whose promotion to *inspecteur d'académie* in the Jura necessitated that this wife Joséphine, a directrice since 1932, take a leave from her reassignment to school inspection. Emma Météraud and her husband were in the resistance in Toulon.[14] In the Gard department, Marie Soboul, retired by Vichy, joined the Mouvement de Libération Nationale (M.L.N.), adopting the alias "Valerie."[15]

Several older directrices who had retired before the war were also recognized for supporting the resistance in ways that included passing on messages, providing temporary shelter, or burying the dead. In the town of Uzès in the Gard, septuagenarian Jeanne Palanque once vowed not to go outside until the reestablishment of the Republic, but she broke that pledge and, observed by curious onlookers, went out to welcome back from prison a teenaged girl, Évelyne Hammel (the future sociologist Évelyne Sullerot), who had been arrested for criticizing Pétain. After the war Radical republicans like Édouard Herriot recommended Palanque for the Legion of Honor.[16] The sister of retiree Berthe Parayre, Amélie Matisse (wife of painter Henri Matisse), was jailed because of resistance work, as was her daughter, who narrowly avoided deportation.[17] Among prewar directrices not active in resistance, it is likely that a number, whether they headed a wartime professional institute or held a different post, shared the sentiments expressed after the war by Jane Chevillard, relocated from the normal school in Angers to head the IFP in Rennes in 1941. Under Vichy, she told Rennes alumnae in 1947, she continued to try to develop students' ability to think independently.[18]

Directrices and Normal Schools on Postwar France

After the liberation of France in the summer of 1944, directrices forced to retire because of Vichy's women's work law began seeking readjustment of their service records in order to increase their pensions, and some sought reinstatement. Other directrices reassigned by Vichy to work in a different capacity also sometimes asked to return to the normal schools, which reopened in 1944 and 1945. Of the 27 directrices retired by Vichy, 13 obtained upward adjustments in retirement dates, which 4 others evidently did not request; 5 became inspectresses; and only 5 resumed directing a normal school. Jeanne Hirtz, the younger of the two dismissed Jewish directrices, asked not to return to Nancy. She ended her career in school inspection in Paris and was again president of the Fontenay alumnae association. Her older colleague, Constance Weill Douillet, was assigned briefly to a teaching post and retired in September 1945.[19] Twelve of the directrices reassigned by Vichy to other posts returned to directing a normal school, 8 remained in or moved to inspection posts, and 4 finished careers in secondary schools. Finally, the largest group of Third Republic directrices who headed postwar normal schools consisted of 29 of the 32 directrices of Vichy's professional institutes, 15 of them remaining in the same town or city.[20] By the end of 1945, 61 women's normal schools had reopened, 18 of them led by women not previously directrices.[21]

For some of the Third Republic's directrices, securing adjustments of their service records was easier to obtain than reinstatements, first authorized by an ordinance of October 2, 1943, issued in Algiers by Charles de Gaulle's provisional government. Alphonsine Sélince, born in 1890, asked to return to her post in the Jura in November 1944 and, receiving no response, appealed to the Conseil d'État in 1945. The minister of education, René Capitant, then informed the Conseil d'État that because the closing of normal schools in 1941 had led to the premature retirement of more than 350 women, restoring all of them to their former posts was problematic. Thus, as of May 1945, only about fifty professors or directrices who requested reintegration had been accommodated. Capitant believed, or wanted to believe, that most of the 350 women had readjusted their lives because their retirement seemed definitive in 1941 and so did not want to return to work. Sélince was finally reinstated as the directrice in Lons-le-Saunier in September 1945.[22]

In the case of Antoinette Cuminal, a widow forced by Vichy to retire at age fifty-four, Capitant denied her request to return to the normal school in the

EPILOGUE 223

Drôme because he wished to retain Jeanne Vèdrine, directrice there of the Vichy IFP. Instead, Cuminal became a school inspectress and retired in 1947. Similarly, Louise Gaillard became an inspectress in 1945 and did not return to the normal school in Tours, as she had requested, because the administration wanted that post for a younger directrice, Hélène Brulé, reassigned by Vichy to school inspection. Anna Roig, the prewar directrice in the Landes, also wanted to return to the normal school and protested that the inspection post offered instead would be too physically difficult. Eventually she accepted an adjustment of her retirement date from 1941 to 1946. Emma Météraud and Germaine Salducci also could not regain their normal school posts, but Salducci, downgraded by Vichy to professorial rank, had her status improved with an appointment to school inspection in Nice. Georgette Tubiana, resident in Algeria, returned to directing the Oran normal school in January 1944 but received no back pay for several years because some effects of the Vichy women's work law were not rectified until January 1946.[23]

Changes in the postwar political landscape affected the organization of the normal schools to which just over half (forty-six) of the last Third Republic directrices returned. Under De Gaulle's provisional government, the first national elections in October 1945 for a constitutional assembly indicated a pronounced shift to the left and rejection of the conservative forces associated with Vichy. Communists and Socialists each won about a quarter of the vote, and the Popular Republican Movement (MRP), a new party with a Catholic base, won another quarter. The makeup of a second constitutional assembly, elected in June 1946, was comparable. The Radical republicans, blamed by many for the military defeat in 1940, never regained their previous strength. Not surprisingly, the left-leaning coalition of parties favored reforms to correct the old structural and social barriers between primary and secondary education, hoping to build on the prewar plans for broader access to educational opportunity advocated by Jean Zay, who was murdered by the Milice in June 1944. Thus the postwar Fourth Republic retained the Vichy policy of having future primary school teachers first obtain the baccalauréat, and it extended the normal school from three to four years to provide adequate time for that academic preparation before a final year for professional training.

In postwar France, women finally possessed the right to vote and to hold elective office. The provisional government in Algiers had issued an ordinance supporting women's suffrage on April 21, 1944, and De Gaulle, head of the Committee of National Liberation, reaffirmed this on October 5. Women

224   WOMEN AND THE POLITICS OF EDUCATION IN FRANCE

voted for the first time in the April 29, 1945 municipal elections. By then, some former and current normal school directrices already had assumed roles in the organization of local affairs since the liberation, and some were also among the first women elected as municipal councilors and as mayors or deputy mayors (*adjoint[e]s*), who were chosen by fellow council members.

Among the retired directrices elected to office were Hélène Odoul, mayor of Ruynes-en-Margeride in Cantal; Jeanne Palanque, the first postwar mayor of Uzès (Gard) for two years; and former directrice and retired inspectress general Jeanne Géraud, *adjointe* to the mayor of Mongeron in the Seine-et-Oise.[24] Marie Soboul represented a resistance group on the Gard department's liberation committee and served on the Nîmes municipal council from 1947 to 1959.[25] Louise Gaillard, reinstated in 1945 as a school inspectress, was elected and reelected mayor of Saint-Cyr-sur-Loire near Tours, where she had directed the normal school until Vichy retired her. Antoinette Cuminal, also retired by Vichy, won election to the municipal council in Valence on the Socialist list. Bernarde Poujade, forced to retire as directrice in Épinal in 1941, spent the rest of the war in the Tarn-et-Garonne, her birthplace, and after the liberation was the *adjointe* to the mayor of Montech.[26] Before the war, Soboul, Gaillard, Cuminal, and Poujade had actively supported the Action Démocratique et Laïque des Femmes (ADLF). Géraud, Odoul, Cuminal, and Mir had worked on behalf of the Union Française pour le Suffrage des Femmes (UFSF), Cuminal as president of its Ardèche group in 1930, and Mir as vice president of the Angoulême group in the mid-1930s.[27]

Resistance leader Mathilde Mir was among the most politically active of the former or current directrices in local government. She was one of the first twelve members of the Charente department's liberation committee (Comité departemental de libération, CDL), which, like the CDL in other departments, was charged by the National Council of Resistance with providing transitional local leadership after the collapse of Vichy. The CDL represented resistance groups, anti-Vichy political parties, and labor and professional organizations. Women were nearly 8 percent of CDL members across France and numbered at least 125 (including 38 educators), but only Mir and one other woman ever presided over a CDL. Mir assumed the role in July 1945 after the previous Charente president died. She was also appointed to the Angoulême city council in March 1945, and in April won election to it and became *adjointe* to the mayor. In addition, she and other resistance colleagues started the journal *Charente libre* in September 1944, the word

EPILOGUE 225

"libre" in the title chosen because of concern that the word "républicaine" might still be too controversial in the department.[28]

Mir's sixty editorials in the journal during its first year made her socialist and feminist views well known, but she failed to win election to the constitutional assembly in October 1945 when she headed a list of women in republican resistance that won only 4 percent of the Charente's votes. Disappointed and in poor health, Mir asked in 1946 to leave the normal school in Angoulême for a post in the Paris region, and in 1948 became a school inspectress in the Seine-et-Oise, retiring in 1955. She also left the Socialist party and leaned toward the Communists because she disapproved of Socialist cooperation with the MRP to check Communist influence, a political evolution similar to that of Marie Soboul.[29]

The public action of some postwar directrices also included participation in the *syndicat* for normal school directors, revived after Vichy. Yvonne Fabre, the prewar assistant secretary, had been retired as the directrice in Arras in 1941 after an inspector general reported that she was an active "militante" who exemplified the "esprit syndicaliste" that, he alleged, had greatly harmed French education. In November 1944 she was ready to take up the cause of women whom Vichy had dismissed before the "normal" retirement age of sixty, but her eventual reintegration as a primary school inspectress in Paris meant that she no longer belonged to the directors' *syndicat*.[30] The women active in the postwar *syndicat* included Henriette Bontemps, retired by Vichy and reintegrated in 1945 as directrice in Chartres, and three younger directrices—Cécile François, Paule Parent, and Marguerite Chardon—previously heads of Vichy's professional institutes.[31]

Whether they remained normal school directrices or became inspectresses, the directrices appointed during the Third Republic continued after 1945 to display their expertise in professional publications. They contributed to textbooks and addressed pedagogical topics in journals and books. Like inspectresses general Kergomard before 1914 and Maucourant between the wars, seven of the postwar inspectresses general wrote specialized texts for teachers in *écoles maternelles*. Marguerite Picard, a prewar directrice of three normal schools and a primary school inspectress in Paris from 1941 to 1958, wrote or coauthored fifteen textbooks, published between 1949 and 1970, for the teaching of reading, grammar, and vocabulary. Marcelle Dechappe, ousted by Vichy as the directrice in Lyon and reinstated in 1945 as an inspectress in Paris, and her husband Lucien, a professor and later an inspector, resumed the collaboration begun during the 1920s with books of

226 WOMEN AND THE POLITICS OF EDUCATION IN FRANCE

documents for teaching history. With other colleagues they coauthored history and geography textbooks, issued in multiple editions between the 1940s and 1960s. A younger directrice, Alice Juredieu, also collaborated with her husband, a primary school inspector, on readers and grammar textbooks. For children from non-French families, Madeleine Boué-Iba-Zizen, the directrice in Miliana (Algeria) from 1937 to 1940 and then an inspectress for indigène girls' education, coauthored a beginning-level reader with inspector general Émile Prigent.[32]

Postwar directrices and inspectresses, like their predecessors, also discussed the special features of the education of girls and young women and the relationship of education to life after schooling. In France, as in other Western countries, including the United States, the postwar birthrate rose dramatically, and there was renewed emphasis on women's domestic roles, even as many women who worked during the war remained in the work force. *Le Rôle de la femme dans éducation familiale et sociale* (1950) by Hélène Brulé, directrice of the normal school in Tours, reflected that domestic emphasis with lessons on moral and civic education to be used in normal and secondary schools. Much of her commentary on familial, civic, and patriotic obligations echoed themes in Third Republic textbooks, and the last chapter concerned the teaching of home economics. She also made some traditional assumptions about gender differences: a wife brought "grace, carefulness and *douceur*" to a marriage, thereby making life "more agreeable," and expected from her husband "vigor, initiative, bold ideas, sure judgment." Spouses should recognize their obligation to have children and avoid "the social malady of the only child" that began during the nineteenth century. Family allocations, increased after the war, were designed to raise the birthrate.[33]

Yet Brulé clearly recognized that "a modern woman" did not see herself as weaker than a man and expected to be treated as an equal partner, not as a servant. Although article 213 of the civil code termed the husband the "head" (*chef*) of the family, the fact that since 1938 it no longer stipulated wifely obedience was one of the progressive gains that she attributed to "feminism." Apart from the reference to feminism, Brulé, the daughter of Haute-Savoie teachers sympathetic to socialism and widow of a resistance leader, did not indicate ideological leanings in this book.[34]

Women's participation in postwar political life was the focus of *L'Éducation civique des femmes* (1954) by Henriette Sourgen, the directrice of three normal schools before becoming an inspectress general of *écoles maternelles* in November 1940. Although the book was published under the auspices of

UNESCO and recorded that women could now vote and hold public office in more countries than ever before, Sourgen drew extensively on French data, which revealed that women, particularly older and rural women, were less likely to vote than men. She disputed the belief that "civic virtue is not feminine," as she had decades earlier when she discussed that same belief in an essay for the examination that qualified her to become a normal school professor in 1916. Differences between men's and women's voting tendencies were related, she argued, to sex, heredity, and habits tied to different activities in life. To encourage women's political participation, she recommended adapting civic education to their "nature, to their habits of feeling and thinking" and thus linked to "questions which give women's life its essential value: love of home, concern about children and the future of humanity, and the preservation of peace, the safeguard of the future."[35]

Sourgen also considered women's current access to a wider range of employment opportunities since 1900. A prewar participant in the UFSF and ADLF, Sourgen remarked that "[t]he long crusade that feminists have led through the nineteenth and earlier twentieth centuries is not finished" because women might still find it harder to be hired for jobs for which they were qualified and might be paid less, despite the acceptance of the principle of equal pay for equal work. Thus she suggested the need for new laws to guarantee women's access to some types of employment. Like many earlier French feminists, Sourgen and Brulé coupled notions of equality with assumptions about gender differences but did not believe that such differences justified excluding women from political life or certain occupations.[36]

The recognition that many postwar women worked also clearly influenced the choice of selections that former directrice Jeanne Seguin and teacher Pauline Millet made for *Pour nos filles* (1957), a reader for eleven-year-old girls. It was unusual as a primary school textbook because it showed women engaged in a wide range of occupations and activities. The daughter of teachers and graduate of the Haute-Marne normal school in 1914, Seguin headed four normal schools before becoming a school inspectress in Paris in 1945. Although half of the 106 selections depicted girls and women in familial settings and offered behavioral advice, those on women at work featured not only many traditional occupations—farm wife, laundress, seamstress, embroiderer, store clerk, secretary—but also various professions. The latter included a teacher, secondary school professor, lawyer, doctor, scientist, and aviatrix as well as women famed for contributions to literature, art, and theater. The book also featured two heroines in the wartime resistance.

228 WOMEN AND THE POLITICS OF EDUCATION IN FRANCE

Because she expected that many girls reading the book would come from working-class backgrounds, Seguin judged it important and realistic to depict women's activities outside the home.[37] Like Brulé and Sourgen, she presented a mix of traditional and newer gender roles that exemplified the transitional nature of the Fourth Republic for French women.

Directrice Brulé also contributed an account of the training of teachers to a volume on teachers' education in England, France, and the United States, published by UNESCO in 1953. After a brief historical review highlighting Third Republic policies, she treated the Vichy regime's abolition of normal schools as "a political measure" with effects that complicated their postwar reopening not only because many of their personnel had been reassigned to other posts but also because Vichy had broken up libraries and given scientific equipment-and some buildings to other establishments. Of Vichy's "alleged reform," there remained only the substitution of the baccalauréat, popularly called the *bac*, for the *brevet supérieur*, now abolished. Unsurprisingly, obtaining the *bac* also had the effect of redirecting the ambitions of some students, especially male students, toward more prestigious careers than primary school teaching because it opened the way to study at a university. Fontenay-aux-Roses and Saint-Cloud, the *écoles normales supérieures* that previously prepared students to teach in normal schools and higher primary schools, now also prepared them for certification as secondary school professors. What Brulé described in 1953 would undergo substantial change in future decades. So, too, would students' experiences in normal schools, still marked during the 1950s by more regulation of the lives of women students than of male counterparts.[38]

France's Fourth Republic collapsed in May 1958 after an uprising in Algiers staged by angry citizens of European descent and members of the army, both groups unhappy with the course of the Algerian war started in November 1954 by Muslim nationalists seeking independence. The Fifth Republic under President Charles de Gaulle, ushered in after a referendum in September 1958, made important changes in education policies inherited from the Third Republic. Although normal schools were not altered immediately, they figured in a continuing debate about the relationship between primary education, for which normal schools prepared teachers, and secondary education. For pupils beginning primary school in 1959, the new government raised the age for leaving school from fourteen to sixteen, and it began reconfiguring the primary curriculum because of plans to replace the last primary class and *cours complémentaire* with an intermediate school, a collège, which all students would attend for four years. The colléges would also orient students toward appropriate academic or vocational paths in secondary education, the demand for which had expanded greatly since 1945 as parents saw additional schooling as a key to a better future for children. Instructors for the new collèges would receive training in regional pedagogical centers, created because the diverse backgrounds of students in the intermediate schools necessitated an attention to pedagogy that was lacking in the traditional academic preparation of secondary school professors, accustomed to teaching middle- and upper-class students. The reforms went far toward realizing the interwar goal of an *école unique* to break down structural barriers impeding many students' advancement from primary to secondary schools.[39]

The other major change in educational policy in 1959 was the Debré law of December 31, which provided government financing for private schools, religious or lay, that agreed to operate under a contract obligating them to follow the curriculum for public schools. Although the Fourth Republic had taken a step in this direction in 1951 by giving private schools allocations for equipment and subsidies for some students, the 1959 law was more far-reaching and a boon to many private schools with precarious finances.[40] Its passage signified the Gaullists' wish to end old church-state quarrels at a time of national crisis, for the Algerian war and conflicting opinions about its conduct and how to end it would continue until 1962.

Former directrice Madeleine Iba-Zizen admitted the possibility of more than one outcome for the Algerian conflict when she spoke about Algerian Muslim women at a meeting of French social workers in February 1959, although her sympathies for "Algérie française" were well known. She was the wife of a Kabyle lawyer who converted to Catholicism after his military service in World War I and strongly supported maintaining Algeria's ties to France. Citing her experience as a normal school directrice and inspectress in Algeria for twenty years, before her recent retirement, she discussed the impact of customs and laws on Muslim women and also argued that their contacts with the French through schools and workplaces had benefited some of them. She detected a growing preference for western dress and even home furnishings. Finally, she underscored the importance of Muslim women as well as men now having the vote. Indeed, she reported, three Muslim women had been elected to the new French national assembly, and premier Michel Debré had appointed a Muslim woman to his cabinet.[41] The cabinet member, Nafissa Sid-Cara, was a teacher who had studied at

230   WOMEN AND THE POLITICS OF EDUCATION IN FRANCE

the Constantine normal school in the late 1920s and appreciated directrice Muraccioli.[42]

Post-1958 reforms did not, of course, diminish the drive for Algerian independence, proclaimed in 1962. Teachers were part of the exodus from Algeria of most Europeans and their Algerian supporters. Unlike Mme Iba-Zizen, another woman who had taught at the Miliana normal school, and briefly directed it in 1925, would indicate in the early 1960s that her ten years in Algeria had aroused in her "a profound indignation against colonialism, which is in reality an unjust and scornful exploitation." Whatever positive actions the French had taken in Algeria, they were, she wrote, "insufficient and in large part *égoistes.*"[43]

The next major upheaval in France, in May 1968, led to more changes in educational policies. As student demonstrations spread from universities to the streets of Paris and other cities, millions of workers also went on strike to protest against the government of the Fifth Republic under President De Gaulle. Subsequent educational reforms were focused on universities but also affected normal schools. Most notably, normal schools would no longer prepare students for the baccalauréat. Their new two-year curriculum covered only pedagogical and professional preparation. During the 1970s the requirement that students live at the normal school in an *internat* was phased out, and students, now older than their Third Republic counterparts, no longer had to be unmarried or, as of September 1970, to ask permission to marry. Normal schools also became *écoles mixtes*, enrolling women and men in one facility. By 1978 all departmental normal schools were coeducational, except in Paris, where the change occurred in 1981. Already during the 1950s, as secondary education expanded, many newly opened secondary schools were coeducational, and by the mid-1970s the last single-sex primary schools also gave way to *écoles mixtes.*[44] A single normal school for a department required only one director, either a woman or a man, and increasingly the administrative duties of a director or directrice outweighed the pedagogical.

Not surprisingly, commentators reported that normal schools were losing much of their original identity.[45] This was also the case in the United States, but instead of losing a role in academic preparation, American normal schools in the mid-twentieth century were renamed state teachers' colleges and then state colleges.

By the time of the 1968 upheaval, all but one of the interwar normal school directrices whose careers ended in normal schools had retired, and the last one did so in September 1968 at the age of sixty-five. Inspectresses general could continue working until age seventy, but only two of the interwar directrices promoted to the rank in the 1960s—Brulé, born in 1902, and Antoinette Guerrini, born in 1903—were still working after 1968. At the end of their careers, many interwar directrices had received Legion of Honor recognition: before 1940, at least 15 of those appointed after 1914; after 1945, at least 32.[46] By July 1989, when the Jospin law slated normal schools for abolition and announced their replacement with university institutes of professional formation (IUFM, *instituts universitaires de formation des maîtres*), nearly all of the last generation of Third Republic directrices had died. Recognition of their contributions lingered, however, in the obituaries published in the alumnae bulletins of Fontenay-aux-Roses and departmental normal schools.

After 1989, the old title of *instituteurs* or *institutrices* for primary schoolteachers was also replaced by the designation *professeur(e)s d'école*, who were required, like secondary school professors, to hold a university *licence*, and as of 2010 also needed a master's degree for tenure. The professional institutes (IUFM), established in the now twenty-nine administrative "academies" for education in France and overseas, initially retained many normal school personnel and utilized 130 sites (including old normal school buildings), but the administrative title offered to former normal school directors and directrices was typically that of *adjoint(e)s*. Unlike the normal schools of the Third Republic, the Fifth Republic institutes provided initial pedagogical training for secondary as well as primary school educators, and they also offered opportunities for teachers' continuing professional development.[47]

From the outset the IUFM were often criticized by commentators, including politicians, who judged their various pedagogical approaches a hindrance, rather than a help, in preparing new teachers to convey academic content. They were also sites where the cultures of personnel from primary education, secondary education, and universities clashed.[48] Interchanges between defenders of the IUFM and their critics frequently echoed themes familiar in interchanges in American universities between faculty in schools of education and faculty in the liberal arts and sciences. Considered to be "*universitaires*" without being part of universities,[49] the IUFM were replaced in 2013 with *écoles supérieures du professorat et de l'éducation* (ESPE), redesignated *instituts nationaux supérieurs du professorat et de l'éducation* (INSPE) in 2019.[50]

232 WOMEN AND THE POLITICS OF EDUCATION IN FRANCE

Few members of the last generation of Third Republic directrices were alive to witness the demise of normal schools after 1989. But as plans for replacements emerged during a decade of commemorating and critically evaluating the founding of the republican school a century earlier,[51] normal school alumnae and associations published articles and brochures looking back at their history and recalling the accomplishments of predecessors.[52]

The first generations of republican normal school directrices played a vital role in the successful creation of women's normal schools after the Bert law of 1879 mandated them for each French department. Founded "amidst a storm of protests and invective," the new normal schools and the women who staffed were often surrounded by controversy.[53] Jules Ferry and other republican leaders saw public primary schools and their provision of civic and moral instruction as vital to the survival of the new democratic government that many monarchists and Catholic traditionalists opposed. Thus republicans wanted schools and their teachers to win over the hearts and minds of women who could influence children, husbands, and other family members. As republicans secularized the curriculum and moved to replace nuns teaching in public schools with laywomen, trained in normal schools run by laywomen, their opponents attacked public schools and normal schools as institutions "sans Dieu."

Of necessity, the circumstances of the 1880s and later decades led women working in normal schools to develop political awareness. Their positions depended upon the Third Republic and its survival. With lessons in civic education, they prepared normal school students to teach about the functioning of government and citizens' rights and duties. Although many schoolteachers before 1914, as well as later, gained credentials without attending a normal school, the normal school was considered the *voie royale* (royal road) to a teaching career.[54]

The training of women normal school personnel at Fontenay-aux-Roses and the training they, in turn, dispensed in departmental normal schools to future teachers emphasized women's intellectual competence and encouraged critical and independent thinking. That training assured women that they were fully equal to men as human beings but also presented them with certain constraints tied to prevailing assumptions about gender. The behavior of normal school directrices, their personnel, and their students was expected to be exemplary so that critics could not fault their conduct with allegations of immorality or unfeminine activity. The school itself functioned behind closed doors and high walls, imposing a daily schedule not unlike that of religious convents, but without religious observances. Some former students remembered their directrices as maternal and the normal school atmosphere as familial; others recalled authoritarian personalities and a confining atmosphere. Directrices and professors in normal schools were role models for their students, some of them clearly more engaging and influential than others.

Beyond the normal school, directrices, like male normal school directors, participated in the deliberations of their department's education council, as did two men and two women teachers. In a provincial department, the normal school directrice's role made her the most visible and important woman representing public primary education. Like colleagues in secondary schools and inspectorates, or women trailblazing in law and medicine, normal school directrices and professors were among the women of the late nineteenth and early twentieth centuries who helped create a new model for the professional woman, a woman whose education gave her an occupation that commanded respect, entailed significant responsibility, and, ideally, led to financial independence.

After 1900, the women staffing normal schools, like thousands of women primary schoolteachers, became more vocal about the injustice of receiving unequal pay for doing the same work as male colleagues with the same qualifications. While women teachers sought support for equal pay from male colleagues in the increasingly active teachers' *amicales* and the more assertive (but then technically illegal) *syndicats*, normal school directrice Albertine Eidenschenk, a member of the Conseil Supérieur de l'Instruction Publique, drew attention to this central issue and other inequities. The discussion of why unequal pay was allowed led some women educators to conclude that lawmakers simply ignored them because women lacked the right to vote. Accordingly, some normal school directrices and professors, along with *institutrices* and secondary school professors, joined feminist organizations, including the Union Française pour le Suffrage des Femmes. Although French feminists typically accepted many prevailing notions about gender differences in personalities and familial roles, they denied that such differences justified restricting women's rights and activities. Their version of "equality in difference" was thus more expansive than that of male pedagogues and commentators who accorded women moral and even intellectual equality with men but denied them a role in public affairs.

After the Great War, many women educators retained feminist convictions and were joined by younger colleagues, hopeful at first that France would

234   WOMEN AND THE POLITICS OF EDUCATION IN FRANCE

follow the example of other Western countries that had granted the vote to women, and then frustrated by the Third Republic's refusal to act. The curricular revisions of 1920 allowed for discussions of women's suffrage in normal schools, and the new dress code modernized the public image of normal school personnel and students. Yet older feminist directrices like Émilie Flayol also recognized that the weight of cultural traditions still affected many women's attitudes toward involvement in public life. For "women of our generation," she wrote, there was a restraint on initiative exerted by the belief, fostered in family circles, that it was "bad" for a woman "to draw attention to herself, and to leave the obscurity suitable for her sex."[55]

International developments and crises also heightened the political awareness of normal school directrices and professors, and indeed of public school educators at all levels. Furthermore, the militancy of various rightwing leagues and parties during the 1930s and their recruiting of women as well as men drew attention to the Third Republic's vulnerability, prompting some staunchly republican women educators, directrices among them, to join the Action Démocratique et Laïque des Femmes. The Popular Front victory in 1936 buoyed the hopes of those supporting the political Left, as increasing numbers of educators did after 1918. Women's participation with male colleagues in professional organizations further heightened political awareness. Yet some women still felt detached from politics and scorned politicians' machinations. On a daily basis, normal school directrices necessarily focused on their duties as educators, but they sometimes offered observations on public issues in the bulletins of alumnae associations.

During World War II, the realities of life under the German occupation and the collaborationist Vichy regime, which abolished normal schools, understandably dismayed and outraged many directrices, even as they, like the population in general, had to function from day to day. They worked in the new professional institutes and in other schools and inspectorates. That some directrices participated in acts of wartime resistance and in postwar local governments might not have been anticipated by those who educated them decades earlier, but such exceptional actions were consistent with the republican values of liberty, equality, and fraternity that their education had emphasized. As leaders of other women in educational institutions, they had acquired a confidence in their abilities that they could bring to other situations.

After 1945, the last generation of normal school directrices trained during the Third Republic continued to prepare future women teachers to combine

EPILOGUE 235

a professional role with societal expectations for them as wives and mothers. They recognized the importance of work outside the home in many women's lives and acknowledged a new political equality, but they also articulated longstanding assumptions about gendered differences in personalities and societal roles that many women might not challenge until a decade or more later when a second wave of feminist thinking and action arrived in a number of Western countries, France included.[56] Controversy in 1989 and later over some Muslim girls' wearing of headscarves in school would also spur renewed interest in the history of the policy of *laïcité* framed in the era of Jules Ferry to separate the public school from religious advocacy and display.[57]

Notes

Abbreviations

ActFmst	*Action féministe*
ADLF	Action Démocratique et Laïque des Femmes
ADP	Archives de Paris
AEP	*Annuaire de l'enseignement primaire*
AN	Archives Nationales
BAADEN	*Bulletin de l'Association amicale des directrices et directeurs d'écoles normales*
BAAENI	*Bulletin de l'Association amicale des anciennes élèves de l'école normale d'institutrices de* (name of city or department)
BAIP	*Bulletin administratif de l'instruction publique*
BAIPDEN	*Bulletin de l'Association amicale des inspecteurs primaires et des directeurs d'écoles normales*
BMD	Bibliothèque Marguerite Durand
BulFR	*Bulletin de l'Association amicale des anciennes élèves de Fontenay-aux-Roses* (retitled in 1923, *Bulletin de l'Association amicale des anciennes élèves de l'École normale supérieure de Fontenay-aux-Roses*)
CAF	Centre des Archives du Féminisme
CNFF	Conseil National des Femmes Françaises
CSIP	Conseil Supérieur de l'Instruction Publique
ÉN	*École nouvelle*
FFU	Fédération Féministe Universitaire
GFU	Groupe Féministe Universitaire
GGA	Gouvernement Général de l'Algérie
INRP	Institut National de Recherche Pédagogique
IR	*L'Instituteur républicain*
JI	*Journal des instituteurs*
LF	*La Française*
Mf/UFSF	"Mouvement féministe, Union Française pour le Suffrage des Femmes"
MGP	*Manuel général de l'instruction primaire*
MIP	Ministère de l'Instruction Publique
MUNAE	Musée National de l'Éducation
OCM	Organisation Civile et Militaire
REP	*Revue de l'enseignement primaire et primaire supérieur*
RP	*Revue pédagogique*
UFSF	Union Française pour le Suffrage des Femmes

238 NOTES TO PAGES 1–3

Introduction

1. Archives Nationales de France [hereinafter AN] F17/22893 (dossier Granet née Vidier).

2. Studies of the Third Republic and *laïcité* include Pierre Ognier, *Une école sans Dieu? 1880–1895: L'Invention d'une morale laïque sous la IIIe République* (Toulouse: Presses universitaires du Mirail, 2008); Patrick Cabanel, *Le Dieu de la République: Aux sources protestantes de la laïcité (1860–1900)* (Rennes: Presses universitaires de Rennes, 2003).

3. Gordon Wright, *France in Modern Times*, 5th ed. (New York: W. W. Norton, 1995), 223.

4. Ognier, *Une école sans Dieu?*

5. Ferdinand Buisson, *Nouveau dictionnaire de pédagogie et d'instruction primaire* (Paris: Hachette, 1911), s.v. "normales primaires (écoles)"; Jean-François Condette, *Histoire de la formation des enseignants en France (XIXe–XXe siècles)* (Paris: L'Harmattan, 2011), 38–109. The division of France into departments (*départements*) for administration dated from 1790.

6. E. Jacoulet, *Notice historique sur les écoles normales d'instituteurs et d'institutrices* in *Recueil des monographies pédagogiques publiées à l'occasion de l'Exposition universelle de 1889* (Paris: Imprimerie nationale, 1889), 2:442–51. See chapter 1, n. 9, 10, 61, on numbers of normal schools.

7. Françoise Mayeur, *L'Éducation des filles en France au XIXe siècle* (Paris: Hachette, 1977); Anne T. Quartararo, *Women Teachers and Popular Education in Nineteenth-Century France: Social Values and Corporate Identity at the Normal School Institution* (Newark: University of Delaware Press, 1995); Rebecca Rogers, *From the Salon to the Schoolroom: Educating Bourgeois Girls in Nineteenth-Century France* (University Park: Pennsylvania State University Press, 2005); Patrick J. Harrigan, "Women Teachers and the Schooling of Girls in France: Recent Historiographical Trends," *French Historical Studies* 21 (Fall 1998): 593–610.

8. François Furet and Jacques Ozouf, *Lire et écrire: L'Alphabétisation des français de Calvin à Jules Ferry*, 2 vols. (Paris: Éditions de Minuit, 1977); Raymond Grew and Patrick J. Harrigan, *School, State, and Society: The Growth of Elementary Schooling in Nineteenth-Century France—A Quantitative Analysis* (Ann Arbor: University of Michigan Press, 1991); Harrigan, "Women Teachers," 607–10.

9. The French term *directrice* is used throughout this study (and not subsequently italicized), rather than English alternatives such as the gender-neutral term "principal" (which in American usage refers to the head of a primary school for young children as well as to the head of a secondary school) or the more old-fashioned terms "directress" or "headmistress."

10. Rogers, *From the Salon to the Schoolroom*; Françoise Mayeur, *L'Enseignement secondaire des jeunes filles sous la Troisième République* (Paris: Presses de la Fondation nationale des sciences politiques, 1977); Jo Burr Margadant, *Madame le Professeur: Women Educators in the Third Republic* (Princeton: Princeton University Press, 1990).

11. Jacques Ozouf and Mona Ozouf, with Véronique Aubert and Claire Steindecker, *La République des instituteurs* (Paris: Gallimard/Le Seuil, 1992); Sharif Gemie, *Women*

NOTES TO PAGES 3–8   239

and Schooling in France: Gender, Authority and Identity in the French Schooling Sector (Keele: University of Keele Press, 1995); Persis Charles Hunt, "Revolutionary Syndicalism and Feminism among Teachers in France, 1900–1921" (PhD diss., Tufts University, 1975). For a comprehensive historiographical overview of French women educators, see Rebecca Rogers, "L'Éducation des filles: Un siècle et demi d'historiographie," *Histoire de l'éducation*, nos. 115–16 (September 2007): 37–79.

12. Quartararo, *Women Teachers*.

13. Thomas Neville Bonner, *To the Ends of the Earth: Women's Search for Education in Medicine* (Cambridge, MA: Harvard University Press, 1992); James C. Albisetti, "Portia ante Portas: Women and the Legal Profession in Europe, ca. 1870–1925," *Journal of Social History* 33 (Summer 2000): 825–57; Linda L. Clark, *Women and Achievement in Nineteenth-Century Europe* (Cambridge: Cambridge University Press, 2008), chapter 6; Sylvie Schweitzer, *Femmes de pouvoir: une histoire de l'égalité professionnelle en Europe XIXe–XXIe siècle* (Paris: Payot, 2010); Juliette Rennes, *Le Mérite et la nature: L'Accès des femmes aux professions de prestige* (Paris: Fayard, 2007).

14. Mayeur, *L'Enseignement secondaire des jeunes filles*; Margadant, *Madame le Professeur*.

15. Félix Pécaut, "La Directrice d'école normale," *Annuaire de l'enseignement primaire* 8 (1892): 313.

16. "Inauguration de l'école normale d'institutrices de Saint-Germain-en-Laye (9 novembre 1913)," *Bulletin de l'association amicale des anciennes élèves de Fontenay-aux-Roses*, no. 63 (March 1914): 35–39, quotation, 37.

17. Rebecca Rogers, ed., *La Mixité dans l'éducation, Enjeux passés et présents* (Lyon: ENS Éditions, 2004).

18. Patricia Legris, "Les Écoles normales primaires de 1945 aux années 1970: les contradictions progressives d'une institution à deux vitesses," in *La Formation des maîtres de 1940 à 2010*, ed. Antoine Prost (Rennes: Presses universitaires de Rennes, 2014), 55–70.

Chapter 1

1. "Il faut que la femme appartienne à l'éducation ou qu'elle appartienne à l'église." Jules Ferry, "Discours sur l'égalité d'éducation," excerpt in Antoine Prost, *Histoire de l'enseignement en France, 1800–1967* (Paris: A. Colin, 1968), 268–69 (speech to the Société pour l'Instruction Élémentaire).

2. Ferry was minister of public instruction in four different cabinets for a total of fifty months: February 4, 1879–November 13, 1881 (under premiers William Waddington and Charles de Freycinet); September 23, 1880–November 13, 1881 (Ferry also premier); January 10–August 6, 1882 (Freycinet cabinet); February 21–November 20, 1883 (second Ferry cabinet). He was premier and minister of foreign affairs, November 20, 1883–April 3, 1885.

3. Ferry, quoted in Prost, *Histoire de l'enseignement*, 268–69. On religion and marital relationships, see Theodore Zeldin, "The Conflict of Moralities," in *Conflicts in French Society: Anticlericalism, Education and Morality in the Nineteenth Century*, ed. Zeldin (London: G. Allen and Unwin, 1970), 13–50.

240 NOTES TO PAGES 9–12

4. Prost, *Histoire de l'enseignement*, 218; Jean Dietz, "Jules Ferry et les traditions républicaines," *Revue politique et parlementaire* 41, no. 161 (October 1934): 129, 134. On inaccuracies in education statistics, see Jean-Noël Luc, *La Statistique de l'enseignement primaire 19e-20e siècles: Politique et mode d'emploi* (Paris: Institut de recherche pédagogique (INRP)/Économica, 1985), and Grew and Harrigan, *School, State, and Society*.

5. Claude Langlois, *Le Catholicisme au féminin: Les Congrégations à supérieure générale au XIXe siècle* (Paris: Cerf, 1984); Ralph Gibson, *A Social History of French Catholicism, 1789–1914* (New York: Routledge, 1989).

6. Sandra Horvath-Peterson, *Victor Duruy and French Education: Liberal Reform in the Second Empire* (Baton Rouge: Louisiana State University Press, 1984); Sandra A. Horvath, "Victor Duruy and the Controversy over Secondary Education for Girls," *French Historical Studies* 9 (Spring 1975): 83–104.

7. "Syllabus Errorum,The Syllabus of the Principal Errors of Our Time, Which Are Stigmatized in the Consistorial Allocutions, Encyclicals, and Other Apostolic Letters of Our Most Holy Father Pope Pius IX," in *The Posture of Europe, 1815–1940: Readings in European Intellectual History*, ed. Eugene Charlton Black (Homewood, IL: Dorsey Press, 1954), 394.

8. Patrick Cabanel, *Ferdinand Buisson, Père de l'école laïque* (Geneva: Éditions Labor et Fides, 2016).

9. E. Jacoulet, *Notice historique sur les écoles normales d'instituteurs et d'institutrices* in *Recueil des monographies pédagogiques publiées à l'occasion de l'Exposition universelle de 1889* (Paris: Imprimerie nationale, 1889), 2: 442–51. Jacoulet cited 19 women's normal schools (8 pre-1870, 11 1872–79) but contradicted that number with a note that the Côte-d'Or department had a *cours normal* until 1880. I exclude the Côte-d'Or from the pre-August 1879 total. The pre-1870 normal schools run by religious orders were in the Orne, Doubs, Loiret, Ardennes, Corse, Haute-Savoie; by laywomen, the Jura, Bouches-du-Rhône. The post-1870 lay schools were in the Isère, Eure-et-Loir, Saône-et-Loire, Yonne, Allier, Seine, Alger, Hérault, Somme. The Rhône department presents a problem for counting. Jacoulet dated it from 1876, as did Buisson's first *Dictionnaire* (1882–87) and recently Jean-François Condette's *Histoire de la formation des enseignants en France* (Paris: L'Harmattan, 2011), but the normal school designation was also disputed in the late 1870s because the ministry of public instruction had no oversight of the budget or staff of the facility owned by a religious order. Thus the dossier of the directrice who opened the Rhône's republican normal school in 1879 indicated that it replaced a *cours normal* (Archives nationales [hereinafter AN], F17/22050, Porte).

10. Jacoulet, *Notice historique*, 429–51. Jacoulet records 82 women's normal schools in early 1889; 5 more were added in 1889 and 1890.

11. The national government paid the salaries of normal school personnel; departments paid for buildings and upkeep. Women's normal schools not located in a department's administrative center were in the Bouches-du-Rhône (Aix), Manche (Coutances), Nord (Douai), Haute-Savoie (Rumilly), and Alger (Miliana).

12. AN F17/20109 (C. Baudry); Alphonse Baudry, inspector in the Yonne (1862–74), and later in the Rhône.

NOTES TO PAGES 12–18 241

13. AN F17/22872 (Friedberg); Clarisse Coignet, *Mémoires* (Lausanne: Constant-Varidel, 1899–1904), 4: 289, 293.

14. AN F17/22862 (Ferrand); Une directrice d'école normale, "Mademoiselle Ferrand," *Revue pédagogique* [hereinafter *RP*] 24 (June 1894): 379–81.

15. AN F17/22050 (Porte); "Mademoiselle Porte," *Bulletin de l'Association amicale des anciennes élèves de l'école normale du Rhône* 18 (December 1931): 4–7.

16. AN F17/21065 (Lanaud), Lissajous letter, August 30, 1879; F17/9752, Jura. For educational adminstration France was divided into sixteen *académies*, each headed by a rector, and a seventeenth *académie* served the three departments in Algeria.

17. AN F17/20109 (Baudry), 22754/B (Bonnet), 22872 (Friedberg), 20795 (Garcin), 21144 (Lemercier), 22050 (Porte), 21682 (Sage).

18. AN F17/20795 (Garcin), 21144 (Lemercier), 21682 (Sage). Ferrand died in 1894; Sage retired in 1895, Porte in 1907. On Sage see also pp. 123, 138.

19. AN F17 22050 (Porte); "Mademoiselle Porte," *Bulletin de l'Association amicale des anciennes élèves de l'école normale supérieure de Fontenay-aux-Roses* [hereinafter *BulFR*], no. 25 (December 1931): 28.

20. "Décret relatif à la nomination définitive aux fonctions de l'enseignement dans les écoles normales primaires d'instituteurs ou d'institutrices (5 juin)," *Manuel général de l'instruction primaire* [hereinafter *MGP*], no. 24 (December 12, 1880): 387.

21. AN F17/22016/B (Murique nèe François), Buisson letter, February 1880, to director of primary education of the Seine; F17/21413 (Olivaint née Pons), rector of academy of Montpellier, letter, August 1882.

22. Félix Pécaut, "La Directrice d'école normale," *Annuaire de l'enseignement primaire* [hereinafter *AEP*] 8 (1892): 299–325, quotations, 323; partially reprinted in Pécaut, *L'Éducation publique et la vie nationale*, 3rd ed. (Paris: Hachette, 1907), 163–77. See also pp. 44, 82, 83 on Pécaut's article.

23. Leslie Page Moch, "Government Policy and Women's Experience: The Case of Teachers in France," *Feminist Studies* 14 (1988): 301–24; Linda L. Clark, *The Rise of Professional Women in France: Gender and Public Administration since 1830* (Cambridge: Cambridge University Press, 2000), 75, 161.

24. Rogers, *From the Salon to the Schoolroom*.

25. AN F17/23060 (Rey).

26. AN F17/22806 (Cougoul).

27. AN F17/22912 (Hippeau née Delacour).

28. AN F17/21991 (Tailleur), 22740/B (Bergin), 21983/A (Moret), 22034 (Doisnel). 21980/B (Lusier); for Georgin, AN AJ16/1100 and Archives départementales de Paris [hereinafter ADP] 551.

29. AN F17/22791 (Chasteau née Saigne); Alain Quella-Villéger, *Belles et rebelles, Le Roman vrai des Chasteau-Tinayre* (Bordeaux: Aubéron, 2000), 63.

30. AN F17/21022/B (Karquel).

31. AN F17/22893 (Granet née Vidier).

32. AN F17/22893 (Granet née Vidier). See the Introduction for the bishop's protest and Ferry's response.

242 NOTES TO PAGES 18-21

33. "Discours de M. F. Buisson," *BulFR*, no. 11, special issue, *M. Félix Pécaut* (November 1898): 14–21 (funeral oration); Patrick Cabanel, "Pensées pour une république, Introduction," to Félix Pécaut, *Quinze ans d'éducation (notes écrites au jour le jour)*, ed. Élie Pécaut (1902) (Paris: Le Bord de l'eau, 2008), 7–73; Yvonne Oulhiou, *L'École normale supérieure de Fontenay-aux-Roses à travers le temps* (Fontenay-aux-Roses: Cahiers de Fontenay, 1981), 7, 30.

34. S. Lauriol, president of the Fontenay alumnae association, at Pécaut's funeral, *BulFR*, no. 11 (1898): 13.

35. Cabanel, "Pensées," in Pécaut, *Quinze ans d'éducation*; Oulhiou, *L'École normale supérieure*. See also pp. 50–50, 51–53 on moral instruction.

36. Pécaut, *Quinze ans d'éducation*, 364, 386, talks at Fontenay, August 6, 1896, November 1894.

37. AN F17/22273 (Floutier née Béridot), Lacroix, August 19, 1889, letter on Floutier's behalf.

38. AN F17/22791 (Chasteau); Drawing on the papers of Chasteau's daughter Marcelle Tinayre, Quella-Villéger (*Belles et rebelles*, 89–90) suggests a clash of personalities and a family story that Chasteau refused to let a prominent male visitor enter a dormitory. Buisson considered assigning her in 1881 to Martinique or Tahiti, but her husband, an engraver, objected to such a move; in 1886 Buisson wrote that he could not name her to another post.

39. Oulhiou, *L'École normale supérieure*, 2, 30; Pécaut, *L'Éducation publique*, 263, 273–89, 306.

40. R. Jalliffier, "A.-E. Jacoulet," *RP* 55 (December 1909): 505; Jean-Noël Luc and Alain Barbé, *Des normaliens: Histoire de l'École normale supérieure de Saint-Cloud* (Paris: Presses de la Fondation nationale des sciences politiques, 1982).

41. On anti-Protestantism, see Oulhiou, *L'École normale supérieure*, 112–15; Steven C. Hause, "Anti-Protestant Rhetoric in the Early Third Republic," *French Historical Studies* 16 (Spring 1989): 185–201; Jean Baubérot and Valentine Zuber, *Une haine oubliée: L'antiprotestantisme avant le "pacte laïque" (1870–1905)* (Paris: Albin Michel, 2000).

42. Jacqueline Gautherin, "Une polyphonie protestante dans le concert de la 'Science de l'éducation,'" *Histoire de l'éducation*, no. 110 (2006): 91–110.

43. Linda L. Clark, *Schooling the Daughters of Marianne: Textbooks and the Socialization of Girls in Modern French Primary Schools* (Albany: State University of New York Press, 1984).

44. Henri Marion, *Leçons de morale*, 2nd ed. (Paris: A. Colin, 1884), 305–6 (1st ed., 1882), based on notes taken by Fontenay students). On "equality in difference," see Karen Offen, "Ernest Legouvé and the Doctrine of 'Equality in Difference' for Women: A Case Study of Male Feminism in Nineteenth-Century France," *Journal of Modern History* 58 (June 1986): 452–84, and Nicole Mosconi, "Henri Marion et l'égalité dans la différence,'" *Le Télémaque*, no. 41 (2012): 133–50.

45. Pécaut, "La Directrice," 300, 312, 318–19; Pécaut, *L'Éducation publique*, 278.

46. Seth Koven and Sonya Michel, eds., *Mothers of a New World: Maternalist Politics and the Origins of Welfare States* (New York: Routledge, 1992), 2, authors' italics.

NOTES TO PAGES 21–26   243

47. Oulhiou, *L'École normale supérieure*, 20–23; AN 20020184/1, Fontenay-aux-Roses, Registre des élèves, 1880–1913. The preparation of professors was extended from two to three years in the mid-1890s but after 1915 was again two years. The number of students admitted through the annual *concours* varied, typically ranging between twenty-five and thirty-two (AN 20020184, Registre).

48. The first *répétitrice* in 1881, Camille Layet, was a normal school *maîtresse* who became a directrice in 1882 (AN F/17 23916, Garonne née Layet). Subsequently the post went to Fontenay alumnae.

49. AN 20020123/7, Fontenay-aux-Roses, Conférences des élèves directrices, 1882–83, 1886–87. On future directrices' presentations, see also pp. 51, 52, 55. After 1882 the number admitted to the directrices' year ranged from a low of four (1884) to a high of twelve in 1889 (AN 20020184/1).

50. AN F17/22586 (Expilly), 22967 (Logé née Hervé).

51. AN F17/22752 (Boissière née Stromeyer); 22775 (Calloch). Boissière, widow of a professor, was the sister-in-law of the rector of Alger; Calloch, daughter of a primary school inspector (deceased), was backed by the prefect of the Loire-Inférieure.

52. AN F17/21280/A (Mathieu).

53. AN F17/21898 (Bourguet née Muret); Octave Gréard, "Une éducatrice laïque," *MGP*, no. 2 (January 9, 1904): 13–16.

54. AN F17/21898 (Bourguet née Muret); Gréard, "Une éducatrice laïque."

55. On the École Pape-Carpantier and *écoles maternelles*, see Colette Cosnier, *Marie Pape-Carpantier: De l'école maternelle à l'école des filles* (Paris: L'Harmattan, 1993); Jean-Noël Luc, ed., *La petite enfance à l'école, XIXe-XXe siècles* (Paris: INRP/ Économica, 1982), and Luc, *L'Invention du jeune enfant: De la salle d'asile à l'école maternelle* (Paris: Belin, 1997). From 1886 until closed in January 1891 the École Pape-Carpantier, relocated to Versailles, trained directrices for *écoles annexes*, the primary schools and *écoles maternelles* attached to normal schools.

56. AN F17/21898 (Bourguet), Buisson letter, March 1894, to minister of public instruction.

57. AN F17/22543/A (Saffroy); Christine Courtis, "Le Cheminement de Lucie Saffroy, une Auxerroise dévouée à la cause de l'instruction des filles du peuple," unpublished ms., courtesy of author.

58. AN F17/22543/A (Saffroy); Oulhiou, *L'École normale supérieure*, 78–79; Lucien Carrive, ed., *Lettres de Jules Steeg à Maurice Schwalb, 1851–1898: Un Pasteur républicain au XIXe siècle* (Paris: Éditions de la nouvelle Sorbonne, 1993), 479, 484; Linda L. Clark, "A Battle of the Sexes in a Professional Setting: The Introduction of Inspectrices Primaires, 1889–1914," *French Historical Studies* 16 (Spring 1989): 113; Haryett Fontanges, *La Légion d'honneur et les femmes décorées, étude d'histoire et de sociologie féminine* (Paris: Alliance coopérative du livre, 1905), 148, 153–56; "Nécrologie," *BulFR*, no. 44 (March 1946): 18–20; "Une lettre de M. Paul Dupuy," *BulFR*, no. 45 (January 1947): 56–58.

59. AN F17/22316/B (Dejean de la Bâtie née Lacoste); ADP D1T1 198 (Lacoste).

60. AN F17/22316/B (Dejean de la Bâtie née Lacoste); Carrive, ed. *Lettres de Jules Steeg*, 484. Similarly, the higher normal school in Sèvres had no male director of studies after 1896.

244 NOTES TO PAGES 27–33

61. The last women's normal school opened before 1900, Albi (Tarn) in 1890, brought the number of women's schools to 87. Three schools with small enrollments soon closed, their students sent to neighboring departments: Avignon (Var) and Auch (Gers), both opened 1886, closed 1891; Montauban (Tarn-et-Garonne), opened 1883, closed 1899. New schools in Nice (Alpes-Maritimes), 1907, and Constantine (Algeria), 1908, raised the number to 86.

62. Statistical analysis for collective profiles in this section based on *dossiers personnels* of 193 directrices (AN F17, ADP D1T1), 124 appointed in the 1880s, 69 from 1890 to 1914.

63. Furet and Ozouf, *Lire et écrire*; Grew and Harrigan, *School, State, and Society*.

64. Pécaut, "La Directrice," 322.

65. Ozouf and Ozouf, *La République des instituteurs*, 33–45; Margadant, *Madame le Professeur*, 51. There is no study detailing backgrounds of Fontenay-aux-Roses students.

66. Ozouf and Ozouf, *La République des instituteurs*, 148; Luc and Barbé, *Des normaliens*, 247. Information on 189 fathers of 193 directrices (including four pairs of sisters) is drawn from the *état civil* (birth, marriage, death records) and *dossiers personnels* of directrices. Four birth certificates record no father. Three pairs of sisters had fathers in education.

67. Pierre Bourdieu, *The State Nobility: Elite Schools in the Field of Power*, trans. Laurette C. Clough (Stanford: Stanford University Press, 1996), 5; Pierre Bourdieu and Jean-Claude Passeron, *Reproduction in Education, Society and Culture*, trans. Richard Nice (London: Sage, 1977), 73–76.

68. Luc and Barbé, *Des normaliens*, 247; Ozouf and Ozouf, *La République des instituteurs*, 348. As a group the women teachers in the Ozoufs' study came from families somewhat better off than those of male teachers.

69. AN/F17 22517 (Bancilhon), 23685 (Dollé née Tourret), 21972 (Desportes), 22743/B (Mondet née Bertrand), 22498/A (M. Marsy).

70. AN, series F17, and ADP, series D1T1; AN F17/23911/B (Escande née Conte), 22618/A (Guny).

71. Félix Martel, "Les Instituteurs et l'inspection primaire," *MGP*, no. 12 (March 19, 1892): 98–100.

72. Data on marital status, age for first appointment as directrice, and career trajectories drawn from 193 *dossiers personnels*. In 1901, women were nearly 35 percent of the French work force, and 40 percent of women workers were married; in 1911 women were 37 percent of all workers, and 43 percent of women workers were married. See T. Deldycke, H. Gelders, J.-M. Limbor, *La Population active et sa structure*, ed. P. Bairoch (Brussels: Éditions de l'Institut de l'Université libre de Bruxelles, 1968), 167, 169.

73. AN F17/23901 (Chaudron née Tassin, 24052 (E. Chaudron); 23784 (Menat née Vaillant), 24013 (P. Menat); 24089 (Mazert née Cligny and J. Mazert).

74. AN F17/22289 (Pieyre née Nivoley).

75. AN F17/22893 (Granet), 23076 (Roy née Piot), 22812/A (Cuttoli née Pélissier).

76. Leslie Page Moch, *Moving Europeans: Migration in Western Europe since 1650*. 2nd ed. (Bloomington: Indiana University Press, 2003), 130; Moch, *The Pariahs of Yesterday: Breton Migrants in Paris* (Durham: Duke University Press, 2012). Frenchmen were more likely than women to migrate from their department of birth before 1900, women more likely by 1914.

NOTES TO PAGES 33–39 **245**

77. AN F17/23916 (Garonne née Layet), 22273 (Floutier née Béridot).

78. AN F17/22240 (Paringaux née Fontes), 22616/B (Ginier).

79. AN F17/22529/B (Frugier).

80. AN F17/22242 (Rambault née Martellière), 21960 (J. Rambault); 23685 (Dollé née Tourret and F. Dollé); 23784 (Menat née Vaillant), 24013 (P. Menat).

81. AN F17/23157 (Slawinska), 1898 resignation.

82. Twenty-three directrices died before retirement, 4 died while in other schools. Eight retired as *inspectrices générales* of écoles maternelles, 2 as departmental *inspectrices* of écoles maternelles, and 6 as *inspectrices primaires*.

83. AN F17/22517 (Bancilhon), 22576/A (Landais), 22498/A (Marsy), 23033/A (A. Petit), comments from qualifying examination for directrices, 1887. See also pp. 59–60.

84. "Documents législatifs, Chambre des députés, séances du 15, 17 mars 1884," *MGP*, no. 12 (March 22, 1884): 197–99, 203; "Sénat, séance du 29 mars 1886," *MGP*, no. 15 (April 10, 1886): 425; "Chambre des députés, séance du 26 octobre 1886," *MGP*, no. 45 (November 6, 1886): 786.

85. "Les Élections au Conseil supérieur de l'instruction publique," *MGP*, no. 50 (December 11, 1886): 866; Linda L. Clark, "Feminist Maternalists and the French State: Two Inspectresses General in the Pre-World War I Third Republic," *Journal of Women's History* 12 (Spring 2000): 32–59.

86. *Congrès international de l'enseignement primaire, analyse des mémoires*, in Musée pédagogique, *Mémoires et documents scolaires*, fascicule 91 (Paris: Delagrave and Hachette, 1889); Pauline Kergomard, "Les Femmes dans l'enseignement primaire," *RP* 14 (May 1889): 417–27, reprinted in *MGP*, no. 21 (May 25, 1889): 265–69.

87. AN 71AJ/81 (Ferdinand Buisson papers), 47 original *mémoires*; summaries of 45 *mémoires* in *Congrès international de l'enseignement primaire, analyse des mémoires*, 199–230.

88. In 1887, men taught 71 percent of *écoles mixtes*; in 1906, 65 percent. André Balz, "L'Expansion féminine dans l'enseignement primaire," *MGP*, no. 47 (August 25, 1906): 559.

89. AN 71AJ/81 (Buisson papers), report by Szumlanska; *Congrès international, Mémoires*, 98–99.

90. AN 71AJ/81, report by Mlle Verdeilhan, April 4, 1889 ; *Congrès international, Mémoires*, 101–02.

91. AN 71AJ/81, *mémoire* by Mme Gaudefroy, April 30, 1889; *Congrès international, Mémoires*, 84–85.

92. AN 71AJ/81 report by Mlle L. Gaudel on meeting, April 12, 1889, of personnel of the men's and women's normal schools, Perpignan; *Congrès international, Mémoires*, 85.

93. AN 71AJ/81, *mémoire* by Simboiselle; *Congrès international, Mémoires*, 98.

94. Clark, "A Battle of the Sexes in a Professional Setting," 96-104.

95. *Congrès international de l'enseignement primaire, Compte rendu des séances*, in Musée pédagogique, *Mémoires et documents scolaires*, fascicule 95 (Paris: Delagrave and Hachette, 1889), 23–24, 62–66, 73–75, quotations, 65.

96. *Congrès international, Compte rendu*, 73–74.

246   NOTES TO PAGES 39–45

97. Ozouf and Ozouf, *La République des instituteurs*, 352 (56 percent of retired women teachers but only 35 percent of men teachers identified themselves as Catholic; 28 percent of women were freethinkers or atheists, 49 percent of men; 4 percent of respondents were Protestant; 1 percent, other religions; 11 percent, no response).

98. For a defense of a directrice's religious practice, AN F17/20916 (Guttron). For exceptions to the rarity of criticism of directrices' religious practice in personnel files after the 1880s, see p. 98 on Slawinska, p. 121 on Moret-, pp. 201–202 on Combes née Buisson and Valin.

99. *Congrès international, Compte rendu*, 69.

100. Pécaut, "La Directrice," 299.

101. *Congrès international, Compte rendu*, 74–75 (Heurtefeu). On Heurtefeu, see Maurice Bouchor, "Préface," to *Pour nos institutrices*, by Mlle Heurtefeu (Pau: Imprimerie Garet, 1901), v–xii, and Mme Dollé, "Avant-Propos," in ibid., xiii–xix.

102. "Congrès international de l'enseignement primaire, liste des délégués étrangers, répartition par sections des délégués de France," *MGP*, no. 27 (July 6, 1889): 387–89, and "Seconde liste d'adhérents étrangers et français," *MGP*, no. 29 (July 20, 1889): 422–23; *Congrès international, Mémoires*, 201. Eleven directrices participated in the section discussing *écoles annexes*, three contributing *mémoires*, but only Mme Murique's opinions appear in the summary of debates.

103. *Congrès international, Compte rendu*, 73, 76. Lebrun, later Mme Goué, became a normal school directrice in 1911; Rauber became the second *inspectrice primaire*, replacing Dejean de la Bâtie in 1892.

104. Ibid., 76, 89–90. On Gréard, see Stéphanie Dauphin, *Octave Gréard, 1828–1904* (Rennes: Presses universitaires de Rennes, 2016).

105. *Congrès international, Compte rendu*, 93–94.

106. Rémi Dalisson, *Paul Bert: L'Inventeur de l'école laïque* (Paris: A. Colin, 2015), 112, 116.

Chapter 2

1. Eugen Weber, *Peasants into Frenchmen: The Modernization of Rural France, 1870–1914* (Stanford: Stanford University Press, 1976).

2. Schedules in N. Julien and J. Naudan, *Histoire des écoles normales de l'Aveyron 1835–1936* (Rodez: Subervie, 1936), 287–90; Jeanne-Luce Marcouly, *Le Périgord à l'école de la République: Les Écoles normales de la Dordogne, un siècle de laïcité* (Périgueux: Copédit, 2005), 122; Enquête Ozouf @Réseau-Canopé-Musée national de l'éducation, Rouen [hereinafter Enquête Ozouf, MUNAE] 1994.01219, "Historique de l'école normale" (Coutances).

3. Pécaut, "La Directrice d'école normale," *AEP* 8 (1892): 299.

4. AN F17/22893 (Granet); Georges Dumas, "L'École normale d'institutrices de la Marne de 1853 à 1939," *Travaux de l'Académie de Reims* 161 (1982): 165."

5. AN F17/22113/A (Mazier née Barbat), examination for future directrices.

NOTES TO PAGES 45–52   247

6. Quartararo, *Women Teachers and Popular Education*.

7. AN F17/22895 (Martin née Schaefer); Z., "Notes d'une directrice d'école normale," *RP* 8 (June 1886): 504–15. The *RP* index (1878–92) lists Martin-Schaefer as the author. Born in 1853, she taught privately before entering Fontenay.

8. Z., [Martin], "Notes d'une directrice."

9. AN F17/22967 (Loiret née Griess), May 1886 comment on Martin; 22242 (Rambault), 1894, inspector general Leyssenne; 22644/B (Athané née Terrial).

10. Koven and Michel, eds., *Mothers of a New World: Maternalist Politics*.

11. AN F17/22050 (Porte), 21898 (Bousquet), 21991 (Tailleur).

12. AN F17/22243 (Sagnier), March 1891; 22545/B (Thiébault), March 1901; 22291/A (Laurain), May 1911.

13. AN F17/21989/B (Ruby née Legros), 22322/B (Jacquemin).

14. AN F17/21922 (Boulinier née Pieyre), 22337/A (Bourgoise), 25907 (Sabatier née Lacassagne).

15. AN F17/22488/B (Hoël).

16. AN F17/22967 (Loiret née Griess). On assessments of students' "affectionate" conduct, see Quartararo, *Women Teachers*, 134–35, and Sharif Gemie, *Women and Schooling in France, 1815–1914* (Keele: University of Keele Press, 1995), 108, 195–96. On Mme Loiret, see also pp. 88, 95–96.

17. ANF17/22543/A (Saffroy), October 1881 examination.

18. AN F17 21850/A (Veyron-Lacroix).

19. AN F17/21413 (Olivaint), 21280/A (Mathieu), 22107/A (Guinier). For exam questions, AN F17/23076 (Roy née Piot), 1886; 24418 (Stolzenberg née Chambre), 1906.

20. L.-M. Compain, *L'Un vers l'autre* (Paris: P.-V. Stock, 1903), serialization starting October 1909; É. Albert and C. Arnaud, *Normaliennes* (Marseille: C. Arnaud, 1914), serialization starting October 1911.

21. AN F17/21413 (Olivaint), 1888; 22034 (Doisnel), 1888; 21280/A (Mathieu), 1889; 23063 (Viennot née Tournier), 1897; 22337/A (Bourgoise), 1905; 22240 (Paringaux), 1906; 23901 (Chaudron née Tassin), 1906; 22213/A (Viaud), 1907.

22. Clark, *Schooling the Daughters*; "Noms des auteurs et manuels d'instruction morale et civique," *MGP*, no. 47 (24 November 1883): 453; Z. [Martin], "Notes d'une directrice," 505.

23. *Catalogue des bibliothèques des écoles normales* in Musée pédagogique, *Mémoires et documents scolaires, fascicule* 32 (Paris: Hachette and Delagrave, 1887), 26; Marion's texts published by A. Colin, Paris.

24. Jacquelin Gautherin, *Une discipline pour la République: la science de l'éducation en France (1882–1914)* (Bern: Peter Lang, 1902).

25. AN 20020123/7, Fontenay-aux-Roses, Conférences des élèves directrices (1882–83), 32–33, 58–64.

26. "Plan d'études des écoles primaires publiques (27 juillet 1882)," *MGP*, no. 31 (August 5, 1882): 486–87. In a famous interchange with Simon in 1881 on "duties to God," Ferry asked which God (Dietz, "Jules Ferry et les traditions républicaines," 137).

27. Ognier, *Une école sans Dieu?*

248 NOTES TO PAGES 52–57

28. "Circulaire aux instituteurs," *MGP*, no. 47 (November 24, 1883): 451; Jean-Marie Mayeur, "Jules Ferry et la laïcité," in *Jules Ferry, fondateur de la République*, ed. François Furet (Paris: Éditions de l'École des hautes études en sciences sociales, 1985), 156.

29. AN 20020123/7, Fontenay-aux-Roses. Conférences (1886–87), 112–22. The phrase "dualité de la nature humaine" appeared in decrees on normal school curricula, August 3, 1881, and January 10, 1889. See Marcel Grandière, Rémi Paris, and Daniel Galloyer, eds., *La Formation des maîtres en France 1792–1914: Recueil de textes officiels* (Lyon: Institut national de recherche pédagogique, 2007), 307, 471.

30. AN F17/22517 (Bancilhon).

31. AN F17/22258 (Ruet).

32. AN F17/23799 (Sahuc née Sarradet).

33. Gabriel Compayré, *L'Instruction civique, cours complet suivi de notions d'économie politique à l'usage des écoles normales primaires*, 8th ed. (Paris: Delaplane, 1888), 64, 19th ed. (1912), 64. Compayré's *Éléments d'instruction morale et civique* (1880) for primary schools sold nearly a million copies and was one of four moral instruction textbooks put on the Index in 1882.

34. Ministère de l'instruction publique et des beaux-arts [hereinafter MIP], *Règlements et programmes d'études des écoles normales d'instituteurs et d'institutrices* (Paris: Imprimerie nationale, 1886), 89, 109; MIP, *Organisation pédagogique et programmes d'enseignement des écoles maternelles, des écoles primaires élémentaires, des écoles primaires supérieures et des écoles normales* (Paris: Imprimerie nationale, 1891), 63, 89–90 (January 10, 1889, curriculum). See also Grandière, Paris, Galloyer, *La Formation*, 332, 490.

35. AN F17/22698 (Prieur née Lacroix), 1900; 24109 (Six née Polge), 1903; François de Salignac de la Mothe Fénelon, *De l'éducation des filles* (at least 25 editions published between 1880 and 1914, including 10 edited by Charles Defodon for Hachette); Françoise d'Aubigné marquise de Maintenon, *Extraits de ses lettres, avis, entretiens, conversations et proverbes sur l'éducation*, ed. Octave Gréard (Paris: Hachette, 1884; 6th ed., 1905); Pécaut, *Quinze ans d'éducation*, 161–63, 170, 173, 215, 236–37.

36. Gabriel Compayré, *Histoire de la pédagogie*, 4th ed. (Paris: Delaplane, 1886), 323; 21st ed. (1910).

37. MIP, *Règlements* (1886), 89, MIP, *Organisation pédagogique*, 95; AN 20020123/7, Fontenay-aux-Roses, Conférences (1882–83), 20–27. On civic education, see Alain Mougniotte, *Les Débuts de l'instruction civique en France* (Lyon: Presses universitaires de Lyon, 1991)

38. AN F17/22113/A (Mazier).

39. AN F17/22107/A (Guinier); 24320 (Odoul); 24692 (Olanier), P. Pécaut report. On Breton normal schools, see chapter 4.

40. Z. [Martin], "Notes d'une directrice," 511–12.

41. "Notes d'une directrice d'école normale," *BulFR*, no. 4 (May 1896): 138–42.

42. F. Buisson, "Des lectures pour les veillées," *RP* 11 (November, December 1885): 397–412, 490–98. "L.S." (possibly Lucie Saffroy, Rouen).

43. Buisson, "Des lectures," 497–98; AN 71AJ/74 (Buisson papers), Lacoste letter.

44. AN F17/22316/B (Dejean de la Bâtie née Lacoste), Leyssenne, May 1886.

NOTES TO PAGES 58–67   249

45. AN F17/22183/A (Lacroix), 22488/B (Hoël), 21898 (Bousquet).

46. AN F17/22490/A (Janin née Magnier), 22322/B (Jacquemin).

47. AN F17/22337/A (Bourgoise); Paula Gillett, *Musical Women in England, 1870–1914: "Encroaching on All Men's Privileges"* (New York: St. Martin's Press, 2000), 78; AN F17/22576/B (Larivière), 1904–07.

48. AN 20020123/7, Fontenay-aux-Roses, Conférences (1882–83), 112–17.

49. Ibid.; F17/22851 (Dutilleul née Peltier).

50. AN F17/23685 (Dollé née Tourret), 23654/A (Sicre), 22337/A (Bourgoise). A law of July 14, 1901, made all tenured teachers eligible for the council.

51. "Candidats reçus aux différents examens supérieurs de l'enseignement primaire, année 1887," *AEP* 4 (1888): 358–59; AN F17/22517 (Bancilhon), 23685 (Dosser), 22107/B (Heigny née Marie).

52. AN F17/23033/A (Petit), 21989/B (Ruby née Legros).

53. Dalisson, *Paul Bert*, 116, 120.

54. AN F17/22243 (Sagnier); Mlle Sagnier, *L'Institutrice, Conseils pratiques* (Paris: Colin, 1895), 5–82, preface by Jules Steeg, ii–iv. On Sagnier, see also pp. 99, 103, 109, 110, 123, 165.

55. Sagnier, *L'Institutrice*, 83–85, 90–95, 124.

56. Sagnier, *L'Institutrice*, 102–07, 112–13, 125.

57. Léon Frapié, *L'Institutrice de province* (Paris: E. Fasquelle, 1897); Francisque Sarcey, "L'Institutrice de province," *Annales politiques et littéraires* 28 (May 2, and May 23, 1897): 274–75, 322–23; Sarcey, "Les Institutrices," ibid. 29 (July 4, 1897): 2–3.

58. AN 71AJ/81 (Buisson papers), 58 letters to Sarcey; excerpts from letters in Ida Berger, ed., *Lettres d'institutrices rurales d'autrefois, rédigées à la suite de l'enquête de Francisque Sarcey en 1897* (Paris: Association des amis du Musée pédagogique, c.1960).

59. AN 71AJ/81, Rambault to Sarcey, May 25, 1897.

60. AN 71AJ/81, March to Sarcey, undated; Desportes to Sarcey, April 29, 1897, but likely May 29.

61. Maurice Talmeyr, "Les Femmes qui enseignent," *Revue des deux mondes* 141 (June 1, 1897): 633–54, quotations, 646; Ferdinand Buisson, "Les Femmes qui enseignent et la 'Revue des deux mondes,'" *MGP*, no. 25 (19 June 1897): 289–90, no. 26 (June 26, 1897): 301–5, and ibid., *RP* 31 (July 1897): 12–26; S. Lauriol, "Au sujet d'un article récent," *BulFR*, no. 7 (July 1897): 294–98. Ozouf and Ozouf (*La République des instituteurs*, 355) report 65 percent of teachers surveyed read the *Manuel général*.

62. Édouard Petit, "Pour l'école," *Le Radical*, June 28, 1897. Barrès's controversial novel was first serialized in the *Revue de Paris*, May 15–August 15,1897.

63. Mme Eidenschenk, *Petits et grands secrets de bonheur* (Paris: Delagrave, 1907), 4–45; AN F17/23836 (Eidenschenk née Patin).

64. Mme Eidenschenk, *Petits et grands secrets de bonheur*, 52–76.

65. AN F17 23836 (Eidenschenk née Patin), 22193/A (Laurent Eidenschenk).

66. Eidenschenk, *Petits et grands secrets*, 117, 121, 124, 132, 138.

67. "Actes officiels," *MGP*, no. 48 (December 1, 1900): 768, no. 2 (January 12, 1901): 27.

68. "Réforme des programmes," *BulFR*, no. 20 (July 1901): 117–26; "Notes sur la révision des programmes des écoles normales," *BulFR*, no. 21 (November 1901): 175–90; Mlle Kieffer, "Réponses à Mlle Baertschi," *MGP*, no. 30 (July 29, 1899): 332. Also in

250 NOTES TO PAGES 67–71

BulFR: E. Chalon, "À propos de la réforme des programmes, les langues vivantes dans les écoles normales," no. 23 (May 1902): 315–17; J. Zgraggen, "Les Raisons pour et les raisons contre l'enseignement des langues vivantes," no. 27 (March 1903): 31–40; M. Martin, "Quelques réflexions sur la révision des programmes de sciences," no. 31 (April 1904): 69–72.

69. "Décret relatif aux écoles normales primaires, Arrêté relatif aux écoles normales primaires, Tableau de la repartition des matières de l'enseignement, Programmes," *Bulletin administratif de l'instruction publique* [hereinafter *BAIP*] 78, no. 1688 (September 2, 1905), 519–656, quotation 637.

70. "Décret . . . écoles normales (1905): 628, 647.

71. J. E. S. Hayward, "The Official Social Philosophy of the French Third Republic: Léon Bourgeois and Solidarity," *International Review of Social History* 6 (1961): 19–48; Judith F. Stone, *The Search for Social Peace: Reform Legislation in France, 1890–1914* (Albany: State University of New York Press, 1985); "Discours prononcé par M. Léon Bourgeois, president de la Ligue de l'enseignement à la séance d'ouverture du congrès de la Ligue," *RP* 27 (October 1895): 302–19.

72. Clark, *Schooling*, 30–34; Jean-Paul Martin, *La Ligue de l'Enseignement, Une histoire politique (1866–2016)* (Rennes: Presses universitaires de Rennes, 2016). Founded in 1867 by Jean Macé, the Ligue had more than 200,000 members in 1,500 local chapters by 1886.

73. Mme Sourdillon, "L'Enseignement ménager à l'école primaire," *AEP* 18 (1902): 448–77.

74. "Dénatalité: l'antériorité française (1800–1914)," special issue, *Communicatons*, no. 44 (1986); Karen Offen, "Depopulation, Nationalism, and Feminism in Fin-de-Siècle France," *American Historical Review* 89 (June 1984): 648–76; "Forum, Population and the State in the Third Republic," *French Historical Studies* 19 (Spring 1996): 633–734.

75. "La Puériculture à l'école de filles," *Journal des instituteurs* [hereinafter *JI*], no. 51 (17 September 1905): 201 (Dollé); *Rapports et délibérations du Conseil général du Loiret* (August 1906): 67; "Institut de puériculture fondé par la Société maternelle parisienne 'La Pouponnière,'" *Revue philanthropique* 30 (January 1912): 315–16; Mme Barthas, *L'Enseignement scolaire de la puériculture* (Paris: A. Michalon), 37–53; Mme Kergomard, "Éducation sexuelle," *L'Action féminine, Bulletin officiel du Conseil national des femmes françaises*, no. 22 (June 1912): 380; "Écoles normales, Programmes," *BAIP* 78 (1905): 584, 646.

76. Mary Lynn Stewart, *For Health and Beauty: Physical Culture for Frenchwomen 1880s–1930s* (Baltimore: Johns Hopkins University Press, 2001), 159–62; A. Dollé, "La Gymnastique rationnelle," *AEP* 23 (1907): 528–56; Philippe Tissié, *Une Oeuvre nationale par les normaliennes de Pau: Le Moteur humain* (n.p., 1913), 1; Mme Murique, *Gymnastique des jeunes filles* (Paris: Hachette, 1906, 3rd ed., 1908).

77. AN F17/22213/A (Viaud); 24213 (Perseil née Verdier); 24858 (Carion), 1908 examination for *économes*; 24418 (Stolzenberg).

78. AN F17/22280 (Kieffer); O. Laguerre, "Les Écoles normales d'institutrices," *La Fronde*, December 1, 1903, January 1, February 1, March 1, April 1, May 1, 1904 (Paringaux).

79. A. Dollé, "La Surveillance dans les écoles normales d'institutrices," *MGP*, no. 10 (March 8, 1902): 146–47; E. Denoël and S. Épinoux, "L'Éducation sociale dans les écoles normales primaires de filles," *MGP*, no. 27 (July 5, 1902): 417–19.

NOTES TO PAGES 71–76   251

80. AN F17/23836 (Eidenschenk née Patin).
81. "Circulaire relative à l'admission d'auditeurs et d'auditrices libres dans les écoles normales—du 18 juin," *BAIP* 79, no. 1729 (June 23, 1906): 701–3. The August 13, 1897 ban cancelled the May 3, 1892 circular opening normal schools to auditors.
82. AN F17/22520/B (Bonnefon).
83. AN F17/23028 (Peltier née Simboiselle), 1906; 23439 (Modrin); 24154 (J. Marie), 1911.
84. L. B. [Brossolette], "L'Énergie désirable," *Association amicale des professeurs des écoles normales d'instituteurs et des écoles normales d'institutrices de France, Bulletin triemestriel*, no. 14 (July 1906): 34–38, no. 15 (October 1906), 17–20; Daniel Vincent, "Sur le service de l'internat," ibid., no. 17 (April 1907): 22–24, and letters from professors, ibid., 25–29; A. Goué, "La Surveillance dans les écoles normales d'institutrices," *BulFR*, no. 42 (July 1907): 70–78; *Annuaire de l'instruction publique* (1890, 1909), for marital status.
85. A. Eidenschenk, "La Surveillance dans les écoles normales, Rapport présenté à M. le Ministre de l'instruction publique," *BulFR*, no. 61 (April 1907): 25–32; "Conseil supérieur de l'instruction publique. . . séance du 21 juillet," *BAIP* 86, no. 1908 (December 18, 1909): 1295; "Décret modifiant. . . décret du 19 juillet 1890, en ce qui concerne la surveillance dans les écoles normales d'institutrices," ibid., no. 1909 (December 25, 1909): 1321–22; "Circulaire relative à l'organisation de la surveillance dans les écoles normales d'institutrices," *BAIP* 87, no. 1919 (March 12, 1910): 324–28.
86. A. Laugier, "Conseil supérieur de l'instruction publique, La surveillance dans les écoles normales d'institutrices, Session de juillet 1909," *École nouvelle* [hereinafter *EN*] 13, no. 2 (October 9, 1909): 22–23.
87. On schoolteachers' demands, see pp. 156, 165, 169.
88. Ozouf and Ozouf, *La République des instituteurs*; Enquête Ozouf, MUNAE.
89. AN F17.21047 (Lafforgue), May 15, 1899 letter; "Le Vingtenaire de l'école normale," *La Charente*, May 26, 1904; Augustine Guillemiau, "Ma première année à l'école normale, Le Mans, 1882–1883," ed. Gérard Boeldieu, *Bulletin de la Société d'agriculture, sciences et arts de la Sarthe, Mémoires* (1989) : 41–64; AN F17/22322/B (Jacquemin).
90. Enquête Ozouf, MUNAE, institutrices, Cher (M), Pas-de-Calais (L), Seine-et-Marne (C), Basses-Alpes (C), Côtes-du-Nord (G, Q), Nord (J, S), Haute-Saône (P), Côte-d'Or (M), Cher (A). The rules for use of the Enquête Ozouf do not permit citing respondents' names or file numbers.
91. Enquête Ozouf, MUNAE, Eure-et-Loir (O, M). See also Association amicale normalienne de Chartres, *Hommage à Mademoiselle Bonnefon* (Vendôme: S. Doucet, 1934), 23–26.
92. Enquête Ozouf, MUNAE, Eure (P, C), Seine/Paris (M).
93. Enquête Ozouf, MUNAE, Seine/Paris (L), citing école normale, Corrèze; Aude (M).
94. Enquête Ozouf, MUNAE, Puy-de-Dôme (G), Gironde (D), Sarthe (B), Bouches-du-Rhône (C), Marne (J), Cher (B), Doubs (S). On Gebelin, see also Ozouf and Ozouf, *La République des instituteurs*, 263–64.
95. Enquête Ozouf, MUNAE, Charente-Maritime (Charente-Inférieure) (D).
96. Enquête Ozouf, MUNAE, Saône-et-Loire (C).

252 NOTES TO PAGES 76–82

97. AN F17/23836 (Eidenschenk née Patin); Enquête Ozouf, MUNAE, Nord (J, P).

98. AN F17/25907 (Sabatier).

99. Goué, "La Surveillance," 72.

100. Enquête Ozouf, MUNAE, Cher (M), Hautes-Pyrénées (A); Benjamin Lutringer and Pierre Rothiot, *Cent cinquante ans au service du peuple* (Charmes: G. Feuillard, 1978), 1: 280; Enquête Ozouf, Rhône (B), Charente Inférieure (1192); B. G., "La Normalienne de Grenoble," *Les Temps nouveaux*, no. 13 (16 May 1908): 6. The Tarbes directrice until 1913 was Protestant.

101. Rachel Albert, "Réponse à Mme O. Laguerre," *La Fronde*, December 1, 1903.

102. Ozouf and Ozouf, *La République des instituteurs*, chapter 6; Enquête Ozouf, MUNAE, Charente (H, M), Finistère (S, P), Hautes-Pyrénées (D), Jura (T), Pas-de-Calais (P).

103. Jean Gonthier, ed., *Thérèse Billard dit adieu à Montgelas, L'Institutrice (1910–1924)* (Montmélian: Arc-Isère, 1990), 20, 64.

104. Enquête Ozouf, MUNAE, Deux-Sèvres (B), Indre-et-Loire (C), Ille-et-Vilaine (M).

105. AN F17/23901 (Chaudron née Tassin), 23474 (Pommeret). For exceptions to ignoring the Dreyfus Affair, see pp. 98, 99.

106. Enquête Ozouf, MUNAE, Vendée (S), Seine-et-Marne (G).

107. Ozouf and Ozouf, *La République des instituteurs*, 191–201, 352. Only 8 percent of men and women respondents regularly attended church.

108. *Dixième congrès international des femmes, Oeuvres et institutions féminines, Droits des femmes, 2–8 juin 1913, compte rendu des travaux*, ed. Mme Avril de Sainte-Croix (Paris: Giard et Brière, 1914), 148–51, quotations in Varlet report. Varlet, a directrice since 1890, was named to Lyon in 1907 (AN F17/22709).

109. *Dixième congrès international des femmes*, 148.

110. *Dixième congrès international des femmes*, 147.

111. AN F17/24323 (Petit-Dutaillis née Desvignes).

112. *Dixième congrès international des femmes*, 152–53.

113. Oulhiou, *L'École normale supérieure de Fontenay-aux-Roses*, 300 n.174; Enquête Ozouf, MUNAE, Haute-Savoie (L), Meuse (V), Tarn (A), Oise (M).

114. Lutringer and Rothiot, *Cent cinquante ans*, 1: 279; Enquête Ozouf, MUNAE, Côtes-d'Armor (formerly Côtes du Nord) (L).

Chapter 3

1. Pécaut, "La Directrice d'école normale," 305–6.

2. Ibid., 300–1. On inspectors general, rectors, and *inspecteurs d'académie*, see Guy Caplat, ed., *Les Inspecteurs généraux de l'instruction publique: Dictionnaire biographique 1802–1914* (Paris: INRP/Éditions du CNRS, 1986); Jean-François Condette, *Les Recteurs d'académie en France de 1808 à 1940*, 3 vols. (Lyon: Service d'histoire de l'éducation/INRP, 2006–09); Dominique Lerche and Gilles Pétreault, eds. *L'Inspecteur d'académie, deux siècles au service de l'éducation* (Paris: Centre national de documentation pédagogique, 2008).

NOTES TO PAGES 83–92   253

3. Pécaut, "La Directrice d'école normale," 324.

4. AN F17/24428 (Stolzenberg). A *décret* of March 29, 1890, governed the *conseil d'administration.*

5. Pécaut, "La Directrice d'école normale," 313; Luc and Barbé, *Des normaliens*, 49.

6. Clark, "A Battle of the Sexes in a Professional Setting," 108–10, evaluations of 75 male and 8 female inspectors in the Seine and Seine-et-Oise, many of them former normal school directors.

7. Pécaut, "La Directrice d'école normale," 310.

8. AN F17/21991 (Tailleur), 22213/A (Viaud), 21922 (Boulisset née Pieyre), 22312/B (Bourgoin).

9. AN F17/22812/A (Cuttoli née Pélissier), 22050 (Porte), 23403 (N. Robert), 23028 (Peltier née Simboiselle), 22545/A (Sourdillon née Simboiselle). For officials' comments on appearance and social origins of women secondary school professors, see Margadant, *Madame le Professeur*, 188–90.

10. AN F17/22240 (Paringaux née Fontes).

11. AN F17/22201/A (Laurain), 23903 (Combes nèe Buisson), 24174 (R. Albert).

12. AN F17/22243 (Sagnier), 22113/A (Mazier), 22449/A (Jalambic).

13. AN F17/22337/A (Bourgoise), 22107/A (Guinier).

14. AN F17/22743/B (Mondet née Bertrand), marriage 1899; "Nécrologie—Mme Mondet," *RP* 44 (March 1904): 274–76.

15. AN F17/21989/B (Ruby née Legros), marriage 1897.

16. AN F17/23784 (Meant née Vaillant), 24088 (Mayaud). Of these five directrices, all born during the 1860s, only Menat became a directrice during the difficult formative years of the 1880s.

17. AN F17/22525/A (Cruvellier), 24213 (Perseil née Verdier).

18. AN F17/23971 (Billotey); *Denise Billotey, directrice honoraire de l'école normale d'institutrices de la Seine* (Paris: n.p., 1949).

19. AN F17/22967 (Loiret née Griess); 22985 (Martin née Schaefer), 23136/B (A. Martin); 23836 (Eidenschenk née Patin), 22193/A (L. Eidenschenk); 24109 (Six née Polge), 24330 (G. Six); 22644/B (Athané née Terrial), 21942/B (U. Terrial); 24323 (Petit-Dutaillis née Desvignes).

20. AN F17/25907 (Sabatier née Lacassagne), 22510/A (A. Sabatier); 23647/B (A. Rollet), Duplan on Rollet's marriage to Mlle Courbières.

21. AN F17/21980/B (Lusier)

22. AN F17/21980/B (Lusier).

23. AN F17/23301 (Ebren née Planchard), 25770 (H. Ebren).

24. AN F17/23301 (Ebren née Planchard); *BAIP* 51, no. 1007 (May 14, 1892): 522, no. 1013 (June 25, 1892): 663.

25. AN F/17/22529/B (Frugier).

26. AN F17/22529/B (Frugier); François Mayoux, *Marie et François Mayoux, instituteurs pacifistes et syndicalistes, Mémoires* (Chamalières: Canope, 1992).

27. AN F17/22107/A (A. Guinier). A. Gunier was a teacher and normal school professor before becoming a directrice in Aix, Perpignan, and Draguignan; H. Guinier was named to Draguignan in 1900.

254 NOTES TO PAGES 92-101

28. AN F17/22107/A (A. Guinier). Ginoux also tried to block a teachers' *syndicat* in the Var (AN Base Léonore, Ginoux).

29. AN F17/22107/A (A. Guinier).).

30. Pécaut, "La Directrice d'école normale," 323.

31. AN F17/22050 (Porte). On religious schooling in Lyon, see Sarah A. Curtis, *Educating the Faithful: Religion, Schooling, and Society in Nineteenth-Century France* (DeKalb: Northern Illinois University Press, 2000).

32. AN F17/23087 (Semmartin); "Nécrologie," *Bulletin de l'instruction primaire du département du Loiret* 19 (1911): 85; AN F17/21989/B (Ruby née Legros), 22012/A (Lauriol), 21922 (Boulisset née Pieyre).

33. AN F17/22442/A (Crouzel née Fontecave), 22851 (Dutilleul née Peltier), 22012/A (Lauriol).

34. AN F17/22490/A (Janin née Magnier), 23384 (Languéry), 22090/A (L. Thomas).

35. AN F17/22442/A (Crouzel née Fontecave).

36. AN F17/22967 (Loiret née Griess).

37. AN F17/22967 (Loiret née Griess); "Docteurs, licenciés et bacheliers féminins," *La Gazette des femmes*, no. 53 (April 10, 1879). Mlle Griess was briefly at Fontenay until delegated to Melun, January 17, 1881.

38. AN F17/22967 (Loiret née Griess).

39. Ibid.; *Journal officiel de la République française*, Chambre des députés, July 13, 1889, 2000-02.

40. AN F17/23157 (Slawinska).

41. Caplat, ed., *Les Inspecteurs généraux de l'instruction publique*, 540; Cabanel, *Ferdinand Buisson*, 482, n. 27; Mélanie Fabre, "Marie Baertschi-Fuster, une intellectuelle et une éducatrice au service du progrès social," *Études sociales*, nos. 167–68 (2018): 397–446; AN F17/23692 (Fuster née Baertschi).

42. Marie Aynié, "'J'admire . . . ,' Lettres de soutien à Émile Zola dans l'affaire Dreyfus," *Cahiers naturalistes*, no. 82 (2008): 8; Paul Brenet and Félix Thureau, eds., *Hommage des artistes à Picquart* (Paris: Société libre d'édition des gens de lettres, 1899), 3–142.

43. Brenet and Thureau, eds., *Hommage des artistes à Picquart*, 3–142 (directrices, 106, 111); *L'Aurore*, December 3, 1898 (Slawinska).

44. A. Eidenschenk, "La Neutralité," *BulFR*, no. 14 (December 1899): 110–14; "Obsèques de M. Pécaut," *BulFR*, no. 11 (November 1898): 14–18; Cabanel, *Ferdinand Buisson*, 313–16.

45. Ozouf and Ozouf, *La République des instituteurs*, 161–64; Enquête Ozouf, MUNAE, Jura (T), Isère (E), Hautes-Pyrénées (D), Rhône (C), Saône-et-Loire (L), Cher (A); *Livre du cinquantenaire de l'école normale de La Roche-sur-Yon (1884–1934)* (La Roche-sur-Yon: Pottier, 1934), 52, Mme Teillaud-Barbier, 1898–1901.

46. AN F17.22916/B (Murique née François).

47. AN F17/22148/B (J. V. Thomas).

48. AN F17/22918/A (Jacquin née Morand), 22573/B (Léon Jacquin).

49. AN F17/22918/A (Jacquin née Morand).

50. AN F17/23176 (M. Allégret); Cabanel, *Ferdinand Buisson*, 267; Paul Desjardins, "Mlle Marie-Thérèse Allégret," *Bulletin de l'Union pour l'action morale* 6, nos. 1–3 (November 1, 15, December 1, 1897): 37–47, 76–96, 113–44.

NOTES TO PAGES 102–109   255

51. AN F17/21972 (Desportes). Desportes was one of only eight women with a *baccalauréat-ès sciences* as of 1879.

52. AN F17/22337/A (Bourgoise).

53. AN F17/22243 (Sagnier), 22447/B (Grauvogel).

54. AN F17/22545/B (Thiébault), 23775/A (Labergère née Dalon), 23901 (C. Chaudron née Tassin), 24052 (E. Chaudron).

55. AN F17/23901 (Chaudron née Tassin).

56. AN F17 23901 (Chaudron née Tassin), 24052 (E. Chaudron).

57. AN F17/23901 (Chaudron née Tassin).

58. AN F17/23901 (Chaudron née Tassin).

59. AN F17/23901 (Chadron née Tassin).

60. "Nécrologie—Mme Mondet;" Jacques Ozouf, "Les Instituteurs de la Manche au début du XXe siècle," *Revue d'histoire moderne et contemporaine* 13 (January–March 1966): 103–4, citing Crouzel's article in *Annuaire de l'enseignement primaire de la Manche* (1897); "L'Association des anciennes élèves de l'école normale d'institutrices de Saint-Brieuc," *RP* 38 (May 1901): 486–88. On student associations at various levels, see Véronique Castagnet-Lars, ed., *Les Associations d'élèves et d'étudiants: Entre socialisation et apprentissages (XVIe–XXe siècle)* (Toulouse: Presses universitaires du Midi, 2020), including Johann-Günther Egginger, "Entre renseignements mutuels et expression d'une pensée pédagogique: L'Association amicale des anciennes élèves de l'école normale d'institutrices de Beauvais (1898–1990)," 173–89.

61. E. Legros, "Création d'une association amicale des anciennes élèves de l'école normale d'institutrices de La Roche-sur-Yon," *BulFR*, no. 6 (April 1897): 266–70; AN F17/ 22322/B (Jacquemin). *Amicales* identified in personnel files, *amicale* bulletins, and *AEP*.

62. A. R., "A propos d'un livre récent," *Bulletin de l'association amicale des anciennes élèves de l'école normale d'institutrices de Limoges*, no. 18 (June 1905): 461–67. [Hereinafter *BAAENI* for *amicale* bulletin titles.]

63. "Compte rendu de la réunion générale 17 mai 1906," *BAAENI de la Seine-Inférieure*, no. 23 (1907): 28; J. Palanque, "Causeries de fin d'année," *BAAENI de la Vendée*, no. 17 (1912): 4–5; *BAAENI de la Seine*, no. 4 (1911); *BAAENI de Melun*, nos. 44, 45 (1911), 47 (1912).

64. M. Thiébault, "Article de Mademoiselle Thiébault," *BulFR*, no. 34 (January 1905): 62–66; E. Flayol, "Une question d'éducation sociale," *BulFR*, no. 41 (April 1907): 17–24.

65. Eidenschenk, "La Neutralité;" Pauline Kergomard, "Choses de l'enseignement," *La Fronde*, September 22, 1899.

66. Mlle Sagnier, *La Fillette bien élévée* (Paris: A. Colin, 1896); J. Mayaud, *Politesse et bonne tenue* (Paris: E. Cornély, 1904, 1908); Mme Murique, *Maman et petite Jeanne* (Paris: Hachette, 1891) and *Économie domestique et hygiène, à l'usage des écoles primaires de filles* (Paris: Delalain, 1894, 7th ed., 1911); Mme Eidenschenk-Patin, *Les premières lectures des petites filles* (1911), *Les deuxièmes lectures des petites filles* (1912), *Les troisièmes lectures des petites filles* (1913) (all Paris: C. Delagrave). Also by directrices: Lucie Saffroy and Georges Noël, eds., *Les Écrivains de l'antiquité, extraits des œuvres de Xénophon, Platon, Aristote, Quintilien, Plutarque* (Paris: Nathan, 1897);

256   NOTES TO PAGES 109–113

Mme Goué and E. Goué, *Comment faire observer nos élèves* (Paris: Nathan, 1911, 4th ed., 1920). Numbers of copies from archives of Colin, Hachette, Delagrave.

67. Alcide Lemoine and Juliette Marie, *La jeune française, 200 Lectures alternées pour les jeunes filles* (Paris: Larousse, 1910), 5; 33,000 copies by 1912 (archives of Larousse). See also p. 180 on this textbook.

68. The Bibliothèque Nationale de France catalogue has 188 entries for textbooks by Gauthier (Mme Échard as of 1911), some coauthored with L. Perseil, all published in Paris by F. Nathan.

69. Ozouf and Ozouf, *La République des instituteurs*, 395; Pierre Caspard, Pénélope Caspard-Karydis, and André Chambon, eds., *La Presse d'éducation et d'enseignement, XVIIIe siècle–1940* (Paris: INRP/Éditions du CNRS, 1981–91), 3: 77; Condette, *Les Recteurs d'académie*, vol. 2, *Dictionnaire biographique* (2006), 311.

70. Mlle Heurtefeu, *Pour nos institutrices, conseils pratiques* (Pau: n.p., 1901). Heurtefeu (AN F17/22911) and Dollé (AN F17/23685) were *maîtresses* at the normal school in Melun in 1881–83 and later directrices in adjacent departments, Heurtefeu in Hautes-Pyrénées (1888–93) and Landes (1893–98), Dollé in Basses-Pyrénées.

71. "Discours prononcé par Mlle Denise Billotey, professeur à l'école supérieure de jeunes filles Edgar Quinet, à Paris," *RP* 31 (November 1897): 535–39.

72. "L'Houmeau-Pontouvre," *La Charente*, August 13, 1902; "Un discours," *La Fronde*, August 23, 1902; Harlor, "Deux discours," ibid., August 25, 1902; Henri Brissac, "Lien des deux questions," *L'Aurore*, August 24, 1902; "Deux discours," *La Charente*, September 4, 1902.

73. R. Lecomte, "Le Patronage des ouvrières et apprenties de la ville du Puy," *RP* 29 (November 1896): 515–19; AN F17/23810 (Armanet née Beugnon).

74. AN F17/22616/B (Ginier), 22442/A (Crouzel), 23301 (Ebren), 22918/A (Jacquin), 25907 (Sabatier), 23911/B (Escande née Conte), 21922 (Boulisset née Pieyre); 23087 (Semmartin), Orléans; 23751 (Combe), citing directrice Guny, Blois.

75. AN F17/21911/A (Léveillé).

76. *Congrès international de l'enseignement primaire du 2 au 5 août 1900, Programme. . . Délégués. . . Membres* (Paris: Imprimerie E. Kapp, 1900), 18–69, attended by 45 directrices and 5 former directrices.

77. "Deux voeux sociaux," *Le Radical*, November 22, 1899; D. Billotey, "La Femme éducatrice," *RP* 64 (June 1914): 530–38.

78. Jean-Paul Martin, "Entre philanthropie et féminisme: Le Comité des dames de la Ligue de l'enseignement (1901–1914)," in *Le Pouvoir du genre: Laïcités et religions 1905–2005*, ed. Florence Rochefort (Toulouse: Presses universitaires du Mirail, 2007), 47–63; M. Ferdinand-Dreyfus, "L'École républicaine et le patronage féminin," *Revue politique et parlementaire* 29 (August 1901): 263–89.

79. "Coopération feminine," *RP* 38 (March 1901): 308–10; Bibliothèque Marguerite Durand (Paris) [hereinafter BMD], DOS 362 COO, Coopération féminine.

80. "Liste des sociétaires au 1er juillet 1907," *Bulletin, Société libre pour l'étude psychologique de l'enfant* 7 (1906–07): 184–200. Buisson held the Sorbonne chair after Marion's death in 1896.

NOTES TO PAGES 114–117　257

81. Desjardins, "Mlle Marie-Thérèse Allégret," 45; "Liste des membres de l'Union," *Bulletin de l'Union pour la vérité* (1908), 1–60; Jean-Elisabeth Pedersen, "'Speaking Together Openly, Honestly and Profoundly': Men and Women as Public Intellectuals in Early Twentieth-Century France," *Gender and History* 26 (April 2014): 36–51; A. Eidenschenk, "De la neutralité politique et religieuse à l'école publique," *Bulletin de l'Union pour l'action morale* 12, no. 7 (February 1, 1904): 289–310. I thank Jean Pedersen for the membership list of l'Union pour la vérité, formerly l'Union pour l'action morale.

82. Fédération internationale de la libre pensée, *Congrès de Paris. . . septembre 1905* (Paris: n.p., 1905), 34–35.

83. "Nos instituteurs en Suisse," *Le petit parisien*, October 11, 1903; "La Société d'études et de correspondance internationale," *Le Figaro*, December 20, 1903; "Le Comité international d'études pédagogiques," *Le Radical*, January 6, 1904; "Tourisme universitaire," *Bulletin trimestriel de l'amicale des instituteurs et institutrices de l'Ardèche* (June 1909), 17; AN F17/22337/A (Bourgoise). On French educators and international congresses, see Damiano Matasci, *L'École républicaine à l'étranger: Une histoire internationale des réformes scolaires en France 1870–1914* (Lyon: ENS Éditions, 2015).

84. *Bulletin de l'Association des inspecteurs primaires et des directeurs d'écoles normales* [hereinafter *BAIPDEN*], no. 1 (May 1905): 7–9.

85. Condette, *Histoire de la formation des enseignants*, 136–41; *MGP*, nos. 11, 12, 13 (16, 23, 30 December 1905), 121–23, 133–35, 147–48, letters from Laugier, Bousquet, F. Henry, directors of men's normal schools, and directrice Eidenschenk; A. Eidenschenk, "Les Écoles normales et le projet de M. Massé," *BulFR*, no. 39 (April 1906): 98–104.

86. "Membres," *BAIPDEN*, no. 8 (October 1907): 341–45, no. 24 (May 1912): 528–32. Between 1905 and 1914 at least 70 directrices joined, but a number left with retirement or for unspecified reasons; 12 more joined after the 1912 list was published.

87. Marie Rauber, "De la part des institutrices dans la représentation primaire au Conseil supérieur de l'instruction publique," *JI*, no. 21 (May 14, 1896): 475–78.

88. Forty CSIP seats were filled by election. The minister of public instruction appointed other members, including four from *enseignement libre* who participated in discussions concerning private schools. Mathilde Salomon, head of a private girls' school in Paris, was long a member.

89. AN F17/23836 (Eidenschenk née Patin); Enquête Ozouf, MUNAE, Nord (J).

90. "Élection au Conseil supérieur de l'instruction publique," *JI*, no. 37 (7 June 1903): 483–84, Eidenschenk née Patin statement.

91. "Élection au Conseil supérieur," *JI*, no. 37 (June 7, 1903); "Candidature de Mme Eidenschenk, née Patin," *MGP*, no. 21 (May 21, 1904): 253–54.

92. Odette Laguerre, "Portrait de femme, Mme Eidenschenk," *La Fronde*, 1 July 1904.

93. AN F17/23694 (Géhin), "La Question scolaire dans la Meuse," *L'Union verdunoise*, April 5, 1911.

258 NOTES TO PAGES 118–126

Chapter 4

1. Jean-François Chanet, *L'École républicaine et les petites patries* (Paris: Aubier, 1996). See also Robert Gildea, *Education in Provincial France 1800–1914: A Study of Three Departments* (Oxford: Clarendon Press, 1983).
2. On Brittany, see Caroline Ford, *Creating the Nation in Provincial France: Religion and Political Identity in Brittany* (Princeton: Princeton University Press, 1993).
3. On Algeria, see Charles-Robert Ageron, *Les Algériens musulmans et la France 1871–1919*, 2 vols. (Paris: Presses universitaires de France, 1968) and Ageron, *Histoire de l'Algérie contemporaine*, 11th ed. (Paris: Presses universitaires de France, 1999).
4. I. Carré, "De la manière d'enseigner les premiers éléments du français dans les écoles de la Basse-Bretagne," *RP* 12 (March 1888): 21–36, and "De la manière d'enseigner les premiers éléments du français aux indigènes, dans nos colonies et dans les pays soumis à notre protectorat," *RP* 18 (April 1891): 289–314.
5. MIP, *Statistique de l'enseignement primaire* 4 (1886–1887), 32–24. The Côtes-du-Nord was renamed Côtes-d'Armor in 1990.
6. MIP, *Statistique* 3 (1881–1882), 106–9.
7. MIP, *Statistique* 4 (1886–1887), 304–6.
8. AN F17/21983/A (Moret); F17/9572, Moret report, July 20, 1886, to the *inspecteur d'académie* and local surveillance committee.
9. AN F17/21983/A (Moret); *Le petit parisien*, October 18, 1892, citing Bourgeois. The Loire-Inférieure was renamed Loire-Atlantique in 1957.
10. MIP, *Statistique* 7 (1901–1902), 124–27, 137–39.
11. AN F17/21983/A (Moret); Condette, *Les Recteurs*, vol. 2, *Dictionnaire biographique*, 226.
12. AN F17/21983/A (Moret); Condette, *Les Recteurs*, vol. 2, *Dictionnaire biographique*, 353; Enquête Ozouf, MUNAE, Loire-Inférieure (B); AN F17/23911/B (Escande).
13. AN F17/22113/A (Mazier née Barbat).
14. AN F17/2113/A (Mazier); MIP, *BAIP* 48 (October 18, 1890): 783, Ditandy retirement.
15. AN F17/22289 (Pieyre née Nivoley), 22459/A (C. Robert), 22243 (Sagnier), 21989/B (Ruby née Legros), 21682 (Sage). On Sage, see below.
16. AN F17/22298 (Voinet), quotation May 1890.
17. AN F17.22107/B (Heigny née Marie), Jarry, 1891.
18. AN F17/23028 (Peltier née Simboiselle). On Peltier's background see pp. 38, 84. Mme Marie Peltier should not be confused with Marie Peltier Dutilleul (p. 59).
19. Dumans, *L'École normale, 100 ans à Laval* (Laval: Silöe, 1989), 54; Janine Salbert and Jean-Louis Dumans, "Centenaire de l'école normale d'institutrices de la Mayenne," *303, La Revue des pays de la Loire*, no. 16 (1988): 64.
20. AN F17/22488/B (Hoël), 22555/B (Brocard).
21. Yannic Rome, *Séminaires laïques: Écoles normales, normaliens, normaliennes en Morbihan (1831–1991)* (Le Faouët: Liv'Éditions, 2013), 80–85.
22. *Rapports du préfet et délibérations du conseil général du Morbihan*, séance du 20 août 1897, 154–59; Rome, *Séminaires*, 80–85; AN F17/23174 (Aignan).

NOTES TO PAGES 126–133   259

23. Rome, *Séminaires*, 85–88; *L'Arvor*, June 3, 1898, and *Croix du Morbihan*, cited in Rome, *Séminaires*; *La Dépêche de Brest*, June 1 and 3, 1898; *Le Figaro*, June 5, 1898; *La Fronde*, June 6, 1898; *L'Univers*, June 7, 1898; *Le Radical*, June 7, 1898.

24. AN F17/23033/A (A. Petit).

25. "Nécrologie," *L'Avenir du Morbihan*, June 3, 1898; "Triaize," *Le Patriote de la Vendée, organe d'Union républicaine)*, June 16, 1898.

26. Rome, *Séminaires*, 86–88. The court discarded one complaint concerning an orphan, reducing the number to thirty-five.

27. "Procès des normaliennes de Vannes contre *L'Arvor*," *L'Enseignement pratique* 3 (July 10, 1898): 397–98; A. Balz, in *Le Rappel*, July 25, 1898, and *Le dix-neuvième siècle*, July 27, 1898. See also Clemenceau's *L'Aurore*, July 8, 1899.

28. Rome, *Séminaires*, 88; Joseph Galtier, "Au pays Breton, la concurrence scolaire," *Le Volume* 15 (October 10, 1903): 219.

29. AN F17/23415 (Mahaut), quotation from J. Steeg, May 19, 1897; F17/22576/A (Landais).

30. AN F17/23903 (Combes née Buisson), inspecteur d'académie, April 26, 1911, on "mentalité;" F17/24602 (Hui), inspector general Pierre Pécaut, 1914, on "civil war."

31. AN F17/22545/B (Thiébault).

32. AN F17/22545/B (Thiébault).

33. AN F17/23836 (Eidenschenk née Patin).

34. AN F17/23836 (Eidenschenk née Patin), June 26, 1903, report on parents' responses, and Nouet correspondence, July 1, 3, 7, and 11, 1903; AN F17/21957/B (Nouet), *inspecteur d'académie*, Côtes-du-Nord since 1892.

35. AN F17/22193/A (L. Eidenschenk); Alain Prigent, *Les Instituteurs des Côtes-du-Nord: Laïcité, amicalisme et syndicalisme (sous la IIIe république)* (Sables-d'Or-les-Pins: Éditions Astoure, 2005), 233.

36. MIP, *Statistique* 7 (1901–1902), 124–27, 136–39; Grew and Harrigan, *School, State, and Society*, chapters 4 and 5.

37. MIP, *Statistique* 3 (1881–1882), 166–69, and 7 (1901–1902), 178–81.

38. Ibid. For national statistics, see also J.-P. Briand, J.-M. Chapoulie, F. Huguet, J.-N. Luc, and A. Prost, *L'Enseignement primaire et ses extensions, Annuaire statistique, 19e-20e siècles, Écoles maternelles, primaires, primaires supérieures et professionnelles* (Paris: INRP/Économica, 1987).

39. MIP, *Statistique* 8 (1906–1907), 266–69.

40. MIP, *Statistique* 8 (1906–1907), 298, 304. By 1906, 96.5 percent of army conscripts were rated literate, but three Breton departments had somewhat lower rates. On literacy in Finistère, see Ford, *Creating the Nation*, 61–66.

41. MIP, *Statistique* 8 (1906–1907), 124–27.

42. MIP, *Statistique* 8 (1906–1907), 136–39; Jean Peneff, *Écoles publiques, écoles privées dans l'Ouest, 1880–1950* (Paris: L'Harmattan, 1987).

43. AN F17/23028 (Peltier née Simboiselle); MIP, *Statistique* 7 (1901–1902), 180–81; Enquête Ozouf, MUNAE, Mayenne (J), Vienne (C).

44. MIP, *Statistique* 7 (1901–1902), 178–79; AN F17/23911 (Escande).

45. AN F17/23895 (Bouige), 22457/A (Pingaud née Épinoux).

260 NOTES TO PAGES 133–137

46. MIP, *Statistique* 4 (1886–1887), 304–7; 5 (1891–1892), 252–55; 6 (1896–1897), 274–77; 7 (1901–1902), 280–83; 8 (1906–1907), 280–83.

47. Enquête Ozouf, MUNAE, Côtes-du-Nord (B, L), Finistère (Q), Vendée (S).

48. Enquête Ozouf, MUNAE, Finistère (S), Ille-et-Vilaine (F, P, S), Maine-et-Loire (M), Mayenne (B).

49. Enquête Ozouf, MUNAE, responses of 96 women teachers from 7 Breton departments and Vendée.

50. Enquête Ozouf, MUNAE, Ille-et-Vilaine (L, F, P), Maine-et-Loire (M).

51. Enquête Ozouf, MUNAE, Maine-et-Loire (B, L, F), Côtes-du-Nord (H).

52. A. Eidenschenk, "La religieuse Bretagne," *AEP* 22 (1906): 438–58. On characterizations of Breton resistance to national policies, see Ford, *Creating the Nation*, chapter 6.

53. A. Eidenschenk, "La religieuse Bretagne," 457–58.

54. AN F17/23895 (Bouige), 1912; 24204 (Lallier), evaluation by Olanier; 22457/A (Pingaud), May 1911.

55. AN, base Léonore, Légion d'honneur, 1980035/1176/36194 (Palanque née Massip).

56. J. Palanque, "Causeries de fin d'année," *BAAENI de la Vendée*, no. 17 (1912): 5.

57. Nupur Chaudhuri and Margaret Strobel, eds., *Western Women and Imperialism: Complicity and Resistance* (Bloomington: Indiana University Press, 1992); Antoinette Burton, *Burdens of History: British Feminists, Indian Women, and Imperial Culture, 1865–1915* (Chapel Hill: University of North Carolina Press, 1994); Julia Clancy Smith and Frances Gouda, eds., *Domesticating the Empire: Race, Gender, and Family Life in French and Dutch Colonialism* (Charlottesville: University Press of Virginia, 1999): Lora Wildenthal, *German Women for Empire, 1884–1945* (Durham: Duke University Press, 2001).

58. Claudine Robert-Guiard, *Des Européennes en Algérie 1830–1939* (Aix-en-Provence: Publications de l'Université de Provence, 2009); Marie-Paule Ha, *French Women and Empire: The Case of Indochina* (Oxford: Oxford University Press, 2014).

59. Ageron, *Les Algériens musulmans et la France*, 2: 943.

60. Ibid., 1: 583–600; Geneviève Dermenjian, *Juifs et européens d'Algérie: L'antisémitisme oranais, 1892–1905* (Jerusalem: Institut Ben-Zvi, 1983); Sophie B. Roberts, *Citizenship and Antisemitism in French Colonial Algeria* (Cambridge: Cambridge University Press, 2017). I use the term *indigène* to reflect contemporary sources.

61. AN F17/20966 (Huet née Leveillé), February 15, 1875.

62. Aimé Dupuy, *Bouzaréa: Histoire illustrée des écoles normales d'instituteurs d'Alger-Bouzaréa* (Alger: Fontana, n.d.); Fanny Colonna, *Instituteurs algériens (1883–1939)* (Paris: Presses de la Fondation nationale des sciences politiques, 1975); AN F17/9713, MIP, *arrête*, August 30, 1875, implementing *décret* of December 18, 1874.

63. Mohammed Soualah, *La Société indigène de l'Afrique du nord* (Alger: Jules Carbonel, 1937), 386; Malika Lemdani-Belkaïd, *Normaliennes en Algérie* (Paris: L'Harmattan, 1998), 99; Robert-Guiard, *Des Européennes*, 221.

64. AN F17.20966 (Huet); 22723 (Aucher), rector Boissière to Buisson, March 8, 1883.

65. Zénaïde Tsourikoff, *L'Enseignement des filles en Afrique du nord* (Paris: A. Pedone, 1935), 69.

NOTES TO PAGES 137–141   261

66. Miliana had 8 directrices, Oran 10, Constantine 2, but 2 directrices served in two Algerian schools.

67. AN F17/21047 (Lafforgue), rector Jeanmaire, August 1898.

68. AN F17/22152 (E. Allégret).

69. From 1875 to 1900, 170 (68 percent) of 251 Miliana students for whom there is data were born in Algeria, 78 were born in France, 3 in other countries or another colony. From 1884 to 1900, 87 percent of 168 Oran students were born in Algeria. Tabulations from student lists in AN F17/9278, 9753, 22974 (Maillier), 20200 (Boissière); *Bulletin universitaire de l'académie d'Alger; Bulletin de l'instruction primaire du département d'Alger* [hereinafter *BIPA*]; *Bulletin de l'instruction publique du département d'Oran* [hereinafter *BIPO*]; *état civil* for Algeria, AN, Centre des archives d'outre-mer (CAOM), anom.archivesnationales.culture.gouv.fr.

70. Félix Hémon, "Les Écoles normales de l'Afrique française," *RP* 46 (June 1905): 517–47, quotation, 540; "Nouvelles de Fontenay," *BulFR*, no. 35 (April 1905): 140.

71. AN F17/23147 (Compagnon), 1901.

72. AN F17/20966 (Huet), 22974 (Maillier).

73. AN F17/20966 (Huet), rector's note on Sage; 21682 (Sage); F17/9713, quotations; F17/9753, Conseil général d'Alger, April 13, 1883; *Déplacement de l'école normale de filles de Miliana* ("Extrait du Registre des délibérations du Conseil municipal de la commune de Miliana . . . du 10 mars 1883") (Miliana, 1883).

74. Caplat, *Les Inspecteurs généraux*, 625–26; AN F17/21940 (Thomas née Matrat); F17/20200 (Boissière), June 8, 1884, letter signed by thirty-two students and *Le petit colon algérien*, June 23, 1884, seven students' letter, published without names. For an incident of male normal school students' protest in Algiers in 1881, see Kyle Francis, "'Algeria for the Algerians': Public Education and Settler Identity in the Early Third Republic," *French Politics, Culture & Society* 36 (Spring 2018): 26–51.

75. "Le Scandale de Miliana," *La Vigie algérienne*, June 13, 1884; AN F17/20200 for Lamy letters to ministry, June 11, 18, 1884, and Boissière letter to ministry June 9, 1884; AN F17/22723 (Aucher née Legrelle); 21940 (Thomas née Matrat), July 2, 1884, report; press clippings in Matrat and Boissière dossiers.

76. AN F17/22135 (Guillot); Fontanges, *La Légion d'honneur et les femmes*, 165. The Tunisian post entailed a detachment to the ministry of foreign affairs.

77. AN F17/21047 (Lafforgue).

78. AN F17/22273 (Floutier née Béridot), 22128/A (Lacroix), 20916 (Guttron).

79. AN F17/22576/B (Larivière); 23836 (Eidenschenk née Patin); 22193/A (L. Eidenschenk), professor of German in Alger (1882–90) and Paris (1890–93), *inspecteur d'académie*, Oran (1893–97), coauthor with M. Cohen-Solal, *Mots usuels de la langue arabe accompagnés d'exercices* (Alger: Jourdan, 1897).

80. AN F17/22659/A (M.-T. Champomier).

81. AN F17/22274 (Fuchs née Falk), July 4, 1898, August 1, 1899; 22309 (Sabouret née Falk); 22168/B (Jeanmaire), report to governor general, June 14, 1900, report to director of enseignement supérieur, June 16, 1900. On antisemitic riots in Algeria, see Roberts, *Citizenship and Antisemitism*, 80–110. For allegations linking antisemitic bias among teachers in Algeria to the non-French European population, see J. Lenormand, *Le Péril étranger* (Paris: André, 1899), 64, 409–11.

262 NOTES TO PAGES 142-146

82. AN F17/23799 (Sahuc née Sarradet); 20200 (Boissière), Sarradet letter to Matrat, June 19, 1884.

83. Patricia Lorcin, *Imperial Identitites: Stereotyping, Prejudice and Race in Colonial Algeria* (London: I. B. Tauris, 1995); Alfred Rambaud, "L'Enseignement primaire chez les indigènes musulmans d'Algérie, notamment dans la Grande-Kabylie," *RP* 19 (November–December 1891): 385–99, 495–515; ibid. 20 (January, February 1892): 28–36, 111–33.

84. *Le petit colon algérien*, June 19, 1885; A. Pressard, "En Algérie (Notes de voyage)," *RP* 9 (August, September 1886): 130–33, 226–27; Ferdinand Buisson, "Nos pionniers en Afrique," *RP* 10 (June 1887): 499.

85. Alfred Rambaud, "Les Écoles françaises d'Algérie chez les kabyles," *L'Illustration* (August 22, 1891), and "Les Écoles françaises en Kabylie," *La Science illustrée* 8 (November 21, 1891): 312–15; AN 81AP/5 (Rambaud papers), dossier 1, "Mon inspection dans la Grande Kabylie," 75, and dossiers 2, 4.

86. C. Jeanmaire, "Sur l'instruction des indigènes en Algérie, observations de M. Jeanmaire, recteur de l'académie d'Alger," *RP* 19 (July 1891): 10–36, quotations, 11.

87. Gouvernement général de l'Algérie [hereinafter GGA], *Statistique générale de l'Algérie (1894–1896)* (Alger, 1897), 161.

88. AN 81AP/5 (Rambaud papers), dossier 2, October–December 1892, manuscript, 165.

89. Henri Pensa, *L'Algérie, voyage de la délégation de la commission sénatoriale d'études des questions algériennes* (Paris: J. Rothschild, 1894); Tsourikoff, *Enseignement*, 43–44.

90. AN F17/23154 (Malaval), 23211 (Blanc), 23518 (Simon); Fadhma Aïth Amrouche, *Histoire de ma vie* (Paris: François Maspéro, 1968), 50–51 (as told to Jean Amrouche).

91. AN F17/23799 (Sahuc née Sarradet); Tsourikoff, *Enseignement*, 73.

92. Rambaud, "L'Enseignement primaire chez les indigènes," 112, 131–33; P. Foncin, "En Kabylie, épilogue de l'histoire de la monitrice Fatma," *RP* 20 (March 1892): 238–39; Pensa, *L'Algérie*, 413.

93. GGA, *Statistique (1894–1896)*, 186; AN F17/24747 (Larab); Hémon, "Les Écoles normales," 537. Larab, with additional credentials, later became a professor of Arabic in higher primary schools, the first indigène woman appointed at this level.

94. AN F17/23799 (Sahuc); Mme Sahuc, " Poupée kabyle," in *Musée des poupées*, ed. Marie Koenig (Paris: Hachette, 1909), 217–22.

95. AN F17/23799 (Sahuc); Hémon, "Les Écoles normales," 536.

96. AN F17, *dossiers personnels* of 24 professors at normal and higher primary schools in Algeria; F17/24801 (Fraysse née Bergerat), Miliana student 1901–04.

97. AN, base Léonore, Légion d'honneur, 19800035/750/85006 (Sahuc), letters of deputy A. Mallarmé, 1929, 1930.

98. *BIPO*, no. 203 (August 1902): 381, no. 209 (August–September 1903): 261, annual reports of inspecteur d'académie, citing Allégret; AN F17/23176 (E. Allégret).

99. Enquête Ozouf, MUNAE, Hautes-Pyrénées (J).

100. Charlotte Ann Legg, *The New White Race: Settler Colonialism and the Press in French Algeria, 1860–1914* (Lincoln: University of Nebraska Press, 2021).

101. AN F17/23941 (Palanque née Massip), inspection reports, April 1, 1908, and in Vendée, March 1912; Palanque, "Causeries," 6.

NOTES TO PAGES 146–150 263

102. A. Roux, "L'Éducation esthétique de la démocratie, compte rendu de la conférence de Mme Palanque," *L'Instituteur républicain* [hereinafter *IR*], no. 32 (September–October 1910): 252–53; J. Palanque, "L'Enseignement de la morale à l'école primaire," *IR*, no. 26 (February 1910): 308–19; J. Palanque, "Impressions d'examens," *IR*, no. 39 (May 1911): 308–10; J. Palanque, "Correction du devoir donné aux aspirants au certificat d'aptitude pédagogique," *BIPO*, no. 238 (January 1908): 70.

103. Palanque, "Causeries," 6; AN F17/23941 (Palanque), letter to rector, May 22, 1911.

104. Anissa Hélie, "Former à son image: normes de genre et institutions européennes en Algérie colonisée," in *L'École aux colonies, les colonies à l'école*, ed. Gilles Boyer, Pascal Clerc, and Michelle Zancarini-Fournel (Lyon: ÉNS éditions, 2013), 57–68.

105. MIP, *Statistique* 5 (1891–1892), 117; 7 (1901–1902), 127; 8 (1906–1907), 126, 133.

106. MIP, *Statistique* 8 (1906–1907), 280–83; "Rapport de l'inspecteur d'académie," *BIPO* no. 250 (July 1909), 171–72, citing *brevet* exam results.

107. GGA, *Situation de l'enseignement pendant l'année scolaire 1907–1908, Rapport de M. le recteur de l'académie d'Alger* (Alger: Imprimerie Heintz, 1909), 34–38.

108. AN F17/24407 (Pontal née Vallet); Jeanne Bottini-Honot, *Parmi des inconnus* (Constantine: Éditions de l'Académie Numidia, 1929), 54, 98.

109. French educators assigned to colonies in the Caribbean, Africa, and Asia received "detachments" to the ministry of colonies. Tunisia, a protectorate, was under the ministry of foreign affairs.

110. AN F17/24465 (Muraccioli née Sposito), Lamy report, November 1913.

111. Félix Hémon, "Les Écoles d'art indigène et l'enseignement primaire des filles en Algérie," *RP* 50 (April 1907): 315–17; Maurice Poulard, *L'Enseignement pour les indigènes en Algérie* (Alger: Cojosso, 1910), 280–83; Tsourikoff, *Enseignement*, 71; AN, Base Léonore, Légion d'honneur 19800035/744/84430 (Quetteville).

112. Rebecca Rogers, *A Frenchwoman's Imperial Story: Madame Luce in Nineteenth-Century Algeria* (Stanford: Stanford University Press, 2013); Julia Clancy-Smith, "A Woman without Her Distaff: Gender, Work, and Handicraft Production in Colonial North Africa," in *Social History of Women and Gender in the Modern Middle East*, ed. Margaret L. Meriwether and Judith B. Tucker (Boulder, CO: Westview Press, 1999), 25–62. See also Tsourikoff, *Enseignement*, and Émilienne Conybeare-Grézel, "La Scolarisation des filles musulmanes," in *1830–1962: Des enseignants d'Algérie se souviennent de ce qu'y fut l'enseignement primaire*, ed. Lucette Besserve Bernollin et al. (Toulouse: Privat, 1981), 281–337.

113. Kamel Kateb, *École, population et société en Algérie* (Paris: L'Harmattan, 2005), 29; Tsourikoff, *Enseignement*, 43–44, 80; *Annuaire statistique de la France* 34 (1914–15), 376. The larger percentage of indigène girls than boys attending European schools (44 percent girls, 13 percent boys) is related to the difference in numbers of schools for indigène boys (299 by 1910) and girls (15); in 1931, 561 for boys, 32 for girls.

114. For memoirs on the persistence of Breton see Pierre-Jakez Hélias, *The Horse of Pride*, trans. June Guicharnaud (New Haven: Yale University Press, 1978), and Mona Ozouf, *Composition française: Retour sur une enfance bretonne* (Paris: Gallimard, 2009).

115. "Concours d'admission à l'école normale de Miliana," *BIPA*, no. 453 (October–December 1916): 180, 183; AN F17/24664 (Cacciaguerra).

264 NOTES TO PAGES 151–154

116. Enquête Ozouf, MUNAE, Somme (F), response of a teacher in Algeria, 1914–25.
117. Quoted without author's name in Félix Hémon, "Les Écoles primaires supérieures dans l'Afrique française," *RP* 47 (November 1905): 420.
118. For contemporary views on prejudice in Algeria, see Lenormand, *Le Péril étranger*; Louis Durieu, *Les juifs algériens (1870–1901): études de démographie algérienne* (Paris: Cerf, 1902), 186, 445.

Chapter 5

1. "Le Mouvement féministe," *La Française* [hereinafter *LF*], no. 311, March 21, 1914.
2. Steven C. Hause with Anne R. Kenney, *Women's Suffrage and Social Politics in the French Third Republic* (Princeton: Princeton University Press, 1984), 134–35; AN F7/13266, police report, April 14, 1915.
3. Karen Offen, *European Feminisms 1700–1950: A Political History* (Stanford: Stanford University Press, 2000); Clark, *Women and Achievement in Nineteenth-Century Europe*, chapter 7, and "Les Femmes dans les professions qualifiées et le féminisme, des années 1880 aux années 1930," in *Les Féministes de la première vague*, ed. Christine Bard (Rennes: Presses universitaires de Rennes, 2015), 119–29.
4. Claire Goldberg Moses, *French Feminism in the Nineteenth-Century* (Albany: State University of New York Press, 1984); Patrick Kay Bidelman, *Pariahs Stand Up! The Founding of the Liberal Feminist Movement in France, 1858–1889* (Westport, CT: Greenwood Press, 1982).
5. Karen Offen, "Sur l'origine des mots 'féminisme' et 'féministe,'" *Revue d'histoire moderne et contemporaine* 34 (1987): 492–96, and "On the French Origins of the Words *Feminism* and *Feminist*," *Feminist Issues* 9, no. 2 (Fall 1988): 45–51.
6. Steven C. Hause, *Hubertine Auclert: The French Suffragette* (New Haven: Yale University Press, 1987).
7. *Congrès international des oeuvres et institutions féminines, Paris 12–18 juillet 1889, Actes* (Paris: Société des éditions scientifiques, 1890); *Deuxième congrès international des oeuvres et institutions féminines, 18–23 juin 1900*, ed. Mme Pegard (Paris: C. Blot, 1902).
8. Hause with Kenney, *Women's Suffrage*, 269; Mary Louise Roberts, *Disruptive Acts: The New Woman in Fin-de-Siècle France* (Chicago: University of Chicago Press, 2002), 74, 278 n. 3. Circulation fell to 14,660 in late 1899 and 2,250 in 1902.
9. AN F17/22263 (Bontems née Winter), inspector general Carré; 22529/B (Frugier), inspecteur d'académie Orth; 23259 (Thimer), inspector Gilles.
10. Pauline Kergomard, "L'Égalité des traitements des instituteurs et des institutrices," *MGP*, no. 11 (March 17, 1888): 145; A. Eidenschenk, "Élection au Conseil supérieur de l'instruction publique," *JI*, no. 37 (7 June 1903): 484; A. Eidenschenk née Patin, "Candidature," *MGP*, no. 21 (May 21, 1904): 253–54.
11. Maria Vérone, "Le Personnel des écoles normales," *La Fronde*, 20 August 1902.
12. Hause with Kenney, *Women's Suffrage*, 126; Odette Laguerre, "Dans l'enseignement," *La Fronde*, June 1, 1904.

NOTES TO PAGES 154–156   265

13. Marie Guérin, "Historique de la Fédération féministe universitaire," *Action féministe* [hereinafter *ActFmst*} (August–September 1913), reprinted in Marguerite Bodin, *L'Institutrice* (1922), new ed. (Paris: L'Harmattan, 2012), 305–10; Francoeur, "Pour tous, par tous, Le Congrès de Lille," *ÉN* 9 (November 4, 1905): 59–60; "Extrait de la loi portant fixation du budget général des dépenses et des recettes de l'exercice 1905 (loi du 22 avril 1905)," *BAIP* 77, no. 1670 (April 29, 1905): 538. The 1905 pay scale for male primary teachers ranged from 1,100 to 2,200 francs; for women, 1,100 to 2,000 francs.

14. H. Murgier, "La 'Revue' à Clermont," *Revue de l'enseignement primaire et primaire supérieur* [hereinafter *REP*], no. 49 (September 1, 1907): 595–96; H.M., "Les Élections au conseil départemental, la campagne des suffragettes," *REP*, no. 14 (December 29, 1907): 165–68; H. Murgier, "Chronique électorale," *REP*, no. 15 (January 5, 1908): 177–79; "Élections au conseil départemental," *REP*, no. 17 (January 19, 1908): 203; nos. 19, 21, 22 (February 2, 16, 23, 1908): 227, 249, 264 André Balz, "Le Réveil des femmes," *MGP*, no. 22 (February, 22, 1908): 339–40. The equal pay tactic also drew a majority of women voting in Haute-Loire, Hérault, Ardèche, Vaucluse and support in Landes, Lot-et-Garonne, Meurthe-et-Moselle, Maine-et-Loire, Oise, Vosges.

15. Hause with Kenney, *Women's Suffrage*, 126–28; Laurence Klejman and Florence Rochefort, *L'Égalité en marche: Le Féminisme sous la Troisième République* (Paris: Presses de la Fondation nationale des sciences politiques/Des Femmes, 1989), 179–82; Marie Guérin, "L'Égalité des traitements," *MGP*, no. 19 (February 6, 1909): 293; Marcel Borit, "Les Groupes féministes universitaires," *Pages libres*, no. 427 (March 6, 1909): 266–70, and "Les Groupes féministes universitaires," *Grande revue* 70 (December 25, 1911): 801–17; Denise Karnaouch, "Marie Guérin," and "Marguerite Bodin," in *Dictionnaire des féministes en France XVIIIe–XXIe siècle*, ed. Christine Bard with Sylvie Chaperon (Paris: Presses universitaires de France, 2017), 690–92, 171–72; Karnaouch, "Avant-propos, Marguerite Bodin, Pédagogue, militante du féminisme et de l'école laïque (1869–1940)," in Bodin, *L'Institutrice*, xvi.

16. "Un document à examiner, les statuts provisoires du G.F.U.," *REP*, no. 33 (May 10, 1908): 398; Marie Guérin, "Statuts de la Fédération féministe primaire," *JI*, no. 9 (November 21, 1909): 66–67.

17. "Un conflit inexplicable, Les A. prennent ombrage et méfiance des G. F.," *REP*, no. 37 (June 7, 1906): 444; "Un petit congrès dans les colonnes de la 'Revue,'" *REP*, no. 15 (January 9, 1910): 126 (Jeanne Déghilage, vice president of federation of *amicales*, criticizing feminist "separatism"); Charles Dessez, "Le Congrès de Nancy," *RP* 55 (October 1909): 301–12.

18. Peter V. Meyers, " From Conflict to Cooperation: Men and Women Teachers in the Belle Epoque," in *The Making of Frenchmen: Current Directions in the History of Education in France, 1679–1979*, ed. Donald N. Baker and Patrick J. Harrigan (Waterloo, ON: Historical Reflections Press, 1980), 493–505.

19. Karnaouch, "Marie Guérin," 691; "Dans les groupes," *ActFmst*, no. 29 (January 1914), citing 54 departmental groups; Marie Guillot, "Nos plus grands ennemis," in ibid.

20. Hause with Kenney, *Women's Suffrage*, 39, 135; Bibliothèque Marguerite Durand [hereinafter BMD], Dos 396 CON, Conseil national des femmes françaises, liste des sociétés affiliées (1907), 78–82; *L'Action féminine*, no. 25 (December 1912): 430.

266 NOTES TO PAGES 156–160

21. Borit, "Les Groupes féministes universitaires," 815–16.

22. Marilyn J. Boxer, "Rethinking the Socialist Construction and International Career of the Concept of 'Bourgeois Feminism,'" *American Historical Review* 112 (February 2007): 131–58. On divisions between pro-syndicalist women teachers and those in *amicales*, see Persis Charles Hunt, "Revolutionary Syndicalism and Feminism among Teachers in France" (PhD diss., Tufts University, 1975).

23. "Note du secrétariat," *ActFmst*, no. 7 (May 1910); L. Bouvrain, "Les Groupements féministes et les bourses du travail," *REP*, no. 31 (April 30, 1911): 357–68; Marie Vidal, "Les Ouvrières dans la C. G. T. et les bourses du travail, 1re réponse à Mme Bouvrain," and "Bourgeoises et ouvrières ont des intérêts opposés," ibid., nos. 33, 38 (May 14, June 18, 1911): 391–92, 452; L. Bouvrain, "Une riposte à Marie Vidal," ibid., no. 40 (July 2, 1911): 473–74; Hunt, "Revolutionary Syndicalism," 84–85.

24. G. Avril de Sainte-Croix, "Rapport de la secrétaire générale," *Action féminine*, no. 11 (August 1910): 171; M. Pichon-Landry, "La Fédération féministe primaire," ibid., 174–79. Pichon-Landry, one of two CNFF secretaries and in 1914 president of its legislative section.

25. Rachel Albert, "L'Extension universitaire en Angleterre," *BulFR*, no. 13 (July 1899): 86.

26. Clark, "A Battle of the Sexes in a Professional Setting."

27. M. M., "Féminisme, route barrée," *BulFR*, no. 38 (January 1906): 42–45; E. Kieffer, untitled note, ibid.: 45–46.

28. E. K., "Conseil national des femmes," *BulFR*, no. 50 (October 1909): 231–37, quotation, 235; "Compte rendu, réunion générale," ibid., no. 53 (October 1910): 135–39; E. Kieffer, "Conseil national des femmes," ibid., no. 58 (July 1912): 125–27.

29. "Compte rendu, réunion générale, 18 May 1911," *BAAENI de la Seine-Inférieure*, no. 28 (March 1912): 41, unanimous decision of 284 members present; "Liste des sociétés affiliées et leurs déléguées," *Action féminine*, no. 31 (December 1913): 580–81.

30. "Nota," *BulFR*, no. 54 (April 1911): 81; A. Rees-Martin, "Aline Zeller," ibid., new series, no. 92 (November 1971): 29.

31. "Adhésions universitaires," *Femme nouvelle* 1 (April 15, 1904): 4; A. Eidenschenk, "La Femme nouvelle," ibid., 22–25 (May 1, 1904): 86–89; A. Eidenschenk, "La Femme française et la République," ibid. 2 (May 15, 1905): 65–72; Rachel Mesch, *Having It All in the Belle Epoque: How French Women's Magazines Invented the Modern Woman* (Stanford: Stanford University Press, 2013). I thank Mélanie Fabre for the reference to *La Femme nouvelle* (1904–6).

32. "En faveur de l'unification des traitements, Déposition de Mme Eidenschenk, directrice d'école normale, devant la Commission extraparlementaire de coordination des traitements," *IR*, no. 6 (March 15, 1908): 42–43; A. Eidenschenk, "La Surveillance dans les écoles normales," *BulFR*, no. 41 (April 1907): 25–32.

33. "Discussions universitaires, Professeurs femmes et professeurs hommes," *La Lanterne* (Paris), February 6, 1911; Eidenschenk quoted by E. Cottet, "L'Égalité des traitements dans l'enseignement primaire," *JI*, no. 32 (May 2, 1909): 381.

34. A. Eidenschenk, "Rapport présenté à M. le Ministre de l'instruction publique sur la question de la surveillance dans les écoles normales d'institutrices," *BulFR*, no. 41 (April 1907): 25–32, quotation, 27.

NOTES TO PAGES 160–163   267

35. "Conseil supérieur de l'instruction publique ... séance du 21 juillet," *BAIP* 86, no. 1908 (December 18, 1909): 1295; "Décret modifiant ... [le] décret du 19 juillet 1890, en ce qui concerne la surveillance dans les écoles normales d'institutrices," ibid., no. 1909 (December 25, 1909): 1321–22; "Circulaire relative à l'organisation de la surveillance dans les écoles normales d'institutrices," ibid. 87, no. 1919 (March 12, 1910): 124–28.

36. "Élections au Conseil supérieur du 17 mai 1912, Candidature de Mme Eidenschenk," *JI*, no. 34 (May 12, 1912): 281.

37. E. Cottet, "Les Groupes féministes universitaires," *JI*, no. 26 (March 21, 1909): 304–5; "Fédération féministe universitaire," *REP*, no. 23 (March 7, 1909): 274–75; Bûcheron [H. Murgier], "Le Sexe faible," ibid., no. 29 (April 18, 1909): 332; "Au ministère de l'instruction publique," ibid., no. 33 (16 May 1909): 388.

38. Mme Eidenschenk "Démarches entreprises en vue d'obtenir l'égalité des traitements," *ÉN* 12 (May 22, 1909): 191–92; "Égalité des traitements des instituteurs et institutrices," *MGP*, no. 41 (July 10, 1909): 574.

39. Karen Offen, *Debating the Woman Question in the French Third Republic, 1870–1920* (Cambridge: Cambridge University Press, 2018), 327–30.

40. "Congrès féministe," *ActFmst*, no. 1 (October 1909); Dessez, "Le Congrès de Nancy," 309; E. Cottet, "Le Congrès de Nancy," *JI*, no. 4 (October 17, 1909): 28, noting several hundred official delegates and over a thousand auditors; Cécile Panis, "Revendications morales et matérielles des institutrices primaires et maternelles," *ActFmst*, no. 9 (July 1910).

41. Marie Guérin and P. Guérin, "À l'œuvre," *ActFemst*, no. 5 (February 1910); "Budget de l'instruction publique," *ÉN* 13 (February 19, 1910): 284.

42. "Extrait de. . . . la Loi de finances du 13 juillet 1911," *BAIP* 90, no. 1989 (July 19, 1911): 223–24. For normal school professors the 6-step pay scale for men ranged from 2900 to 4900 francs, for women 2500 to 4500 francs (previously 2500 to 3700, men; 2500 to 3400, women). For directors and directrices, the professors' pay scale became a base to which an indemnity of 1000 to 1600 francs would be added.

43. Offen, *Debating the Woman Question*, 440–41; *ActFmst*, nos. 21, 22 (March, April 1913); AN 71 AJ/73, Buisson papers, also including FFU groups' letters to Buisson.

44. A. C., "Nos traitements," *MGP*, no. 42 (June 28, 1913): 499, pay increases to take effect, 1913 to 1917; J. Méo, "Pourquoi l'égalité," *ActFmst*, no. 23 (May 1913); "Audiences du 15 et du 29 janvier," ibid., no. 30 (February 1914); "Assemblée générale de la Fédération," ibid., no. 33 (May 1914).

45. A. Eidenschenk, "La Femme française et la République," *Femme nouvelle* 2 (January 15, 1905): 65–72. On her 1907 book, see p. 64.

46. A. Eidenschenk, "À propos de quelques idées sur le féminisme, réponse à Mme Roger-Lévy," *MGP, no.* 29 (April 17, 1909): 433; Jeanne Roger-Lévy, "Quelques idées sur le féminisme," *MGP*, no. 26 (March 27, 1909): 393–95.

47. A. Eidenschenk, "Le Féminisme universitaire," *ActFmst*, no. 7 (March 1911).

48. Murgier, "La 'Revue' à Clermont," (1907); "Une grande manifestation du féminisme universitaire," *LF*, September 17, 1911; Hause with Kenney, *Women's Suffrage*, 128.

49. A. Eidenschenk, "Pour nos filles, Préparation à la vie," MGP, October 18; November 1, 15; December 6, 13, 27, 1913; January 10, 24; February 7, 21; March 7, 21; April 4, 18;

268 NOTES TO PAGES 163–169

May 2, 1914. Quotations from Eidenschenk letter in Émile Bugnon, "Le Désaccord entre l'école et la nation, II. Les Institutrices," *Grande Revue* 84 (April 25, 1914): 729.

50. Ferdinand Buisson, *Le Vote des femmes* (Paris: Dunod et Pinat, 1911).

51. Offen, *Debating the Woman Question*, 519; Hause with Kenney, *Women's Suffrage*, 52–53, 59, 84–86, 116, 122, 136; Odile Sarti, *The Ligue Patriotique des Françaises, 1902–1933: A Feminine Response to the Secularization of French Society* (New York: Garland, 1992).

52. *Dixième congrès international des femmes, oeuvres et institutions féminines, droits des femmes*, 147–52, 390. On reports by Varlet and Martin, see pp. 78–79. On the congress, see also Offen, *Debating the Woman Question*, 319–20.

53. *Dixième congrès international des femmes*, 577; L. Sagnier, "À propos du 10e Congrès international des femmes," *Le Volume* 25 (June 28, 1913): 673–74. Sagnier retired as a higher primary school professor in Paris.

54. Bugnon, "Le Désaccord entre l'école et la nation, I. Les Instituteurs," *Grande revue* 82 (November 25, 1913): 349–76 (*Pages libres*, 673–704), and "II. Les Institutrices," ibid. 84 (April 25, 1914): 713–33 (*Pages libres*, 225–41), quotation, 725.

55. Bugnon, "Le Désaccord, II. Les Institutrices," *Grande revue* 84 (April 25, 1914): 728–29.

56. "Le Mouvement féministe," *LF*, no. 311, March 21, 1914; BMD, DOS 396 UNI, *Bulletin trimestriel de l'Union française pour le suffrage des femmes* (January–March 1914), 7–8.

57. "Communications du comité central," *LF*, March 21, 1914.

58. Hause with Kenney, *Women's Suffrage*, 138–45; AN F7/13266, police report, April 14, 1915, UFSF central committee members and Paris-area leaders.

59. BMD, DOS 396 UNI, UFSF *Bulletin* (1912), 85: "Le Mouvement féministe, Union française pour le suffrage des femmes" [hereinafter "Mf/UFSF"], "Aube," *LF*, no. 257, 30 November 1912; Offen, *European Feminisms*, 116–17.

60. Marie-Dominique Leclerc, "Union française pour le suffrage des femmes, le groupe de l'Aube," *La Vie en Champagne*, no. 28 (October–December 2001): 20–31; Hause with Kenney, *Women's Suffrage*, 181.

61. Cécile Panis, "Revendications," *ActFmst*, no. 5 (February–March 1910), no. 9 (July 1910); "Groupe féministe primaire ardéchois," *Bulletin trimestriel de l'Amicale des instituteurs et institutrices de l'Ardèche*, no. 24 (December 1909): 16; Hunt, "Revolutionary Syndicalism and Feminism," 278.

62. AN F17/23993 (Flayol). On controversy about women riding bicycles, see Christopher Thomson, "Un troisième sexe? Les bourgeoises et la bicyclette dans la France fin de siècle," *Le Mouvement social*, no. 192 (2000): 9–39.

63. BMD, DOS 396 UNI, UFSF, *Bulletin trimestriel* (July–October 1913), 8, and (January–March 1914), 4. The UFSF required at least twenty-five members for an official "group" (Hause with Kenney, *Women's Suffrage*, 135).

64. "Action auprès des conseils municipaux, des conseils d'arrondissement et des conseils généraux," *LF*, no. 317, May 9, 1914.

65. AN F17/23993 (Flayol). On a syndicalist professor at the men's normal school, see Paul Boissel, "Le Syndicaliste," in *Une belle figure vivaroise, Élie Reynier (1875–1953)* (Aubenas: Lienhart, 1967), 43–47.

NOTES TO PAGES 169–172   269

66. "UFSF, réunion du comité central," *LF*, no. 260, December 21, 1912; BMD, DOS 396 UNI, UFSF *Bulletin* (July–October 1913), 9; "Communication de l'U.F.S.F., Voyage de propagande," *LF*, no. 304, January 31, 1914.

67. "Communication de l'U.F.S.F., Voyage de propagande," *LF*, no. 304, January 31, 1914; "Groupe de Charente," *LF*, no. 283, June 14, 1913.

68. Hause with Kenney, *Women's Suffrage*, 144; "Dans les groupes," *ActFmst*, no. 21 (March 1913); "Troisième congrès national," ibid., no. 23 (May 1913); "Groupe féministe du sud-ouest," *LF*, no. 286, July 12, 1913; "Fédération féministe du sud-ouest," *LF*, no. 313, April 4, 1914; "Organisation féministe régionale," *ActFmst*, no. 34 (June 1914).

69. Enquête Ozouf, MUNAE, Charente (M); AN F17/23529 (Thimer).

70. AN F17/22529/B (Frugier); Renée Lebel, "Mme Frugier," *LF*, no. 965, February 14, 1931.

71. AN F17/24827 (Rebour née Boyenval), March 1904.

72. "Tournée de propagande de Mme Brunschwicg [sic]," *LF*, no. 270, March 8, 1913 (Jeanne Géraud, Orne directrice); "Eure-et-Loir," *Le Droit des femmes*, no. 1 (January 1913): 12; "Mf/UFSF," *LF*, no. 279, May 17, 1913; Centre des Archives du Féminisme, Angers [hereinafter CAF], papers of Cécile Brunschvicg, 1AF 67, Drôme UFSF members; J. Le Guillon, "Quimper," *LF*, no. 283, June 14, 1913; AN F17/22457/A (Pingaud née Épinoux); "Mf/UFSF," *LF*, no. 272, March 29, 1913, no. 286, July 12, 1913 (Marseille UFSF); *LF*, no. 240, 26 May 1912 (Vienne). On UFSF organizing in Brittany, see Isabelle Le Boulanger, *À l'origine du féminisme en Bretagne, Marie Le Gac-Salonne* (Rennes: Presses universitaires de Rennes, 2017), 65–83.

73. Cécile Brunschvicg, "Rapport," *Actes du Congrès féministe international de Bruxelles 1912*, ed. Marie Popelin (Brussels: C. Bulens, 1912), 138; "Mf/UFSF," *LF*, no. 260, December 21, 1912 (Brunschvicg at Fontenay *mairie*); BMD DOS 396 UNI, UFSF *Bulletin* (1912), 12.

74. "Conférence faite à l'Association des anciennes élèves de Fontenay le 1 août 1911," *BulFR*, no. 56 (December 1911): 203–15, reprinted in *Le Monde féminin*, no. 2 (August 30, 1912): 17–23.

75. M. Ginier, "L'Inspection féminine des écoles maternelles et des écoles de filles," *RP* 58 (March 1911): 217–29; "L'Inspection féminine des écoles," *MGP*, *no.* 35 (May 13, 1911): 419–20; P. Rebour, "L'Inspection féminine," *ÉN* 15 (June 24, 1911): 540; M. Ginier, "Note sur la question de l'inspection féminine des écoles de filles," *BulFR*, no. 57 (April 1912): 58–60; *REP* (1911–12), extensive discussion of Ginier's controversial article; "Le Banquet," *Le Droit des femmes*, no. 14 (July–August 1911): 7–8.

76. "Communication de l'U.F.S.F., Voyage de propagande," *LF*, no. 304, 31 January 1914; AN F17/24268 (E. Périères), 23636/B (G. Périères); A. Privat, "Dans les groupes, Basses-Pyrénées," *ActFmst*, no. 54 (October 1917).

77. "Communication de l'U.F.S.F." *LF*, 31 January 1914; AN F17/22576/A (Landais), 24937 (Veveaud). See also Julia-Pauline Larose, "Le Suffragisme au milieu rural dans l'entre-deux-guerres: l'action de l'UFSF dans les Deux-Sèvres," *Genre & Histoire* (on line), no. 21 (Spring 2018) and Albéric Verdon, *Féminisme et suffragisme en Deux-Sèvres jusqu'en 1945* (n.p.: bookelis, 2019).

78. BMD, DOS 396 UNI, UFSF, *Bulletin* (July–October 1913), 13; CAF, 1AF 112, UFSF membership, Rhône, and 1AF 107, Basses-Pyrénées. In 1912, 13 percent of Rhône

270   NOTES TO PAGES 172–176

members were women educators, mostly in primary schools; in Basses-Pyrénées, 40 percent were women educators (including two at the normal school), 7 percent male educators.

79. BMD, DOS 396 UNI, UFSF *Bulletin* (July–October 1913), 13; CAF, 1AF 107 (Basses-Pyrénées); AN F17/23695 (Dollé née Tourret and F. Dollé); Enquête Ozouf, MUNAE, Basses-Pyrénées (G).

80. BMD, DOS 396 UNI, UFSF *Bulletin* (January–March 1914), 3–10; J.M., "Les Disparus: Mme Vincent," *LF*, no. 308, February 28, 1914. On male feminists, see Alban Jacquemart, *Les Hommes dans les mouvements féministes: Socio-histoire d'un engagement improbable* (Rennes: Presses universitaires de Rennes, 2015).

81. BMD, DOS 396 UNI, UFSF *Bulletin* (January–March 1914), 3–10. Nine of the ten women on both the central committee and a departmental list were from the Seine. The other women identified by occupation but not educators or named above were a lawyer, a nurse, a singer, a postal clerk, and two workers. See Bard, ed., *Dictionnaire des féministes*, for Brunschvicg, Chéliga, Misme, Pichon-Landry, Vérone, Viollis. On Le Gac-Salonne, Le Boulanger, *À l'origine du féminisme en Bretagne*.

82. BMD DOS 396 UNI, UFSF *Bulletin* (January–March 1914); "Dans les groupes, Indre," *ActFmst*, no. 28 (December 1913), 67 members in the Indre GFU; Hunt, "Revolutionary Syndicalism," 292, citing 700 teachers in the Indre *amicale* in 1906.

83. AN F17/23593/B (Fontvieille-Moller), 22125/A (L. Bernard); "Une doyenne du féminisme," *LF*, no. 954, November 8, 1930.

84. AN F17/22446/A (Galzanadat), 23918 (Goepp), both Nord directrices; 23774 (Jumau); 23745 (Camplo), Ardèche; Mme Poizat (Haute-Savoie); "Groupe de Drôme," *LF*, no. 352, 14 February 1914; AN F17/24172 (Verguet); 24848 (Batier née Jacquot-Doney), Belfort; 24735 (Fradet), Tours; Mlle Mittaine, Alençon.

85. AN F17/24827 (Rebour née Boyenval), ADP D1T1/703 (P. Rebour); "Groupe féministe primaire supérieur," *ActFmst*, no. 9 (July 1910); P. Rebour, "Chronique féministe," ibid. (1913–14). Pauline Rebour also obtained a *licence* in law; Raoul Rebour was a *rédacteur* at the ministry of public works by 1915 (AN F7/13266, UFSF).

86. BMD DOS 396 UNI, UFSF *Bulletin* (January–March 1914), 3; Charles Sowerwine, *Sisters or Citizens: Women and Socialism in France since 1876* (Cambridge: Cambridge University Press, 1982), 131, 139; Albéric Verdon, *Marguerite Martin née Brunet (1877–1956): Première militante féministe des Deux-Sèvres et de la Vendée* (n.p.: bookelis, 2018); AN F17/23335 (Girard née Bourdon), ADP D1T1/552 (Girard).

87. BMD DOS 396 UNI, UFSF *Bulletin* (January–March 1914), 3–10; J. M., "Une réforme qui ne coûterait rien à l'état," *MGP*, no. 38 (May 31, 1913): 450. For women with no occupation noted on the UFSF list, identification as educator from *ActFmst*, *LF*, *AEP, Annuaire de l'instruction publique et des beaux-arts*, and *Journal officiel de la République française*.

88. On Guérin, Bigot, Guillot, see Bard, ed., *Dictionnaire des féministes*. On Guérin, Méo, Pichorel, Bigot, Panis, Pellat-Finet, Guillot, see Jean Maîtron, ed., *Dictionnaire biographique du mouvement ouvrier*, maitron-en-ligne, univ-paris.fr/spip.php?; AN F17/22263 (Bouchet née Renaudin).

NOTES TO PAGES 176–180   271

89. Marthe Bigot, "Craintes," *ActFmst*, no. 34 (June 1914).

90. BMD, DOS 396 UNI, UFSF *Bulletin* (January–March 1914), 5; Enquête Ozouf, MUNAE, Gironde (F), Dordogne (L); "Groupe féministe périgourdin," *ActFmst*, no. 51 (May 1917); Bernard Dougnac, *Suzanne Lacore, biographie 1875–1975: Le Socialisme-femme* (Périgueux: Institut acquitain d'études sociales-Éditions Fanlac, 1996). Lacore, as a socialist, favored "feminism" but not "bourgeois" feminism.

91. Noélie Drous (pseud.), "En passant," *ActFmst*, no. 31 (March 1914); Enquête Ozouf, MUNAE, Vienne (S), Charente (M). On Sourd, see entry in maitron-en-ligne.

92. "UFSF Groupe de Seine-et-Marne," *LF*, no. 275, April 19, 1913; Marie Charpentier, "Féminisme en action," *BAAENI de Melun*, no. 44 (1911): 947–48; F. Buisson, "Le Vote des femmes," ibid., no. 47 (1912): 1035–42.

93. C. L. Brunschvicg, "Tournée de propagande," *LF*, no. 297, December 6, 1913; Lemoine and Marie, *La jeune française*, 5.

94. B. Netter-Gidon, "Groupe de Caen et de Calvados," *LF*, no. 308, February 28, 1914; CAF, 1AF 55 (Calvados), Schreck letter to Brunschvicg, January 1923; "Groupe de l'Yonne," *LF*, no. 312, March 28, 1914; AN F17/24320 (Odoul), 24271 (Py); CAF, 1AF 70 (Finistère), J. Marot letter to Brunschvicg, May 12, 1918.

95. "Groupe d'Alger," *LF*, no. 316, May 2, 1914; "Union française pour le suffrage des femmes," *L'Écho d'Alger*, April 24, 1914.

96. J. Thimer, "Groupe de la Haute-Vienne, Un beau succès pour l'Union," *LF*, no. 325, July 5, 1914.

97. "Un nouveau groupe féministe," *Le Journal*, July 22, 1914; AN F17/24047 (Bringuier née Thévenet).

98. Jane Misme, "Pour le suffrage des femmes, Le congrès de Lyon," *LF*, no. 321, June 6, 1914; Pauline Rebour, "Chronique suffragiste," *ActFmst*, no. 34 (June 1914), no. 35 (July 1914); *Le Journal*, May 5, 1914, reporting 505,972 votes for women's suffrage, 114 against. On suffrage campaigns in 1914, see Hause with Kenney, *Women's Suffrage*, 169–90; Klejman and Rochefort, *L'Égalité en marche*, 285–87; Offen, *Debating the Woman Question*, 533–39.

99. Pauline Rebour, "Chronique suffragiste," *ActFmst*, no. 32 (April 1914), no. 33 (May 1914); Pauline Rebour, "Le 3e Congrès national de la Fédération féministe universitaire, Rapport général," ibid., no. 26 (October 1913); Raoul Rebour, "L'Éducation civique des femmes," ibid., no. 34 (June 1914); Pauline Rebour, "Chronique suffragiste," ibid., no. 35 (July 1914).

100. Helen Chenut, "Attitudes toward Women's Suffrage on the Eve of World War I," *French Historical Studies* 41 (October 2018): 711–40.

101. Misme, "Pour le suffrage des femmes"; Rebour, "Chronique suffragiste," June, July 1914.

102. D. Billotey, "La Femme éducatrice," *RP* 64 (June 1914): 530.

103. E. Glay, "Le Congrès de Nantes," *REP*, no. 1 (1 October 1911): 1–2; Bûcheron [pseud.], "Le Congrès féministe," *REP*, no. 50 (September 14, 1913): 50–51.

104. Ferdinand Buisson, ed., *Nouveau dictionnaire de pédagogie et d'instruction primaire* (Paris: Hachette, 1911), s.v. "Femme."

272 NOTES TO PAGES 180–187

105. Bûcheron [pseud.], "Institutrices, debout!" *REP*, no. 5 (26 October 1913): 50–51; G. Persigout, "Le Tournol féministe," *REP*, no. 12 (December 14, 1913): 131–32; Marie Guillot, "Nos plus grands ennemis," *ActFmst*, no. 29 (January 1914).

106. Ozouf and Ozouf, *La République des instituteurs*, 129–32, 230, 351. Only 49 percent of teachers in the survey stated an opinion about women's access to new occupations.

107. Lemoine and Marie, *La jeune française*, 125–26.

108. AN F17/26512/B (Magnat née Delacquis), 28383 (Sourgen).

109. AN F17/26512/B (Magnat), 28383 (Sourgen).

110. Hause with Kenney, *Women's Suffrage*, 184–89. *La Française*, July 5, 1914, announced the planned demonstration.

Chapter 6

1. Françoise Thébaud, *La Femme au temps de la guerre de 14* (Paris: Stock, 1986); Laura Lee Downs, *Manufacturing Inequality: Gender Division in the French and British Metalworking Industries, 1914–1919* (Ithaca: Cornell University Press, 1995); Margaret H. Darrow, *French Women and the First World War: War Stories of the Home Front* (Oxford and New York: Berg, 2000).

2. Jean-Louis Robert, "Women and Work in France during the First World War," in *The Upheaval of War: Family, Work and Welfare in Europe, 1914–1918*, ed. Richard Wall and Jay Winter (Cambridge: Cambridge University Press, 1988), 262; Jane Misme, "La Guerre et le rôle des femmes," *Revue de Paris* 23 (November 1, 1916): 204.

3. Alain Vincent, *Des hussards de la République aux professeurs des écoles: L'école normale* (Joué-lès-Tours: Alan Sutton, 2016), 73.

4. Condette, *Les Recteurs d'académie*, vol. 2, *Dictionnaire biographique*, 263.

5. AN F17/23685 (Dosser), 24521 (Maucourant), 24154 (J. Marie), 22498/A (Marsy), 23836 (Eidenschenk née Patin). On the war's impact on schooling, see Jean-François Condette, ed., *La Guerre des cartables (1914–1918): Élèves, étudiants et enseignants dans la Grande Guerre en Nord-Pas-de-Calais* (Villeneuve-d'Ascq: Presses universitaires du Septentrion, 2018), including Johann-Günther Egginger, "Raconter et témoigner: la vie des élèves-maîtres et maîtresses des départements du Nord et du Pas-de-Calais pendant la Grande Guerre . . . et après (1914–1925)," 351–68.

6. A. Eidenschenk, "En pays envahi, Douai 1914–1918," *BulFR*, no. 74 (December 1920): 29–36; *Madame Eidenschenk-Patin 1864–1942* (Douai: Amicale des anciennes élèves de l'école normale d'institutrices du Nord, 1978), 34, chapter by J. Mauschassat-Eidenschenk; AN F17/23836 (Eidenschenk née Patin).

7. AN F17/24136 (Évard), 24678 (Grunfelder), 24978 (Valin), 24213 (Perseil).

8. AN F17/22709 (Varlet), 24873 (Échard née Gauthier), 23840 (Foulet née Martin), 22447/B (Grauvogel).

9. Lutringer and Rothiot, *Cent cinquante ans au service du peuple*, vol. 1, 284.

10. AN F17/23941 (Palanque): AN, Base Léonore, Légion d'honneur, 19800035/1176/ 3614 (Palanque); Fernand Tardif, *Un département pendant la guerre* (La Roche-sur-Yon: Guigné-Hurtaud, 1917), 48.

11. AN F17 22529/B (Frugier).

12. J. R., "La Crise de l'inspection primaire," *BAIPDEN*, no. 40 (June 1917): 50.

13. AN F17/23901 (Chaudron), 24320 (Odoul), 23836 (Eidenschenk).

14. J. R., "Crise de l'inspection," 50; AN F17 dossiers of directrices appointed 1915–19.

15. Linda L. Clark, *The Rise of Professional Women in France: Gender and Public Administration since 1830* (Cambridge: Cambridge University Press, 2000), 239. In 1930, there were 15 primary school inspectresses and 20 departmental nursery school inspectresses; in 1939, 29 and 23, respectively.

16. "Enquête sur le service d'inspection," *Bulletin de l'association amicale des directeurs et des directrices d'écoles normales* [hereinafter *BAADEN*], no. 24 (November 1928): 20–23.

17. Legion of Honor indicated in AN F17, *dossiers personnels*; AN Base Léonore, Légion d'honneur; and *Journal officiel de la République française*.

18. AN F17, *dossiers personnels* for 118 directrices, and AJ16/6012 (Guerrini), 9079 (Brulé née Delavenay). Parents' occupations identified from *dossiers personnels* and departments' *état civil*; occupations for 119 fathers, 54 mothers. Two directrices were sisters.

19. Karen Offen, "Body Politics: Women, Work and the Politics of Motherhood in France, 1920–1950," in *Maternity and Gender Policies: Women and the Rise of the European Welfare States, 1880s–1950*, ed. Gisela Bock and Pat Thane (London: Routledge, 1991), 138–59.

20. "Arrêté [du 18 août] modifiant les programmes des écoles normales primaires," *BAIP* 108, no. 2442 (September 18, 1920): 769, 812; "Arrêté [du 18 août] modifiant les programmes des écoles primaires supérieures," ibid., 730.

21. In colonial settings other than Algeria and Tunisia more than one model for training women teachers existed; the directrices in this study did not lead such training in Asia or sub-Saharan Africa. Secondary schools housed some training courses, as in Morocco and Martinique; an *institutrice* might also direct training, as in the early 1920s at an *école normale* in Hanoi, or at a new *école normale* in 1938 in Senegal, studied by Pascale Barthélémy. For most colonies French teachers were detached from the education ministry to the ministry of colonies.

22. S. Paul, "Une Étape," *BAAENI de Digne*, nos. 7–8 (1932–33): 5; M. Chardron, "Images et souvenirs," *BAAENI de Poitiers*, no. 59 (1969): 22.

23. "Arrêté [du 18 août] modifiant . . . l'arrêté organique du 18 janvier 1887," and "Arrêté . . . programmes des écoles normales," 701–27, 764–813; "Instructions [du 30 septembre] relatives à l'organisation des cours complémentaires, des écoles primaires supérieures et des écoles normales, décret et arrêtés du 18 août 1920," *BAIP*, no. 2450 (November 13, 1920): 1426–97, quotation, 1494.

24. "Arrêté . . . programmes des écoles normales," 769–70; "Instructions," 1475.

25. Roger Geiger, "La Sociologie dans les écoles normales primaires: Histoire d'une controverse," *Revue française de sociologie* 20 (1979): 257–67.

26. "Arrêté . . . programmes des écoles normales," 769–70.

27. A. Hesse and A. Gleyze, *Notions de sociologie appliquée à la morale et à l'éducation*, 2nd ed. (Paris F. Alcan, 1925), 102–3, ibid., 8th ed. (1938). Hesse taught economic

274   NOTES TO PAGES 193-200

history in the écoles d'arts et métiers; Gleyze, director of the men's normal school in Aix, was married to normal school professor Éva Astruc.

28. Hesse and Gleyze, *Notions de sociologie*, 179–80; ibid., 8th ed. (1938), 179.

29. AN F17/23775/A (Labergère née Dalon), 24206 (Rollet), 24920 (Privat).

30. AN F17/24268 (Périères), inspector's signature illegible.

31. "Arrêté [du 18 août] modifiant . . . 18 janvier 1887," 723–24; "Instructions," 1464–66.

32. "Arrêté [du 18 août] modifiant," 723–24; "Instructions," 1464–66.

33. Mary Louise Roberts, *Civilization without Sexes: Reconstructing Gender in Postwar France, 1917–1927* (Chicago: University of Chicago Press, 1994).

34. AN F17/24281 (Omnès), 22586/B (Omnès née Texier); Mlle Omnès, "Histoire de l'école normale d'institutrices de La Roche-sur-Yon," in *Livre du cinquantenaire*, 21–40: Mme B., "39e promotion 1921–1924," in ibid., 59–61.

35. Yvonne Dagand, "L'École normale d'institutrices de Rumilly (1922–1925)," *Revue savoisienne* 118 (1978): 88–102.

36. Lutringer and Rothiot, *Cent cinquante ans au service*, vol. 1, 281–306, quotations 291–92.

37. Jean-Louis Dumans, *L'École normale, 100 ans à Laval*, 50–51.

38. *Centenaire de l'école normale d'institutrices de Lyon 1883–1983, témoignages recueillis par l'amicale des anciens élèves des écoles normales d'institutrices et d'instituteurs de Lyon* (Lyon: Centre régional de la documentation pédagogique, 1985), 20.

39. *Manifestation de sympathie à l'occasion du départ de Mademoiselle Marie* (Arras: n.p., 1930). 25.

40. Oulhiou, *L'École normale supérieure de Fontenay-aux-Roses*, 190. Marguerite Dard, directrice in Bordeaux, succeeded Grauvogel in 1935.

41. AN F17/24852 (Billot née Kay).

42. AN F17/27099 (François nèe Pheulpin).

43. H. Alimen, "Mademoiselle Blanche Maucourant," *BulFR*, no. 73 (April 1962): 5.

44. E. Flayol, *La Méthode Montessori en action* (Paris: F. Nathan, 1921); E. Flayol, "La Coopération dans une école normale de jeunes filles," *Nouvelle éducation* 7 (1928): 55–60; E. Flayol, *Le Dr. O. Decroly, éducateur* (Paris: F. Nathan, 1934).

45. Mme Gaillard, "L'Introduction de la méthode active à l'école traditionnelle," *Nouvelle éducation* 11 (June 1932): 96–105.

46. M. Angles, "Quelques réflexions au sujet du Congrès d'éducation nouvelle," *BulFR*, no. 29 (December 1932): 71–77; F. Seclet-Riou, "Mademoiselle Flayol," *BulFR*, no. 66 (November 1958): 15–19.

47. E. Flayol, "Réflexions sur l'éducation civique," *BulFR*, no. 8 (March 1926): 35; Madame Périères, Baumont, V. Delfolie, Lucien-Gérard, Périères, and Rongau, *Les Six, Livre de lecture de l'école unique* (Paris: Delalain, 1929, 1934).

48. John E Talbott, *The Politics of Educational Reform in France, 1918–1940* (Princeton: Princeton University Press, 1969), 118–20, 226–27; Jean-Michel Barreau, Jean-François Garcia, and Louis Legrand, *L'École unique (de 1914 à nos jours)* (Paris: Presses universitaires de France, 1998).

49. Judith Wishnia, *The Proletarianizing of the Fonctionnaires: Civil Service Workers and the Labor Movement under the Third Republic* (Baton Rouge: Louisiana State

University Press, 1990), 238–39; Jeanne Siwek-Pouydesseau, *Le Syndicalisme des fonctionnaires jusqu'à la guerre froide 1848–1948* (Lille: Presses universitaires de Lille, 1989); Jacques Girault, *Instituteurs, Professeurs: Une culture syndicale dans la société française (fin XIXe–XXe siècle* (Paris: Publications de la Sorbonne, 1996); M. Delmas, "Du rôle des instituteurs dans la république," *A.D.L.F., L'Action démocratique et laïque des femmes*, no. 8 (June 1937): 105; Anne-Marie Sohn, *Féminisme et syndicalisme: Les Institutrices de la Fédération unitaire de l'enseignement de 1919 à 1935* (Paris: Hachette/ Bibliothèque Nationale, 1975).

50. "Conseil d'administration," *BAIPDEN*, no. 46 (December 1918): 15; *BAADEN*, nos. 1–25 (1918–29); *Bulletin mensuel du syndicat national des directeurs et directrices d'écoles normales*, nos. 1–51 (1929–40). In 1933 the CSIP membership was enlarged from 54 to 81; primary education representation rose from 6 to 12.

51. "Une lettre de Madame la directrice de l'école normale de l'Yonne à la section du S. N. des instituteurs," *L'Université, Journal officiel de la Fédération générale de l'enseignement* 4 (March–April 1932): 2; AN F17/25259/A (Fabre), 24827 (Renault).

52. Stephen L. Harp, *Learning to Be Loyal: Primary Schooling as Nation Building in Alsace and Lorraine, 1850–1940* (DeKalb: Northern Illinois University Press, 1998), 183–95.

53. AN F17/23903 (Combes née Buisson), 23904 (J. Combes).

54. AN F17/23903 (Combes née Buisson), 23904 (J. Combes).

55. AN F17/27978 (Valin), quotations, E. Bernard, February 15, 1921, April 12, 1924; inspector general (name illegible), May 9, 1923.

56. AN F17/24978 (Valin), quotation, inspector general A. Aubin, July 2, 1932.

57. AN F17/25573 (Gambey née André); "En Alsace et Lorraine," *L'Oeuvre*, December 17, 1922.

58. AN F17.27019 (G. Martin); Wanda Marchal, *Nous serons maîtresses d'école . . . du couvent des grands-carmes à l'École normale d'institutrices de Metz* (Metz: Éditions Serpenoise, 1990).

59. AN F17/24521 (Maucourant); B. Maucourant and J. Toutain, "Le Séjour des institutrices alsaciennes et lorraines à Saint-Germain-en-Laye," *BulFR*, no. 74 (November 1920): 21–29. Ninety men attended a similar program at the Seine-et-Oise men's normal school.

60. Yves Bisch, *Écoles d'Alsace: Les Leçons d'histoire* (Besançon: Éditions du Rhin, 1996), 141–45.

61. AN F17/24602 (Hui).

62. "Une Alsacienne 'libre-penseuse' peut-elle devenir institutrice?" *L'Oeuvre*, July 27, 1932; Albert Bayet, "L'Affaire Fouilleron, un défi aux droits de l'homme et aux libertés alsaciennes," *Le Midi syndicaliste*, October 1932. See also *Le Quotidien*, August 11, 1932; *Le Peuple*, August 18, 1932.

63. Mlle Maucourant, "L'Organisation des écoles normales d'institutrices en Alsace et Lorraine," *BAADEN*, no. 3 (July 1919): 7; Jules Senger and Paul Barret, *Bismarck chez Jules Ferry: Le Problème scolaire en Alsace et en Lorraine, le régime confessionnel, le bilinguisme* (Paris: EDIMAF, 2001), 84 (1st ed., 1948), citing one Jewish student in an Alsatian normal school, 1947.

276   NOTES TO PAGES 204–208

64. Harp, *Learning*, 193–94; Bisch, *Écoles d'Alsace*, 154–56; Alison Carrol, "Regional Republicans: The Alsatian Socialists and the Politics of Primary Schooling in Alsace, 1918–1939," *French Historical Studies* 34 (Spring 2011): 299–325.

65. Marie Silve, "Témoignage sur une origine," in *Les Davidées*, ed. Jean Guitton (Paris: Casterman, 1967), 45–81.

66. Marceau Pivert, *Un des aspects de l'offensive cléricale, le noyautage de l'enseignement public par les Davidées* (Paris: Groupe fraternel de l'enseignement, 1930); Jules Bonnet, "Les Davidées," *La Fronde*, September 16, 1926; Marie Guillot, "Les Cléricaux dans l'enseignement, les Davidées," *La Révolution prolétarienne* 6 (December 5, 1930): 327–32.

67. AN F17/24914 (Paul), 24321 (Parayre), 25206 (Cuminal née Leschi), 24873 (Échard née Gauthier), 25465 (Sélince née Marseille), 26883 (Hue), 24281 (Omnès).

68. Peneff, *Écoles publiques, écoles privées*, 15, 198–99; Harry W. Paul, *The Second Ralliement: The Rapprochement between Church and State in France in the Twentieth Century* (Washington, D.C.: Catholic University of America Press, 1967), 87–88; Prost, *Histoire de l'enseignement*, 294.

69. AN F17/24819 (Morel), March 1916, February 1931; 24602 (Hui), August 14, 1931; 26982 (Drouin née Royère, veuve Fassou), April 1932; 28418 (Beunot).

70. *Livre du cinquantenaire*, 75 (G. Benattar-Paineau).

71. AN 103AJ/2, Sid-Cara papers, draft of talk for Legion of Honor ceremony, 1998.

72. In 1937, 83,400 indigène schoolboys (18,771 of them in European schools); 14,945 indigène schoolgirls (7,645 in European schools). See René Lespès, *Pour comprendre l'Algérie* {Alger: Gouvernement général, 1937), 187–89.

73. AN F17/24465 (Muraccioli), 25665 (Tubiana née Raynaud).

74. CAF (Angers), 1AF 58 (Charente-Inférieure). The department's only prewar UFSF group was in Saintes.

75. "La Propagande suffragiste," *LF*, no. 932, April 12, 1930; "Les Conférences de l'U.F.S.F.," *LF*, no. 1001, December 12, 1931.

76. CAF, 1AF 50 (Ariège), April 1932, Goron; 1AF 55 (Calvados), January 11, 1923, Schreck; 1AF 70 (Finistère), January 1922, Huber-Fortin.

77. Pierre Flandin, "Ce qu'il faut penser de l'esprit clérical féminin," *LF*, no. 624, June 23, 1923.

78. Hause with Kenney, *Women's Suffrage*, 134; Paul Smith, *Feminism and the Third Republic: Women's Political and Civil Rights in France, 1918–1945* (Oxford: Clarendon Press, 1996), 16, 26, 39; Françoise Blum, Colette Chambelland, and Michel Dreyfus, "Mouvements de femmes (1919–1940): Guide des sources documentaires," special issue, *Vie sociale*, nos. 11–12 (November–December 1984): 559, 563. See also Christine Bard's comprehensive *Les Filles de Marianne: Histoire des féminismes, 1914–1940* (Paris: Fayard, 1995).

79. Smith, *Feminism*, 18, 44–52, 58–59; Blum. Chambelland, and Dreyfus, "Mouvements de femmes," 566; Klejman and Rochefort, *L'Égalité en marche*, 205; Emily Machen, "Catholic Women, International Engagement and the Battle for Suffrage in Interwar France: The Case of the Action Sociale de la Femme and the Union Nationale pour le Vote des Femmes," *Women's History Review* 26 (April 2017): 291.

NOTES TO PAGES 208–213   277

80. Siân Reynolds, *France between the Wars: Gender and Politics* (London: Routledge, 1996), 132–203; Évelyne Diebolt, *Les Femmes dans l'action sanitaire, sociale et culturelle, 1901–2001: Les Associations face aux institutions* (Paris: Femmes et Associations, 2001).

81. Membership or leadership roles noted in *La Française* and Brunschvicg's records (CAF, 1AF 45–131), with UFSF membership lists for some departments; "La Campagne suffragiste en Corrèze," *LF*, no. 909, October 26, 1929; "Mme Prieur," *LF*, no. 1287, June 3–10, 1939.

82. "Comité central," *Droit des femmes* (1920–35); reports in *La Française* and CAF, 1AF; "Le Mans," *Droit des femmes* 27 (October 1931): 239; "Congrès d'Amiens," *Droit des femmes* 29 (August–September 1933): 198. Directrice Chauvin was not the pioneering lawyer Jeanne Chauvin.

83. "Assemblée générale," May 19, 1927, *BAAENI de Blois* (1927): 7–8.

84. E. Morel, "Aux anciennes," *BAAENI des Côtes-du-Nord*, no. 6 (1926), 22–23; CAF, 1AF 62 (Côtes-du-Nord).

85. Jean Grispoux, "Les Écoles normales de Perpignan," *Études roussillonnaises* 11 (1992): 211.

86. "Journée du cinquantenaire de l'amicale," assemblée générale, April 21, 1976, *BAAENI de Poitiers*, no. 70 (March 1977), unpaginated, with excerpts from earlier issues; "La Bataille suffragiste," *Droit des femmes* 24 (April 1928): 438–39; Fernande Granvaud Jourdanneau, *Images et vie de l'école normale d'institutrices de Poitiers, 1887–1991* (Poitiers: Éditions du Pont-Neuf, 1994), 146–49.

87. "Notre féminisme," *Après l'école normale, BAAENI de Rumilly* (1934): 11–12; "Féminisme et suffrage," ibid. (1936): 10–12.

88. "Conférence féministe," *Amicale normalienne des institutrices de la Lozère, Bulletin*, no. 6 (June 1932): 35–36.

89. *Feu follet, Revue mensuelle de l'école normale d'institutrices de Cahors*, nos. 3, 7, 12, 17 (December 1930, April, December 1931, April 1932).

90. S. Paul, "Que veut la jeunesse," *MGP*, nos. 36, 37, 39 (June 2, 9, 23, 1934): 679, 697, 730.

91. AN F17/26695 (Naud née Ithurbide); Mlle J. Ithurbide, "Féminisme et suffrage," *LF*, no. 1177, February 1, 1936.

92. Ithurbide, "Féminisme"; Smith, *Feminism*, 22, 67–85. On the limited numbers of women in political parties, other than the rightwing Parti social français, see also Geoff Read, *The Republic of Men: Gender and Political Parties in Interwar France* (Baton Rouge: Louisiana State University Press, 2014), 168–79.

93. Mona Siegel, *The Moral Disarmament of France: Education, Pacifism, and Patriotism, 1914–1940* (Cambridge: Cambridge University Press, 2004), 197; "Assemblée générale," *Bulletin mensuel du Syndicat national des directeurs et directrices d'écoles normales*, no. 27 (April 1934): 6.

94. Joel Colton, *Leon Blum: Humanist in Politics* (New York: Knopf, 1966); Julian Jackson, *The Popular Front in France: Defending Democracy, 1934–1938* (Cambridge: Cambridge University Press, 1987); Vicki Caron, *Uneasy Asylum: France and the Jewish Refugee Crisis, 1933–1942* (Stanford: Stanford University Press, 1999).

278　NOTES TO PAGES 213–215

95. "Trois femmes au ministère," *BAAENI de Vesoul*, no. 36 (June 1936): 36–38; "Le Banquet de l'après-midi," *BulFR*, no. 38 (December 1937): 8; Siân Reynolds, "Women and the Popular Front: The Case of the Three Women Ministers," *French History* 8 (1994): 196–224; Smith, *Feminism*, 145–47.

96. *Commémoration du cinquantenaire de l'école normale d'institutrices et du centenaire de l'école normale d'instituteurs de Rennes* (Rennes: n.p., 1937), 43.

97. Cécile Formaglio, *"Féministe d'abord": Cécile Brunschvicg (1877–1946)* (Rennes: Presses universitaires de Rennes, 2014), 253–70.

98. Norman Ingram, *The Politics of Dissent: Pacifism in France, 1919–1939* (Oxford: Clarendon Press, 1991); Marie-Michèle Doucet, "Prise de parole au féminin: La Paix et les relations internationales dans les revendications du mouvement de femmes pour la paix en France (1919–1934)," (PhD. Diss., Université de Montréal, 2015); Reynolds, *France between the Wars*, 181–203; Siegel, *Moral Disarmament*; Bard, *Filles de Marianne*, 289–313.

99. M. Angles, "Quel rôle pour les femmes dans la propagande pour la Société des Nations," *BulFR*, no. 15 (June 1928): 38–45, "L'Éducation de la jeunesse en vue de la collaboration internationale," *BulFR*, no. 17 (March 1929): 15–21, "Les 'Moins de vingt ans' et la guerre," *BulFR*, no. 22 (December 1930): 64–76; A. Eidenschenk-Patin, "Ligue internationale des mères et des éducatrices pour la paix," *BulFR*, no. 19 (December 1929): 61–65.

100. A. Eidenschenk-Patin, "La Ligue internationale des mères et des éducatrices pour la paix en 1930–1931," *BulFR*, no. 25 (December 1931): 43–55; AN F17/22447/B (Grauvogel).

101. Blum, Chambelland, and Dreyfus, "Mouvements de femmes," 585–86; Camille Drevet, *Sur les routes humaines* (Paris: l'auteur, 1936), 59–61.

102. M. Dudon, "La Paix par l'éducation," *BulFR*, no. 2 (May 1930): 43–55; Dudon, "L'Action pour la paix à Nice," *Le Poilu républicain* (December 1931) : 2; Dudon, "Développement de l'action feminine," *BAAENI de Nice*, no. 3 (December 1931): 3–5, and "Quand les femmes font des congrès," ibid., no. 14 (October 1934): 17–20; Dudon, *Un ministre de la paix* (Nice: César Ventura, 1937); AN, Base Léonore (Palanque).

103. "Réunion amicale," *Bulletin annuel de l'AAENI de Digne*, nos. 6–7 (1930–31): 4; S. Paul, "Sur la paix," *MGP*, no. 7 (November 8, 1930): 139–40.

104. "Ligue internationale des mères et des éducatrices pour la paix," *BAAENI de Clermont-Ferrand*, no. 6 (May 1929): 19–21, no. 16 (June 1934): 16–18; J. M., "Conférence de Mme Eidenschenk," *AAENI d'Orléans, Bulletin* 6 (1932): 21–22; A. Eidenschenk-Patin, "Ligue internationale des méres et des éducatrices pour la paix," *BAAENI de Rennes*, no. 5 (May 1933): 48–50.

105. AN F17/26989 (Flamant).

106. Hesse and Gleyze, *Notions de sociologie*, 8th ed. (1938), 289, 313–14.

107. "Action démócratique et laïque des femmes," *LF*, no. 1095, March 3, 1934; Smith, *Feminism*, 85, 141.

108. A.D.L.F., *L'Action démocratique et laïque des femmes*, nos. 2–14 (1935–39).

NOTES TO PAGES 215–219 279

109. M. Soboul, "Importance de l'éducation des femmes dans une démocratie Causerie faite aux membres de l'Action démocratique et laïque des femmes, Groupe du Gard, le 20 novembre 1935," *BAAENI du Gard*, no. 9 (May 1936): 48–56, quotations, 56.

110. "La Vie de la section Tourangelle de l'A.D.L.F. en 1935–1937," *A.D.L.F.*, no. 8 (June 1937): 5.

111. Caroline Campbell, "Building a Movement, Dismantling the Republic: Women, Gender, and Political Extremism in the Croix de Feu/Parti Social Français, 1927–1940," *French Historical Studies* 35 (Fall 2012): 691–726; Campbell, *Political Belief in France, 1927–1945: Gender, Empire, and Fascism in the Croix de Feu and Parti Social Français* (Baton Rouge: Louisiana State University Press, 2015); Kevin Passmore, "'Planting the Tricolor in the Citadels of Communism': Women's Social Action in the Croix de feu and Parti social français," *Journal of Modern History* 71 (December 1999): 814–51 (membership, 817).

112. Madame Gaillard, "Éducation civique des jeunes filles," *A.D.L.F.*, no. 6 (January–February 1937): 4–7; M. Schwab, "Réflexions après le congrès," *A.D.L.F.*, no. 10 (February 1938): 1–2; "Notre 4ème congrès," *A.D.L.F.*, no. 14 (January 1939): 4–5.

113. "La Ligue des femmes pour la paix," *Feuilles libres de la quinzaine* 4, no. 64 (September 30, 1938): 237.

114. "Adresse au président du conseil," *BAAENI de Poitiers*, no. 22 (December 1938): 14.

115. "XIVe Congrès national de la paix, à Tours 26–29 mai 1938, Discours de Mme Gaillard," *A.D.L.F.*, no. 12 (June 1938), 3–4; L. Gaillard, "Lettre de Province," *A.D.L.F.*, no. 13 (October 1938): 3.

116. Prost, *Histoire de l'enseignement*, 394.

Epilogue

1. Rémy Handourtzel, *Vichy et l'école 1940–1944* (Paris: Noêsis, 1997).

2. Mona Siegel, *Moral Disarmament*, 213. Alain Vincent cites 500 teachers killed in battle in 1940 and13,000 prisoners of war (*L'École normale: Des hussards de la République aux professeurs des écoles* [Joué-les-Tours: A. Sutton, 2001], 79).

3. Quoted in Christine Persyn, *Une grande éducatrice, Madame Eidenschenk-Patin 1864–1942* (Avesnes: L'Observateur, 1950), 21.

4. Yvette Delsaut, *La Place du maître: une chronique des écoles normales d'instituteurs* (Paris: L'Harmattan, 1992), 108, 127; Handourtzel, *Vichy et l'école*; Jean-François Condette, "Former des maîtres sous Vichy: Les instituts de formation professionnelle et leur échec (1940–1944)," in *La Formation des maîtres de 1940 à 2010*, ed. Antoine Prost (Rennes: Presses universitaires de Rennes, 2014), 39–54.

5. Linda L. Clark, "Higher-Ranking Women Civil Servants and the Vichy Regime: Firings and Hirings, Collaboration and Resistance," *French History* 13 (September 1999): 332–59; Marc Olivier Baruch, *Servir l'État français: L'administration en France de 1940 à 1944* (Paris: Fayard, 1997); Francine Muel-Dreyfus, *Vichy et l'éternel féminin, contribution à une sociologie de l'ordre des corps* (Paris: Seuil, 1996); Miranda Pollard, *Reign of Virtue: Mobilizing Gender in Vichy France* (Chicago: University of Chicago Press, 1998).

280 NOTES TO PAGES 219–224

6. Handourtzel, *Vichy et l'école*, 96; AN F17/25465 (Sélince née Marseille), education minister René Capitant, May 19, 1945, letter.
7. AN F17, dossiers personnels of directrices; F17/25665 (Tubiana née Raynaud).
8. AN F17/25385 (Moitessier), 26883 (Hue), 26518 (Mir).
9. AN F17/ 26833 (Bar née Desbordes), 27872 (Météraud née Beulaygue), 26512/B (Magnat née Delacquis), 27017 (Malivert).
10. AN F17/24915 (MP).
11. AN F17/25555 (NB), 28065 (OT).
12. AN F17/26518 (Mir); Mathilde Mir, *Quand la terre se soulève* (Angoulême: Coquemard, 1948); Yvette Renaud, *Mathilde Mir en Charente, l'engagement d'une femme dans son temps* (Angoulême: Centre départemental de documentation pédagogique, 1996), 25–29; René Pomeau, *Mémoires d'un siècle entre XIXe et XXIe* (Paris: Fayard, 1999), 291–96.
13. AN F17/27099 (François née Pheulpin); Jean-Marie Fossier, *Zone interdite: mai 1940–mai 1945, Nord-Pas-de-Calais* (Paris: Éditions sociales, 1977), 259–64.
14. AN AJ16/9079 (Brulé née Delavenay); F17/28309 (Grandjeat née Charrot), 27872 (Météraud).
15. Pierre Mazier, *Quand le Gard se libérait: Un ancien du C.D.L. raconte* (Nîmes: C. Lacour, 1992), 20.
16. "Mlle Hélène Odoul," *BulFR*, no. 16 (November 1963): 6–7; Margaret Collins Weitz, *Sisters in the Resistance: How Women Fought to Free France* (New York: John Wiley, 1995), 132–33; Évelyne Sullerot and Bernard Morlino, *L'Insoumise: Femmes, familles, les combats d'une vie* (Paris: L'Archipel, 2017); AN, Base Léonore, Légion d'honneur 1980035/1176/3614 (Palanque).
17. S. Paul, "Mlle Parayre," *BulFR*, no. 46 (January 1947): 35–36.
18. J. Chevillard, "En est-il donc moins vrai que la lumière existe?" *BAAENI de Rennes*, no. 14 (April 1947): 3.
19. AN F17/26882 (Hirtz), 25122 (Douillet née Weill); Enquête Ozouf, MUNAE, Bouches-du-Rhône (D).
20. One IFP directrice retired in 1942 (Valin), one died, and one became an inspectress in Paris.
21. Ministère de l'éducation nationale, *Tableau de classement par ordre d'ancienneté de classe du personnel de l'inspection académique, de l'inspection primaire, des écoles normales, arrêté le 31 décembre 1945* (Paris: Imprimerie nationale, 1946), 32, 46–48.
22. AN F17/25465 (Sélince), Capitant letter to Conseil d'Etat, May 19, 1945.
23. AN F17/25206 (Cuminal née Leschi), 24879 (Gaillard née Joly), 24925 (Roig), 27872 (Météraud), 28051 (Salducci née Latty), 25665 (Tubiana).
24. "Discours de Maurice Montel, maire et conseiller général de Ruynes-de-Margeride," in "Hommage à Mademoiselle Odoul," *BAAENI de Clermont-Ferrand*, no. 16 (March 1963): 27–29; AN, Légion d'honneur (Palanque); "Géraud, Marie-Louise-Jeanne," in Guy Caplat, ed., *L'Inspection générale de l'instruction publique au XXe siècle: Dictionnaire biographique des inspecteurs généraux et des inspecteurs de l'Académie de Paris, 1914–1939* (Paris: Institut national de recherche pédagogique/ Économica, 1987), 299.
25. AN F17/24849 (Usciati née Soboul); Mazier, *Quand le Gard se libérait*, 52, 144.

NOTES TO PAGES 224–229 281

26. AN F17/24878 (Gaillard), 25285 (Poujade née Rey); Jacques Girault and Julien Veyret, "Gaillard, Louise, Suzanne," maîtron-en-ligne.univ.paris1.fr/spip.php? article23914; Justinien Raymond, Maurice Moissonnier, and Roger Pierre, "Cuminal, Paul," ibid., article107609.

27. *La Française*, May 17, 1913 and February 3, 1923 (Géraud); March 28, 1914 (Odoul); April 12, 1930 (Cuminal); December 14, 1935 (Mir).

28. Renaud, *Mathilde Mir*, 39–41; Charles-Louis Foulon, "Les Femmes dans les comités départementaux de la libération," in *Les Femmes dans la résistance*, ed. Henriette Bidouze et al. (Monaco: Éditions de Rocher, 1977). 272–76; Claire Andrieu, "Les Résistantes, perspectives de recherche," *Le Mouvement social*, no. 180 (July–September 1997): 92–93; Pomeau, *Mèmoires*, 299.

29. Renaud, *Mathilde Mir*; Jacques Girault, "Mir Mathilde," and "Soboul Marie, femme Usciati," maîtrron-en-ligne... articles 145106, 173471.

30. AN F17/25259/A (Fabre).

31. Jacques Girault, "Bontemps Henriette, Léontine, Valérie"; "François Cécile"; "Parent Paule, Henriette, Joséphine, Victorine"; Alain Dalançon and Jacques Girault, "Chardon Marguerite, Louise, Marie," all in maîtron-en-ligne... articles 17248 (HB), 23986 (CF), 147477 (PP), 190129 (MC).

32. Bibliothèque nationale de France, Catalogue général, for book titles and numbers of editions by authors named above and by inspectresses general Bandet-Estève, Boscher, Brulé, Drouin, Mezeix, Sourgen, Thomet.

33. AN AJ16/9079 (Brulé née Delavenay); Hélène Brulé, *Le Rôle de la femme dans l'éducation familiale et sociale* (Paris: Foucher, 1950), quotations, 29, 43.

34. Brulé, *Le Rôle de la femme*, quotations, 33, 36; Émile Delavenay, *Témoignage: d'un village savoyard au village mondial, 1905–1991* (Aix-en-Provence: Édisud, 1992).

35. H. Sourgen, *L'Éducation civique des femmes: quelques suggestions pratiques* (Paris: UNESCO, 1954), 16–17, 20, 95; AN F17/28383 (Sourgen), 1916. UNESCO also issued books in English and Spanish on women's civic education.

36. Sourgen, *L'Éducation civique*, 63–64; *LF*, December 23, 1933, Tunis UFSF.

37. AN F17/27516 (Seguin); Jeanne Seguin and Pauline Millet, *Pour nos filles, recueil de lectures* (Paris: Larousse, 1957); letter from Seguin, June 1981. On the history of textbooks for girls, see Clark, *Schooling the Daughters*.

38. Hélène Brulé, "The Education of Teachers in France," in *The Education of Teachers in England, France, and the U.S.A.*, by C. A. Richardson, Hélène Brulé and Harold E. Snyder (Paris: UNESCO), 1953), 131–211, citations 137, 156; also published as *La Formation du personnel enseignant: Angleterre, France, États-Unis* (Paris: UNESCO, 1954); Jean-Claude Bouthau, *En cravate et blouse grise: Mémoires d'un normalien* (Saint-Brieuc: Breizh-Compo, 1986), 60–69; Micheline Hermine, *Les Poulettes de la République: Journal d'une normalienne ingénue* (Paris: L'Harmattan, 2003), 31.

39. Prost, *Histoire de l'enseignement*, 443–43.

40. Prost, *Histoire*, 476–77.

41. AN F17/27003 (Iba-Zizen née Boué); Mme Iba-Zizen, "La Condition des femmes musulmanes en Algérie," *Association des surintendantes d'usines et de services sociaux, Assemblée générale, 10 février 1959* (Paris: 1959), 25–39; Augustin Ibazizen, *Le Testament d'un berbère, un itinéraire spirituel et politique* (Paris: Albatros, 1984).

282   NOTES TO PAGES 230–235

42. Jean Pascal, *Les Femmes députés de 1945 à 1988* (Paris: Jean Pascal, 1990), 302; AN 103AJ/2, Nafissa Sid-Cara papers, Légion d'honneur.

43. Enquête Ozouf, MUNAE, Bouches-du-Rhône (G née Albert).

44. On coeducation, see Rebecca Rogers, ed., *La mixité dans l'éducation: Enjeux passés et présents* (Lyon: ENS Éditions, 2004). On men's predominance heading coeducational secondary schools, see Marlaine Cacouault-Bitaud, *La Direction des collèges et des lycées: Une affaire d'hommes? Genre et inégalités dans l'éducation nationale* (Paris: L'Harmattan, 2008).

45. J. Athol Hunt, "The Preparation of Primary School Teachers in France since World War II" (Ph.D. diss., University of Hobart, 1977); Delsaut, *La Place du maître*, 127–51; Patricia Legris, "Les Écoles normales primaires de 1945 aux années 1970: Les Contradictions progressives d'une institution à deux vitesses," in *La Formation des maîtres*, ed. Prost, 55–70; Hervé Terral, *Profession: professeur, Des écoles normales maintenues aux instituts universitaires de formation des maîtres (1945–1990)* (Paris: Presses universitaires de France, 1997), 83.

46. The number of interwar directrices so honored is likely greater because not all personnel files note the information and AN, Base Léonore does not yet include many interwar recipients.

47. Annette Bon, "Des débuts difficiles: Naissance et construction des IUFM, 1990–1997," in *La Formation des maîtres*, ed. Prost, 227–42.

48. Bon, "Des débuts difficiles;" Annette Bon, "Pavane pour une infante défunte: les IUFM de 1990 à 2009," in *La Formation des maîtres*, ed. Prost, 259–72; Prost, "Les IUFM au milieu du gué: Diversité et convergences," in ibid., 243–58.

49. Prost, "Les IUFM," 247.

50. Prost, "Conclusion," in *La Formation des maîtres*, ed. Prost, 277; Bernard Cornu, "Teacher Education in France: Universitisation and Professionalization—from IUFMs to ESPEs," *Education Inquiry* 6 (September 2015), https://doi.org/ 10.3402/edui.v6.28649.

51. Furet, ed., *Jules Ferry*; Willem Frijhoff, ed., *L'Offre d'école: Éléments pour une étude comparative des politiques éducatives au XIXe siècle* (Paris: I.N.R.P., 1983).

52. For example, Granvaud-Jourdanneau, *Images et vie de l'école normale d'institutrices de Poitiers, 1887–1891*; Marchal, *Nous serons maîtresses d'école . . . du couvent des grands-carmes à l'école normale d'institutrices de Metz.*

53. Gabriel Compayré, "Les Discours scolaires de Jules Ferry," *RP* 28 (June 1896): 483.

54. Ozouf and Ozouf, *La République des instituteurs*, 83.

55. E. Flayol, "Réflexions sur l'éducation civique," *BulFR*, no. 8 (March 1928): 32.

56. Christine Bard, ed., *Les Féministes de la deuxième vague* (Rennes: Presses universitaires de Rennes, 2012).

57. Joan Wallach Scott, *The Politics of the Veil* (Princeton: Princeton University Press, 2007).

Selected Bibliography

Archives and Manuscript Sources

Archives Départementales de Paris
  D1T1 198, 551, 552, 703, Dossiers personnels
Archives Nationales de France
  AJ16/559, 1100, 6012, 9070 Académie de Paris, Dossiers
  F17 Ministère de l'Instruction publique, Ministère de l'Éducation nationale
  F17 9278 Inspection générale, Algeria
  F17 9572, 9574, 9614, 9620 Écoles normales, various topics
  F17 9643–9645 Écoles normales, inspections 1880s
  F17 9670–9681 Écoles normales, curriculum
  F17 9684–9687, 9698, Écoles normales, personnel
  F17 9744–9759 Écoles normales d'institutrices
  F17 10865, 10891 Écoles maternelles, École Pape-Carpantier
  F17 12325–12337 Enseignement primaire, Algeria
  F17 20001– Dossiers personnels
  71AJ Ferdinand Buisson papers
  103AJ Nafissa Sid-Cara papers
  81AP Alfred Rambaud papers
  20020123/7 École normale supérieure Fontenay-aux-Roses, conférences des élèves directrices
  20020184/1, 2 École normale supérieure Fontenay-aux-Roses, régistres des élèves
    Légion d'honneur, Base de données Léonore, www.leonore.archives-nationales.culture.gouv.fr
Bibliothèque Marguerite Durand, Paris
  DOS 362 COO Coopération Féminine
  DOS 396 UNI Union Française pour le Suffrage des Femmes
Centre des Archives du Féminisme,
  Angers, Bibliothèque de l'université
  1AF Cécile Brunschvicg papers, Union Française pour le Suffrage des Femmes
Musée National de l'Éducation, Rouen
  Enquête Ozouf, questionnaires completed by pre-1914 teachers, Enquête Ozouf @Réseau-Canopé.fr

Periodicals

Action féminine, Bulletin officiel du Conseil national des femmes françaises
Action féministe, Bulletin mensuel de la Fédération féministe universitaire de France
A.D.L.F., Action Démocratique et Laïque des Femmes
Annuaire de l'enseignement primaire

284 SELECTED BIBLIOGRAPHY

Annuaire de l'instruction publique et des beaux-arts
Annuaire général de l'université
Association amicale des professeurs des écoles normales d'instituteurs et des écoles normales d'institutrices, Bulletin trimestriel
Bulletin de l'Association amicale des anciennes élèves de Fontenay-aux-Roses, later *Bulletin de l'Association amicale des anciennes élèves de l'école normale supérieure de Fontenay-aux-Roses*
Bulletin de l'Association amicale des directrices et directeurs d'écoles normales
Bulletin de l'Association des inspecteurs primaires et des directeurs d'écoles normales
Bulletin de l'Enseignement des indigènes
Bulletin de l'Union pour l'action morale, subsequently *Bulletin de l'Union pour la vérité*
Bulletin du Syndicat national des directeurs et directrices d'écoles normales
Bulletin, Société libre pour l'étude psychologique
Correspondance générale de l'instruction primaire
Droit (Le) des femmes
École (L') émancipée
École (L') et la vie
École (L') nouvelle
Femme (La) nouvelle
Française (La)
Fronde (La)
Histoire de l'éducation
Instituteur (L')
Instituteur (L') républicain
Journal des instituteurs
Manuel général de l'instruction primaire
Nouvelle (La) éducation
Revue de l'enseignement primaire et primaire supérieur
Revue pédagogique, L'Enseignement public
Volume (Le)

Selected issues of *Bulletins* of Associations amicales des anciennes élèves des écoles normales d'institutrices, at Bibliothèque Nationale de France (titles use name of department or city): Albi, Angers, Aube, Auxerre, Aveyron, Beauvais, Blois, Bourg, Caen, Cahors, Chartres, Châteauroux, Clermont-Ferrand, Côtes-du-Nord, Coutances, Digne, Évreux, Gard, Gironde, Grenoble, Guéret, Limoges, Lozère, Mâcon, Melun, Meurthe-et-Moselle, Nantes, Nice, Nord, Orléans, Perpignan, Poitiers, Rennes, Rumilly, Saint-Brieuc, Seine, Seine-Inférieure, Strasbourg, Tarbes, Vendée, Vesoul

Official Publications

Bulletin administratif de l'instruction publique
Bulletin de l'instruction primaire du département d'Alger
Bulletin de l'instruction publique du département d'Oran
Gouvernement général de l'Algérie. *Situation de l'enseignement pendant l'année scolaire 1907–1908, Rapport de M. le recteur de l'Académie d'Alger*. Alger, 1909.
Gouvernement général de l'Algérie. *Statistique générale de l'Algérie (1894–1896)*. Alger, 1897.

Ministère de l'Éducation nationale. *Tableau de classement par ordre d'ancienneté de classe du personnel de l'inspection académique, de l'inspection primaire, des écoles normales, arrêté le 31 décembre 1945*. Paris: Imprimerie nationale, 1946. *Tableau de classement. . . arrêté le 31 décembre 1948*. Paris: Imprimerie nationale, 1949.

Ministère de l'Instruction publique et des Beaux-arts. *Organisation pédagogique et Programmes d'enseignement des écoles maternelles, des écoles primaires élémentaires, des écoles primaires supérieures et des écoles normales*. Paris: Imprimerie nationale, 1891.

Ministère de l'Instruction publique et des Beaux-arts. *Règlements et programmes d'études des écoles normales d'instituteurs et d'institutrices*. Paris: Imprimerie nationale, 1886.

Ministère de l'Instruction publique et des Beaux-arts. *Statistique de l'enseignement primaire*. Vols. 1–8 (1876–1877, 1829–1877, 1881–1882, 1886–1887, 1891–1892, 1896–1897, 1901–1902, 1906–1907). Paris: Imprimerie nationale, 1878–1909.

Ministère de l'Instruction publique et des Beaux-arts. *Tableau de classement par ordre d'ancienneté de classe du personnel de l'inspection académique, de l'inspection primaire, des écoles normales et des écoles primaires supérieures* (1919–26). Paris: Imprimerie nationale, 1920–1927.

Books and Articles Published before 1940

Actes du Congrès féministe international de Bruxelles 1912. Edited by Marie Popelin. Brussels: C. Bulens, 1912.

Albert, E., and C. Arnaud. *Normaliennes*. Marseille: C. Arnaud, 1914.

Association amicale des anciennes élèves de l'école normale de Nîmes. *Cinquantenaire de l'école normale d'institutrices de Nîmes 1883–1933*. Nîmes: G. Teissier, 1934.

Association amicale des anciennes élèves de l'école normale de Rouen. *À la mémoire de Madame Menat 1863–1936*. Rouen, 1936.

Association amicale normalienne de Chartres. *Hommage à Mademoiselle Bonnefon*. Vendôme: S. Doucet, 1934.

Barthas, Mme. *L'Enseignement scolaire de la puériculture*. Paris: A. Michalon, 1909.

Bodin, Marguerite. *L'Institutrice: Une féministe militante à la Belle Epoque*. Reprint of 1922 edition with "avant-propos" by Denise Karnaouch. Paris: L'Harmattan, 2012.

Borit, Marcel. "Les Groupes féministes universitaires," *Pages libres*, no. 427 (March 6, 1909): 266–70.

Borit, Marcel. "Les Groupes féministes universitaires." *Grande revue* 70 (December 1911): 801–17.

Bottini-Honot, Jeanne. *Parmi les inconnus*. Constantine: Éditions de l'Académie Numidia, 1929.

Brenet, Paul, and Félix Thureau, eds. *Hommage des artistes à Picquart. . . Liste des protestataires*. Paris: Société libre d'édition des gens de lettres, 1899.

Bugnon, Émile. "Le Désaccord entre l'école et la nation," I. "Les Instituteurs." II. "Les Institutrices." *Grande revue* 82 (November 25, 1913): 673–704, 84 (April 25, 1914): 713–33.

Buisson, Ferdinand, ed. *Dictionnaire de pédagogie et d'instruction primaire*. 4 vols. Paris: Hachette, 1882–87.

Buisson, Ferdinand, ed. *Nouveau dictionnaire de pédagogie et d'instruction primaire*. Paris: Hachette, 1911.

Buisson, Ferdinand. *Le Vote des femmes*. Paris: Dunod et Pinat, 1911.

286 SELECTED BIBLIOGRAPHY

Catalogue des bibliothèques des écoles normales. Musée pédagogique, *Mémoires et documents scolaires. Fascicule* 32. Paris: Delagrave and Hachette, 1887.

Coignet, Clarisse. *Mémoires.* 4 vols. Lausanne: Constant-Varidel, 1899–1904.

Commémoration du cinquantenaire de l'école normale d'institutrices et du centenaire de l'école normale d'instituteurs de Rennes. Rennes: n.p., 1937.

Compain, L.-M. *L'Un vers l'autre.* Paris: P.-V. Stock, 1903.

Compayré, Gabriel. *Histoire de la pédagogie.* 4th ed. Paris: Delaplane, 1886.

Compayré, Gabriel. *Instruction civique, cours complet suivi de notions d'économie politique à l'usage des écoles normales primaires.* 7th ed. Paris: Delaplane, 1888.

Congrès international de l'enseignement primaire, analyse des mémoires. Musée pédagogique, *Mémoires et documents scolaires. Fascicule* 91. Paris: Delagrave and Hachette, 1889.

Congrès international de l'enseignement primaire, compte rendu des séances. Musée pédagogique. *Mémoires et documents scolaires. Fascicule* 95. Paris: Delagrave and Hachette, 1889.

Congrès international de l'enseignement primaire du 2 au 5 août 1900, Programme du congrès, Délégués du Ministère de l'instruction publique et des gouvernements étrangers, Membres adhérents. Paris: Imprimerie E. Kapp, 1900.

Congrès international des œuvres et institutions féminines, Paris 12–18 juillet 1889, Actes. Paris: Société des éditions scientifiques, 1890.

Dechappe, M. *Cinquantenaire de l'école normale d'institutrices de Clermont-Ferrand.* Aurillac: Imprimerie Moderne, 1938.

Deuxième congrès international des œuvres et institutions féminines, 18–23 juin 1900. 4 vols. Edited by Mme Pegard. Paris: C. Blot, 1902.

Dietz, Jean. "Jules Ferry et les traditions républicaines." *Revue politique et parlementaire* 41 (October 1934): 122–41.

Dixième congrès international des femmes, Œuvres et institutions féminines, droits des femmes, 2–8 juin 1913, compte rendu des travaux. Edited by Mme Avril de Sainte-Croix. Paris: Giard et Brière, 1914.

Dupuy, Aimé. *Bouzaréa, Histoire illustrée des écoles normales d'instituteurs d'Alger-Bouzaréa.* Alger: Fontana, n.d.

Eidenschenk, Mme. *Petits et grands secrets de bonheur.* Paris: Delagrave, 1907.

Eidenschenk-Patin, Mme. *Les troisièmes lectures des petites filles,* Paris: Delagrave, 1913.

Farrington, Frederic E. *The Public Primary School System of France with Special Reference to the Training of Teachers.* New York: Teachers College, Columbia University, 1906.

Fédération internationale de la libre pensée. Congrès de Paris, 3, 4, 5, 6, 7 septembre 1905. Paris: n.p., 1905.

Flayol, E. *La Méthode Montessori en action.* Paris: F. Nathan, 1921.

Fontanges, Haryett. *La Légion d'honneur et les femmes décorées, Études d'histoire et de sociologie féminine.* Paris: Alliance coopérative du livre, 1905.

Frapié, Léon. *L'Institutrice de province.* Paris: E. Fasquelle, 1897.

Hesse, A., and A. Gleyze. *Notions de sociologie appliquée à la morale et à l'éducation.* 2nd ed. Paris: Alcan, 1924. 8th ed., 1938.

Heurtefeu, Mlle. *Pour nos institutrices.* Pau: Garet, 1901.

Jacoulet, E. *Notice historique sur les écoles normales d'instituteurs et d'institutrices.* In Ministère de l'Instruction publique et des Beaux-arts, *Recueil des monographies pédagogiques publiées à l'occasion de l'Exposition universelle de 1889.* Vol. 2, 373–451. Paris: Imprimerie nationale, 1889.

SELECTED BIBLIOGRAPHY 287

Julien, B., and J. Naudan. *Histoire des écoles normales de l'Aveyron 1835–1936*. Rodez: Subervie, 1936.

Koenig, Marie, ed. *Musée des poupées*. Paris: Hachette, 1909.

Lemoine, Alcide, and Juliette Marie. *La jeune française, 200 lectures alternées pour les jeunes filles*. Paris: Larousse, 1910.

Lespès, René. *Pour comprendre l'Algérie*. Alger: Gouvernement général, 1937.

Livre du cinquantenaire de l'école normale d'institutrices de La Roche-sur-Yon (1884–1934). La Roche-sur-Yon: n.p., 1934.

Manifestation de sympathie à l'occasion du départ de Mademoiselle Marie. Arras: n.p., 1934.

Marion, Henri. *Leçons de morale*. 2nd ed. Paris: A. Colin, 1884.

Mayaud, Julia. *Politesse et bonne tenue*. Paris: E. Cornély, 1904.

Murique, Mme. *Économie domestique et hygiène à l'usage des écoles primaires de filles*. 4th ed. Paris: Delalain, 1904.

Murique, Mme. *Gymnastique des jeunes filles, exercices calisthéniques*. Paris: Hachette, 1906.

Murique, Mme. *Maman et petite Jeanne*. Paris: Hachette, 1891.

Palanque, J. *Vents de l'esprit, souffles du cœur*. Paris: E. Figuière, 1935.

Pécaut, Félix. "La Directrice d'école normale." *Annuaire de l'enseignement primaire* 8 (1892): 299–325.

Pécaut, Félix. *L'Éducation publique et la vie nationale*. 3rd ed. Paris: Hachette, 1907.

Pécaut, Félix. *Quinze ans d'éducation, pensées pour une république laïque* (Paris: Delagrave, 1902). Edited by Patrick Cabanel. Paris: Le Bord de l'Eau, 2008.

Pensa, Henri. *L'Algérie, voyage de la délégation de la commission sénatoriale d'études des questions algériennes*, Paris: J. Rothschild, 1894.

Pinard, Adolphe. *La Puériculture du premier âge*. 6th ed. Paris: A. Colin, 1913.

Pivert, Marceau. *Un des aspects de l'offensive cléricale, le noyautage de l'enseignement public par les Davidées*. Paris: Groupe fraternel de l'enseignement, 1930.

Poulard, Maurice. *L'Enseignement pour les indigènes en Algérie*. Alger: Cojosso, 1910.

Sagnier, Mlle. *La Fillette bien élevée, livre de lecture à l'usage des écoles de filles*. Paris: A. Colin, 1896.

Sagnier, Mlle. *L'Institutrice, Conseils pratiques*. Paris: A. Colin, 1895.

Sarcey, Francisque. "L'Institutrice de province." *Annales politiques et littéraires* 28 (May 2, 23 1897): 274–75, 322–23; 29 (July 4, 1897): 2–3.

Soualah, Mohammed. *La Société indigène de l'Afrique du nord*. Alger: Jules Carbonel, 1937.

Talmeyr, Maurice. "Les Femmes qui enseignent." *Revue des deux mondes* 141 (June 1, 1897): 633–54.

Tardif, Fernand. *Un département pendant la guerre*. La Roche-sur-Yon: Guigné- Hurtaud, 1917.

Tsourikoff, Zénaïde. *L'Enseignement des filles en Afrique du nord*. Paris: A. Pedone 1935.

Books and Articles Published since 1940

Ageron, Charles-Robert. *Les Algériens musulmans et la France*. 2 vols. Paris: Presses universitaires de France, 1968.

Ageron, Charles-Robert. *Histoire de l'Algérie contemporaine 1830–1999*. 11th ed. Paris: Presses universitaires de France, 1999.

Amicale des anciens élèves des écoles normales d'institutrices et d'instituteurs de Lyon. *Centenaire de l'école normale d'institutrices de Lyon 1883–1983, Témoignages*. Lyon: Centre régional de la documentation pédagogique, 1985.

288 SELECTED BIBLIOGRAPHY

Amicale des anciennes élèves de l'école normale de Douai. *Madame Eidenschenk-Patin 1854–1942, Directrice de l'école normale de Douai 1905–1926*. Douai: n.p., 1978.

Amrouche, Fadhma Aïth Mansour. *Histoire de ma vie*. Edited by Jean Amrouche. Paris: François Maspéro, 1968.

Association amicale des anciennes élèves de l'école normale d'institutrices d'Arras. *Spécial centenaire*. Arras, 1984.

Bard, Christine. *Les Filles de Marianne: Histoire des féminismes 1914–1940*. Paris: Fayard, 1995.

Barreau, Jean-Michel, Jean-François Garcia, and Louis Legrand. *L'École unique de 1914 à nos jours*. Paris: Presses universitaires de France, 1998.

Barthélémy. Pascale. *Africaines et diplômées à l'époque coloniale (1918–1957)*. Rennes: Presses universitaires de Rennes, 2010.

Baruch, Marc Olivier. *Servir l'État français: L'Administration en France de 1940 à 1944*. Paris: Fayard, 2007.

Béguier-Magne, Claudine. *Se souvenir des écoles normales des Deux-Sèvres: Histoire iconographique de l'école normale de filles de Niort et de l'école de garçons de Parthenay*. La Crèche: Geste, 2011.

Béguier-Parrot, Claudine. *Les Instituteurs des Deux-Sèvres du début du XXe siècle*. La Crèche: Geste, 2007.

Belly, Marlène, ed. *1914–1918, Les Femmes en Poitou et en Charentes*. La Crèche: La Geste, 2018.

Berger, Ida, ed. *Lettres d'institutrices rurales d'autrefois, rédigées à la suite de l'enquête de Francisque Sarcey en 1897*. Paris: Association des amis du Musée pédagogique, 1960.

Besserve Bernollin, Lucette, et al., *1830–1962: Des enseignants d'Algérie se souviennent de ce qu'y fut l'enseignement primaire*. Toulouse: Privat, 1981.

Bidault, Jean-Pierre. *Mémoire des écoles normales de l'Eure: Histoire essentielle et anecdotique des EN de l'Eure de 1832 à 1991*. Évreux: J.-P. Bidault, 2012.

Bidelman, Patrick Kay. *Pariahs Stand Up! The Founding of the Liberal Feminist Movement in France*. Westport, CT: Greenwood Press, 1982.

Bisch, Yves. *Écoles d'Alsace: Les Leçons d'histoire*. Besançon: Éditions du Rhin, 1996.

Bourdieu, Pierre. *The State Nobility: Elite Schools in the Field of Power*. Translated by Lauretta C. Clough. Stanford: Stanford University Press, 1996.

Bourdieu, Pierre, and Jean-Claude Passeron. *Reproduction in Education, Society and Culture*. Translated by Richard Nice. London: Sage, 1977.

Bouthau, Jean-Claude. *En cravate et blouse grise: Mémoires d'un normalien*. Saint-Brieuc: Breizh-Compo, 1986.

Bouyer, Christian. *La grande aventure des écoles normales d'instituteurs*. Paris: Le Cherche Midi, 2003.

Boxer, Marilyn J. "Rethinking the Socialist Construction and International Career of the Concept of 'Bourgeois Feminism.'" *American Historical Review* 112 (February 2007): 131–58.

Briand, Jean-Pierre, and Jean-Michel Chapoulie. *Les Collèges du peuple: L'Enseignement primaire supérieur et le développement de la scolarisation prolongée sous la Troisième République*. Paris: CNRS/INRP/ENS Fontenay–Saint Cloud, 1992.

Briand, Jean-Pierre, Jean-Michel Chapoulie, F. Huguet, J.-N. Luc, and A. Prost. *Enseignement primaire et ses extensions, Annuaire statistique, 19e–20e siècles, Écoles maternelles, primaires, primaires supérieures et professionnelles*. Paris: Économica and INRP, 1987.

SELECTED BIBLIOGRAPHY 289

Brulé, Hélène. *Le Rôle de la femme dans l'éducation familiale et sociale*. Paris: Foucher, 1950.

Burton, Antoinette. *Burdens of History: British Feminists, Indian Women, and Imperial Culture, 1865–1915*. Chapel Hill: University of North Carolina Press, 1994.

Cabanel, Patrick. *Le Dieu de la République: Aux sources protestantes de la laïcité (1860–1900)*. Rennes: Presses universitaires de Rennes, 2003.

Cabanel, Patrick. *Ferdinand Buisson: Père de l'école laïque*. Geneva: Labor et Fides, 2016.

Cacouault-Bitaud, Marlaine. *La Direction des collèges et des lycées: Une affaire d'hommes? Genre et inégalités dans l'éducation nationale*. Paris: L'Harmattan, 2008.

Cacouault-Bitaud, Marlaine. *Professeurs . . . mais femmes: Carrières et vies privées des enseignantes du secondaire au XXe siècle*. Paris: Éditions de la Découverte, 2007.

Caillaouze, S., J. L. Nembrini, and P. Polivka, eds. *La Formation des maîtres au XIXe siècle: Les écoles normales de Lot-et-Garonne de F. Guizot à J. Ferry*. Agen: Archives départementales du Lot-et-Garonne, 1983.

Campbell, Caroline. "Building a Movement, Dismantling the Republic: Women, Gender, and Political Extremism in the Croix de Feu/Parti Social Français, 1927–1940." *French Historical Studies* 35 (Fall 2012): 691–726.

Campbell, Caroline. *Political Belief in France, 1927–1945: Gender, Empire, and Fascism in the Croix de Feu and Parti Social Français*. Baton Rouge: Louisiana State University Press, 2015.

Caron, Vicki. *Uneasy Asylum: France and the Jewish Refugee Crisis, 1933–1942*. Stanford: Stanford University Press, 1999.

Carrive, Lucien, ed. *Lettres de Jules Steeg à Maurice Schwalb, 1851–1898: Un Pasteur républicain au XIXe siècle*. Paris: Éditions de la nouvelle Sorbonne, 1993.

Carrol, Alison. "Regional Republicans: The Alsatian Socialists and the Politics of Primary Schooling in Alsace, 1918–1939." *French Historical Studies* 34 (Spring 2011): 299–325.

Caspard, Pierre, Jean-Noël Luc, and Rebecca Rogers, eds. "L'Éducation des filles XVIIIe-XXIe siècles, Hommage à Françoise Mayeur." Numéro spécial, *Histoire de l'éducation*, nos. 115–16 (September 2007).

Centenaire de l'école normale d'institutrices, Montpellier 1876–1976. Montpellier: C.R.D.P., 1976.

Chanet, Jean-François. *L'École républicaine et les petites patries*. Paris: Aubier. 1996.

Chanet, Jean-François. "Vocation et traitement, réflexions sur la 'nature sociale' du métier de l'instituteur dans la France de la 3e République." *Revue d'histoire moderne et contemporaine* 47 (July–September 2000): 581–603.

Chapoulie, Jean-Michel. *L'École d'État conquiert la France: Deux siècles de politique scolaire*. Rennes: Presses universitaires de Rennes, 2010.

Chaudhuri, Nupur, and Margaret Strobel, eds. *Western Women and Imperialism: Complicity and Resistance*. Bloomington: Indiana University Press, 1992.

Chenut, Helen. "Attitudes toward Women's Suffrage on the Eve of World War I." *French Historical Studies* 41 (October 2018): 711–40.

Clancy-Smith, Julia. "A Woman without Her Distaff: Gender, Work, and Handicraft Production in Colonial North Africa." In *Social History of Women and Gender in the Modern Middle East*, edited by Margaret Meriwether and Judith E. Tucker, 25–62. Boulder, CO: Westview Press, 1999.

Clancy-Smith, Julia, and Frances Gouda, eds. *Domesticating the Empire: Race, Gender, and Family Life in French and Dutch Colonialism*. Charlottesville: University of Virginia Press, 1998.

290 SELECTED BIBLIOGRAPHY

Clark, Linda L. "A Battle of the Sexes in a Professional Setting: The Introduction of *Inspectrices Primaires*, 1889–1914." *French Historical Studies* 16 (Spring 1989): 95–125.

Clark, Linda L. "Feminist Maternalists and the French State: Two Inspectresses General in the Pre-World War I Third Republic." *Journal of Women's History* 12 (Spring 2000): 32–59.

Clark, Linda L. *The Rise of Professional Women in France: Gender and Public Administration since 1830*. Cambridge: Cambridge University Press, 2000.

Clark, Linda L. *Schooling the Daughters of Marianne: Textbooks and the Socialization of Girls in Modern French Primary Schools*. Albany: State University of New York Press, 1984.

Clark, Linda L. *Women and Achievement in Nineteenth-Century Europe*. Cambridge: Cambridge University Press, 2008.

Clary, Maryse. "Les Écoles normales du Gard à l'époque des lois laïques." *Études sur l'Hérault* 1 (1985): 33–38.

Clavel, Julien. *Histoire de l'école normale d'institutrices de Grenoble*. Grenoble: Allier, 1969.

Colonna, Fanny. *Instituteurs algériens (1883–1939)*. Paris: Presses de la Fondation nationale des sciences politiques, 1975.

Condette, Jean-François. *Histoire de la formation des enseignants en France (XIXe–XXe siècles)*. Paris: L'Harmattan, 2011.

Condette, Jean-François. *Les Recteurs d'académie en France de 1808 à 1940*. 3 vols. Lyon: Service d'histoire de l'éducation/Institut national de recherche pédagogique, 2006–09.

Condette, Jean-Francois, ed. *Les Chefs d'établissement: Diriger une institution scolaire ou universitaire XVIIe–XXe siècle*. Rennes: Presses universitaires de Rennes, 2015.

Condette, Jean-François, ed. *Les Personnels d'inspection: Contrôler, évaluer, conseiller les enseignants, Retour sur une histoire, France-Europe (XVIIIe–XXe siècle)*. Rennes: Presses universitaires de Rennes, 2017.

Condette, Jean-François, and Gilles Rouet, eds. *Un siècle de formation des maîtres en Champagne-Ardennes: Écoles normales, normaliens, normaliennes et écoles primaires de 1880 à 1980*. Reims: CRDP Champagne-Ardennes, 2008.

Cosnier, Colette. *Marie Pape-Carpantier: De l'école maternelle à l'école de filles*. Paris: L'Harmattan, 1993.

Courtis, Christine. "L'École normale d'institutrices (Auxerre 1912)." *Bulletin de la Société des sciences historiques et naturelles de l'Yonne*, no. 132 (2000): 183–98.

Criblez, Lucien, and Rita Hofstetter, eds. *La Formation des enseignant(e)s primaires: Histoire et réformes actuelles*. Berne: Peter Lang, 2000.

Cubizolle, Monique. "À propos d'un centenaire: l'école normale d'institutrices de la Haute-Loire." *Cahiers de la Haute-Loire (Le Puy)* (1983), 181–201.

Curtis, Sarah A. *Educating the Faithful: Religion, Schooling, and Society in Nineteenth-Century France*. DeKalb: Northern Illinois University Press, 2000.

Dagand, Yvonne. "L'École normale d'institutrices de Rumilly (1922–1925)." *Revue savoisienne* 118 (1979): 88–102.

Dalisson, Rémi. *Paul Bert: L'Inventeur de l'école laïque*. Paris: A. Colin, 2015.

Darrow, Margaret. *French Women and the First World War: War Stories of the Home Front*. Oxford and New York: Berg, 2000.

Dauphin, Stéphanie. *Octave Gréard 1828–1904*. Rennes: Presses universitaires de Rennes, 2016.

Deldycke, T., H. Gelder, and J.-M. Limbor. *La Population active et sa structure*. Edited by P. Bairoch. Brussels: Institut de l'Université libre de Bruxelles, 1968.

SELECTED BIBLIOGRAPHY 291

Delhome, Danielle, Nicole Gault, and Josiane Gonthier, eds. *Les premières institutrices laïques*. Paris: Mercure de France, 1980.

Delsaut, Yvette. *La Place du maître: une chronique des écoles normales d'instituteurs*. Paris: L'Harmattan, 1992.

Denise Billotey, directrice honoraire de l'école normale d'institutrices de la Seine. Paris: n.p., 1949.

Dermenjian, Geneviève. *Juifs et européens d'Algérie: L'Antisémitisme oranais*. Jerusalem: Institut Ben-Zvi, 1983.

Devigne, Mathieu. *L'École des années noires: Une histoire du primaire en temps de guerre, entre Vichy et république, 1938–1948*. Paris: Presses universitaires de France, 2018.

Diebolt, Evelyne. *Les Femmes dans l'action sanitaire, sociale et culturelle, 1901–2001: Les Associations face aux institutions*. Paris: Femmes et associations, 2001.

Dieux, Laurence. "Les Écoles normales primaires d'Auxerre de 1833 à 1939." *Bulletin de la Société des sciences historiques et naturelles de l'Yonne*, no. 132 (2000): 163–81.

Dougnac, Bernard. *Suzanne Lacore, biographie 1875–1975: Le Socialisme-femme*. Périgueux: Institut aquitain d'études sociales-Éditions Fanlac, 1996.

Downs, Laura Lee. *Manufacturing Inequality: Gender Division in the French and British Metalworking Industries, 1914–1919*. Ithaca: Cornell University Press, 1996.

Dumans, Jean-Louis. *L'École normale, 100 ans à Laval*. Laval: Siloé, 1989.

Dumas, Georges. "L'École normale d'institutrices de la Marne de 1853 à1939." *Travaux de l'Académie nationale de Reims* 161 (1982): 159–68.

Dumas, Georges. "Histoire de l'école normale d'institutrices de la Marne, comparée à celle de l'école normale d'instituteurs 1854–1939." *Mémoires de la Société d'agriculture, commerce, sciences et arts du département de la Marne* 97 (1982): 263–97.

Egginger, Johann-Günther. "Les Directeurs et directrices des écoles normales de l'Oise (1884–1940): Première approche prosopographique d'un corps professionnel." In *Les Chefs d'établissement: Diriger une institution scolaire ou universitaire XVII–XXe siècle*, edited by Jean-François Condette, 107–29. Rennes: Presses universitaires de Rennes, 2015.

Egginger, Johann-Günther. "Entre renseignements mutuels et expression d'une pensée pédagogique: Le *Bulletin de l'Association amicale des anciennes élèves de l'école normale d'institutrices de Beauvais* (1898–1990)." In *Les Associations d'élèves et d'étudiants: Entre socialisation et apprentissages (XVIe–XXe siècle)*, edited by Véronique Castagnet-Lars, 173–89. Toulouse: Presses universitaires du Midi, 2020.

Egginger, Johann-Günther. "Raconter et témoigner: la vie des élèves-maîtres et maîtresses des départements du Nord et du Pas-de-Calais pendant la Grande Guerre . . . et après (1914–1925)." In *La Guerre des cartables (1914–1918): Élèves, étudiants et enseignants dans la Grande Guerre en Nord-Pas-de-Calais*, edited by Jean-François Condette, 351–68. Villeneuve d'Ascq: Presses universitaires du Septentrion, 2018.

Essen, Mineke van, and Rebecca Rogers, eds. "Les Enseignantes: Formations, identités, représentations XIXe-XXe siècles." Numéro special, *Histoire de l'éducation*, no. 98 (May 2003).

Fabre, Mélanie. "Éduquer pour la République, Jeanne Desparmet-Ruello, une intellectuelle au temps de Jaurès." *Cahiers Jaurès*, nos. 235–36 (2020): 115–39.

Fabre, Mélanie. "Marie Baertschi-Fuster, une intellectuelle et une éducatrice au service du progrès social." *Études sociales*, nos. 167–68 (2019): 397–446.

Figeac-Monthus, Marguerite. "La Formation des institutrices à Bordeaux dans la seconde moitié du XIXe siècle." *Revue historique de Bordeaux et du département de la Gironde*, nos. 13–14 (2008): 83–96.

292 SELECTED BIBLIOGRAPHY

Ford, Caroline. *Creating the Nation in Provincial France: Religion and Political Identity in Brittany*. Princeton: Princeton University Press, 1993.

Formaglio, Cécile. *"Féministe d'abord": Cécile Brunschvicg (1877–1946)*. Rennes: Presses universitaires de Rennes, 2014.

Francis, Kyle. "'Algeria for the Algerians': Public Education and Settler Identity in the Early Third Republic." *French Politics, Culture & Society* 36 (Spring 2018): 26–51.

Frijhoff, Willem, ed. *L'Offre d'école: Éléments pour une étude comparative des politiques éducatives au XIXe siècle*. Paris: Institut national de recherche pédagogique, 1983.

Furet, François, ed. *Jules Ferry: Fondateur de la République*. Paris: Éditions de l'École des hautes études en sciences sociales, 1985.

Furet, François, et Jacques Ozouf. *Lire et écrire: L'Alphabétisation des français de Calvin à Jules Ferry*. 2 vols. Paris: Éditions de Minuit, 1977.

Fusina, Jacques et al. *Histoire de l'école en Corse*. Ajaccio: Albania, 2003.

Gallardo, Jean, ed. *Histoire de l'école normale de Foix*. Foix: Ligue de l'enseignement, 2011.

Gautherin, Jacqueline. *Une discipline pour la République: la science de l'éducation en France (1882–1914)*. Bern: Peter Lang, 2002.

Gautherin, Jacqueline. "Une polyphonie protestante dans le concert de la science de l'éducation (1882–1914)." *Histoire de l'éducation*, no. 110 (2006): 91–110.

Gauthier, Marcelle. *Chère école normale de Gap: Vue générale de l'EN*. Grenoble: M. Gauthier, 2005.

Gavoille, Jacques. *Du maître d'école à l'instituteur, la formation d'un corps enseignant du primaire: Instituteurs, institutrices et inspecteurs primaires du département du Doubs (1870–1914)*. Besançon: Presses universitaires de Besançon, 2010.

Geiger, Roger. "La Sociologie dans les écoles normales primaires: Histoire d'une controverse." *Revue française de sociologie* 20 (1979): 257–67.

Gemie, Sharif. *Women and Schooling in France, 1815–1914: Gender, Authority and Identity in the Female Schooling Sector*. Keele: Keele University Press, 1995.

Gibson, Ralph. *A Social History of French Catholicism, 1789–1914*. New York: Routledge, 1989.

Gildea, Robert. *Education in Provincial France, 1800–1914: A Study of Three Departments*. Oxford: Clarendon Press, 1983.

Girault, Jacques. *Instituteurs, professeurs: Une culture syndicale dans la société française fin XIXe–XXe siècles*. Paris: Publications de la Sorbonne, 1996.

Gontard, Maurice. *La Question des écoles normales primaires de la Révolution à 1962*. 2nd ed. Toulouse: Centre régional de documentation pédagogique, 1975.

Gonthier, Jean, ed. *Thérèse Billard dit adieu à Montgelas, L'institutrice (1910–1924)*. Montmélian: Arc-Isère, 1990.

Grandière, Marcel. *La Formation des maîtres en France 1792–1914*. Lyon: Institut national de recherche pédagogique, 2006.

Grandière, Marcel, Rémi Paris, and Daniel Galloyer, eds. *La Formation des maîtres en France 1792–1914, Recueil de textes officiels*. Lyon: Institut national de recherche pédagogique, 2007.

Granvaud-Jourdanneau, Fernande. *Images et vie de l'école normale d'institutrices de Poitiers, 1887–1991*. Poitiers: Éditions du Pont Neuf, 1994.

Grew, Raymond, and Patrick J. Harrigan. *School, State, and Society: The Growth of Elementary Schooling in Nineteenth-Century France—A Quantitative Analysis*. Ann Arbor: University of Michigan Press, 1991.

SELECTED BIBLIOGRAPHY 293

Grispoux, Jean. "Les Écoles normales de Perpignan (1834–1991)." *Études roussillonnaises* 11 (1992): 210–16.

Guillemiau, Augustine. "Ma première année à l'école normale, Le Mans, 1882–1883." Edited by Gérard Boeldieu. *Bulletin de la Société d'agriculture, sciences et arts de la Sarthe, Mémoires* (1989): 41–64.

Ha, Marie-Paule. *French Women and Empire: The Case of Indochina.* Oxford: Oxford University Press, 2014.

Handourtzel, Rémy. *Vichy et l'école 1940–1944.* Paris: Noêsis, 1997.

Harp, Stephen L. *Learning to Be Loyal: Primary Schooling as Nation Building in Alsace and Lorraine, 1850–1940.* DeKalb: Northern Illinois University Press, 1998.

Harrigan, Patrick J. "Women Teachers and the Schooling of Girls in France: Recent Historiographical Trends." *French Historical Studies* 21 (Fall 1998): 593–610.

Hause, Steven C. "Anti-Protestant Rhetoric in the Early Third Republic." *French Historical Studies* 16 (Spring 1989): 185–201.

Hause, Steven C. *Hubertine Auclert: The French Suffragette.* New Haven: Yale University Press, 1987.

Hause, Steven C., with Anne R. Kenney. *Women's Suffrage and Social Politics in the French Third Republic.* Princeton: Princeton University Press, 1984.

Hayward, J. E. S. "The Official Social Philosophy of the French Third Republic: Léon Bourgeois and Solidarity." *International Review of Social History* 6 (1961): 19–48.

Hélias, Pierre-Jakez. *The Horse of Pride.* Translated by June Guicharnaud. New Haven: Yale University Press, 1978.

Hélie, Anissa. "Former à son image: normes de genre et institutrices européennes en Algérie colonisée (1910–1940)." In *L'École aux colonies, les colonies à l'école,* edited by Gilles Boyer, Pascal Clerc, and Michelle Zancarini-Fournel, 57–68. Lyon: ENS Éditions, 2013.

Hermine, Micheline. *Les Poulettes de la République: Journal d'une normalienne ingénue.* Paris: L'Harmattan, 2003.

Hirtz, Colette. "École primaire supérieure de Fontenay: des protestants aux sources de la laïcité française." *Bulletin de la Société d'histoire du protestantisme français,* no. 135 (April–June 1989): 281–90.

Horvath, Sandra A. "Victor Duruy and the Controversy over Secondary Education for Girls." *French Historical Studies* 9 (Spring 1975): 83–104.

Horvath-Peterson, Sandra. *Victor Duruy and French Education: Liberal Reform in the Second Empire.* Baton Rouge: Louisiana State University Press, 1984.

Humbert, Jean-Louis. "La Fondation de l'école normale d'institutrices de Sainte-Savine (1880)." *Les Cahiers aubois d'histoire de l'éducation,* no. 17 (2000): 17–27.

Iba-Zizen, Mme. "La Condition des femmes musulmanes en Algérie." In *Association des surintendantes d'usine et de services sociaux, Assemblée générale 10 février 1959,* 25–39. Paris, 1959.

Ingram, Norman. *The Politics of Dissent: Pacifism in France, 1919–1939.* Oxford: Clarendon Press, 1991.

Jackson, Julian. *The Popular Front in France: Defending Democracy, 1934–1938.* Cambridge: Cambridge University Press, 1987.

Jacquemart, Alban. *Les Hommes dans les mouvements féministes: Socio-histoire d'un engagement improbable.* Rennes: Presses universitaires de Rennes, 2015.

Karnaouch, Denise. "Le Féminisme universitaire à l'époque des amicales." *Cahiers du centre fédéral de la Fédération de l'éducation nationale,* no. 5 (March 1993): 7–56.

294 SELECTED BIBLIOGRAPHY

Kateb, Kamel. *École, population et société en Algérie*. Paris: L'Harmattan, 2005.

Klejman, Laurence, and Florence Rochefort. *L'Égalité en marche: Le Féminisme sous la Troisième République*. Paris: Presses de la Fondation nationale des sciences politiques/ Des Femmes, 1989.

Koven, Seth, and Sonya Michel, eds. *Mothers of a New World: Maternalist Politics and the Origins of Welfare States*. New York: Routledge, 1993.

Krop, Jérôme. *Les Fondateurs de l'école républicaine: La première génération des instituteurs sous la IIIe République*. Villeneuve d'Ascq: Presses universitaires du Septentrion, 2016.

Langlois, Claude. *Le Catholicisme au féminin: Les Congrégations à supérieure générale au XIXe siècle*. Paris: Cerf, 1984.

Laprévote, Gilles. *Les Écoles normales primaires en France 1879–1979: Splendeurs et misères de la formation des maîtres*. Lyon: Presses universitaires de Lyon, 1984.

Le Boulanger, Isabelle. *À l'origine du féminisme en Bretagne, Marie Le Gac-Salonne 1878– 1974*. Rennes: Presses universitaires de Rennes, 2017.

Leclerc, Marie-Dominique. "Union française pour le suffrage des femmes." *La Vie en Champagne*, no. 28 (October–December 2001): 20–31.

Legg, Charlotte Ann. *The New White Race: Settler Colonialism and the Press in French Algeria, 1860–1914*. Lincoln: University of Nebraska Press, 2021.

Lemdani Belkaïd, Malika. *Normaliennes en Algérie*. Paris: L'Harmattan, 1998.

Lemercier, Mme. "La Création de l'école normale d'institutrices interconfessionnelles de Montpellier et sa mutation en école normale laïque (1871–1890)." *Études sur l'Hérault* 1 (1985): 27–32.

Lerch, Dominique, and Gilles Pétreault, eds. *L'Inspecteur d'académie, deux siècles au service de l'éducation*. Paris: Centre national de documentation pédagogique, 2008.

Lethierry, Hugues, ed. *Feu les écoles normales (et les I.U.F.M.?)*. Paris: L'Harmattan, 1994.

Liszek, Slava. *Marie Guillot: De l'émancipation des femmes à celle du syndicalisme*. Paris: L'Harmattan, 1994.

Lorcin, Patricia. *Imperial Identities: Stereotyping, Prejudice and Race in Colonial Algeria*. London: I. B. Tauris, 1995.

Luc, Jean-Noël. *L'Invention du jeune enfant: De la salle d'asile à l'école maternelle*. Paris: Belin, 1997.

Luc, Jean-Noël. *La petite enfance à l'école, XIXe–XXe siècles*. Paris: Institut national de recherche pédagogique/Économica, 1982.

Luc, Jean-Noël. *La Statistique de l'enseignement primaire 19e–20e siècles: Politique et mode d'emploi*. Paris: Institut national de recherche pédagogique/Économica, 1985.

Luc, Jean-Noël, and Alain Barbé. *Des normaliens: Histoire de l'école normale de Saint-Cloud*. Paris: Presses de la Fondation nationale des sciences politiques, 1982.

Lutringer, Benjamin, and Pierre Rothiot. *Cent cinquante ans au service du peuple*. 2 vols. Charmes: Feuillard, 1978.

Machen, Emily. "Catholic Women, International Engagement and the Battle for Suffrage in Interwar France: The Case of the Action Sociale de la Femme and the Union Nationale pour le Vote des Femmes." *Women's History Review* 26 (April 2017): 229–44.

Malefon, Rose. *Vivante mémoire 1883–1985: École normale d'institutrices de Limoges*. Limoges: Touron, 1987.

Marchal, Wanda. *Nous serons maîtresses d'école . . . du couvent des grands-carmes à l'école normale d'institutrices de Metz*. Metz: Éditions Serpenoise, 1990.

Marcouly, Jeanne-Luce. *Le Périgord à l'école de la République, l'enseignement de la Révolution aux IUFM: Les écoles normales de Dordogne, un siècle de laïcité*. Périgueux: Copédit, 2005.

SELECTED BIBLIOGRAPHY 295

Margadant, Jo Burr. *Madame le Professeur: Women Educators in the Third Republic.* Princeton: Princeton University Press, 1990.

Martin, Jean-Paul. *La Ligue de l'enseignement: Une histoire politique (1866–2016).* Rennes: Presses universitaires de Rennes, 2016.

Martinez, Michel. "Les Écoles normales primaires de l'Académie de Montpellier dans les années 1880." *Études sur l'Hérault* 1 (1995): 39–42.

Matasci, Dominique. *L'École républicaine à l'étranger: Une histoire internationale des réformes scolaires en France 1870–1914.* Lyon: ENS Éditions, 2015.

Mayeur, Françoise. *L'Éducation des filles en France au XIXe siècle.* Paris: Hachette, 1979.

Mayeur, Françoise. *L'Enseignement secondaire des jeunes filles sous la Troisième République.* Paris: Presses de la Fondation nationale des sciences politiques, 1977.

Mayeur, Jean-Marie. "Jules Ferry et la laïcité." In *Jules Ferry, Fondateur de la République*, edited by François Furet, 147–60. Paris: Éditions de l'École des hautes études en sciences sociales, 1985.

Mayoux, François. *Marie et François Mayoux, Instituteurs pacifistes et syndicalistes.* Chamalières: Éditions Canope, 1992.

Mazataud, Pierre. *Institutrices, sœurs laïques de la République?* Rennes: Éditions Ouest-France, 2006.

Mazier, Pierre. *Quand le Gard se libérait: Un ancien du C.D.L. raconte.* Nîmes: C. Lacour, 1992.

Mesch, Rachel. *Having It All in the Belle Epoque: How French Women's Magazines Invented the Modern Woman.* Stanford: Stanford University Press, 2013.

Meyers, Peter V. "From Conflict to Cooperation: Men and Women Teachers in the Belle Epoque." In *The Making of Frenchmen: Current Directions in the History of Education in France, 1679–1979*, edited by Donald N. Baker and Patrick J. Harrigan, 493–505. Waterloo, ON: Historical Reflections Press, 1980.

Mir, Mathilde. *Chronique des jours heureux.* Angoulême: Coquemard, 1947.

Mir, Mathilde. *Quand la terre se soulève.* Angoulême: Coquemard, 1948.

Moch, Leslie Page. "Government Policy and Women's Experience: The Case of Teachers in France." *Feminist Studies* 14 (1988): 301–24.

Moch, Leslie Page. *Moving Europeans: Migration in Western Europe since 1650.* 2nd ed. Bloomington: Indians University Press, 2003.

Moch, Leslie Page. *Pariahs of Yesterday: Breton Migrants in Paris.* Durham: Duke University Press, 2012.

Mole, Frédéric. *L'École laïque pour une république sociale: Controverses pédagogiques et politiques (1900–1914).* Rennes: Presses universitaires de Rennes, 2010.

Montacié, Jean, and François Moulin. *Nos écoles de Nancy.* Nancy: Renaudot, 2011.

Mosconi, Nicole. "Henri Marion et 'l'égalité dans la différence.'" *Le Télémaque*, no. 41 (2012): 133–50.

Moses, Claire Goldberg. *French Feminism in the Nineteenth Century.* Albany: State University of New York Press, 1984.

Mougniotte, Alain. *Les Débuts de l'instruction civique en France.* Lyon: Presses universitaires de Lyon, 1991.

Muel-Dreyfus, Francine. *Vichy et l'éternel féminin, Contribution à une sociologie de l'ordre des corps.* Paris: Seuil, 1995.

Nique, Christian. *L'impossible gouvernement des esprits: Histoire politique des écoles normales primaires.* Paris: Nathan, 1991.

"Numéro spécial du centenaire de l'école normale de filles." *Le Normalien dijonnais*, no. 7/3 (1982).

296   SELECTED BIBLIOGRAPHY

Offen, Karen. "Body Politics: Women, Work and the Politics of Motherhood in France, 1920–1950." In *Maternity and Gender Policies: Women and the Rise of the European Welfare States 1880s–1950s*, edited by Gisela Bock and Pat Thane, 138–59. London: Routledge, 1991.

Offen, Karen. *Debating the Woman Question in the French Third Republic, 1870–1920*. Cambridge: Cambridge University Press, 2018.

Offen, Karen. "Depopulation, Nationalism, and Feminism in Fin-de-Siècle France." *American Historical Review* 89 (June 1984): 648–76.

Offen, Karen. "Ernest Legouvé and the Doctrine of 'Equality in Difference' for Women: A Case Study of Male Feminism in Nineteenth-Century France." *Journal of Modern History* 58 (June 1986): 452–84.

Offen, Karen. *European Feminisms 1700–1950: A Political History*. Stanford: Stanford University Press, 2000.

Offen, Karen. "Sur l'origine des mots 'féminisme' et 'féministe.'" *Revue d'histoire moderne et contemporaine* 34 (1987): 492–96.

Ognier, Pierre. *Une école sans Dieu? 1880–1905: L'Invention d'une morale laïque sous la IIIe République*. Toulouse: Presses universitaires du Mirail, 2008.

Oulhiou, Yvonne. *L'École normale supérieure de Fontenay-aux-Roses: À travers le temps 1880–1980*. Fontenay-aux-Roses: Cahiers de Fontenay, 1981.

Ozouf, Jacques. "Les Instituteurs de la Manche au début du XXe siècle." *Revue d'histoire moderne et contemporaine* 13 (January–March 1966): 95–114.

Ozouf, Jacques, ed. *Nous les maîtres d'école: Autobiographies d'instituteurs de la Belle Époque*. Paris: Gallimard-Juilliard, 1973.

Ozouf, Jacques, and Mona Ozouf, with Véronique Aubert and Claire Steindecker. *La République des instituteurs*. Paris: Gallimard/Le Seuil, 1992.

Ozouf, Mona, ed. *La Classe ininterrompue: Cahiers de la famille Sandre 1780–1960*. Paris: Hachette, 1979.

Ozouf, Mona. *Composition française: Retour sur une enfance bretonne*. Paris: Gallimard, 2009.

Pascal, Jean. *Les Femmes députés de 1945 à 1988*. Paris: Jean Pascal, 1990.

Paul, Harry W. *The Second Ralliement: The Rapprochement between Church and State in France in the Twentieth Century*. Washington, D.C.: Catholic University Press of America, 1967.

Pedersen, Jean Elisabeth. "'Speaking Together Openly, Honestly and Profoundly': Men and Women as Public Intellectuals in Early Twentieth-Century France." *Gender and History* 26 (April 2014): 36–51.

Peneff, Jean. *Écoles publiques, écoles privées dans l'ouest 1880–1950*. Paris: L'Harmattan, 1987.

Persyn, Christiane. *Une grande éducatrice: Madame Eidenschenk-Patin 1864–1942*. Avesnes: Éditions de l'Observateur, 1950.

Piéra, Pascal. *L'École normale d'institutrices du Puy-de-Dôme*. Clermont-Ferrand: Un, Deux... Quatre Éditions, 2005.

Ploud, Odette. *Filles du Morvan: Ma Man et Moi*. Mâcon: Éditions Rhône-Alpes, 1976.

Poitou, Christian. *Centenaire de l'école normale d'institutrices d'Orléans 1887–1987*. Orléans: École normale mixte d'Orléans, 1987.

Pollard, Miranda. *Reign of Virtue: Mobilizing Gender in Vichy France*. Chicago: University of Chicago Press, 1998.

Prigent, Alain. *Les Instituteurs des Côtes-du-Nord sous la IIIe République: Laïcité, amicalisme et syndicalisme*. Sables- d'Or-les-Pins: Astoure, 2005.

SELECTED BIBLIOGRAPHY 297

Prost, Antoine. *Histoire de l'enseignement en France, 1800–1967*. Paris: A. Colin, 1968.

Prost, Antoine, ed. *La Formation des maîtres de 1940 à 2010*. Rennes: Presses universitaires de Rennes, 2014.

Quartararo, Anne T. *Women Teachers and Popular Education in Nineteenth-Century France: Social Values and Corporate Identity at the Normal School Institution*. Newark: University of Delaware Press, 1995.

Read, Geoff. *The Republic of Men: Gender and Political Parties in Interwar France*. Baton Rouge: Louisiana State University Press, 2014.

Réal, Isabelle. "L'Ariège et ses premières institutrices laïques (1881–1930)." *Bulletin de la Société ariégoise des sciences, lettres et arts* 50 (1995): 51–72.

Renaud, Yvette. *Mathilde Mir (1896–1958) en Charente (de 1932 à 1948): L'Engagement d'une femme dans son temps*. Angoulême: Centre départemental de documentation pédagogique de la Charente, 1996.

Rennes, Juliette. *Le Mérite et la nature, une controverse républicaine: L'Accès des femmes aux professions de prestige*. Paris: Fayard, 2007.

Reynier, Élie, and Louise Abrial. *Les Écoles normales primaires de l'Ardèche (1831–1944, 1882–1944)*. Privas: L. Volle, 1945.

Reynolds, Siân. *France between the Wars: Gender and Politics*. London: Routledge, 1996.

Reynolds, Siân. "Women and the Popular Front: The Case of the Three Women Ministers." *French History* 8 (1994): 196–224.

Richardson, C. A., Hélène Brulé, and Harold E. Snyder. *The Education of Teachers in England, France and the U.S.A.* Paris: UNESCO, 1953.

Robert, Jean-Louis. "Women and Work in France during the First World War." Translated by Jay Winter. In *The Upheaval of War: Family, Work and Welfare in Europe, 1914–1918*, edited by Richard Wall and Jay Winter, 251–66. Cambridge: Cambridge University Press, 1988.

Robert-Guiard, Claudine. *Des Européennes en situation coloniale: Algérie 1830–1939*. Aix-en-Provence: Publications de l'Université de Provence, 2009.

Roberts, Mary Louise. *Civilization without Sexes: Reconstructing Gender in Postwar France, 1917–1927*. Chicago: University of Chicago Press, 1994.

Roberts, Mary Louise. *Disruptive Acts: The New Woman in Fin-de-siècle France*. Chicago: University of Chicago Press, 2002.

Roberts, Sophie B. *Citizenship and Antisemitism in French Colonial Algeria*. Cambridge: Cambridge University Press, 2017.

Rochefort, Florence, ed. *Le Pouvoir du genre: Laïcité et religions 1905–2005*. Toulouse: Presses universitaires du Mirail, 2007.

Rogers, Rebecca. "L'Éducation des filles: un siècle et demi d'historiographie." *Histoire de l'éducation*, nos. 115–16 (September 2007): 37–79.

Rogers, Rebecca. *A Frenchwoman's Imperial Story: Madame Luce in Nineteenth-Century Algeria*. Stanford, CA: Stanford University Press, 2013.

Rogers, Rebecca. *From the Salon to the Schoolroom: Educating Bourgeois Girls in Nineteenth-Century France*. University Park: Pennsylvania State University Press, 2005.

Rogers, Rebecca, ed. *La Mixité dans l'éducation: Enjeux passés et présents*. Lyon: ENS Éditions, 2004.

Rome, Yannic. *La Guerre scolaire en Morbihan, 1820–1940*. 2 vols. Le Faouët: Liv'éditions, 2007–8.

Rome, Yannic. *Séminaires laïques: Écoles normales, normaliens, normaliennes en Morbihan (1831–1991)*. Le Faouët: Liv'éditions, 2013.

298 SELECTED BIBLIOGRAPHY

Royer, Marie. "En marge du centenaire de l'école normale de Maxéville (fondée en 1879)." *Revue Lorraine populaire*, no. 30 (October 1979): 279–81.

Rozières-Stépaniantz, Alice. *Le Pied de cuve*. Paris: Le Cerf-Volant, 1957.

Ruimy, Laurence. "La *Revue de l'enseignement primaire et primaire supérieur*, 1890–1914." *Jean Jaurès, Cahiers trimestriels*, no. 146 (October–December 1998): 17–28.

Sarti, Odile. *The Ligue Patriotique des Françaises, 1902–1933: A Feminine Response to the Secularization of French Society*. New York: Garland, 1992.

Schweitzer, Sylvie. *Femmes de pouvoir: une histoire de l'égalité professionnelle en Europe (XIXe–XXIe siècle)*. Paris: Payot, 2010.

Scott, Joan Wallach. *The Politics of the Veil*. Princeton: Princeton University Press, 2007.

Seguin, Jeanne, and Pauline Millet. *Pour nos filles, recueil de lectures*. Paris: Larousse, 1957.

Siegel, Mona. *The Moral Disarmament of France: Education, Pacifism, and Patriotism, 1914–1940*. Cambridge: Cambridge University Press, 2004.

Silve, Marie. "Témoignage sur une origine." In *Les Davidées*, edited by Jean Guitton, 45–81. Paris: Casterman, 1967.

Siwek-Pouydesseau, Jeanne. *Le Syndicalisme des fonctionnaires jusqu'à la guerre froide 1848–1948*. Lille: Presses universitaires de Lille, 1989.

Smith, Paul. *Feminism and the Third Republic: Women's Political and Civil Rights in France, 1918–1945*. Oxford: Clarendon Press, 1996.

Sohn, Anne-Marie. "Exemplarité et limites de la participation féminine à la vie syndicale: Les institutrices de la C.G.T.U." *Revue d'histoire moderne et contemporaine* 24 (July–September 1977): 391–414.

Sohn, Anne-Marie. *Féminisme et syndicalisme: Les Institutrices de la Fédération unitaire de l'enseignement de 1919 à 1935*. Paris: Hachette/Bibliothèque Nationale (microfiche), 1975.

Sourgen, H. *L'Éducation civique des femmes: Quelques suggestions pratiques*. Paris: UNESCO, 1954.

Sowerwine, Charles. *Sisters or Citizens? Women and Socialism in France since 1876*. Cambridge: Cambridge University Press, 1982.

Stewart, Mary Lynn. *For Health and Beauty: Physical Culture for Frenchwomen 1880s–1930s*. Baltimore: Johns Hopkins University Press, 2001.

Stock-Morton, Phyllis. *Moral Education for a Secular Society: The Development of "Morale Laïque" in Nineteenth-Century France*. Albany: State University of New York Press, 1988.

Stone, Judith F. *The Search for Social Peace: Reform Legislation in France, 1890–1914*. Albany: State University of New York Press, 1985.

Sueur-Hubert, Gabrielle. *Un siècle de vie de pensionnaires: De la communale à l'école normale*. Lunéray: Bertout, 1983.

Talbott, John E. *The Politics of Educational Reform in France, 1918–1940*. Princeton: Princeton University Press, 1969.

Terral, Hervé. *Profession: professeur, Des écoles normales maintenues aux instituts universitaires de formation des maîtres (1945–1990)*. Paris: Presses universitaires de France, 1997.

Thébaud, Françoise. *La Femme au temps de la guerre de 14*. Paris: Stock, 1986.

Thivend, Marianne. *L'École républicaine en ville: Lyon, 1870–1914*. Paris: Belin, 2006.

Tilburg, Patricia A. *Colette's Republic: Work, Gender, and Popular Culture in France, 1870–1914*. New York: Berghahn Books, 2009.

SELECTED BIBLIOGRAPHY **299**

Verdon, Albéric. *Féminisme et suffragisme en Deux-Sèvres jusqu'en 1945*. N.p.: Bookelis, 2019.

Verdon, Albéric. *Marguerite Martin née Brunet (1877–1956)*. N.p.: Bookelis, 2018.

Verneuil, Yves. *Les Agrégés: Histoire d'une exception française*. Paris: Belin, 2005.

Verneuil, Yves. "La Société des agrégées, entre féminisme et esprit de catégorie (1920–1948)." *Histoire de l'éducation*, nos. 115–16 (2007): 195–224.

Villin, Marc. *Les Chemins de la communale: Regards sur l'école et les maîtres d'autrefois*. Paris: Éditions du Seuil, 1981.

Villin, Marc and Pierre Lesage. *La Galerie des maîtres d'école et des instituteurs 1820–1945*. Paris: Plon, 1987.

Vincent, Alain. *L'École normale: Des hussards de la République aux professeurs des écoles*. Joué-les-Tours: Alan Sutton, 2001.

Weber, Eugen. *Peasants into Frenchmen: The Modernization of Rural France*. Stanford: Stanford University Press, 1976.

Weisbecker, Yvette. *Mémoire et engagement: Des mauvais hivers 1940–1944 à l'éclatant printemps 1947–1957*. Paris: Le Manuscrit, 2012.

Weitz, Margaret Collins. *Sisters in the Resistance: How Women Fought to Free France, 1940–1945*. New York: John Wiley, 1995.

Wildenthal, Lora. *German Women for Empire, 1884–1945*. Durham: Duke University Press, 2001.

Wishnia, Judith. *The Proletarianizing of the Fonctionnaires: Civil Service Workers and the Labor Movement under the Third Republic*. Baton Rouge: Louisiana State University Press, 1990.

Wright, Gordon. *France in Modern Times*. 5th ed. New York: W.W. Norton, 1995.

Zeldin, Theodore, ed. *Conflicts in French Society: Anticlericalism, Education and Morals in the Nineteenth Century*. London: George Allen and Unwin, 1970.

Reference Works and Biographical Dictionaries

Bard, Christine, with Sylvie Chaperon, eds. *Dictionnaire des féministes en France XVIIIe–XXIe siècle*. Paris: Presses universitaires de France, 2017.

Blum, Françoise, Colette Chambelland, and Michel Dreyfus. "Mouvements de femmes (1919–1940): *Guide des sources documentaires*." Special issue, *Vie sociale*, nos. 11–12 (November–December 1984).

Caplat, Guy, ed. *Les Inspecteurs généraux de l'instruction publique, Dictionnaire biographique 1802–1914*. Paris: Institut national de recherche pédagogique/Éditions du CNRS, 1985.

Caplat, Guy, ed. *L'Inspection générale de l'instruction publique au XXe siècle: Dictionnaire biographique des inspecteurs généraux et des inspecteurs de l'Académie de Paris, 1914–1939*. Paris: Institut national de recherche pédagogique/Économica, 1997.

Caspard, Pierre et al. *La Presse d'éducation et d'enseignement (XVIIIe–1940)*. 4 vols. Paris: Institut national de recherche pédagogique/Éditions du CNRS, 1981–1991.

Maîtron,, Jean, et al., eds. *Dictionnaire biographique du mouvement ouvrier français*. maître-en-ligne.univ-paris1.fr

300   SELECTED BIBLIOGRAPHY

Unpublished Manuscripts and Dissertations

Courtis, Christine. "Le Cheminement de Lucie Saffroy, une Auxerroise dévouée à la cause de l'instruction des filles du peuple."

Doucet, Marie-Michèle. "Prise de parole au féminin: La Paix et les relations internationales dans les revendications du mouvement de femmes pour la paix en France (1919–1934)." PhD. diss., Université de Montréal, 2015.

Hélie, Anissa. "Maîtresses et mission coloniale en Méditerranée, Trajectoires d'institutrices européennes en Algérie coloniale 1874–1949: Émanciper les écolières ou féminiser les 'Fatmas'"? Thèse de doctorat, École des hautes études en sciences sociales, 2006.

Hunt, J. Athol. "The Preparation of Primary School Teachers in France since World War II." Ph.D. diss., University of Hobart, 1977.

Hunt, Persis Charles. "Revolutionary Syndicalism and Feminism among Teachers in France, 1900–1921." Ph.D. diss., Tufts University, 1975.

Marcheboeuf, Agnes. "Former et éduquer institutrices et instituteurs: La vie dans les écoles normales de Lyon de 1879 à 1941." Mémoire de maîtrise, Université de Lyon, 1997.

Index

For the benefit of digital users, indexed terms that span two pages (e.g., 52–53) may, on occasion, appear on only one of those pages.

Figures are indicated by *f* following the page number

academy, *académie*, 82, 231, 241n.16
   of Clermont-Ferrand, 27–28
   of Lille, 184–85
   of Nancy, 27–28, 185–86
   of Paris, 27–28, 93–94
   of Rennes, 27–28, 93–94, 118–19
   of Toulouse, 94–95
Action Démocratique et Laïque des
      Femmes (ADLF), 215–16, 224
Action feminine (L'), 157
Action féministe (L'), 155–56, 158, 160–61,
      162–63, 165–66, 174–75, 176–77,
      178–79, 181–82
agrégée des lettres, 25–26
Albert, Élise (Mme Gouin), 49, 230
Albert, Rachel, 76–77, 85, 157
Algeria, 118–19, 135–51, 177, 206–7,
      228–30
Allégret, Éva, 144–46
Allégret, Marie-Thérèse, 101
Alsace-Lorraine, 23, 201, 202–4
alumnae associations, normal schools
      (*associations amicales des
      anciennes élèves*), 62–63, 106–8,
      154
   and feminism, 158, 177, 209–11
   and pacifism, 214, 216–17
amicales, teachers, 106, 114, 116–17, 154,
      159, 165, 168–69, 179–80, 199–200
   congress, 1907, 154–55
   congress, 1909, 155–56, 160–61,
      267n.40
   congress, 1911, 163
Angles, Marguerite, 199, 213, 215
Annuaire de l'enseignement primaire,
      14–15, 56–57, 69, 82, 134–35

Annuaire de l'instruction publique, 56–57
antisemitism, 77–78, 99, 127, 212–13, 219
   in Algeria, 136, 141, 148–49, 207,
      261n.81
Arabic, teaching of, 137, 144–46
Ardaillon, Édouard, 104–6, 146–47, 177
Armanet, Charlotte, 112
Association des inspecteurs primaires
      et directeurs d'écoles normales
      (AIPDEN), 114, 115, 200–1
Associations Law (1901), 114, 132
Athané, Gabrielle, 46–47, 88
Aucher, Carmen, 139–40
Auclert, Hubertine, 53–54, 152–53, 156
Aurore (L'), 98–99, 100, 112–13
Avril de Sainte-Croix, Ghénia, 157

baccalauréat (*bac*), 218–19, 223, 228, 230
Baertschi, Marie, 98–99
Bancilhon, Aglaë, 29–30, 52–53, 60,
      189–90
Bar, Yvonne, 220
Barthou, Louis, 5
bas-bleus (bluestockings), 57–58
Baudry, Césarine, 12, 13
Bayet, Charles, 66, 83–84, 98, 128–29
Bérard, Léa, 158–59, 167
Bérard, Léon, 192–93
Bergerat, Jeanne. *See* Fraysse-Auriol
Bergin, Anna, 16–17
Béridot, Ernestine (Mme Floutier), 33,
      140–41, 242n.37
Bernard, Louise, 174
Bert, Paul, 8–9, 12, 17, 25, 153
Bert law, 2–3, 8–9, 10–11, 35, 120
Berthelet, Anaïs, 209

302 INDEX

Bertrand, Cornélie, 29–30, 74, 86
Beunot, Amélie, 205–6
Bigey, Hélène, 203
Bigot, Marthe, 176
Billot-Kay, Marthe, 197–98
Billotey, Denise, 74–75, 88, 111–12, 113, 114, 179
Blum, Léon, 212–13
Bodin, Marguerite, 154–55
Boissière, Caroline, 23, 243n.51
Boissière, Gustave, 139–40
Bonbled, Émilie, 13
Bonnefon, Magdeleine, 74–75, 170–71
Bonnel, Clara, 60, 96
Bonnet, Victorine, 13, 16–17
Bonnevial, Marie, 163, 164
Bontemps, Henriette, 225
Bordas, Marie, 177–78, 196–97
Bouige, Maria, 133–34, 135
Bourgeois, Léon, 67–68, 89–90, 121
Bourgoin, Berthe, 83–84
Bourgoise, Nathalie, 48, 58, 60, 102, 114
Bourguet, Zoé, 23–24
Bousquet, Herminie, 47, 57–58
Bouvrain, Lucie, 156–57, 169, 176
brevets (élémentaire, supérieur), 12, 21, 30, 67, 133, 147, 228
Briand, Aristide, 71, 105–6
Bringuier, Annette, 177–78, 207–8, 210
Brittany, 55–56, 93–94, 118–35, 150–51, 205–6
Brocard, Émilie, 125–26
Brugalières, Emma, 200–1, 210–11
Brulé, Hélène, 221, 222–23, 226, 228, 230–31
Brunschvicg, Cécile, 163, 164, 166–68, 169, 170–71, 172–73, 177
   interwar roles, 207–9, 210–11, 213
Bugnon, Émile, 165–66
Buisson, Ferdinand, 10, 99, 179–80
   in Chamber of Deputies, 114, 115, 161, 168
   as director of primary education, 10, 11, 14, 15–16, 17–18, 20, 23, 56–57, 85, 86–87, 89, 93–94, 95–96
   equal pay campaign, 161
   as professor of pedagogy, 63–64, 113
   women's suffrage, 163–64, 168, 171, 177

Buisson, Marie-Louise. See Combes (née Buisson)

Cacciaguerra, Jéromine, 150
Calloch, Eugénie, 23, 243n.51
Capitant, René, 222
Carré, Irénée, 86–87, 119, 122–23, 134–35
Cartel des Gauches, 192–93, 199–200, 204
Cassagnac, Paul de, 95, 96
Castaing, Jeanne, 174
Catholic church, and politics, 2, 8, 97, 118–19
Catholic hostility to republican education, 1, 2, 93–95, 96, 121, 126, 127, 205
certificate for normal school directors, 12, 22
certificate for normal school professors, 12
certificate of primary studies (c.e.p.), 29, 126, 131
Champomier, Marie-Thérèse, 141
Chardon, Marguerite, 210, 216–17, 225
Chasteau, Louise, 17, 19, 242n.38
Chaudron, Cécile (née Tassin), 103–6, 167–68, 174, 187–88
Chauvin, Jeanne (directrice), 208–9
Chevillard, Jane, 221
civic instruction, 1–2, 50, 53–54, 55, 166–67, 178–79, 181, 215, 226–27
Claude, Marie, 74
Clemenceau, Georges, 92, 98
Clément, Marguerite, 169–70, 175
Cligny, Gabrielle, 114
Coeducation. See mixité
Collet, Hélène, 191
colonization, directrices' views on, 105–6, 229–30
Combe, Delphine, 196–97
Combes, Émile, 143–44
Combes, Marie-Louise (née Buisson), 85, 127–28, 201–2
Comité international des études pédagogiques, 114
communism, 192–93
Communist party, 199–200, 201, 212–13, 223, 225
Compain, Louise, 49, 173–74
Compayré, Gabriel, 50–51, 53–55, 84–85, 181, 248n.33

INDEX 303

Confédération Générale du Travail (CGT), 199–201, 212–13
Congress on primary education, international, 1889, 34, 36–41
Congress on primary education, international, 1900, 113, 256n.77
conseil d'administration (advisory committee), for normal school, 83
conseil départemental (departmental council of primary education), 35–36, 59–60, 186
conseil général (departmental), 83, 96–97, 120
Conseil National des Femmes Françaises (CNFF), 152–53, 156–58, 160–61, 162–64, 165–66, 174–75, 208
Conseil Supérieur de l'Instruction Publique (CSIP, Higher Council of Public Instruction), 36, 51, 65–66, 72–73, 115–16, 154–55, 159, 160, 192–93, 200–1, 275n.50
Conte, Joséphine. *See* Escande (née Conte)
Coopération feminine, 113
Correspondance générale de l'instruction primaire, 52, 110–11
Cougoul, Anna, 16
cours complémentaire, 29, 121, 124, 228–29
cours normal, 2–3, 10–11, 12, 23, 25, 30
Nîmes (Gard), 1, 17, 23–24, 27–28, 29–30
"couvents laïques" (lay convents), 5, 43–44, 73, 80, 82, 117
Crouzel, Marie (née Fontecave), 95, 106–7, 112–13
Cruvellier, Marcelline, 87–88
culture générale, 58–59, 218–19
Cuminal, Antoinette, 205, 215, 222–23, 224

Dalon, Élise. *See* Labergère (née Dalon)
Davidées, 202, 204–5
Debré, Michel, 229–30
Dechappe, Marcelle, 225–26
De Gaulle, Charles, 222, 223–24, 228–29, 230
Déghilage, Jeanne, 115–16, 265n.17

Dejean de la Bâtie, Jeanne (née Lacoste), 25–26, 57, 66, 113, 171, 188–89
depopulation and birthrate, 68, 191
Desportes, Émilie, 29–30, 63, 102
Desvignes, Joséphine. *See* Petit-Dutaillis (née Desvignes)
DeWitt-Schlumberger, Marguerite, 164, 166–67, 170–71, 173, 175
directrices of normal schools, 3–7
advice to teachers, 59–62, 64–66
careers, length of, 34, 188–89, 191, 230–31
duties of, 43
educational backgrounds, 30–31, 189–90
evaluations of, 82, 83–93, 121
family backgrounds, 28–30, 189
geographical origins, 27–28, 137, 189
marriage, 12, 14–15, 31–32, 47, 88–89, 190–91
and children, 32, 191
and husbands' professions, 32, 190–91
number of posts held, 26–27, 33
prior teaching experience, 12, 15–17, 22–24, 25, 30–31, 62–63, 70–71, 88, 120, 138–39, 148–49, 190
publications, 61–62, 64–66, 109–11, 198–99, 225–28
Doisnel, Pélagie, 16–17
Dollé, Jeanne, 189, 204
Dollé, Adèle (née Tourret), 29–30, 33–34, 52, 59–60, 68–69, 71, 110–11, 113–14, 172–73, 189
Dosser, Marie, 60–61, 184–85
Douillet née Weill, Constance, 222
Doumergue, Gaston, 92–93, 160
Dreyfus Affair, 63–64, 77–78, 97–101, 107, 108–9, 121, 127, 141
Dudon, Marcelle, 214
Duplan, Edmond, 69–70, 71–72, 88–89, 101, 103, 170
Duruy, Victor, 9

Ebren, Pauline (née Planchard), 90–91, 99–100, 112–13
Échard, Blanche (née Gauthier), 110, 186, 205

304 INDEX

école annexe, 36, 54–55, 72–73, 192
École (L') et la vie, 198–99
École (L') libératrice, 200–1
école maternelle, 24–25, 198–99
école mixte (coeducational school), 36–38, 39, 40, 230
École normale supérieure, 11, 83
École (L') nouvelle, 73, 110–11, 174–75
École Pape-Carpantier, 24–25, 243n.55
école primaire supérieure (higher primary school). 12, 29, 174–75, 199, 219–20
école unique, 199, 218–19, 228–29
économe, 49, 69–70, 72
éducation nouvelle, 198–99
Eidenschenk, Albertine (née Patin), 65, 65f, 68–69, 75–76, 113–14, 116, 129–30, 141, 184–85, 187–88, 218
  advice to teachers, 64–66
  Conseil Supérieur de l'Instruction publique (CSIP), 65–66, 72–73, 115–16, 160
  equal pay, 116–17, 154, 159–61
  feminism, 117, 162–63, 165–66, 174, 181
  pacifism, 213–14, 216
  publications, 64, 108–9, 110–11, 113–14, 134–35, 158–59, 163, 180
  students' appreciation of, 74, 80, 116, 141–42
Eidenschenk, Laurent, 65, 88, 99, 129–30, 141, 185, 261n.79
enseignement libre. See private schools
Épinoux, Suzanne. *See* Pingaud (née Épinoux)
"equality in difference," 20–21, 59–60, 167–68, 181, 193, 227
equal pay for women educators, 116–17, 153–57, 159–61, 179–80, 265n.13, 265n.14, 267n.42
Escande, Joséphine (née Conte), 30, 112–13, 121–22, 133
Espiau, Antoinette, 196–97
Estates General of Feminism, 1929, 208
Évard, Rose (née Lecomte), 112, 185–86, 188–89, 215
Expilly, Marthe, 22–23

Fabre, Yvonne, 200–1, 210, 225
Faillières, Armand, 41, 96–97
Falloux law, 9, 35, 201, 203
fascism, 214–15
Fassou, Berthe, 205–6
Favre, Julie, 20
Fédération Féministe du Sud-Est (FFSE), 167, 169–70, 176
Fédération Féministe du Sud-Ouest (FFSO), 169–70, 172
Fédération Féministe Universitaire (FFU), 155–57, 160–61, 162–63, 165, 174–75, 178–80, 266n.22
  and UFSF, 167, 174, 176
Fémina, 158–59
feminism, 70–71, 117, 152–82, 207–12, 226, 227
  and normal school personnel, 107–8, 112, 153, 194, 209–12 (*see also* Union Française pour le Suffrage des Femmes [UFSF])
  and normal school students, 169, 170–71, 176–78, 210–11
  and teachers (*see* Fédération Féministe Universitaire)
Femme nouvelle (La), 158–59, 162
Fénelon, abbé, 54, 57, 248n.35
Ferrand, Léonie, 12, 13, 14, 24–25, 86–87, 107
Ferry, Jules, 1–2, 8, 11, 20, 24–25, 41, 52, 112, 239n.2
  and appointment of normal school directrices, 1, 11, 14, 15–16, 17–18
Ferry laws, 2, 10, 12–13, 50
Fiévet, Aimée, 164–65
Fifth Republic, 228–29, 230
  education policy, 228–29, 230–31
Flamant, Marthe, 214
Flandin, Pierre, 208, 215
Flayol, Émilie, 108, 168–69, 174, 198–99, 207, 233–34
Fontcave, Marie. *See* Crouzel (née Fontcave)
Fontenay-aux-Roses, *école normale supérieure*, 2–3, 4, 11, 13, 18–22, 18f, 31, 60, 63–64, 80, 181, 190, 228

INDEX 305

alumnae association (*association amicale*), 33, 107, 108
Bulletin of *amicale*, 63–64, 66–67, 72, 99, 108–9, 178, 185, 199, 213, 214
directrices of, 13, 18–19, 25, 26, 66, 82, 190, 197, 274n.40
"esprit" of, 19–20, 113–14
feminism and, 157–58, 171–72
pedagogical instruction, 21–22, 50–53
training for directrices, 22, 31, 51, 55, 190
Fontes, Marguerite. *See* Paringaux (née Fontes)
Foulet, Marguerite (née Martin), 79, 164–65, 186
Fourth Republic, 223, 228–29
Française (La), 152, 166, 167–68, 173, 181–82, 208–9, 210, 215. *See also* Union Française pour le Suffrage des Femmes (UFSF)
François, Cécile, 197–98, 215, 216, 221, 225
Frapié, Léon, 62–63, 107–8
Fraysse-Auriol (née Bergerat), Jeanne, 144, 215
French, teaching of, 55–56, 66–67, 119, 138
Friedberg, Joséphine de, 12, 13, 19, 23–24, 25, 95, 107
Fronde (La), 70–71, 76–77, 108–9, 112, 117, 152–53, 157, 173–74
Frugier, Emma, 33–34, 51, 73–74, 91–92, 187, 189–90
and feminism, 112, 153, 169, 170, 181, 211–12

Gaillard, Louise, 195–96, 198–99, 216–17, 222–23, 224
Gambey, Blanche, 191, 203
Garcin, Amélie, 13, 14
Gard department, 17, 23–24, 27–28, 52–53
Garnier, Marie, 66–67
Gasquet, Amédée, 92–93, 105–6, 129–30, 160
Gaudefroy, Pauline, 37–38, 40, 174–75
Gauthier, Blanche. *See* Échard (née Gauthier)
Gebelin, Joséphine, 75

Géhin, Célina, 106, 117
gender, gender roles,
ideas about, 19, 26, 36–39, 40, 47, 52–53, 60–61, 219, 226–27
teaching of, 4–5, 14–15, 20–21, 41, 43, 53–55, 61, 65–66, 67, 78–79, 110–12, 163, 179, 180, 192, 226, 227–28
geographical mobility, 33, 244n.76
Georgin, Marie-Thérèse, 16–17
Géraud, Jeanne, 215, 224, 269n.72
GFU (groupe féministe universitaire), 155–56, 167, 168–70, 176–77, 270n.82
Ginier, Marguerite, 33, 66–67, 75, 112–13, 157, 158, 161, 171–72, 181
Girard, Jeanne, 175
Goblet, René, 58
Goblet law, 35, 36–37, 59–60, 132
Goron, Sarah, 174, 207–8
Goué, Augustine (née Lebrun), 40, 72, 76
Granet, Hélène, 1, 17–18, 20, 44–45
Grandjeat, Joséphine, 221
Grauvogel, Anne-Marie, 103, 190, 197, 214
Gréard, Octave, 36, 40–41, 100
Groupe Français de l'Éducation nouvelle, 198–99
Grunfelder, Jeanne, 185–86
Guérin, Marie, 154–56, 160–61, 163, 176
Guérin, Paul, 155–57, 160–61
Guerrini, Antoinette, 230–31
Guillot, Denise, 140, 141–42
Guillot, Marie, 176
Guinier, Adrienne, 37–38, 55–56, 92–93
Guizot law, 2–3, 9
Guny, Mathilde, 30
Guttron, Hermance, 140–41

Heigny, Blanche, 60, 123–24
Hémon, Félix, 138, 143–44
Hesse and Gleyze, sociology textbook, 193–94, 209, 214–15
Heurtefeu, Léonie, 40, 56–57, 110–11, 111*f*
higher primary school. See *école primaire supérieure*
Hippeau, Eugénie, 16
Hirtz, Jeanne, 213, 222
History, teaching of, 1–2, 55, 67, 118, 146–47

306 INDEX

Hitler, Adolf, 212–13, 214–15, 216
Hoël, Caroline, 48, 57–58, 125–26
home economics (*économie domestique,
enseignement ménager*), 55, 68,
69–70, 192
Huber-Fortin, Jeanne, 207–8
Hue, Thérèse, 205, 215, 219–20
Huet, Henriette, 137, 138
Hugonnier-Ginet, Marie, 191
Hui, Amélie, 127–28, 204, 205–6, 215

Iba-Zizen, Madeleine (née Boue), 225–26,
229–30
indigènes (Algeria), education of, 118–19,
136–37, 142–44, 149–50, 206,
263n.113
inspecteur d'académie (chief departmental
inspector), 12–13, 35, 62, 65, 82,
83, 88, 89–93
inspecteur primaire (primary
school inspector), 62, 103,
187–88
inspectrice, écoles maternelles, 34, 39, 115,
175–76
directrice appointed as, 16–17, 23,
245n.82
inspectrice générale, écoles maternelles, 19,
38–39, 188–89, 225–26
directrice appointed as, 88, 188–89,
191, 199, 204, 215, 219, 226–27,
230–31, 245n.82
inspectrice primaire (primary school
inspectress), 36–39, 40–41, 115,
157–58, 171–72, 187–88, 191,
273n.15
directrice appointed as, 22, 25, 26, 34,
70–71, 202–3, 219, 221, 222–23,
225–26, 227–28, 245n.82
Instituteur (*L'*), 110–11
institut de formation professionnelle (IFP),
218–19, 220, 221, 222
*institut universitaire de formation des
maîtres* (IUFM), 230–31
institutrice (woman teacher), 61–63, 116,
137, 175–76, 192, 231
internat, 43–45, 49, 70–71, 72, 230
International Congress of Women's
Charities and Institutions, 1889,
1900, 152–53

International Congress of Women's
Charities, Institutions, and Women's
Rights, 1913, 78–80, 158, 164–65
International Council of Women (ICW),
157–58, 164, 165
International Woman Suffrage Alliance
(IWSA), 156, 173
Ithurbide, Jeanne, 210–12, 214–15

Jacoulet, Édouard, 19–20, 83
Jacquemin, Eugénie, 47, 58, 73–74, 107
Jacquin, Honorine, 100–1, 104–5, 112–13
Jacquot, Marguerite, 208–9
Jalambic, Marguerite, 37, 85–86, 114
Janin, Marthe (née Magnier), 58, 74,
94–95, 171–72, 208–9
Jarry, Jules, 121, 123–24, 125–26, 128–29
Jeanmaire, Charles, 140–41, 142–44
Jospin law, 230–31
Jost, Guillaume, 47, 84–85, 86–87, 91,
126–27, 128–29
Journal (*Le*), 168, 178, 271n.98
Journal des instituteurs, 110–11, 191
Juredieu, Alice, 225–26

Kabylia, 141–42, 144
Karquel, Joséphine, 17
Kergomard, Pauline, 20, 25, 36, 40, 78,
108–9, 123–24, 153, 164–65, 175
advocating inspectrices, 36–37, 38–39,
157–58
on CSIP, 36, 115–16
Kieffer, Eugénie, 66–67, 70–71, 113, 157,
158, 164–65

Labergère, Élise (née Dalon), 77–78,
103–4, 133–34
Lacore, Suzanne, 176–77, 213
Lacoste, Jeanne. *See* Dejean de la Bâtie
(née Lacoste)
Lacroix, Aurélie, 19, 57–58, 114, 140, 141
Lafforgue, Marie, 73–74, 99, 140
Lafourcade, Hélène, 75
Laguerre, Odette, 70–71, 76–77
laïcité, 2, 12–13, 35, 41–42, 52, 53, 106–7,
201–3, 204–6, 218–19
resisted by some directrices, 15–16,
22–23, 98, 102, 121–22, 201–2
resisted by some teachers (*see* Davidées)

INDEX 307

Lamy, Georges, 71–72, 84–85, 116, 139–40, 148–49

Lanaud, Victorine, 12–13, 30

Landais, Amélie, 127–28, 172

Languéry, Augustine, 94–95

Lapie, Paul, 192–93, 194–95

Larab, Yamina, 143–44, 262n.93

Larivière, Marie, 58–59, 74–75, 141

Laurain, Marie, 85

Lauriol, Sophie, 18–19, 63–64, 93–94, 99

Layet, Camille (Mme Garonne), 33, 243n.48

League of Nations, 183–84, 214–15

Leblanc, René, 31–32, 86, 102, 129

Lebrun, Augustine. *See* Goué (née Lebrun)

Lecomte, Rose. *See* Évard (née Lecomte)

Le Gac-Salonne, Marie, 173–74

Legion of Honor, and directrices, 25, 91–92, 140, 144, 170, 185, 188–89, 221, 230–31

Legros, Élise, 47, 60–61, 86–87, 93–94, 107, 123, 127

Lemercier, Suzanne, 13, 14

Lemoine, Alcide, 109–10, 180

letter of obedience, 9

Léveillé, Céleste, 112–13

Le Verrier, Marie-Louise, 173, 177–78

Leyssenne, Pierre, 14, 26, 57, 85, 87, 89–90, 91

Liard, Louis, 15–16, 159–60, 164

Ligue de l'Enseignement, 63–64, 68, 112, 113, 144, 154, 156–57, 170, 250n.72

    Comité des dames, 68, 113

Ligue des Droits de l'Homme (League of the Rights of Man), 98–99, 129–30, 160–61, 172

Ligue des Mères et des Éducatrices pour la Paix (LIMEP), 214, 216

Ligue Française pour le Droit des Femmes (LFDF), 156, 160–61, 163, 164, 170–72, 181–82, 208–9

Ligue Patriotique des Françaises, 164, 208

literacy, 27, 119, 131–32

Logé-Hervé, Alice, 22–23

Loiret, Henriette (née Griess), 49, 88, 95–97

Lusier, Marie, 16–17, 77, 89–90

MacMahon, Marshal Patrice de, 10

Magnat, Inès, 220

Magnier, Marthe, *See* Janin (née Magnier)

Mahaut, Marie, 108, 127–28, 157–58

Maillier, Jenny, 138

Maintenon, Mme de, 54, 248n.35

Malaval, Louise, 142, 143

Malivert, Lucie, 220

Manuel général de l'instruction primaire, 63–64, 71, 110–11, 162, 163, 198–99, 211, 214

March, Lucienne, 63, 77–78, 99

Marie, Juliette, 71–72, 109–10, 177, 180, 184–85, 197, 200–1

Marin, Louis, 161, 171

Marion, Henri. 19–21, 50

marriage and women educators, 14–15, 31–32, 64

Marsy, Marie, 29–30, 184–85

Martel, Félix, 69, 86, 125–26

Martin, Germaine, 203

Martin, Louise (née Schaefer), 45–47, 50, 55, 56–57, 88

Martin, Marguerite. *See* Foulet (née Martin)

Martin, Marguerite (née Brunet), 175

Martinique, *cours normal,* 147–48

Massé, Alfred, 115

maternalism, 21, 47

Matrat, Marie, 138–40, 141–42

Mathieu, Emma, 23, 31

Mathieu, Thérèse, 195

Maucourant, Blanche, 184–85, 197–98, 203–4, 225–26

Mayaud, Julia, 5, 68–69, 71, 87, 109, 129

Mayeur, Françoise, 3

mayors, women as, 224

Mayoux, Marie, 91–92

Mazier, Céline, 44–45, 55, 56–57, 85–86, 122–23

Menat, Alcidie, 33–34, 87, 107–8, 158

Méo, Jeanne, 167, 176

Météraud, Emma, 220, 221, 222–23

Mir, Mathilde, 219–20, 221, 224–25

Misme, Jane, 166, 173, 178, 183

mission civilisatrice (civilizing mission), 136, 137, 150–51

308 INDEX

mixité (coeducation), 6, 230
Modrin, Camille, 71–72, 174
Moitessier, Marguerite, 219–20
monitrice indigène, 142, 143–44
moral instruction, *morale*, 2, 4–5, 44–45, 50, 51–53, 192–93, 201–2, 226
Moral Order (*Ordre moral*), 13, 24–25, 121
Morel, Eugénie, 205–6, 210, 213
Moret, Clémence, 16–17, 120–22
municipal council (*conseil municipal*), women on, 224–25
Muraccioli, Félicie, 148–49, 206, 229–30
Murique, Louise, 69, 100, 109
music, in normal schools, 58–59
Mussolini, Benito, 212–13, 214–15

Napoleonic civil code, 20, 65–66, 162, 193, 226
Nivoley, Marguerite. *See* Pieyre (née Nivoley)
normal school (*école normale*), 2–3, 8–9
   curriculum, 4–5, 50–56, 66–69, 192–94
   differences between men's and women's curriculum, 54, 67, 192
   familial atmosphere, 46–47, 49
   foreign languages in, 66–67, 137, 144–46
   numbers of, 2–3, 10–11, 240n.9, 240n.10, 244n.61
   pedagogy, teaching of, 22, 50–51, 54–55, 67
   regulations, 43–44, 194–95, 230
normal school, departmental, for women
   Agen (Lot-et-Garonne), 25–26, 33, 112–13
   Aix-en-Provence (Bouches du Rhône), 14, 48, 75, 189–90, 205
   Ajaccio (Corse), 14, 55–56, 84–85
   Albi (Tarn), 94–95, 164–65, 194, 207–8
   Alençon (Orne), 59, 93–94, 170–71, 174–75, 205
   Amiens (Somme), 12, 16–17, 184–85, 208–9
   Angers (Maine-et-Loire), 33–34, 123, 124, 133, 200–1
   Angoulême (Charente), 33–34, 73–74, 91–92, 153, 169–70, 187, 189–90, 211–12, 225

Arras (Pas-de-Calais), 66–67, 74, 184–85, 197
Auch (Gers), 95
Aurillac (Cantal), 25, 48, 76
Auxerre (Yonne), 12, 25, 177
Avignon (Vaucluse), 33, 86
Bar-le-Duc (Meuse), 45–46, 106, 117, 185–86
Beauvais (Oise), 33, 80, 125–26, 164–65, 195–96, 196f
Besançon (Doubs), 13, 30, 33, 66–67, 75, 205
Blois (Loir-et-Cher), 44–45, 47, 55, 56–57, 73–74, 112–13, 202, 209
Bordeaux (Gironde), 33–34, 58, 75, 96–97, 197–98
Bourg (Ain), 101
Bourges (Cher), 25, 33, 69–70, 74, 75, 76–77, 87–88, 99–100, 102, 110, 125–26, 194, 211–12
Caen (Calvados), 69–70, 98, 177
Cahors (Lot), 33, 200–1, 210–11
Carcassonne (Aude), 16, 30, 37, 74–75, 85–86, 114
Châlons-sur-Marne (Marne), 1, 17–18, 44–45, 75, 184–86
Chambéry (Savoie), 33, 64, 70–71, 77, 154, 176–77
Charleville (Ardennes), 114, 153, 184–85
Chartres (Eure-et-Loir), 33–34, 74–75, 170–71
Châteauroux (Indre), 106, 127, 157–58
Chaumont (Haute-Marne), 87, 93–94, 98, 102
Clermont-Ferrand (Puy-de-Dôme), 16–17, 49, 75
Constantine (Constantine), 136–37, 147–49, 149f, 206, 229–30
Coutances (Manche), 106–7, 112–13
Digne (Basses-Alpes), 29–30, 74, 86, 174, 211
Dijon (Côte-d'Or), 16–17, 74, 98, 128–29
Douai (Nord), 17–18, 64, 66–67, 70–71, 74, 75–76, 85–86, 107, 115–16, 164–65, 184–85
Draguignan (Var), 33, 49, 92–93

INDEX 309

Épinal (Vosges), 13, 76–77, 80, 85,
185–86, 190, 195–96, 198–99
Évreux (Eure), 33–34, 58–59, 74–75,
93–94
Foix (Ariège), 33, 114, 141–42, 207–8
Gap (Hautes-Alpes), 33, 38, 84–85
Grenoble (Isère), 16–17, 33, 61, 76–77,
85, 99–101, 103, 186
Guéret (Creuse), 71–72
Laon (Aisne), 30, 184–85, 197–98, 214
La Roche-sur-Yon (Vendée), 33, 48,
77–78, 86–87, 99–100, 107–8, 124,
127, 133, 135, 146–47, 187, 195,
205
La Rochelle (Charente-Inférieure), 22–
23, 33–34, 75, 76–77, 198–99, 207
Laval (Mayenne), 71–72, 84–86, 120,
122–23, 124, 133, 196–97
Le Mans (Sarthe), 23, 73–74, 75, 86–87,
100, 208–9
Le Puy (Haute-Loire), 86–87, 90, 93–94,
112
Limoges (Haute-Vienne), 33–34, 44f,
45f, 46–47, 56–57, 62–63, 107–8,
177–78, 197–98
Lons-le-Saunier (Jura), 12–13, 30, 33,
99–100, 104–6, 123, 205, 222
Lyon (Rhône), 13, 14, 33–34, 47, 76–77,
78–79, 84–85, 93–94, 189–90,
196–97, 240n.9
Mâcon (Saône-et-Loire), 12, 16–17,
75–76, 83–84, 99–100
Melun (Seine-et-Marne), 13, 33, 69–70,
74, 77–78, 87–88, 96–97, 177,
185–86
Mende (Lozère), 33, 37, 55–56, 103–4,
210–11
Metz (Moselle), 203
Miliana (Alger), 13, 53, 73–74, 136–37,
138–40, 144, 145f, 147–48, 148f,
150, 177, 203, 225–26, 230
Mont-de-Marsan (Landes), 33, 172
Montpellier (Hérault), 15–16, 33, 47,
87–88
Moulins (Allier), 13, 33, 48, 110, 177,
186
Nancy (Meurthe-et-Moselle), 17,
33–34, 63, 107, 185–86

Nantes (Loire-Inférieure), 120–22, 133,
220
Nevers (Nièvre), 33–34, 63
Nice (Alpes-Maritimes), 146, 214
Nîmes (Gard), 24, 79, 80, 101, 164–65,
215
Niort (Deux-Sèvres), 16–17, 33–34, 77,
89–90
Oran (Oran), 33, 64, 136–37, 138, 140–
41, 144–47, 207, 222–23
Orléans (Loiret), 16–17, 30, 33–34, 55,
68–69, 93–94, 112–13, 240n.9
Paris (Seine), 12, 13, 24–25, 63–64,
74–75, 88, 107, 144, 179
Pau (Basses-Pyrénées), 33–34, 68–69,
172–73
Périgueux (Dordogne), 24, 58–59,
176–77
Perpignan (Pyrénées-Orientales), 16,
33, 37–38, 177–78, 207–8, 210
Poitiers (Vienne), 33–34, 176–77, 210,
216–17
Privas (Ardèche), 83–84, 93–94, 169
Quimper (Finistère), 58–59, 86–87, 124,
133, 135, 170–71, 205–6, 207–8
Rennes (Ille-et-Vilaine), 33–34, 77,
123–24, 133, 179–80, 205–6
Rodez (Aveyron), 33, 87–88, 94–95,
201–2, 220
Rouen (Seine-Inférieure), 15–16, 25,
33–34, 87, 107–8, 158, 219–20
Rumilly (Haute-Savoie), 13, 80, 174, 195
Saint-Brieuc (Côtes-du-Nord), 71, 74,
75–76, 80, 106–7, 123, 124, 128–
30, 133, 135, 205–6, 210
Saint-Étienne (Loire), 13, 23, 33, 83–84
Saint-Germain-en-Laye (Seine-et-
Oise), 5, 195–96, 197f
Sélestat (Bas-Rhin), 203
Strasbourg (Bas-Rhin), 203–4
Tarbes (Hautes-Pyrénées), 40, 49, 76–77, 85
Toulouse (Haute-Garonne), 25–26, 33,
57, 85–86, 122–23, 140–41
Tours (Indre-et-Loire), 16–17, 33, 61,
68, 77, 84–85, 226
Troyes (Aube), 17, 33, 49, 71, 95–97,
113, 129, 167–68
Tulle (Corrèze), 37–38, 74–75, 208–9

310 INDEX

normal school, departmental, for women (*cont.*)
  Tunis (Tunisia), 140, 147–48
  Valence (Drôme), 22–23, 49, 56–57, 79, 107, 170–71, 205
  Vannes (Morbihan), 33, 47, 57–58, 85, 123, 124–28, 205–6
  Versailles (Seine-et-Oise), 16–17, 24–25, 68–69, 87, 98–99, 100
  Vesoul (Haute-Sâone), 74, 213
normal school students
  in Algeria, 138, 139
  characterizations of, 15, 45–47, 52, 55–56, 121, 123–24, 128, 135
  church attendance, 14, 39–40, 76–78, 100, 101, 128, 129–30, 133–34, 139, 194
  opinions about normal schools, directrices, 73–78, 80, 91–92, 100, 105, 106, 116, 133–34
  rules for, 43–44, 48, 52, 71, 194–96, 228, 230
  surveillance of, 49, 72–73, 160, 194
  uniform, 43–44, 70*f*, 125*f*, 194–95
Normandy, 93–94

Odoul, Hélène, 55–56, 177, 187–88, 224
Olanier, Émilie, 135
Omnès, Yvonne, 195, 205
Ozouf, Jacques and Ozouf, Mona, survey of teachers, 28–29, 73, 74–78, 80, 99–100, 133–34, 146, 180

pacifism, 114, 176–77, 213–14, 216–17, 218
Palanque, Jeanne, 107–8, 135, 146–47, 187, 214, 221, 224
Panis, Cécile, 160–61, 174, 176
Pape-Carpantier, Marie, 24–25
Parayre, Berthe, 205, 221
Parent, Paule, 225
Paringaux, Marguerite (née Fontes), 33, 70–71, 85, 99, 113
Parti Social Français (PSF), 216
patronage, 112–13, 153, 162–63
Paul, Suzanne, 211, 214
Payot, Jules, 92–93
Pécaut, Félix, 4, 13, 24–25, 28, 44–45, 71–72, 82, 83, 98–99, 108–10, 113–14

advice to directrices, 14–15, 20–21, 82, 83–84, 93
  at Fontenay-aux-Roses, 18–20, 25, 51
  influence on directrices, 18–19, 61, 64, 75, 77–78, 91–92, 116–17, 127–28
Pélissier, Jeanne, 84–85
Pellat-Finet, Vénise, 167, 176
Peltier, Marie (Mme Dutilleul), 59, 93–94
Peltier, (née Simboiselle), Marie, 38, 71–72, 84–85, 124, 125*f*, 133
Périères, Émilie, 172, 174, 194, 199, 207–8
Perseil, Nancy, 69–70, 74, 77–78, 87–88, 99, 110, 177, 185–86
Pétain, Philippe, 217, 218
Petit, Angélina, 35, 60–61, 126–27
Petit-Dutaillis, Charles, 88, 168–69
Petit-Dutaillis, Joséphine (née Desvignes), 79, 88, 170–71
physical education, 69, 70*f*
Picard, Marguerite, 225–26
Pichon-Landry, Marguerite, 157, 164, 169, 173, 266n.24
Pichorel, Marthe, 176
Picquart, Georges, 98–99
Pieyre, Léonie, 48, 55, 84–85, 93–94, 112–13
Pieyre, Marguerite (née Nivoley), 123
Pingaud, Suzanne (née Épinoux), 71, 135, 170–71, 177
Pontal, Juliette (née Vallet), 147–48
Popular Front, 199, 212–13, 215
Popular Republican Movement (MRP), 223, 225
Porte, Marie, 12, 13, 14, 30–31, 47, 84–85, 93–94
Poujade, Bernarde-Marie (née Rey), 190, 215, 224
Prieur-Lacroix, Marie-Eugénie, 208–9
primaires (les), 83–84, 115
Privat, Marie, 194, 200–1
private schools (*écoles libres*), 9, 15, 30–31, 35, 130–31, 132, 205, 229
professeur d'école, 231
Protestants, 20, 27
  directrices, 1, 17, 20, 23–24, 29–30, 52–53, 87–88, 93–94, 100–1, 125–26, 127–28, 204

prominent educational leaders, 10, 13, 20

psychology, teaching of, 20–21, 50, 52, 113

puériculture, 67, 68–69

Quartararo, Anne, 3

Radical (republican) party, 97, 212–13, 215, 223

Rambaud, Alfred, 98, 142–44

Rambault, Alix, 33–34, 46–47, 56–57, 62–63, 107–8, 177–78

Rauber, Marie, 40

Raynaud, Georgette. *See* Tubiana (née Raynaud)

reading, in normal schools, 48, 56–57

Rebour, Pauline, 160–61, 170, 174–75, 176, 178–79, 215, 270n.85

rector, 82, 83, 89, 93

Red Cross, 112–13, 186

religious controversy about normal schools, 15–16, 22–23, 93–94

religious teachers, Catholic, 9, 10–11, 119, 121, 130–31, 132, 133, 147

Goblet law and, 35

law banning from private schools, 1904, 97, 132, 201, 218–19

Renaudet, Marie-Louise, 200–1

Renault, Jeanne, 195

répétitrice, Fontenay-aux-Roses, 21–22, 61, 64, 87–88, 99

Resistance, World War II, 221, 224–25

Revolution of 1789, 1–2, 8, 34, 55

Revue de l'enseignement primaire et primaire supérieur, 156–57, 160

Revue des deux mondes, 57, 63–64

Revue pédagogique, 36, 45–46, 56–57, 63–64, 106–7, 111–12, 171–72

Rey, Léontine, 15–16

Robert, Constance, 75, 99, 123

Robert, Noémie, 84–85

Rogers, Rebecca. 3, 15

Roig, Anna, 223

Rostaing, Hortense, 77

Ruault, Marie, 75

Ruet, Isabelle, 53, 75–76

Russian Revolution of 1917, 183–84, 192–93

Sabatier, Célina, 48, 76, 112–13

Saffroy, Lucie, 25, 31, 74, 87, 115–16, 171–72, 208–9

Sage, Amélie, 13, 14, 123, 138–39

Sagnier, Louise, 61–62, 85–86, 99, 103, 104f, 109, 110–11, 123, 165

Sahuc, Louise, 53, 141–42, 143–44, 145f, 147–48, 150, 177

Saint-Cloud, *école normale supérieure*, 11, 19–20, 28–29, 31, 50–51, 228

Salducci, Germaine, 191, 222–23

salles d'asile, 12, 24–25

Salve, Ernest de, 136–37

Sarcey, Francisque, 62

savantes, 57–58, 65–66

Schreck, Sophie, 177, 207–8

Schwab, Marguerite, 215, 216–17

secondary schools, 4, 9, 28, 199, 228–29, 230

Sée law, 4, 11, 15

Seguin, Jeanne, 227–28

Sélince, Alphonsine, 205, 222

Semmartin, Philippine, 55, 68–69, 93–94

separation of church and state (1905), 52, 75–76, 77–78, 97, 134–35

Sèvres, *école normale supérieure*, 11, 20, 28, 82, 113–14, 171

Sicre, Marguerite, 59–60

Sid-Cara, Nafissa, 206, 229–30

Siegfried, Julie, 164, 165, 174–75

Simboiselle, Marie. *See* Peltier (née Simboiselle)

Simon, Jules, 10, 12, 51

Six, Adrienne (née Polge), 88

Slawinska, Marie Léonie, 98, 99

Soboul, Marie, 164–65, 215, 221, 224, 225

socialism, 97, 100–1, 115, 192–93

Socialist party (SFIO), 212–13, 223, 225

sociology, in normal schools, 192–94

solidarism, 67–68, 112

Sourdillon, Jeanne (née Simboiselle), 68, 77, 84–85

Sourgen, Henriette, 181, 215, 216, 226–27

Spanish Civil War, 214–15, 219–20

Statistics on education, 9, 119, 121, 130–33, 147, 150, 205

Steeg, Jules, 20, 25, 26, 61

Stolzenberg, Marie, 69–70, 215

"Syllabus of Errors," 9

312 INDEX

syndicalism
  normal school personnel, 200–1, 225
  teachers and, 67–68, 92, 115, 156–57,
    165, 169, 268n.65
Syndicat National des Instituteurs (SNI),
  199–201, 218–19

Taddert-ou-Fella (Alger), *cours normal*,
  136–37, 142–44
Tailleur, Berthe, 16–17, 47, 75–76, 83–84
Talmeyr, Maurice, 63–64
Temps, Le, 57, 80
textbooks, primary school, 50, 109–10,
  179, 225–26, 227–28
Thamin, Raymond, 86–87, 121–22,
  128–29
Thiébault, Marie, 74, 103–4, 106–7, 108,
  128–29
Thimer, Juliette, 153, 169–70, 172, 174,
  177–78
Thomas, Jeanne, 75, 100
Thomas, Léona, 94–95
Tourret, Adèle. *See* Dollé (née Tourret)
Tubiana, Georgette (née Raynaud), 207,
  219, 222–23
Tunisia, 119, 137–38, 140, 147–48,
  263n.109

Union Française pour le Suffrage des
  Femmes (UFSF), 152, 156, 158,
  162–63, 164, 165–79, 181–82,
  207–8, 213
  central committee, 173–74, 175,
    270n.81
  normal school personnel in, 152,
    166–73, 174, 177–78, 207–12, 213,
    214, 224
  teachers in, 167, 169, 172–73, 175–77,
    208–9, 269–70n.78
Union Nationale pour le Vote des Femmes
  (UNVF), 208

Union pédagogique (*L'*), 110–11
Union pour la Vérité, 113–14

Valin, Blanche, 80, 185–86, 187, 195–96,
  202–3
Vallet, Juliette. *See* Pontal (nèe Vallet)
Varlet, Marie, 78–79, 79f, 164–65, 186,
  189–90
Védrine, Jeanne, 222–23
Vendée department, 33, 118–19, 135
Vérone, Maria, 160–61, 164, 170–71,
  173–74
Veyron-Lacroix, Sophie, 49
Viaud, Léonie, 69–70, 97
Vichy regime, 218–19, 228
  and normal school directrices,
    219–23
  women's work law, 219
Vincent, Caroline, 195
Voinet, Élise, 123
Volume (*Le*), 110–11, 165

Winter, Marie (Mme Bontems), 153
women's suffrage, 53–54, 152–53,
  156, 162–82, 183–84, 193–94,
  207–9, 210–12, 213, 215, 223–24
  (*see also* Union Française
  pour le Suffrage des Femmes
  [UFSF])
  opposition to, 178, 208, 211–12, 213
World War I, 80, 181–82, 183
  and normal schools, 183–88
  and school inspection, 187–88
World War II, 217, 218. *See also* Vichy
  regime

Yonne department, 12, 25

Zay, Jean, 199, 218–19, 223
Zgraggen, Joséphine, 164–65, 174
Zola, Émile, 48, 98